DEATH AND DYING

END-OF-LIFE CONTROVERSIES

ISSN 1532-2726

DEATH AND DYING

END-OF-LIFE CONTROVERSIES

Sandra M. Alters

INFORMATION PLUS® REFERENCE SERIES
Formerly Published by Information Plus, Wylie, Texas

GALE
CENGAGE Learning™

Detroit • New York • San Francisco • New Haven, Conn • Waterville, Maine • London

Death and Dying: End-of-Life Controversies

Sandra M. Alters

Paula Kepos, Series Editor

Project Editors: Kathleen J. Edgar, Elizabeth Manar

Rights Acquisition and Management: Margaret Abendroth, Kathy Alverson, Vernon English

Composition: Evi Abou-El-Seoud, Mary Beth Trimper

Manufacturing: Cynde Bishop

Product Management: Carol Nagel

For product information and technology assistance, contact us at
Gale Customer Support, 1-800-877-4253.
For permission to use material from this text or product,
submit all requests online at **www.cengage.com/permissions.**
Further permissions questions can be e-mailed to
permissionrequest@cengage.com

Cover photograph: Image copyright Natalia Bratslavsky, 2008. Used under license from Shutterstock.com.

While every effort has been made to ensure the reliability of the information presented in this publication, Gale, a part of Cengage Learning, does not guarantee the accuracy of the data contained herein. Gale accepts no payment for listing; and inclusion in the publication of any organization, agency, institution, publication, service, or individual does not imply endorsement of the editors or publisher. Errors brought to the attention of the publisher and verified to the satisfaction of the publisher will be corrected in future editions.

Gale
27500 Drake Rd.
Farmington Hills, MI 48331-3535

ISBN-13: 978-0-7876-5103-9 (set)   ISBN-10: 0-7876-5103-6 (set)
ISBN-13: 978-1-4144-0748-7   ISBN-10: 1-4144-0748-3

ISSN 1532-2726

This title is also available as an e-book.
ISBN-13: 978-1-4144-3819-1 (set)
ISBN-10: 1-4144-3819-2 (set)
Contact your Gale sales representative for ordering information.

Printed in the United States of America
1 2 3 4 5 6 7 12 11 10 09 08

TABLE OF CONTENTS

PREFACE

Death and Dying: End-of-Life Controversies is part of the *Information Plus Reference Series*. The purpose of each volume of the series is to present the latest facts on a topic of pressing concern in modern American life. These topics include today's most controversial and studied social issues: abortion, capital punishment, care for the elderly, crime, health care, the environment, immigration, minorities, social welfare, women, youth, and many more. Even though this series is written especially for high school and undergraduate students, it is an excellent resource for anyone in need of factual information on current affairs.

By presenting the facts, it is the intention of Gale, a part of Cengage Learning, to provide its readers with everything they need to reach an informed opinion on current issues. To that end, there is a particular emphasis in this series on the presentation of scientific studies, surveys, and statistics. These data are generally presented in the form of tables, charts, and other graphics placed within the text of each book. Every graphic is directly referred to and carefully explained in the text. The source of each graphic is presented within the graphic itself. The data used in these graphics are drawn from the most reputable and reliable sources, in particular from the various branches of the U.S. government and from major independent polling organizations. Every effort has been made to secure the most recent information available. Readers should bear in mind that many major studies take years to conduct, and that additional years often pass before the data from these studies are made available to the public. Therefore, in many cases the most recent information available in 2008 is dated from 2005 or 2006. Older statistics are sometimes presented as well, if they are of particular interest and no more-recent information exists.

Even though statistics are a major focus of the *Information Plus Reference Series*, they are by no means its only content. Each book also presents the widely held positions and important ideas that shape how the book's subject is discussed in the United States. These positions are explained in detail and, where possible, in the words of their proponents. Some of the other material to be found in these books includes historical background; descriptions of major events related to the subject; relevant laws and court cases; and examples of how these issues play out in American life. Some books also feature primary documents, or have pro and con debate sections giving the words and opinions of prominent Americans on both sides of a controversial topic. All material is presented in an even-handed and unbiased manner; readers will never be encouraged to accept one view of an issue over another.

HOW TO USE THIS BOOK

Death is one of the universal human experiences. This and its ultimately unknowable nature combine to make it a topic of great interest to most Americans. How we die and how we deal with the deaths of others evokes profound religious or ethical issues, or both, about which many people hold strong beliefs. When these beliefs are in conflict with those of others, this can result in some of the most serious and divisive controversies in the modern United States. This book examines how Americans deal with death, with a particular focus on the highly charged political and moral issues of living wills, life-sustaining treatments, end-of-life care funding, and physician-assisted suicide.

Death and Dying: End-of-Life Controversies consists of eleven chapters and three appendixes. Each of the chapters is devoted to a particular aspect of death and dying in the United States. For a summary of the information covered in each chapter, please see the synopses provided in the Table of Contents at the front of the book. Chapters generally begin with an overview of the basic facts and background information on the chapter's topic, then proceed to examine subtopics of particular interest. For example, Chapter 3: The End of Life: Ethical Considerations briefly addresses the teachings about death and dying by the major world religions: Roman Catholicism, the Eastern Orthodox Church, Protestantism, Judaism, Islam, Hinduism, and Buddhism. The chapter then focuses on how bioethics and medical practice are intertwined with death and dying. More specifically, it discusses the Hippocratic Oath, the physician's role in death and dying, medical education about death and dying, and contemporary ethical guidelines for physicians. Next, patient autonomy (the right to self-rule) is examined, in which patients have the right to choose among medically recommended treatments and refuse any treatment they do not want. Cultural differences and health-care proxies and surrogate decision makers are covered in this section. Finally, the desire to die by euthanasia or by assisted suicide is addressed briefly. Readers can find their way through a chapter by looking for the section and subsection headings, which are clearly set off from the text. Or, they can refer to the book's extensive index if they already know what they are looking for.

Statistical Information

The tables and figures featured throughout *Death and Dying: End-of-Life Controversies* will be of particular use to readers in learning about this issue. These tables and figures represent an extensive collection of the most recent and important statistics on death, as well as related issues—for example, graphics in the book cover death rates for suicide, reasons for choosing hospice care, Medicare coverage of various end-of-life needs, the rise in life expectancy over the last century, and public opinion about the most fearful aspects of death. Gale, a part of Cengage Learning, believes that making this information available to readers is the most important way to fulfill the goal of this book: to help readers understand the issues and controversies surrounding death and dying in the United States and reach their own conclusions.

Each table or figure has a unique identifier appearing above it, for ease of identification and reference. Titles for the tables and figures explain their purpose. At the end of each table or figure, the original source of the data is provided.

To help readers understand these often complicated statistics, all tables and figures are explained in the text. References in the text direct readers to the relevant statistics. Furthermore, the contents of all tables and figures are fully indexed. Please see the opening section of the index at the back of this volume for a description of how to find tables and figures within it.

Appendixes

Besides the main body text and images, *Death and Dying: End-of-Life Controversies* has three appendixes. The first is the Important Names and Addresses directory. Here readers will find contact information for a number of government and private organizations that can provide further information on aspects of death and dying. The second appendix is the Resources section, which can also assist readers in conducting their own research. In this section, the author and editors of *Death and Dying: End-of-Life Controversies* describe some of the sources that were most useful during the compilation of this book. The final appendix is the detailed index, which facilitates reader access to specific topics in this book.

ADVISORY BOARD CONTRIBUTIONS

The staff of Information Plus would like to extend its heartfelt appreciation to the Information Plus Advisory Board. This dedicated group of media professionals provides feedback on the series on an ongoing basis. Their comments allow the editorial staff who work on the project to continually make the series better and more user-friendly. Our top priorities are to produce the highest-quality and most useful books possible, and the Advisory Board's contributions to this process are invaluable.

The members of the Information Plus Advisory Board are:

- Kathleen R. Bonn, Librarian, Newbury Park High School, Newbury Park, California
- Madelyn Garner, Librarian, San Jacinto College–North Campus, Houston, Texas
- Anne Oxenrider, Media Specialist, Dundee High School, Dundee, Michigan
- Charles R. Rodgers, Director of Libraries, Pasco-Hernando Community College, Dade City, Florida
- James N. Zitzelsberger, Library Media Department Chairman, Oshkosh West High School, Oshkosh, Wisconsin

COMMENTS AND SUGGESTIONS

The editors of the *Information Plus Reference Series* welcome your feedback on *Death and Dying: End-of-Life Controversies*. Please direct all correspondence to:

Editors
Information Plus Reference Series
27500 Drake Rd.
Farmington Hills, MI 48331-3535

CHAPTER 1
DEATH THROUGH THE AGES: A BRIEF OVERVIEW

Strange, is it not? That of the myriads who
Before us pass'd the door of Darkness through,
Not one returns to tell us of the Road,
Which to discover we must travel too.

—Omar Khayyám, *Rubáiyát of Omar Khayyám*

Death is the inevitable conclusion of life, a universal destiny that all living creatures share. Even though all societies throughout history have realized that death is the certain fate of human beings, different cultures have responded to it in different ways. Through the ages, attitudes toward death and dying have changed and continue to change, shaped by religious, intellectual, and philosophical beliefs and conceptions. In the twenty-first century advances in medical science and technology continue to influence ideas about death and dying.

ANCIENT TIMES

Archaeologists have found that as early as the Paleolithic period, about 2.5 million to 3 million years ago, humans held metaphysical beliefs about death and dying—those beyond what humans can know with their senses. Tools and ornaments excavated at burial sites suggest that the earliest ancestors believed that some element of a person survived the dying experience.

Ancient Hebrews (c. 1020–586 B.C.), while acknowledging the existence of the soul, were not preoccupied with the afterlife. They lived according to the commandments of their God, to whom they entrusted their eternal destiny. By contrast, early Egyptians (c. 2900–950 B.C.) thought that the preservation of the dead body (mummification) guaranteed a happy afterlife. They believed a person had a dual soul: the *ka* and the *ba*. The *ka* was the spirit that dwelled near the body, whereas the *ba* was the vitalizing soul that lived on in the netherworld (the world of the dead). Similarly, the ancient Chinese (c. 2500–1000 B.C.) also believed in a dual soul, one part of which

continued to exist after the death of the body. It was this spirit that the living venerated during ancestor worship.

Among the ancient Greeks (c. 2600–1200 B.C.), death was greatly feared. Greek mythology—which was full of tales of gods and goddesses who exacted punishment on disobedient humans—caused the living to follow rituals meticulously when burying their dead so as not to displease the gods. Even though reincarnation is usually associated with Asian religions, some Greeks were followers of Orphism, a religion that taught that the soul underwent many reincarnations until purification was achieved.

THE CLASSICAL AGE

Mythological beliefs among the ancient Greeks persisted into the classical age. The Greeks believed that after death the psyche (a person's vital essence) lived on in the underworld. The Greek writer Homer (c. eighth century–c. seventh century B.C.) greatly influenced classical Greek attitudes about death through his epic poems the *Iliad* and the *Odyssey*. Greek mythology was freely interpreted by writers after Homer, and belief in eternal judgment and retribution continued to evolve throughout this period.

Certain Greek philosophers also influenced conceptions of death. For example, Pythagoras (569?–475? B.C.) opposed euthanasia ("good death" or mercy killing) because it might disturb the soul's journey toward final purification as planned by the gods. On the contrary, Socrates (470?–399? B.C.) and Plato (428–348 B.C.) believed people could choose to end their life if they were no longer useful to themselves or the state.

Like Socrates and Plato, the classical Romans (c. 509–264 B.C.) believed a person suffering from intolerable pain or an incurable illness should have the right to choose a "good death." They considered euthanasia a "mode of dying" that allowed a person's right to take control of an intolerable situation and distinguished it from suicide, an act considered to be a shirking of responsibilities to one's family and to humankind.

THE MIDDLE AGES

During the European Middle Ages (c. 500–1485), death—with its accompanying agonies—was accepted as a destiny everyone shared, but it was still feared. As a defense against this phenomenon that could not be explained, medieval people confronted death together, as a community. Because medical practices in this era were crude and imprecise, the ill and dying person often endured prolonged suffering. However, a long period of dying gave the dying individual an opportunity to feel forewarned about impending death, to put his or her affairs in order, and to confess sins. The medieval Roman Catholic Church, with its emphasis on the eternal life of the soul in heaven or hell, held great power over people's notions of death.

By the late Middle Ages the fear of death had intensified due to the Black Death—the great plague of 1347 to 1351. The Black Death killed more than twenty-five million people in Europe alone. Commoners watched not only their neighbors stricken but also saw church officials and royalty struck down: Queen Eleanor of Aragon and King Alfonso XI (1311–1350) of Castile met with untimely deaths, and so did many at the papal court at Avignon, France. With their perceived "proper order" of existence shaken, the common people became increasingly preoccupied with their own death and with the Last Judgment, God's final and certain determination of the character of each individual. Because the Last Judgment was closely linked to an individual's disposition to heaven or hell, the event of the plague and such widespread death was frightening.

THE RENAISSANCE

From the fourteenth through the sixteenth centuries, Europe experienced new directions in economics, the arts, and social, scientific, and political thought. Nonetheless, obsession with death did not diminish with this "rebirth" of Western culture. A new self-awareness and emphasis on humans as the center of the universe further fueled the fear of dying.

By the sixteenth century many European Christians were rebelling against religion and had stopped relying on church, family, and friends to help ease their passage to the next life. The religious upheaval of the Protestant Reformation of 1520, which emphasized the individual nature of salvation, caused further uncertainties about death and dying.

The seventeenth century marked a shift from a religious to a more scientific exploration of death and dying. Lay people drifted away from the now disunited Christian church toward the medical profession, seeking answers in particular to the question of "apparent death," a condition in which people appeared to be dead but were not. In many cases unconscious patients mistakenly believed to be dead were hurriedly prepared for burial by the clergy, only to "come back to life" during burial or while being transported to the cemetery.

An understanding of death and its aftermath was clearly still elusive, even to physicians who disagreed about what happened after death. Some physicians believed the body retained some kind of "sensibility" after death. Thus, many people preserved cadavers so that the bodies could "live on." Alternatively, some physicians applied the teachings of the Catholic Church to their medical practice and believed that once the body was dead, the soul proceeded to its eternal fate and the body could no longer survive. These physicians did not preserve cadavers and pronounced them permanently dead.

THE EIGHTEENTH CENTURY

The fear of apparent death that took root in the seventeenth century resurfaced with great intensity during the eighteenth century. Coffins were built with contraptions to enable any prematurely buried person to survive and communicate from the grave. (See Figure 1.1.)

For the first time, the Christian church was blamed for hastily burying its "living dead," particularly because it had encouraged the abandonment of pagan burial traditions such as protracted mourning rituals. In the wake of apparent death incidents, more long burial traditions were revived.

THE NINETEENTH CENTURY

Premature and lingering deaths remained commonplace in the nineteenth century. Death typically took place in the home following a long deathbed watch. Family members prepared the corpse for viewing in the home, not in a funeral parlor. However, this practice changed during the late nineteenth century, when professional undertakers took over the job of preparing and burying the dead. They provided services such as readying the corpse for viewing and burial, building the coffin, digging the grave, and directing the funeral procession. Professional embalming and cosmetic restoration of bodies became widely available, all carried out in a funeral parlor where bodies were then viewed instead of in the home.

Cemeteries changed as well. Before the early nineteenth century, American cemeteries were unsanitary, overcrowded, and weed-filled places bearing an odor of decay. That began to change in 1831, when the Massa-

FIGURE 1.1

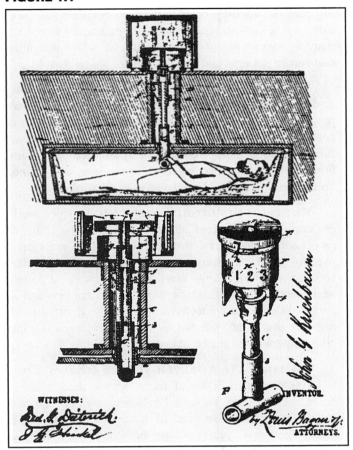

Device for indicating life in buried persons, 1882

chusetts Horticultural Society purchased seventy-two acres of fields, ponds, trees, and gardens in Cambridge and built Mount Auburn Cemetery. This cemetery was to become a model for the landscaped garden cemetery in the United States. These cemeteries were tranquil places where those grieving could visit the graves of loved ones and find comfort in the beautiful surroundings.

Literature of the time often focused on and romanticized death. Death poetry, consoling essays, and mourning manuals became available after 1830, which comforted the grieving with the concept that the deceased were released from worldly cares in heaven and that they would be reunited there with other deceased loved ones. The deadly lung disease tuberculosis—called consumption at the time—was pervasive during the nineteenth century in Europe and the United States. The disease caused sufferers to develop a certain appearance—an extreme pallor and thinness, with a look often described as haunted—that actually became a kind of fashion statement. The fixation on the subject by writers such as Edgar Allan Poe (1809–1849) and the English Romantic poets helped fuel the public's fascination with death and dying. In the late twentieth and early twenty-first centuries the popularization of the

Goth look is sometimes associated with the tubercular appearance.

Spiritualism

By the mid-nineteenth century the romanticizing of death took on a new twist in the United States. Spiritualism, in which the living communicate directly with the dead, began in 1848 in the United States with the Fox sisters: Margaret Fox (1833?–1893) and Catherine Fox (1839?–1892) of Hydesville, New York. The sisters claimed to have communicated with the spirit of a man murdered by a former tenant in their house. The practice of conducting "sittings" to contact the dead gained instant popularity. Mediums, such as the Fox sisters, were supposedly sensitive to "vibrations" from the disembodied souls that temporarily lived in that part of the spirit world just outside the earth's limits.

This was not the first time people tried to communicate with the dead. Spiritualism has been practiced in cultures all over the world. For example, many Native Americans believe shamans (priests or medicine men) have the power to communicate with the spirits of the dead. The Old Testament (I Samuel 28:7–19) recounts the visit of King Saul to a medium at Endor, who summoned the spirit of the prophet Samuel, which predicted the death of Saul and his sons.

The mood in the United States in the 1860s and 1870s was ripe for Spiritualist séances. Virtually everyone had lost a son, husband, or other loved one during the Civil War (1861–1865). Some survivors wanted assurances that their loved ones were all right; others were simply curious about life after death. Those who had drifted away from traditional Christianity embraced this new Spiritualism, which claimed scientific proof of survival after physical death.

THE MODERN AGE

Modern medicine has played a vital role in the way people die and, consequently, the manner in which the dying process of a loved one affects relatives and friends. With advancements in medical technology, the dying process has become depersonalized, as it has moved away from the familiar surroundings of home and family to the sterile world of hospitals and strangers. Certainly, the institutionalization of death has not diminished the fear of dying. Now, the fear of death also involves the fear of separation: for the living, the fear of not being present when a loved one dies, and for the dying, the prospect of facing death without the comforting presence of a loved one.

Changing Attitudes

In the last decades of the twentieth century, attitudes about death and dying slowly began to change. Aging baby boomers (people born between 1946 and 1964), facing the deaths of their parents, began to confront their own mortality. Even though medical advances continue to increase life expectancy, they have raised an entirely new set of issues associated with death and dying. For example, how long should advanced medical technology be used to keep comatose people alive? How should the elderly or incapacitated be cared for? Is it reasonable for people to stop medical treatment, or even actively end their life, if that is what they wish?

The works of the psychiatrist Elisabeth Kübler-Ross (1926–2004), including the pioneering book *On Death and Dying* (1969), have helped individuals from all walks of life confront the reality of death and restore dignity to those who are dying. Considered to be a highly respected authority on death, grief, and bereavement, Kübler-Ross influenced the medical practices undertaken at the end of life, as well as the attitudes of physicians, nurses, clergy, and others who care for the dying.

During the late 1960s medical education was revealed to be seriously deficient in areas related to death and dying. However, initiatives under way in the late twentieth and early twenty-first centuries have offered more comprehensive training about end-of-life care. With the introduction of in-home hospice care, more terminally ill people have the option of spending their final days at home with their loved ones. With the veil of secrecy lifted and open public discussions about issues related to the end of life, Americans appear more ready to learn about death and to learn from the dying.

Hospice Care

In the Middle Ages hospices were refuges for the sick, the needy, and travelers. The modern hospice movement developed in response to the need to provide humane care to terminally ill patients, while at the same time lending support to their families. The English physician Dame Cicely Saunders (1918–) is considered the founder of the modern hospice movement—first in England in 1967 and later in Canada and the United States. The soothing, calming care provided by hospice workers is called palliative care, and it aims to relieve patients' pain and the accompanying symptoms of terminal illness, while providing comfort to patients and their families.

Hospice may refer to a place—a freestanding facility or designated floor in a hospital or nursing home—or to a program such as hospice home care, in which a team of health-care professionals helps the dying patient and family at home. Hospice teams may involve physicians, nurses, social workers, pastoral counselors, and trained volunteers.

WHY PEOPLE CHOOSE HOSPICE CARE. Hospice workers consider the patient and family to be the "unit of care" and focus their efforts on attending to emotional, psychological, and spiritual needs as well as to physical comfort and well-being. With hospice care, as a patient nears death, medical details move to the background as personal details move to the foreground to avoid providing care that is not wanted by the patient, even if some clinical benefit might be expected.

THE POPULATION SERVED. Hospice facilities served 621,100 people in 2000; of these, 85.5% died while in hospice care. (See Table 1.1.) Nearly 80% of hospice patients were sixty-five years of age and older, and 26.5% were eighty-five years of age or older. Male hospice patients numbered 309,300, whereas 311,800 were female. The vast majority (84.1%) was white. Approximately half (46.6%) of the patients served were unmarried, but most of these unmarried patients were widowed. Nearly 79% of patients used Medicare as their primary source of payment for hospice services.

Even though more than half (57.5%) of those admitted to hospice care in 2000 had cancer (malignant neoplasms) as a primary diagnosis, patients with other primary diagnoses, such as Alzheimer's disease and heart, respiratory, and kidney diseases, were also served by hospice. (See Table 1.2.)

TABLE 1.1

Hospice care discharges by length of service, according to selected patient characteristics, 2000

	Discharges		Length of service in days				
			Percent distribution			Average length of service	Median length of service
Discharge characteristic	Number	Percent distribution	Total	Less than 30 days	30 days or more		
Total	621,100	100.0	100.0	62.8	37.2	46.9	15.6
Sex							
Male	309,300	49.8	100.0	66.7	33.3	42.8	14.5
Female	311,800	50.2	100.0	58.9	41.1	50.9	18.1
Age at discharge							
Under 65 years	126,900	20.4	100.0	64.1	35.9	43.9	15.0
65 years and over	494,300	79.6	100.0	62.4	37.6	47.7	16.3
65–74 years	153,100	24.7	100.0	65.0	35.0	41.2	16.4
75–84 years	176,400	28.4	100.0	62.3	37.7	50.6	16.5
85 years and over	164,800	26.5	100.0	60.2	39.8	50.5	15.9*
Race[a]							
White	522,500	84.1	100.0	62.6	37.4	46.7	14.8
Black or African American and other races	64,300	10.3	100.0	68.5	31.5	53.6*	15.8
Black or African American	50,100	8.1	100.0	66.8	33.2	61.1*	14.9*
Unknown	34,400	5.5	100.0	55.5	44.5*	36.7	26.8*
Marital status at discharge							
Married	293,400	47.2	100.0	67.5	32.5	40.0	11.7
Not married	289,500	46.6	100.0	58.8	41.2	54.1	18.5
Widowed	206,400	33.2	100.0	58.7	41.3	53.5	18.4*
Divorced or separated	35,200	5.7	100.0	63.1	36.9	74.8*	14.3*
Single or never married	47,900	7.7	100.0	56.3	43.7	41.5	19.5*
Unknown	38,300	6.2	100.0	56.4*	43.6*	45.3	24.2*
Primary source of payment							
Medicare	488,000	78.6	100.0	61.5	38.5	48.1	16.7
All other sources	133,200	21.4	100.0	67.6	32.4	42.4	10.3*
Medicaid	31,400	5.1	100.0	73.7	26.3*	24.3	5.4*
Private[b]	80,600	13.0	100.0	64.4	35.6	49.4*	11.0*
Other[c]	21,100	3.4	100.0	70.9	29.1*	42.5	7.0*
Reason for discharge							
Died	531,000	85.5	100.0	66.7	33.3	42.4	13.6
Did not die	90,200	14.5	100.0	39.5	60.5	73.1	43.6*
Services no longer needed from agency [d]	49,000	7.9	100.0	29.2*	70.8	86.2	64.7
Transferred to inpatient care[e]	14,500	2.3	100.0	*	63.9*	81.7	71.0
Other and unknown	26,700	4.3	100.0	60.2*	39.8*	44.4	10.0*

*Data do not meet standard of reliability or precision (sample size is less than 30) and are, therefore, not reported. If shown with a number, data should not be assumed reliable because the sample size is 30–59.

[a]Prior to 1998, only one race was recorded. Since 1998, more than one race may be recorded. The categories "white" and "black or African American" include only those discharges for whom that one race was reported. Discharges for whom more than one race was reported are included in "black or African American and other races."

[b]Includes private insurance, own income, family support, Social Security benefits, retirement funds, and welfare.

[c]Includes unknown source and no charge for care.

[d]Includes recovered, stabilized, treatment plan completed, no longer eligible for hospice care, and insurance coverage no longer available.

[e]Includes transferred to hospital, nursing home, or other inpatient or residential care.

Notes: Numbers may not add to totals because of rounding. Percents and average and median lengths of service are based on the unrounded figures.

SOURCE: Barbara J. Haupt, "Table 1. Number and Percent Distribution of Hospice Care Discharges by Length of Service, According to Selected Patient Characteristics: United States, 2000," in "Characteristics of Hospice Care Discharges and Their Length of Service: United States, 2000," *Vital and Health Statistics*, series 13, no. 154, August 2003, http://www.cdc.gov/nchs/data/series/sr_13/sr13_154.pdf (accessed January 28, 2008)

TABLE 1.2

Hospice care discharges, by primary and all-listed diagnoses at admission, 2000

Diagnosis	Primary diagnosis[a]		All-listed diagnoses[b]	
	Number of discharges	Percent	Number of diagnoses	Percent
Total	621,100	100.0	1,437,500	100.0
Infectious and parasitic diseases	11,400*	1.8*	18,900*	1.3*
Human immunodeficiency virus (HIV) disease	9,400*	1.5*	9,700*	0.8*
Neoplasms	363,000	58.4	599,300	41.7
Malignant neoplasms	357,000	57.5	592,000	46.8
Malignant neoplasms of large intestine and rectum	51,500	8.3	60,000	4.7
Malignant neoplasm of trachea, bronchus and lung	120,500	19.4	146,100	11.5
Malignant neoplasm of bone, connective tissue and skin	10,500*	1.7*	46,000	3.6
Malignant neoplasm of breast	16,400	2.6	18,000	1.4
Malignant neoplasm of female genital organs	15,200*	2.5*	15,700*	1.2*
Malignant neoplasm of prostate	20,600	3.3	33,700	2.7
Malignant neoplasm of urinary organs	15,500	2.5	26,900	2.1
Malignant neoplasm of hemotopoietic tissue	22,500	3.6	30,600	2.4
Malignant neoplasm of other and unspecified sites	84,200	13.6	214,900	17.0
Endocrine, nutritional, and metabolic diseases and immunity disorders	*	*	60,100	4.2
Diabetes mellitus	*	*	47,100	3.7
Mental disorders	23,800	3.8	58,600	4.1
Diseases of the nervous system and sense organs	32,100	5.2	64,700	4.5
Alzheimer's disease	16,900*	2.7*	27,600*	2.2*
Diseases of the circulatory system	72,900	11.7	243,100	16.9
Heart disease	42,500	6.8	109,200	8.6
Ischemic heart disease	*	*	21,600*	1.7*
Congestive heart failure	23,500	3.8	49,600	3.9
Cerebrovascular disease	16,900	2.7	37,800	3.0
Other diseases of the circulatory system	29,600	4.8	83,900	6.6
Diseases of the respiratory system	42,800	6.9	124,200	8.6
Chronic obstructive pulmonary disease and allied conditions	27,600	4.4	65,800	5.2
Diseases of the digestive system	12,000*	1.9*	36,100	2.5
Diseases of the genitourinary system	7,600*	1.2*	32,200	2.2
Diseases of the musculoskeletal system and connective tissue	*	*	22,800*	1.6*
Symptoms, signs and ill-defined conditions	34,800	5.6	92,900	6.5
Supplementary classification	*	*	23,700*	1.6*
Posthospital aftercare	*	*	16,600*	1.3*
Unknown or no diagnosis	*	*	—	—

*Figure does not meet standard of reliability or precision because the sample size is less than 30 if shown without an estimate. If shown with an estimate, the sample size is between 0 and 59.
— Category not applicable.
[a]Primary diagnosis is the diagnosis that is chiefly responsible for the discharges's admission to hospice care.
[b]Up to six diagnoses are recorded for each patient at admission.
Notes: Numbers may not add to totals because of rounding. Percentages are based on the unrounded numbers.

SOURCE: "Table 13. Number and Percentage of Hospice Care Discharges, by Primary and All-Listed Diagnoses at Admission: United States, 2000," in *Hospice Care Discharges*, Centers for Disease Control and Prevention, National Center for Health Statistics, February 2004, http://www.cdc.gov/nchs/data/nhhcsd/hospicecaredischarges00.pdf (accessed January 28, 2008)

CHAPTER 2
REDEFINING DEATH

TRADITIONAL DEFINITION OF DEATH

The processes of human life are sustained by many factors, but oxygen is a key to life. Respiration and blood circulation provide the body's cells with the oxygen needed to perform their life functions. When an injury or a disease compromises respiration or circulation, a breakdown in the oxygen supply can occur. As a result, the cells, deprived of essential life-sustaining oxygen, deteriorate. Using the criteria of a working heart and lungs, defining death was once quite simple: a person was considered dead once he or she stopped breathing or was without a detectable heartbeat.

A NEW CRITERION FOR DEATH

Advances in medical science have complicated the definition of death. Life-saving measures such as cardio-pulmonary resuscitation or defibrillation (electrical shock) can restart cardiac activity. The development of the mechanical respirator in the 1950s also prompted a change in the concept of death. An unconscious patient, unable to breathe without assistance, could be kept alive with a respirator and, based on the heart and lung criteria, the patient could not be declared dead.

Further complicating the issue was the transplantation of the first human heart. Experimental organ transplantation has been performed since the early 1900s. In the 1960s transplantation of organs such as kidneys became routine practice. Kidneys could be harvested from a patient whose heart had stopped and who therefore could be declared legally dead. By contrast, a successful heart transplant required a beating heart from a "dead" donor. On December 3, 1967, the South African surgeon Christiaan Barnard (1922–2001) transplanted a heart from a fatally injured accident victim into Louis Washkansky (1913–1967). Washkansky's health declined within a week after the surgery, and he died eighteen days later from pneumonia.

Physicians who had been debating how best to handle patients whose life functions were supported mechanically now faced a new dilemma. With the first successful heart transplant, such patients now became potential heart donors, and it became necessary to ensure that a patient was truly dead before the heart was actually removed. Thus, physicians proposed a new criterion for death: irreversible cessation of brain activity, or what many called brain death.

The Harvard Criteria

In 1968 the Ad Hoc Committee of the Harvard Medical School to Examine the Definition of Brain Death was organized. The goal of the Harvard Brain Death Committee, as it was also known, was to redefine death. On August 5, 1968, the committee published the report "A Definition of Irreversible Coma" (*Journal of the American Medical Association*, vol. 205, no. 6). This landmark report, known as the Harvard Criteria, listed the following guidelines for identifying irreversible coma:

- Unreceptivity and unresponsivity—the patient is completely unaware of externally applied stimuli and inner need. He or she does not respond even to intensely painful stimuli.

- No movements or breathing—the patient shows no sign of spontaneous movements and spontaneous respiration and does not respond to pain, touch, sound, or light.

- No reflexes—the pupils of the eyes are fixed and dilated. The patient shows no eye movement even when the ear is flushed with ice water or the head is turned. He or she does not react to harmful stimuli and exhibits no tendon reflexes.

- Flat electroencephalogram (EEG)—this shows lack of electrical activity in the cerebral cortex.

The Harvard Criteria could not be used unless reversible causes of brain dysfunction, such as drug intoxication and hypothermia (abnormally low body temperature—below 90°F core temperature), had been ruled out. The committee further recommended that the four tests be repeated twenty-four hours after the initial test.

The Harvard committee stated, "Our primary purpose is to define irreversible coma as a new criterion for death." Despite this, the committee in effect reinforced brain death—a lack of all neurological activity in the brain and brain stem—as the legal criterion for the death of a patient. A patient who met all four guidelines could be declared dead, and his or her respirator could be withdrawn. The committee added, however, "We are concerned here only with those comatose individuals who have no discernible central nervous system activity." Brain death differs somewhat from irreversible coma; patients in deep coma may show brain activity on an EEG, even though they may not be able to breathe on their own. People in a persistent vegetative state are also in an irreversible coma; however, they show more brain activity on an EEG than patients in deep coma and are able to breathe without the help of a respirator. Such patients were not considered dead by the committee's definition because they still had brain activity.

Criticisms of the Harvard Criteria

In 1978 Public Law 95-622 established the ethical advisory body called the President's Commission for the Study of Ethical Problems in Medicine and Biomedical and Behavioral Research. President Ronald Reagan (1911–2004) assigned the commission the task of defining death. In *Defining Death: Medical, Legal, and Ethical Issues in the Determination of Death* (July 1981, http://www.bioethics.gov/reports/past_commissions/defining _death.pdf), the commission reported that "the 'Harvard Criteria' have been found to be quite reliable. Indeed, no case has yet been found that met these criteria and regained any brain functions despite continuation of respirator support."

However, the commission noted the following deficiencies in the Harvard Criteria:

- The phrase "irreversible coma" is misleading. Coma is a condition of a living person. A person lacking in brain functions is dead and, therefore, beyond the condition called coma.

- The Harvard Brain Death Committee failed to note that spinal cord reflexes can continue or resume activity even after the brain stops functioning.

- "Unreceptivity" cannot be tested in an unresponsive person who has lost consciousness.

- The committee had not been "sufficiently explicit and precise" in expressing the need for adequate testing of brain stem reflexes, especially apnea (absence of the impulse to breathe, leading to an inability to breathe

spontaneously). Adequate testing to eliminate drug and metabolic intoxication as possible causes of the coma had also not been spelled out explicitly. Metabolic intoxication refers to the accumulation of toxins (poisons) in the blood resulting from kidney or liver failure. These toxins can severely impair brain functioning and cause coma, but the condition is potentially reversible.

- Even though all people who satisfy the Harvard Criteria are dead (with irreversible cessation of whole-brain functions), many dead individuals cannot maintain circulation long enough for retesting after a 24-hour interval.

THE GOVERNMENT REDEFINES DEATH

The President's Commission proposed in *Defining Death* a model statute, the Uniform Determination of Death Act, the guidelines of which would be used to define death:

- [Determination of Death.] An individual who has sustained either (1) irreversible cessation of circulatory and respiratory functions, or (2) irreversible cessation of all functions of the entire brain, including the brain stem, is dead. A determination of death must be made in accordance with accepted medical standards.

- [Uniformity of Construction and Application.] This act shall be applied and construed to effectuate its general purpose to make uniform the law with respect to the subject of this Act among states enacting it.

Brain Death

In *Defining Death*, the President's Commission incorporated two formulations or concepts of the "whole-brain definition" of death. It stated that these two concepts were "actually mirror images of each other. The Commission has found them to be complementary; together they enrich one's understanding of the 'definition' [of death]."

The first whole-brain formulation states that death occurs when the three major organs (heart, lungs, and brain) suffer an irreversible functional breakdown. These organs are closely interrelated, so that if one stops functioning permanently, the other two will also stop working. Even though traditionally the absence of the "vital signs" of respiration and circulation have signified death, this is simply a sign that the brain, the core organ, has permanently ceased to function. Even if individual cells or organs continue to live, the body as a whole cannot survive for long. Therefore, death can be declared even before the whole system shuts down.

The second whole-brain formulation "identifies the functioning of the whole brain as the hallmark of life because the brain is the regulator of the body's integration." Because the brain is the seat of consciousness and the director of all bodily functions, when the brain dies, the person is considered dead.

Reason for Two Definitions of Death

The President's Commission claimed in *Defining Death* that its aim was to "supplement rather than supplant [take the place of] the existing legal concept." The brain-death criteria were not being introduced to define death in a new way. In most cases the cardiopulmonary definition of death would be sufficient. Only comatose patients on respirators would be diagnosed using the brain-death criteria.

Criteria for Determination of Death

The President's Commission did not include in the proposed Uniform Determination of Death Act any specific medical criteria for diagnosing brain death. Instead, it had a group of medical consultants develop a summary of currently accepted medical practices. The commission stated that "such criteria—particularly as they relate to diagnosing death on neurological grounds—will be continually revised by the biomedical community in light of clinical experience and new scientific knowledge." These Criteria for Determination of Death read as follows (with medical details omitted here):

1. An individual with irreversible cessation of circulatory and respiratory functions is dead. A) Cessation is recognized by an appropriate clinical examination. B) Irreversibility is recognized by persistent cessation of functions during an appropriate period of observation and/or trial of therapy.

2. An individual with irreversible cessation of all functions of the entire brain, including the brainstem, is dead. A) Cessation is recognized when evaluation discloses findings that cerebral functions are absent and brainstem functions are absent. B) Irreversibility is recognized when evaluation discloses findings that the cause of coma is established and is sufficient to account for the loss of brain functions; the possibility of recovery of any brain functions is excluded; and the cessation of all brain functions persists for an appropriate period of observation and/or trial of therapy.

The Criteria for Determination of Death further warn that conditions such as drug intoxication, metabolic intoxication, and hypothermia may be confused with brain death. Physicians should practice caution when dealing with young children and people in shock. Infants and young children, who have more resistance to neurological damage, have been known to recover brain function. Shock victims might not test well due to a reduction in blood circulation to the brain.

The Brain-Death Concept and Brain-Death Criteria around the World

Since the development of brain-death criteria in the United States, most countries have adopted the brain-death concept. Nevertheless, determining brain death varies worldwide. One reason has to do with cultural or religious beliefs. For example, in Japan it is believed that the soul lingers in the body for some time after death. Such a belief may influence the length of time the patient is observed before making the determination of death.

Eelco F. M. Wijdicks of the Mayo Medical Center in Rochester, Minnesota, surveyed brain-death criteria throughout the world and reported his results in "Brain Death Worldwide: Accepted Fact but No Global Consensus in Diagnostic Criteria" (*Neurology*, vol. 58, no. 1, 2002). Wijdicks obtained brain-death guidelines for adults in eighty countries and determined that seventy of the eighty countries had guidelines for clinical practice in determining brain death. In examining these guidelines, Wijdicks finds major differences in the procedures used for diagnosing brain death in adults. For example, in some countries brain-death criteria are left up to the physician to determine, whereas in other countries written guidelines are extremely complicated. In some countries confirmatory laboratory tests are mandatory, whereas in others they are not. Because of these and many other differences in brain-death diagnostic criteria across countries, Wijdicks suggests that countries worldwide consider standardizing procedures to determine brain death.

What are the diagnostic criteria for determining brain death in the United States? In "Variability among Hospital Policies for Determining Brain Death in Adults" (*Critical Care Medicine*, vol. 32, no. 6, June 2004), David J. Powner, Michael Hernandez, and Terry E. Rives explain that there is no federally mandated definition for brain death or method for certifying brain death. Thus, states have adopted the Uniform Determination of Death Act as described in the previous section. However, within each hospital clinical practice is determined by the medical staff and administrative committees. The researchers studied six hundred randomly selected hospitals to determine whether differences exist among hospital policies for the certification of brain death. They determine that differences exist and suggest that policies be standardized. Wijdicks and Ronald E. Cranford list in "Clinical Diagnosis of Prolonged States of Impaired Consciousness in Adults" (*Mayo Clinic Proceedings*, vol. 80, no. 8, August 2005) clinical criteria for brain death. (See Table 2.1.)

In the editorial "The Clinical Criteria of Brain Death throughout the World: Why Has It Come to This?" (*Canadian Journal of Anesthesia*, vol. 53, no. 6, June 2006), Wijdicks emphasizes the variability of international brain-death guidelines, as well as the variability of hospital policies and practices in the United States. Wijdicks concludes that "what is required is standardization of policy, appropriate education of staff, introduction of checklists in intensive care units, and brain death examination by designated, experienced physicians who have documented proficiency in brain death examination." David M. Greer et al. confirm in "Variability of Brain

TABLE 2.1

Criteria for brain death

Coma
Absence of motor responses
Absence of pupillary responses to light and pupils at midposition with respect to
   dilatation (4–6 mm)
Absence of corneal reflexes
Absence of caloric responses
Absence of gag reflex
Absence of coughing in response to tracheal suctioning
Absence of respiratory drive at PaCO₂ that is 60 mm Hg or 20 mm Hg above normal
   baseline values

SOURCE: Eelco F.M. Wijdicks and Ronald E. Cranford, "Table 3. Clinical Criteria for Brain Death," in "Clinical Diagnosis of Prolonged States of Impaired Consciousness in Adults," *Mayo Clinic Proceedings*, vol. 80, no. 8, August 2005, http://www.mayoclinicproceedings.com/pdf%2F8008%2F8008-r1%2Epdf (accessed March 25, 2008). Data from E.F.M. Wijdicks, "The Diagnosis of the Brain," *New England Journal of Medicine*, no. 344 (2001): 1215–21.

FIGURE 2.1

Parts of the brain

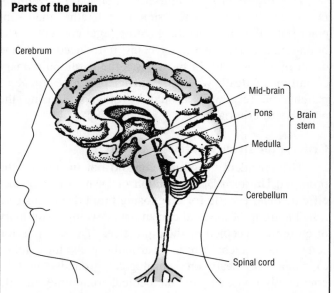

SOURCE: Adapted from "Figure 2. Anatomic Interrelationships of Heart, Lungs, and Brain," in *Defining Death: A Report on the Medical, Legal and Ethical Issues in the Determination of Death*, President's Commission for the Study of Ethical Problems in Medicine and Biomedical and Behavioral Research, July 1981, http://www.bioethics.gov/reports/past_commissions/defining_death.pdf (accessed March 25, 2008)

TABLE 2.2

Criteria for a persistent vegetative state (PVS)

1. No evidence of awareness of themselves or their environment; they are incapable of interacting with others
2. No evidence of sustained, reproducible, purposeful, or voluntary behavioral responses to visual, auditory, tactile, or noxious stimuli
3. No evidence of language comprehension or expression
4. Intermittent wakefulness manifested by the presence of sleep-wake cycles
5. Sufficiently preserved hypothalamic and brainstem autonomic functions to survive if given medical and nursing care
6. Bowel and bladder incontinence
7. Variably preserved cranial nerve (pupillary, oculocephalic, corneal, vestibulo-ocular, and gag) and spinal reflexes

SOURCE: Eelco F.M. Wijdicks and Ronald E. Cranford, "Table 1. Criteria for the Diagnosis of a Persistent Vegetative State," in "Clinical Diagnosis of Prolonged States of Impaired Consciousness in Adults," *Mayo Clinic Proceedings*, vol. 80, no. 8, pp. 1037–1046, August 2005. Reproduced with permission from Dowden Health Media.

Death Determination Guidelines in Leading US Neurologic Institutions" (*Neurology*, vol. 70, no. 4, January 22, 2008) the continuing variation in determining brain death in the United States via a survey of leading neurologic hospitals.

Brain Death and Persistent Vegetative State

In the past people who suffered severe head injuries usually died from apnea. In the twenty-first century rapid emergency medical intervention allows them to be placed on respirators before breathing stops. In some cases the primary brain damage may be reversible, and unassisted breathing eventually resumes. In many cases, however, brain damage is irreversible, and, if the respirator is not disconnected, it will continue to pump blood to the dead brain.

The brain stem, traditionally called the lower brain, is usually more resistant to damage from anoxia (oxygen deprivation). Thus, oxygen deprivation may cause irreversible damage to the cerebrum, or higher brain, but may spare the brain stem. (See Figure 2.1.) When the cerebrum is irreversibly damaged yet the brain stem still functions, the patient goes into a persistent vegetative state, also called persistent noncognitive state. Persistent vegetative state patients, lacking in the higher-brain functions, are awake but unaware. They swallow, grimace when in pain, yawn, open their eyes, and may even breathe without a respirator. Table 2.2 lists the criteria for the diagnosis of the persistent vegetative state.

The case of Karen Ann Quinlan called attention to the ramifications of the persistent vegetative state. In 1975 Quinlan suffered a cardiopulmonary arrest after ingesting a combination of alcohol and drugs. In 1976 Joseph Quinlan was granted court permission to discontinue artificial respiration for his comatose daughter. Even after life sup-

port was removed, Karen remained in a persistent vegetative state until she died of multiple infections in 1985.

A more recent case that has refocused national attention on the persistent vegetative state is that of Terri Schiavo, who entered a persistent vegetative state in 1990, when her brain was deprived of oxygen during a heart attack brought on by an eating disorder. Her husband argued that she would never recover and that his wife would not want to be kept alive by artificial means.

He petitioned a Florida court to remove her feeding tube. In October 2003 a Florida judge ruled that the tube should be removed. However, Schiavo's parents believed their daughter would recover and requested that the Florida governor Jeb Bush (1953–) intervene. The Florida legislature subsequently gave Governor Bush the authority to override the courts, and the feeding tube was reinserted six days after its removal.

In May 2004 the law that allowed Governor Bush to intervene in the case was ruled unconstitutional by a Florida appeals court. The case was then appealed to the U.S. Supreme Court, which in January 2005 refused to hear the appeal and reinstate the Florida law. In March 2005 doctors removed Terri Schiavo's feeding tube. She died thirteen days later. An autopsy showed extensive damage throughout the cerebrum.

Patients in a persistent vegetative state are not dead, and so the brain-death criteria do not apply to them. They can survive for years with artificial feeding and antibiotics for possible infections. The President's Commission reported on a patient who remained in a persistent vegetative state for thirty-seven years: Elaine Esposito lapsed into a coma after surgery in 1941 and died in 1978.

THE NEAR-DEATH EXPERIENCE

The term *near-death experience* was first used by Raymond A. Moody Jr. in *Life after Life: The Investigation of a Phenomenon—Survival of Bodily Death* (1976), a compilation of interviews with people who claimed to have come back from the dead. A decade earlier, Elisabeth Kübler-Ross investigated out-of-body episodes recounted by her patients.

The near-death experience is not a phenomenon limited to modern times. It has been recounted in various forms of mysticism, as well as by well-known historical figures such as the Greek philosopher Plato (428–348 B.C.) and the Benedictine historian and theologian St. Bede (673–735). It appears, however, that the development and administration of emergency resuscitation has contributed to widespread reports of near-death experiences.

Some people who were revived after having been declared clinically dead have recounted remarkably similar patterns of experiences. They report leaving their body and watching, in a detached manner, while others tried to save their life. They felt no pain and experienced complete serenity. After traveling through a tunnel, they encountered a radiant light. Some claim they met friends and relatives who have died; many attest to seeing their whole life replayed and of ultimately being given either a choice or a command to return to their body.

Many people who have had a near-death experience believe they have undergone a spiritual event of great importance. For example, they may believe that they saw, or even entered, the afterlife. Studies conducted during the 1990s indicated that the near-death experience might be related to one or more physical changes in the brain. These changes include the gradual onset of anoxia in the brain; residual electrical activity in the brain; the release of endorphins in response to stress; or drug-induced hallucinations produced by drug therapies used during resuscitation attempts or resulting from previous drug abuse.

Not everyone who has been close to death has had a near-death experience. These experiences are atypical reactions to trauma, and the involvement of the temporal lobes of the brain in these experiences has been explored by researchers for decades. In "Near-Death Experiences and the Temporal Lobe" (*Psychological Science*, vol. 15, no. 4, April 2004), Willoughby Britton and Richard Bootzin discuss the results of their study of temporal lobe functioning in forty-three individuals who had experienced life-threatening events. Of these forty-three participants, twenty-three reported having had near-death experiences during these events. The researchers find that people who reported near-death experiences had more of certain types of temporal lobe activity than those who did not have such experiences. The researchers conclude that "altered temporal lobe functioning may be involved in the near-death experience and that individuals who have had such experiences are physiologically distinct from the general population."

CHAPTER 3
THE END OF LIFE: ETHICAL CONSIDERATIONS

Defining death has become a complex matter. Innovative medical technology, while saving many lives, has also blurred the lines between life and death. The controversy about the definition of death is but one of the ethical issues, or principles of moral conduct, related to end-of-life care and decision making. For example, should a son or daughter request the withdrawal of nutrition and hydration from a parent in a persistent vegetative state, knowing that parent's respect for the sanctity of life? Does a physician honor a patient's do-not-resuscitate request when it goes against the physician's ethical convictions? Who should determine when medical care is futile and no longer benefits the dying patient?

The answers to questions about care at the end of life, as well as decisions made by people who are dying and by their loved ones, vary in response to cultural influences, family issues, and spiritual beliefs. Historical, social, cultural, political, and religious convictions shape ethical beliefs about death and guide the actions of health-care professionals and people who are terminally ill. For people of faith, religious convictions are vitally important when making end-of-life decisions.

RELIGIOUS TEACHINGS

All major religions consider life sacred. When it comes to death and dying, they take seriously the fate of the soul, be it eternal salvation (as in Christian belief) or reincarnation (as in Buddhist philosophy).

Roman Catholicism

According to Catholic teachings, death is contrary to God's plan for humankind. In the Old Testament story of Genesis, when God created human beings, he did not intend for them to die. However, when Adam and Eve (the first humans) disobeyed God in the Garden of Eden, physical death was the consequence of their sin. In the New Testament section of the Bible, Jesus was the Son of God who,

out of love for humankind, was born into the world and died as a man. God raised Jesus from the dead after his crucifixion to live eternally with him in heaven, and Jesus promised humankind the same opportunity. The *Catechism of the Catholic Church* (2003) notes that according to Christian doctrine, Jesus "transformed the curse of death into a blessing."

HISTORY. Early Christians believed God was the giver of life, and therefore he alone could take life away. They viewed euthanasia (hastening the death of a dying, suffering patient who requests death) as usurping that divine right. The early Christian philosopher St. Augustine of Hippo (354–430) taught that people must accept suffering because it comes from God. According to Augustine, suffering not only helps one grow spiritually but also prepares Christians for the eternal joy that God has in store for them. Moreover, the healthy were exhorted to minister to the sick not for the purpose of helping to permanently end their suffering, but to ease their pain.

St. Thomas Aquinas (1225?–1274), who is considered to be one of the greatest Catholic theologians, taught that ending one's suffering by ending one's life was sinful. To help another take his or her life was just as sinful. However, in 1516 Sir Thomas More (1478–1535), an English statesman, humanist, and loyal defender of the Catholic Church, published *Utopia*, which described an ideal country governed by reason. More argued that if a disease is not only incurable but also causes pain that is hard to control, it is permissible to free the sufferer from his or her painful existence. This was a major departure from the medieval acceptance of suffering and death as the earthly price to be paid for eternal life.

PRINCIPLE OF DOUBLE EFFECT. Catholic moral theologians were said to have developed the ethical principle "Rule of Double Effect." According to this principle, "Effects that would be morally wrong if caused intentionally are permissible if foreseen but unintended." For example, a physician prescribes an increased dosage of the painkiller morphine to ease a patient's pain, not to bring about his or her death. However, it is foreseen that a potent dosage may depress the patient's respiration and hasten death. The *Catechism of the Catholic Church* states that "the use of painkillers to alleviate the sufferings of the dying, even at the risk of shortening their days, can be morally in conformity with human dignity if death is not willed as either an end or a means, but only foreseen and tolerated as inevitable."

ON EUTHANASIA. Over the years, Catholic theologians have debated balancing the preservation of God-given life with the moral issue of continuing medical treatments that are of no apparent value to patients. In "The Prolongation of Life" (1957), Pope Pius XII (1876–1958) states that if a patient is hopelessly ill, physicians may discontinue heroic measures "to permit the patient, already virtually dead, to pass on in peace." He adds that if the patient is unconscious, relatives may request withdrawal of life support under certain conditions.

The Committee for Pro-Life Activities of the National Conference of Catholic Bishops states in *Nutrition and Hydration: Moral and Pastoral Reflections* (April 1992, http://www.priestsforlife.org/magisterium/bishops/92-04nutritionandhydrationnccbprolifecommittee.htm) that "in the final stage of dying one is not obliged to prolong the life of a patient by every possible means: 'When inevitable death is imminent in spite of the means used, it is permitted in conscience to take the decision to refuse forms of treatment that would only secure a precarious and burdensome prolongation of life, so long as the normal care due to the sick person in similar cases is not interrupted.'"

The Eastern Orthodox Church

The Eastern Orthodox Church resulted from the division between eastern and western Christianity during the eleventh century. Differences in doctrines and politics, among other things, caused the separation. The Eastern Orthodox Church does not have a single worldwide leader such as the Roman Catholic pope. Instead, national jurisdictions called sees are each governed by a bishop.

Eastern Orthodoxy relies on the Scriptures, tradition, and the decrees of the first seven ecumenical councils to regulate its daily conduct. In matters of present-day morality, such as the debates on end-of-life issues, contemporary Orthodox ethicists explore possible courses of action that are in line with the "sense of the Church." The sense of the church is deduced from church laws and dissertations of the church fathers, as well as from previous council decisions. Their recommendations are subject to further review.

In "The Stand of the Orthodox Church on Controversial Issues" (2005, http://www.goarch.org/en/ourfaith/articles/article7101.asp), the Reverend Stanley Harakas

states, "The Orthodox Church has a very strong pro-life stand which in part expresses itself in opposition to doctrinaire advocacy of euthanasia." However, Harakas notes that "as current Orthodox theology expresses it: 'The Church distinguishes between euthanasia and the withholding of extraordinary means to prolong life. It affirms the sanctity of human life and man's God-given responsibility to preserve life. But it rejects an attitude which disregards the inevitability of physical death.'"

Protestantism

The different denominations of Protestantism have varying positions about euthanasia. Many hold that active euthanasia is morally wrong, but they also believe that prolonging life by extraordinary measures is not necessary. In other words, even though few would condone active euthanasia, many accept passive euthanasia. (Active euthanasia involves the hastening of death through the administration of lethal drugs. Passive euthanasia refers to withdrawing life support or medical interventions necessary to sustain life, such as removing a patient from a ventilator.) Among the Protestant denominations that support the latter view are the Jehovah's Witnesses, the Church of Jesus Christ of Latter-day Saints (Mormons), the Lutheran Church, the Reformed Presbyterians, the Presbyterian Church in America, the Christian Life Commission of the Southern Baptist Convention, and the General Association of the General Baptists.

Some denominations have no official policy on active or passive euthanasia. However, many individual ethicists and representatives within these churches agree with other denominations that active euthanasia is morally wrong but that futile life support serves no purpose. Among these churches are the Seventh-Day Adventists, the Episcopal Church, and the United Methodist Church.

Christian Scientists believe that prayer heals all diseases. They claim that illnesses are mental in origin and therefore cannot be cured by outside intervention, such as medical help. Some also believe that seeking medical help while praying diminishes or even cancels the effectiveness of the prayers. Because God can heal even those diseases others see as incurable, euthanasia has no practical significance among Christian Scientists.

The Unitarian Universalist Association, a union of the Unitarian and Universalist Churches, is perhaps the most liberal when it comes to the right to die. The association states in "The Right to Die with Dignity: 1988 General Resolution" (March 28, 2007, http://www.uua.org/socialjustice/socialjustice/statements/14486.shtml) that "human life has inherent dignity, which may be compromised when life is extended beyond the will or ability of a person to sustain that dignity." Furthermore, "Unitarian Universalists advocate the right to self-determination in dying, and the release from civil or criminal penalties of those who, under proper safeguards, act to honor the right of terminally ill patients to select the time of their own deaths."

Judaism

In the United States there are three main branches of Judaism. The Orthodox tradition adheres strictly to Jewish laws. Conservative Judaism advocates adapting Jewish precepts to a changing world, but all changes must be consistent with Jewish laws and tradition. Reform Judaism, while accepting the ethical laws as coming from God, generally considers the other laws of Judaism as "instructional but not binding."

Like the Roman Catholics, Jews believe that life is precious because it is a gift from God. No one has the right to extinguish life, because one's life is not his or hers in the first place. Generally, rabbis from all branches of Judaism agree that active euthanasia is not morally justified. It is tantamount to murder, which is forbidden by the Torah. Moreover, Jewish teaching holds that men and women are stewards entrusted with the preservation of God's gift of life and therefore are obliged to hold on to that life as long as possible.

PROLONGING LIFE VERSUS HASTENING DEATH. Even though Jewish tradition maintains that a devout believer must do everything possible to prolong life, this admonition is subject to interpretation even among Orthodox Jews.

The Torah and the Talmud (the definitive rabbinical compilation of Jewish laws, lore, and commentary) provide the principles and laws that guide Jews. The Talmud provides continuity to Jewish culture by interpreting the Torah and adapting it to the constantly changing situations of Jewish people.

On the subject of prolonging life versus hastening death, when that life is clearly nearing death, the Talmud narrates a number of situations involving people who are considered "goses" (literally, the death rattle is in the patient's throat, or one whose death is imminent). Scholars often refer to the story of Rabbi Hanina ben Teradyon, who, during the second century, was condemned to be burned to death by the Romans. To prolong his agonizing death, the Romans wrapped him in some wet material. At first, the rabbi refused to hasten his own death; however, he later agreed to have the wet material removed, thus bringing about a quicker death.

Some Jews interpret this Talmudic narration to mean that in the final stage of a person's life, it is permissible to remove any hindrance to the dying process. In this modern age of medicine, this may mean implementing a patient's wish, such as a do-not-resuscitate directive or the withdrawal of artificial life support.

Islam

Islam was founded by the prophet Muhammad (570–632) in the seventh century. The Koran, which is composed of God's revelations to Muhammad, and the sunna, Muhammad's teachings and deeds, are the sources of Islamic beliefs and practice. Even though there are many sects and cultural diversities within the religion, all Muslims (followers of Islam) are bound by a total submission to the will of Allah (God). The basic doctrines of Allah's revelations were systematized into definitive rules and regulations that now comprise the sharia (the religious law that governs the life of Muslims).

Muslims look to the sharia for ethical guidance in all aspects of life, including medicine. Sickness and pain are part of life and must be accepted as Allah's will. They should be viewed as a means to atone for one's sins. By contrast, death is simply a passage to another existence in the afterlife. Those who die after leading a righteous life will merit the true life on Judgment Day. The Koran (chapter 2, verse 28) states, "How do you disbelieve in God seeing you were dead and He gave you life and then He shall cause you to die, then He shall give you life, then unto Him you shall be returned?"

Islam teaches that life is a gift from Allah; therefore, no one can end it except Allah. Muhammad said, "Whosoever takes poison and thus kills himself, his poison will be in his hand; he will be tasting it in Hell, always abiding therein, and being accommodated therein forever" (compiled in *Sahih Bukhari*). While an ailing person does not have the right to choose death, even if he or she is suffering, Muslims heed the following admonition from the *Islamic Code of Medical Ethics* (1981): "[The] doctor is well advised to realize his limit and not transgress it. If it is scientifically certain that life cannot be restored, then it is futile to diligently [maintain] the vegetative state of the patient by heroic means.... It is the process of life that the doctor aims to maintain and not the process of dying. In any case, the doctor shall not take a positive measure to terminate the patient's life."

Hinduism

The Eastern religious tradition of Hinduism is founded on the principle of reincarnation (the cycle of life, death, and physical rebirth). Hindus believe that death and dying are intricately interwoven with life and that the individual soul undergoes a series of physical life cycles before uniting with Brahman (God). Karma refers to the ethical consequences of a person's actions during a previous life, which determine the quality of his or her present life. A person can neither change nor escape his or her karma. By conforming to dharma (religious and moral law), an individual is able to fulfill obligations from the past life. Life is sacred because it offers one the chance to perform good acts toward the goal of ending the cycle of rebirths.

Therefore, a believer in Hinduism views pain and suffering as personal karma, and serious illness as a consequence of past misdeeds. Death is simply a passage to another rebirth, which brings one closer to Brahman. Artificial medical treatments to sustain life are not recommended, and medical intervention to end life is discouraged. Active euthanasia simply interrupts one's karma and the soul's evolution toward final liberation from reincarnation.

Buddhism

Buddhism, like Hinduism, is based on a cycle of reincarnation. To Buddhists, the goals of every life are emancipation from samsara (the compulsory cycle of rebirths) and attainment of nirvana (enlightenment or bliss). Like the Hindus, Buddhists believe that sickness, death, and karma are interrelated. Followers of Siddhartha Gautama (c. 563–483 B.C.), also called Buddha, the founder of Buddhism, claim that Buddha advised against taking too strict a position when it comes to issues such as the right to die.

Tenzin Gyatso (1935–), the fourteenth Dalai Lama, the spiritual leader of Tibetan Buddhism, has commented on the use of mechanical life support when the patient has no chance to recover. Sogyal Rinpoche explains in *The Tibetan Book of Living and Dying* (1992) that rather than advocating or condemning passive euthanasia, the Dalai Lama advises that each case be considered individually: "If there is no such chance for positive thoughts [Buddhists believe that a dying person's final thoughts determine the circumstances of his next life], and in addition a lot of money is being spent by relatives simply to keep someone alive, then there seems to be no point. But each case must be dealt with individually; it is very difficult to generalize."

BIOETHICS AND MEDICAL PRACTICE

Since ancient times, medical practice has been concerned with ethical issues. However, only since the last half of the twentieth century have rapid advances in medicine given rise to so many ethical dilemmas. In matters of death and dying the debate continues on issues such as physicians' honoring a patient's do-not-resuscitate order, withholding food and fluids, and withdrawing artificial respiration.

There are four basic tenets of bioethics: autonomy, beneficence, nonmaleficence, and justice. Autonomy refers to self-rule and self-determination. Beneficence is action that is in the best interest of the patient. Nonmaleficence means to do no harm. Justice is the practice of treating patients in comparable circumstances the same way and refers to equitable distribution of resources, risks, and costs.

Even though bioethics is subject to change and reinterpretation, medical practice continues to rely on these principles to guide the actions of physicians and other health-care providers.

The Hippocratic Oath

The earliest written document to deal with medical ethics is generally attributed to Hippocrates (c. 460–c. 377 B.C.), who is considered the father of medicine. For more than two thousand years, the Hippocratic Oath has been adopted by Western physicians as a code of ethics, defining their conduct in the discharge of their duties. In part, the oath states: "I will follow that method of treatment, which, according to my ability and judgment, I consider for the benefit of my patients, and abstain from whatever is deleterious [harmful] and mischievous. I will give no deadly medicine to anyone if asked, nor suggest any such counsel."

Nonetheless, some scholars claim that the giving of "deadly medicine" does not refer to euthanasia. During the time of Hippocrates, helping a suffering person end his or her life was common practice. Therefore, the oath might have been more an admonition to the medical profession to avoid acting as an accomplice to murder, rather than to refrain from the practice of euthanasia.

Some physicians believe that literal interpretation of the oath is not necessary. It simply offers guidelines that allow for adaptation to twenty-first-century situations. In fact, in 1948 the World Medical Association modified the Hippocratic Oath to call attention to the atrocities committed by Nazi physicians. Known as the Declaration of Geneva (October 14, 2006, http://www.wma.net/e/policy/c8.htm), the document reads in part: "I will practise my profession with conscience and dignity. The health of my patient will be my first consideration.... I will not permit considerations of age, disease or disability, creed, ethnic origin, gender, nationality, political affiliation, race, sexual orientation, social standing or any other factor to intervene between my duty and my patient. I will maintain the utmost respect for human life. I will not use my medical knowledge to violate human rights and civil liberties, even under threat."

The Physician's Role

Even in ancient times, as can be gleaned from the Hippocratic Oath, physicians believed they knew what was best for their patients. Patients relied on their doctors' ability and judgment, and usually did not question the treatments prescribed. Doctors were not even required to tell their patients the details of their illness, even if they were terminally ill.

Beginning in the 1960s many patients assumed a more active role in their medical care. The emphasis on preventive medicine encouraged people to take responsibility for their own health. Physicians were faced with a new breed of patients who wanted to be active participants in their health care. Patients also wanted to know more about modern technologies and procedures that were evolving in medicine. With this new health consciousness, physicians and hospitals assumed the responsibility for informing and educating patients, and increasingly were legally liable for failing to inform patients of the consequences of medical treatments and procedures.

To compound the complexity of the changing patient-physician relationship, modern technology, which could sometimes prolong life, was also prolonging death. Historically, physicians had been trained to prevent and combat death, rather than to deal with dying patients, communicate with the patient and the family about a terminal illness, prepare them for an imminent death, or respond to a patient requesting assisted suicide.

Medical Education in Death and Dying

George E. Dickinson of the College of Charleston in Charleston, South Carolina, studied medical school offerings on end-of-life issues between 1975 and 2005 by mailing brief questionnaires to all accredited medical schools in the United States in 1975, 1980, 1985, 1990, 1995, 2000, and 2005. Table 3.1 shows trends in medical school offerings in death and dying from 1975 to 2005. The percentage of medical schools offering separate courses in death and dying fluctuated over those years, with a low of 7% of medical schools in 1975 to a high of 18% of medical schools in both 1990 and 2000. The percentage of lectures and short courses incorporating death and dying information also fluctuated from 1975 through 2005, with a low of 70% of lectures and short courses incorporating death and dying topics in 1995 to a high of 87% in 2005. Nonetheless, the number of students enrolled in death and dying offerings grew steadily during that time, growing slowly from 71% in 1975 to 77% in 1995. A jump then occurred, with medical schools reporting 96% of their students enrolled in death and dying offerings in both 2000 and 2005.

Table 3.2 shows trends in U.S. medical school offerings in palliative care from 2000 to 2005. (The goal of palliative care is to relieve symptoms and suffering, rather than to treat or cure disease.) In both 2000 and 2005 palliative care training was not covered in separate courses in many U.S. medical schools, with only 11% of schools offering a separate course in 2000 and 8% in 2005. The most popular mode of palliative care training by medical schools was incorporating palliative care topics as modules of larger courses. This was the case in 41% of medical schools in 2000 and in 59% of medical schools in 2005. The percentage of schools that included palliative care training throughout the curriculum and in clerkships in which students are usually assigned patients decreased from 22% in 2000 to 12% in 2005.

TABLE 3.1

Medical school offerings in death and dying, selected years 1975–2005

[In percent]

Year*	Separate D&D course offered	Lecture(s)/ short course	Students in D&D offerings	Schools with multidisciplinary-team approach to D&D
1975	7	80	71	59
1980	13	80	74	64
1985	12	82	75	62
1990	18	73	NA	NA
1995	8	70	77	76
2000	18	82	96	78
2005	16	87	96	82

NA = Not available.
D&D = Death and dying.
*Sample sizes per survey period are as follows: 107 for 1975, 123 for 1980, 113 for 1985, 111 for 1990, 113 for 1995, 112 for 2000, and 99 for 2005.

SOURCE: George E. Dickinson, "Table 1. US Medical School Offerings in Death and Dying (D&D), 1975–2005 (in Percentages)," in "Teaching End-of-Life Issues in US Medical Schools: 1975 to 2005," *American Journal of Hospice and Palliative Medicine*, vol. 23, no. 3, June/July 2006, pp. 197–204, http://ajh.sagepub.com/content/vol23/issue3/ (accessed March 25, 2008). Copyright © 2006 Sage Publications, Inc. Reprinted with permission of Sage Publications, Inc.

TABLE 3.2

Medical school offerings in palliative care, 2000 and 2005

[In percent]

Palliative care addressed in the curriculum	2000 (n = 112)	2005 (n = 99)
Covered in a separate course	11	8
Module of a larger course	41	59
In one or two lectures	25	24
Throughout the curriculum and in clerkships	22	12

n = Sample size.

SOURCE: George E. Dickinson, "Table 5. US Medical School Palliative Care Offerings in the Curriculum, 2000–2005 (in Percentages)," in "Teaching End-of-Life Issues in US Medical Schools: 1975 to 2005," *American Journal of Hospice and Palliative Medicine*, vol. 23, no. 3, June/July 2006, pp. 197–204, http://ajh.sagepub.com/content/vol23/issue3/ (accessed March 25, 2008). Copyright © 2006 Sage Publications, Inc. Reprinted with permission of Sage Publications, Inc.

One program in particular stands out in death and dying education. The Education for Physicians on End-of-Life Care (EPEC) Project (http://www.epec.net/EPEC/webpages/index.cfm) is an ongoing, ambitious training program developed in 1998 by the American Medical Association (AMA). The EPEC Project has a death and dying curriculum that emphasizes the development of skills and competence in the areas of communication, ethical decision making, palliative care, psychosocial issues, and pain and symptom management. The program became fully operational in 1999 and provides curricula to all leaders of medical societies, medical school deans, and major medical organizations. The EPEC Project was supported from 1996 to 2003 with funding from the Robert Wood Johnson Foundation. After 2003 it was sponsored by and housed at Northwestern University's Feinberg School of Medicine in Chicago, with a mission to educate all health-care professionals on the essential clinical competencies in end-of-life care.

Contemporary Ethical Guidelines for Physicians

Physicians are trained to save lives, not to let people die. Advanced medical technology, with respirators and parenteral nutrition (artificial feeding devices that provide nutrition to an otherwise unconscious patient), can prolong the process of dying. Ira Byock admits in *Dying Well: The Prospect for Growth at the End of Life* (1997) that "a strong presumption throughout my medical career was that all seriously ill people required vigorous life-prolonging treatment, including those who were expected to die, even patients with advanced chronic illness such as wide spread cancer, end stage congestive heart failure, and kidney or liver failure. It even extended to patients who saw death as a relief from suffering caused by their illness."

However, more recent medical education is changing this focus. The Council on Ethical and Judicial Affairs of the AMA published guidelines for physicians dealing with dying patients in "Decisions Near the End of Life" (2007, http://www.ama-assn.org/apps/pf_new/pf_online?f_n=browse&doc=policyfiles/HnE/H-140.966.HTM). They were originally written in 1991, reaffirmed in 1996 and 1997, and appended in 2000. The following guidelines are the most recent:

Our AMA believes that:

1. The principle of patient autonomy requires that physicians must respect the decision to forgo life-sustaining treatment of a patient who possesses decision-making capacity. Life-sustaining treatment is any medical treatment that serves to prolong life without reversing the underlying medical condition. Life-sustaining treatment includes, but is not limited to, mechanical ventilation, renal dialysis, chemotherapy, antibiotics, and artificial nutrition and hydration.

2. There is no ethical distinction between withdrawing and withholding life-sustaining treatment.

3. Physicians have an obligation to relieve pain and suffering and to promote the dignity and autonomy of dying patients in their care. This includes providing effective palliative treatment even though it may foreseeably hasten death. More research must be pursued, examining the degree to which palliative care reduces the requests for euthanasia or assisted suicide.

4. Physicians must not perform euthanasia or participate in assisted suicide. A more careful examination of the issue is necessary. Support, comfort, respect for patient autonomy, good communication, and adequate pain control may decrease dramatically the public demand for euthanasia and assisted suicide. In certain carefully defined circumstances, it would be humane to recognize that death is certain and suffering is great. However, the societal risks of involving physicians in medical interventions to cause patients' deaths is too great to condone euthanasia or physician-assisted suicide at this time.

5. Our AMA supports continued research into and education concerning pain management.

The American College of Physicians, another prominent professional medical organization, published its most recent recommendations about end-of-life care in the fifth edition of its code of ethics, *The American College of Physicians Ethics Manual* (2005, http://www.acponline.org/running_practice/ethics/manual/ethicman5th.htm). The guidelines for decision making near the end of life emphasize that capable and informed adults nearly always have the legal and ethical right to refuse treatment. They advise physicians to practice empathy, to compromise, and to negotiate with patients who wish to forgo recommended treatment. The guidelines offer an approach to clinical ethical decision making that not only involves defining the problems and reviewing facts and uncertainties but that also considers patients' wishes as included in written or oral advance care planning (advance directives).

PATIENT AUTONOMY

According to the principle of patient autonomy, competent patients have the right to self-rule—to choose among medically recommended treatments and refuse any treatment they do not want. To be truly autonomous, they have to be told about the nature of their illness, the prospects for recovery, the course of the illness, alternative treatments, and treatment consequences. After thoughtful consideration, a patient makes an informed choice and grants "informed consent" to treatment or decides to forgo treatment. Decisions about medical treatment may be influenced by the patient's psychological state, family history, culture, values, and religious beliefs.

Cultural Differences

Even though patient autonomy is a fundamental aspect of medical ethics, not all patients want to know about their illnesses or be involved in decisions about their terminal care. H. Russell Searight and Jennifer Gafford note in "Cultural Diversity at the End of Life: Issues and Guidelines for Family Physicians" (*American Family Physician*, vol. 71, no. 3, February 1, 2005) that the concept of patient autonomy is not easily applied to members of some racial or ethnic groups. Searight and Gafford explain the three basic dimensions in end-of-life treatment that vary culturally: communication of bad news, locus of decision making, and attitudes toward advance directives and end-of-life care.

Members of some ethnic groups, such as many Africans and Japanese, soften bad news with terms that do not overtly state that a person has a potentially terminal condition. For example, the terms *growth* or *blood disease* may be used rather than telling a person he or she has a cancerous tumor or leukemia. That idea is taken one step further in many Hispanic, Chinese, and Pakistani communities, in which the terminally ill are generally protected from knowledge of their condition. Many reasons exist for this type of behavior, such as viewing the discussion of serious illness and death as disrespectful or impolite, not wanting to cause anxiety or eliminate hope in the patient, or believing that speaking about a condition makes it real. Many people of Asian and European cultures believe it is cruel to inform a patient of a terminal diagnosis.

In "Cultural Differences with End-of-Life Care in the Critical Care Unit" (*Dimensions of Critical Care Nursing*, vol. 26, no. 5, September–October 2007), Jessica Doolen and Nancy L. York add similar cultural scenarios in communication about death and dying to those outlined by Searight and Gafford. Doolen and York note that Koreans generally do not talk about the dying process because it fosters sadness, and they believe such discussions may quicken the dying process. Those in the Filipino culture believe discussions of death will interfere with God's will and, as in the Korean culture, believe such discussions may hasten death.

The phrase "locus of decision making" refers to those making the end-of-life decisions: the physician, the family, and/or the patient. Searight and Gafford explain that the locus of decision making varies among cultures. The North American cultural norm is individual decision for one's own medical care. Koreans and Mexicans often approach end-of-life decision making differently, abiding by a collective decision process in which relatives make treatment choices for a family member without that person's input. East Europeans and Russians often look to the physician as the expert in end-of-life decision making. In Asian, Indian, and Pakistani cultures, physicians and family members may share decision making. Doolen and York add that, in the Afghan culture, health-care decisions are made by the head of the family, possibly in consultation with an educated younger family member.

An advance directive (often called a living will) is a written statement that explains a person's wishes about end-of-life medical care. Completion of advance directives varies among cultures. For example, Searight and Gafford note that approximately 40% of elderly whites have completed advance directives, whereas only 16% of elderly African-Americans have done the same. Doolen and York add that Mexican-Americans, African-Americans, Native Americans, and Asian-Americans do not share the typical American philosophy that end-of-life decisions are the individual's responsibility and are much less likely than the general American population to sign advance directives or do-not-resuscitate orders.

Polly Mazanec and Mary Kay Tyler suggest in "Cultural Considerations in End-of-Life Care: How Ethnicity, Age, and Spirituality Affect Decisions When Death Is Imminent" (*Home Healthcare Nurse*, vol. 22, no. 5, May 2004) that there are many differences among African-Americans, Chinese-Americans, Filipino-Americans, and Hispanics regarding the role of the family at the end of life, the preferences for the environment of the dying person, and the preparation of the body after death. Mazanec and Tyler suggest that often a lack of attention to such cultural needs in end-of-life care can be a predominant factor in a person's experience of dying.

Because of differences among cultures regarding various facets of end-of-life decision making and preparedness, it appears important for physicians to realize patient autonomy is far from a universally held ideal. There are differences of opinion not only among ethnic groups but also within each ethnic group, such as differences with age. People bring their cultural values to bear on decisions about terminal care.

Health-Care Proxies and Surrogate Decision Makers

When a patient is incompetent to make informed decisions about his or her medical treatment, a proxy or a surrogate must make the decision for that patient. Some patients, in anticipation of being in a position of incompetence, will execute a durable power of attorney for health care, designating a proxy. Most people choose family members or close friends who will make all medical decisions, including the withholding or withdrawal of life-sustaining treatments.

When a proxy has not been named in advance, health-care providers usually involve family members in medical decisions. Most states have laws that govern surrogate decision making. Some states designate family members, by order of kinship, to assume the role of surrogates.

THE DESIRE TO DIE: EUTHANASIA AND ASSISTED SUICIDE

Serious diseases such as acquired immunodeficiency syndrome and metastatic cancer have directed societal attention to end-of-life decision making because many patients who are suffering as they die would like their death to be hastened. In "Granted, Undecided, Withdrawn, and Refused Requests for Euthanasia and Physician-Assisted Suicide" (*Archives of Internal Medicine*, vol. 165, no. 15, August 8–22, 2005), Marijke C. Jansen-van der Weide, Bregje D. Onwuteaka-Philipsen, and Gerrit van der Wal reveal characteristics of patients in the Netherlands who explicitly requested euthanasia or physician-assisted suicide between April 2000 and December 2002. More than half the patients requesting euthanasia and assisted suicide (EAS) were male (54%). Most of the patients were diagnosed with cancer (90%). Even though only 9% were diagnosed with depression, 92% were "feeling bad." The three most often cited reasons for requesting EAS were pointless suffering (75%), deterioration or loss of dignity (69%), and weakness or tiredness (60%).

Jansen-van der Weide, Onwuteaka-Philipsen, and van der Wal shed light on reasons physicians were reluctant to grant requests for euthanasia or assisted suicide. Of the 570 patients who had initially requested EAS, 65 died before EAS was administered, 72 died before a final decision was rendered, 68 changed their mind and no longer wanted EAS, 101 were refused, and 253 had their requests carried out. Physicians caring for patients in all five categories were reluctant to grant the EAS request in some cases. Physicians caring for 52% of the "refused" patients cited doubts about their patients' hopeless and unbearable suffering. This doubt was prevalent across groups. Other common doubts expressed by physicians were those about the availability of alternative treatment, personal doubts in particular cases, doubts about the patient being depressed, and doubts about a well-considered and persistent request. Not usually significant in a physician's reluctance to grant EAS were concerns that the patient was too close to death, that the request for EAS was voluntary, and that the family was against EAS.

According to Jansen-van der Weide, Onwuteaka-Philipsen, and van der Wal, the factor most likely to have influenced a physician to refuse an EAS request was the patient not being competent or fully competent (did not have all of his or her mental faculties). Another factor associated with refusal was the physician's perception that the patient's unbearable or hopeless suffering was experienced to a lesser extent than would be necessary to consider EAS. Depression was the reason most likely to have influenced a patient to request EAS and not wanting to burden his or her family was the second-most influential factor.

In "Desire for Euthanasia or Physician-Assisted Suicide in Palliative Cancer Care" (*Health Psychology*, vol. 26, no. 3, May 2007), Keith G. Wilson et al. discuss the results of their study on attitudes of terminally ill patients toward the legalization of EAS. Most (357) had no current interest in a hastened death, whereas a few (22) did. (See Table 3.3.) As in the Jansen-van der Weide, Onwuteaka-Philipsen, and van der Wal study, more than half of those interested in a hastened death were male (54.5% versus 45.5%). However, unlike Jansen-van der Weide, Onwuteaka-Philipsen, and van der Wal, 40.9% were diagnosed with depression. Wilson et al. determine

that the desire for a hastened death was also associated with lower religiosity. Religiosity is the degree to which a person believes in and is involved in religion. It was assessed with three questionnaire items that addressed the patient's religious self-perception, attendance at organized services, and frequency of private prayer. The sum of these items, which could range from 0 to 15, was used as the religiosity index. The higher the score, the higher the religiosity. The religiosity index of those interested in a hastened death was lower (an average of 7.8 out of 15) than those with no current interest in a hastened death (an average of 9.7 out of 15).

Wilson et al.'s study also compares the symptoms and concerns of terminal patients with no interest in a hastened death to those of terminal patients who had interest in a hastened death. Much higher percentages of those interested in a hastened death had social concerns: 59.1% were concerned about being a burden to others as opposed to 23.8% of those not interested in a hastened death. (See Table 3.4.) Many more of those wanting a hastened death felt isolated (31.8% versus 10.4%), had communication problems (13.6% versus 1.4%), and had financial problems (13.6% versus 8.7%) than those not wanting a hastened death. Much higher percentages of patients desiring a hastened death had various physical and psychological symptoms, compared to patients not desiring a hastened death. Also, 54.5% of those wanting a hastened death reported that they were suffering as opposed to 23.8% of patients not desiring a hastened death.

As mentioned earlier, Wilson et al.'s primary goal was to determine the attitudes of terminally ill patients toward the legalization of EAS. The reason cited by the highest percentage of people for the legalization of EAS was a person's right to choose his or her own destiny (39.1%). (See Table 3.5.) The reason cited by the second highest percentage of people was suffering (32.4%). Other reasons cited by more than 10% of people for legalization of EAS were pain (26.1%); terminal illness (26.1%); a merciful, peaceful escape (12.6%); lingering (12.2%); low quality of life, no pleasure (10.9%); and nothing to be done (10.1%). In summary, those in favor of legalizing EAS believed that patients should be able to decide if their death should be hastened in a situation in which they had a painful, lingering, terminal illness with no hope of survival and a low quality of life.

Religious and moral concerns were at the forefront of reasons reported by those who opposed legalizing EAS. Wilson et al. note that 41.8% of people in this group believed that God decides when a person should die and that it is wrong to take a life (32.7%), even if it is your own life. (See Table 3.5.) Other than religious or moral concerns, a small percentage of people were concerned about abuse of such a law (14.3%) and that EAS was an inappropriate role for a physician (12.2%).

TABLE 3.3

Characteristics of terminal cancer patients with and without an interest in physician-assisted suicide, 2001–03

Characteristic	All participants (n = 379)[a]			No current interest in hastened death (n = 357)[a]			Current interest in hastened death n = 22)[b]		
	M	n	%	M	n	%	M	n	%
Age (years)	67.2			67.2			66.6		
Gender									
Men		169	44.6		157	44.0		12	54.5
Women		210	55.4		200	56.0		10	45.5
Religion									
Protestant		147	38.8		137	38.4		10	45.5
Roman Catholic		136	35.9		134	37.5		2	9.1
Other		34	9.0		31	8.7		3	13.6
None		62	16.4		55	15.4		7	31.8
Religiosity index[c]	9.6			9.7			7.8		
Married/living with		195	51.5		182	51.0		13	59.14
Social network size[c]	13.6			13.9			10.8		
Education									
Less than high school		135	35.6		126	35.3		9	40.9
High school graduate		83	21.9		78	21.8		5	22.7
More than high school		161	42.5		153	42.9		8	36.4
Language									
English		320	84.4		300	84.0		20	90.9
French		49	12.9		47	13.2		2	9.1
Other		10	2.6		10	2.8		0	0
Setting									
Palliative care unit		197	52.0		182	51.0		15	68.2
Hospital inpatient		77	20.3		74	20.7		3	13.6
Outpatient, home care		105	27.7		101	28.3		4	18.2
Palliative performance scale[d]	54.6			54.9			48.2		
Medications[d]									
Opioids		292	77.2		273	76.7		19	86.4
Antidepressants		71	18.8		65	18.3		6	27.3
Benzodiazepines		173	45.8		158	44.4		15	68.2
Neuroleptics		68	18.0		60	16.9		8	36.4
Mental disorders									
Depression (any disorder)		78	20.6		69	19.3		9	40.9
Anxiety (any disorder)		52	13.7		46	12.9		6	27.3

Notes: M = Mean (average). Mdn = Median (midpoint). n = Number of patients (total sample size.)
[a]For survival duration, Mdn = 63 days.
[b]For survival duration, Mdn = 55.5 days.
[c]Two participants were missing values.
[d]One participant was missing values.

SOURCE: Adapted from Keith G. Wilson et al., "Table 1. Demographic and Clinical Characteristics of Participants with or without a Current Interest in Physician-Hastened Death," in "Desire for Euthanasia or Physician-Assisted Suicide in Palliative Cancer Care," *Health Psychology*, vol. 26, no. 3, May 2007, http://content.apa.org/journals/hea/26/3/314 (accessed March 26, 2008). Reprinted with permission of the American Psychological Association.

TABLE 3.4

Symptoms and concerns reported by terminal cancer patients with and without an interest in physician-assisted suicide, 2001–03

Symptom or concern	No current interest in hastened death (n = 357)		Current interest in hastened death (n = 22)	
	n	%	n	%
Social concerns				
Isolation	37	10.4	7	31.8
Communication problem	5	1.4	3	13.6
Burden to others	85	23.8	13	59.1
Financial problem[a]	31	8.7	3	13.6
Existential issues				
Spiritual crisis[b]	11	3.1	0	0.0
Difficulty accepting	30	8.4	3	13.6
Dissatisfaction with life	16	4.5	3	13.6
Loss of resilience[b]	27	7.6	7	31.8
Loss of dignity	24	6.7	2	9.1
Loss of control	21	5.9	5	22.7
Physical symptoms				
General malaise	145	40.6	15	68.2
Pain	119	33.3	9	40.9
Drowsiness	109	30.5	13	59.1
Weakness	204	57.1	19	86.4
Nausea	59	16.5	6	27.3
Breathlessness	91	25.5	7	31.8
Psychological symptoms				
Anxiety	51	14.3	7	31.8
Depression	46	12.9	7	31.8
Loss of interest/pleasure[a]	49	13.8	4	18.2
Hopelessness[b]	36	10.1	6	27.3
Global considerations				
Suffering	85	23.8	12	54.5
Desire for death[b]	28	7.9	18	81.8

Note: The severity of symptoms and concerns were rated using a semistructured interview. n refers to the number of participants in each group who were given ratings of "moderate" to "extreme" severity. Ratings of moderate severity represent the threshold at which each symptom or concern was generally regarded as a significant problem.
[a]One participant was missing values.
[b]Two participants were missing values.

SOURCE: Adapted from Keith G. Wilson et al.,"Table 3. Symptoms and Concerns Reported by Participants with or without a Current Interest in Physician-Hastened Death," in "Desire for Euthanasia or Physician-Assisted Suicide in Palliative Cancer Care," *Health Psychology*, vol. 26, no. 3, May 2007, http://content.apa.org/journals/hea/26/3/314 (accessed March 26, 2008). Reprinted with permission of the American Psychological Association.

TABLE 3.5

Reasons given by terminal cancer patients for being for or against the legalization of euthanasia or physician-assisted suicide, 2001–03

Reason given	n	%
Reasons for legalization (n = 238)		
Autonomy		
Right to choose	93	39.1
Control	22	9.2
Suffering		
Suffering	77	32.4
Pain	62	26.1
Low quality of life, no pleasure	26	10.9
Negative outlook, stress	18	7.6
"Can't take it"	16	6.7
Perceived futility		
Terminal illness	62	26.1
Lingering	29	12.2
Nothing to be done	24	10.1
Mental incompetence, vegetative	22	9.2
Functional loss, dependence	13	5.5
Compassion		
Merciful, peaceful, escape	30	12.6
Availability to animals	18	7.6
Dignified	12	5.0
Experience		
Experience of others	23	9.7
Famous cases	18	7.6
Concern for others		
Family stress	19	8.0
Burden to others, health system	16	6.7
Reasons against legalization (n = 99)		
Religious concerns		
God decides	41	41.8
Religious doctrine	12	12.2
Faith	10	10.2
Religious duty to live	9	9.2
Moral opposition		
Wrong to take life	32	32.7
Criminal act	15	15.3
Unnatural death	9	9.2
Sanctity of life	9	9.2
Negative possibilities		
Abuse	14	14.3
Unstable/irrational decisions	10	10.2
Fallible laws	6	6.1
Physician's role		
Inappropriate role	12	12.2
Too much responsibility	5	5.1
Unnecessary action		
Good care is available	8	8.2
Hope for life, cure	6	6.1

Note: Participants could give more than one reason for or against legalization.
n = Sample size.

SOURCE: Keith G. Wilson et al., "Table 2. Reasons for and against the Legalization of Euthanasia or Physician-Assisted Suicide," in "Desire for Euthanasia or Physician-Assisted Suicide in Palliative Cancer Care," *Health Psychology*, vol. 26, no. 3, May 2007, http://content.apa.org/journals/hea/26/3/314 (accessed March 26, 2008). Reprinted with permission of the American Psychological Association.

CHAPTER 4
THE END OF LIFE: MEDICAL CONSIDERATIONS

TRENDS IN CAUSES OF DEATH

The primary causes of death in the United States have changed dramatically over the past century. In the 1800s and early 1900s infectious (communicable) diseases such as influenza, tuberculosis, and diphtheria (a potentially deadly upper respiratory infection) were the leading causes of death. These have been replaced by chronic noninfectious diseases; heart disease, cancer (malignant neoplasms), and stroke (cerebrovascular diseases) were the three leading causes of death in 2005. (See Table 4.1.)

In 2005 the age-adjusted death rate for heart disease, which accounts for changes in the age distribution of the population across time, was 211.1 deaths per 100,000 people, whereas the rate for cancer was 183.8 per 100,000. (See Table 4.2.) Together, these two diseases accounted for 49.4% of all deaths in the United States in 2005. (See Table 4.1.) The American Heart Association indicates in *Heart and Stroke Statistics—2008 Update* (2008, http://www.americanheart.org/downloadable/heart/1200082005246HS_Stats%202008.final.pdf) that the number of deaths from heart disease have been decreasing since 1970 and that the number of deaths from cancer dropped for the first time in 2003. In "For First Time in Decades, Annual Cancer Deaths Fall" (*USA Today*, February 9, 2006), Liz Szabo reports that the death rate (number of deaths per one thousand people) from cancer has been decreasing by about 1% since 1991.

Not surprisingly, the leading causes of death vary by age. For those from birth to thirty-four, accidents and their adverse effects were the leading cause of death from 1999 to 2005, as well as the leading cause of death for those aged thirty-five to forty-four in 2002 through 2005. (See Table 4.2.) For those aged thirty-five to forty-four, cancer was the leading cause of death in 1999, 2000, and 2001, with accidents and their adverse effects second, and heart disease third. Cancer and heart disease caused the most deaths among those forty-five years and older from 1999 to 2005.

Trends in Death Rates Due to HIV/AIDS

The human immunodeficiency virus (HIV) is transmitted when the body fluids (blood, semen, or vaginal secretions) of an HIV-infected person come into contact with the body fluids of an uninfected person through activities such as having anal or vaginal intercourse, sharing HIV-contaminated hypodermic needles, giving birth when the mother is HIV infected, and receiving transfusions of contaminated blood. HIV attacks the body's immune system, and when the immune system becomes sufficiently weakened, the HIV-infected person enters the symptomatic phase of HIV disease. These first symptoms include fever, night sweats, headache, and fatigue. As the immune system becomes further weakened by the virus, the HIV-infected patient develops diseases and conditions typical of the stage of disease known as acquired immunodeficiency syndrome (AIDS). The patient develops a syndrome (pattern) of conditions, infections, and diseases, which may include wasting—a marked loss of weight and a decrease in physical stamina, appetite, and mental activity. He or she may also develop fungal infections of the lungs or brain coverings; Kaposi's sarcoma, a type of cancer; or a viral infection of the retina of the eye. As immune system function declines even further, the risk of death increases. There is no cure for HIV/AIDS, but there are effective treatments that significantly slow the progression of the disease.

In *HIV/AIDS Surveillance Report: U.S. HIV and AIDS Cases Reported through December 1997* (1997, http://www.cdc.gov/hiv/topics/surveillance/resources/reports/pdf/hivsur92.pdf), the Centers for Disease Control and Prevention (CDC) states that a decline occurred in U.S. AIDS deaths for the first time in 1996. This decline removed AIDS as the leading cause of death among people aged twenty-five through forty-four in the United States, which it had been through 1994 and 1995. The decrease was largely due to the growing use of combinations of antiretroviral drugs. According to the CDC, in *HIV/AIDS Surveillance Report: U.S. HIV and AIDS Cases Reported*

TABLE 4.1

Death rates for the 15 leading causes of death, 2005, and percent change, 2004–05

[Death rates on an annual basis per 100,000 population. Age-adjusted rates per 100,000 U.S. standard population.]

Rank[a]	Cause of death	Number	Percent of total deaths	2005 crude death rate	Age-adjusted death rate				
					2005	Percent change 2004 to 2005	Male to female	Black to white	Hispanic[b] to non-Hispanic white
								Ratio	
—	All causes	2,448,017	100.0	825.9	798.8	−0.2	1.4	1.3	0.7
1	Diseases of heart	652,091	26.6	220.0	211.1	−2.7	1.5	1.3	0.7
2	Malignant neoplasms	559,312	22.8	188.7	183.8	−1.1	1.4	1.2	0.7
3	Cerebrovascular diseases	143,579	5.9	48.4	46.6	−6.8	1.0	1.5	0.8
4	Chronic lower respiratory diseases	130,933	5.3	44.2	43.2	5.1	1.3	0.7	0.4
5	Accidents (unintentional injuries)	117,809	4.8	39.7	39.1	3.7	2.2	1.0	0.8
6	Diabetes mellitus	75,119	3.1	25.3	24.6	0.4	1.3	2.1	1.6
7	Alzheimer's disease	71,599	2.9	24.2	22.9	5.0	0.7	0.8	0.6
8	Influenza and pneumonia	63,001	2.6	21.3	20.3	2.5	1.3	1.1	0.8
9	Nephritis, nephrotic syndrome and nephrosis	43,901	1.8	14.8	14.3	0.7	1.4	2.3	0.9
10	Septicemia	34,136	1.4	11.5	11.2	0.0	1.2	2.2	0.8
11	Intentional self-harm (suicide)	32,637	1.3	11.0	10.9	0.0	4.1	0.4	0.4
12	Chronic liver disease and cirrhosis	27,530	1.1	9.3	9.0	0.0	2.1	0.8	1.6
13	Essential (primary) hypertension and hypertensive renal disease	24,902	1.0	8.4	8.0	3.9	1.0	2.6	1.0
14	Parkinson's disease	19,544	0.8	6.6	6.4	4.9	2.2	0.4	0.6
15	Assault (homicide)	18,124	0.7	6.1	6.1	3.4	3.8	5.7	2.8
—	All other causes (residual)	433,800	17.7	146.4	—	—	—	—	—

—Category not applicable.
[a]Rank based on number of deaths.
[b]Data for Hispanic origin should be interpreted with caution because of inconsistencies between reporting Hispanic origin on death certificates and on censuses and surveys.

SOURCE: "Table C. Percentage of Total Deaths, Death Rates, Age-Adjusted Death Rates for 2005, Percentage Change in Age-Adjusted Death Rates from 2004 to 2005, and Ratio of Age-Adjusted Death Rates by Race and Sex for the 15 Leading Causes of Death for the Total Population in 2005: United States," Centers for Disease Control and Prevention, National Center for Health Statistics, 2005, ftp://ftp.cdc.gov/pub/Health_Statistics/NCHS/Publications/NVSR/56_10/table C.xls (accessed January 30, 2008)

through December 1999 (1999, http://www.cdc.gov/hiv/topics/surveillance/resources/reports/pdf/hasr1102.pdf), this downward trend in annual number of deaths due to AIDS continued through 1998, when AIDS dropped to the fifth-leading cause of death among people aged twenty-five through forty-four. The CDC notes in *HIV/AIDS Surveillance Report: Cases of HIV Infection and AIDS in the United States, 2003* (2003, http://www.cdc.gov/hiv/topics/surveillance/resources/reports/2003report/pdf/2003SurveillanceReport.pdf) that from 1999 through 2004 the number of deaths due to AIDS remained relatively steady, with a low of 17,741 deaths in 2001 and a high of 18,491 in 1999. In spite of this drop and leveling off of AIDS deaths, Melonie P. Heron and Betty L. Smith of the CDC explain in "Deaths: Leading Causes for 2003" (*National Vital Statistics Reports*, vol. 55, no. 10, March 15, 2007) that this deadly syndrome was still among the top-ten leading causes of death in 2003 for people aged twenty to fifty-four, ranging from the fifth-leading cause of death in people aged thirty-five to forty-four years to the eighth-leading cause of death in people aged forty-five to fifty-four. In 2005 the number of deaths from HIV/AIDS reached an all-time low of 17,011. (See Table 4.3.)

From 2001 through 2005 most males with AIDS contracted HIV via male-to-male sexual contact or intra-venous drug use. (See Table 4.3.) Most females contracted the virus by heterosexual contact with high-risk partners or intravenous drug use. Children most often contracted the virus perinatally (immediately before and after birth) from infected mothers. The South and the Northeast, respectively, experienced more AIDS deaths during these years than other parts of the United States.

THE STUDY TO UNDERSTAND PROGNOSES AND PREFERENCES FOR OUTCOMES AND RISKS OF TREATMENTS

During the twentieth century in the United States, the process of dying shifted from the familiar surroundings of home to the hospital. Even though hospitalization ensures that the benefits of modern medicine are readily available, many patients dread leaving the comfort of their home and losing, to some extent, control over their end-of-life decisions.

Between 1989 and 1994, in an effort to "improve end-of-life decision making and reduce the frequency of a mechanically supported, painful, and prolonged process of dying," a group of investigators from various disciplines undertook the largest study of death and dying ever conducted in the United States. The project, known as the Study to Understand Prognoses and Preferences for Outcomes and Risks of Treatments (SUPPORT), included

TABLE 4.2

Death rates, by age, for the 15 leading causes of death, 1999–2005

[Rates on an annual basis per 100,000 population in specified group; age-adjusted rates per 100,000 U.S. standard population. Rates are based on populations enumerated as of April 1 for 2000 and estimated as of July 1 for all other years.]

Cause of death and year	All ages[a]	Under 1 year[b]	1–4 years	5–14 years	15–24 years	25–34 years	35–44 years	45–54 years	55–64 years	65–74 years	75–84 years	85 years and over	Age-adjusted rate
All causes													
2005	825.9	692.5	29.4	16.3	81.4	104.4	193.3	432.0	906.9	2,137.1	5,260.0	13,798.6	798.8
2004	816.5	685.2	29.9	16.8	80.1	102.1	193.5	427.0	910.3	2,164.6	5,275.1	13,823.5	800.8
2003	841.9	700.0	31.5	17.0	81.5	103.6	201.6	433.2	940.9	2,255.0	5,463.1	14,593.3	832.7
2002	847.3	695.0	31.2	17.4	81.4	103.6	202.9	430.1	952.4	2,314.7	5,556.9	14,828.3	845.3
2001	848.5	683.4	33.3	17.3	80.7	105.2	203.6	428.9	964.6	2,353.3	5,582.4	15,112.8	854.5
2000	854.0	736.7	32.4	18.0	79.9	101.4	198.9	425.6	992.2	2,399.1	5,666.5	15,524.4	869.0
1999	857.0	736.0	34.2	18.6	79.3	102.2	198.0	418.2	1,005.0	2,457.3	5,714.5	15,554.6	875.6
Diseases of heart													
2005	220.0	8.7	0.9	0.6	2.7	8.1	28.9	89.7	214.8	518.9	1,460.8	4,778.4	211.1
2004	222.2	10.3	1.2	0.6	2.5	7.9	29.3	90.2	218.8	541.6	1,506.3	4,895.9	217.0
2003	235.6	11.0	1.2	0.6	2.7	8.2	30.7	92.5	233.2	585.0	1,611.1	5,278.4	232.3
2002	241.7	12.4	1.1	0.6	2.5	7.9	30.5	93.7	241.5	615.9	1,677.2	5,466.8	240.8
2001	245.8	11.9	1.5	0.7	2.5	8.0	29.6	92.9	246.9	635.1	1,725.7	5,664.2	247.8
2000	252.6	13.0	1.2	0.7	2.6	7.4	29.2	94.2	261.2	665.6	1,780.3	5,926.1	257.6
1999	259.9	13.8	1.2	0.7	2.8	7.6	30.2	95.7	269.9	701.7	1,849.9	6,063.0	266.5
Malignant neoplasms													
2005	188.7	1.8	2.3	2.5	4.1	9.0	33.2	118.6	326.9	742.7	1,637.7	1,637.7	183.8
2004	188.6	1.8	2.5	2.5	4.1	9.1	33.4	119.0	333.4	755.1	1,280.4	1,653.3	185.8
2003	191.5	1.9	2.5	2.6	4.0	9.4	35.0	122.2	343.0	770.3	1,302.5	1,698.2	190.1
2002	193.2	1.8	2.6	2.6	4.3	9.7	35.8	123.8	351.1	792.1	1,311.9	1,723.9	193.5
2001	194.4	1.6	2.7	2.5	4.3	10.1	36.8	126.5	356.5	802.8	1,315.6	1,765.6	196.0
2000	196.5	2.4	2.7	2.5	4.4	9.8	36.6	127.5	366.7	816.3	1,335.6	1,819.4	199.6
1999	197.0	1.8	2.7	2.5	4.5	10.0	37.1	127.6	374.6	827.1	1,331.5	1,805.8	200.8
Cerebrovascular diseases													
2005	48.4	3.1	0.4	0.2	0.5	1.4	5.2	15.0	33.0	101.1	359.0	1,141.8	46.6
2004	51.1	3.1	0.3	0.2	0.5	1.4	5.4	14.9	34.3	107.8	386.2	1,245.9	50.0
2003	54.2	2.5	0.3	0.2	0.5	1.5	5.5	15.0	35.6	112.9	410.7	1,370.1	53.5
2002	56.4	2.9	0.3	0.2	0.4	1.4	5.4	15.1	37.2	120.3	431.0	1,445.9	56.2
2001	57.4	2.7	0.4	0.2	0.5	1.5	5.5	15.1	38.0	123.4	443.9	1,500.2	57.9
2000	59.6	3.3	0.3	0.2	0.5	1.5	5.8	16.0	41.0	128.6	461.3	1,589.2	60.9
1999	60.0	2.7	0.4	0.2	0.5	1.4	5.7	15.2	40.6	130.8	469.8	1,614.8	61.6
Chronic lower respiratory diseases													
2005	44.2	0.8	0.3	0.3	0.4	0.6	2.0	9.4	42.0	160.5	385.6	637.2	43.2
2004	41.5	0.9	0.3	0.3	0.4	0.6	2.0	8.4	40.4	153.8	366.7	601.7	41.1
2003	43.5	0.8	0.3	0.3	0.5	0.7	2.1	8.7	43.3	163.2	383.0	635.1	43.3
2002	43.3	1.0	0.4	0.3	0.5	0.8	2.2	8.7	42.4	163.0	386.7	637.6	43.5
2001	43.2	1.0	0.3	0.3	0.4	0.7	2.2	8.5	44.1	167.9	379.8	644.7	43.7
2000	43.4	0.9	0.3	0.3	0.5	0.7	2.1	8.6	44.2	169.4	386.1	648.6	44.2
1999	44.5	0.9	0.4	0.3	0.5	0.8	2.0	8.5	47.5	177.2	397.8	646.0	45.4

TABLE 4.2

Death rates, by age, for the 15 leading causes of death, 1999–2005 [CONTINUED]

[Rates on an annual basis per 100,000 population in specified group; age-adjusted rates per 100,000 U.S. standard population. Rates are based on populations enumerated as of April 1 for 2000 and estimated as of July 1 for all other years.]

Cause of death and year	All ages[a]	Under 1 year[b]	1–4 years	5–14 years	15–24 years	25–34 years	35–44 years	45–54 years	55–64 years	65–74 years	75–84 years	85 years and over	Age-adjusted rate
Accidents (unintentional injuries)													
2005	39.7	26.4	10.3	6.0	37.4	34.9	38.6	43.2	35.8	46.3	106.1	279.5	39.1
2004	38.1	25.8	10.3	6.5	37.0	32.6	37.3	40.7	33.2	44.0	103.7	276.7	37.7
2003	37.6	23.6	10.9	6.4	37.1	31.5	37.8	38.8	32.9	44.1	101.9	278.9	37.3
2002	37.0	23.5	10.5	6.6	38.0	31.5	37.2	36.6	31.4	44.2	101.3	275.4	36.9
2001	35.7	24.2	11.2	6.9	36.1	29.9	35.4	34.1	30.3	42.8	100.9	276.4	35.7
2000	34.8	23.1	11.9	7.3	36.0	29.5	34.1	32.6	30.9	41.9	95.1	273.5	34.9
1999	35.1	22.3	12.4	7.6	35.3	29.6	33.8	31.8	30.6	44.6	100.5	282.4	35.3
Diabetes mellitus													
2005	25.3	*	*	0.1	0.5	1.5	4.7	13.4	37.2	86.8	177.2	312.1	24.6
2004	24.9	*	*	0.1	0.4	1.5	4.6	13.4	37.1	87.2	176.9	307.0	24.5
2003	25.5	*	*	0.1	0.4	1.6	4.6	13.9	38.5	90.8	181.1	317.5	25.3
2002	25.4	*	*	0.1	0.4	1.6	4.8	13.7	37.7	91.4	182.8	320.6	25.4
2001	25.1	*	*	0.1	0.4	1.5	4.3	13.6	37.8	91.4	181.4	321.8	25.3
2000	24.6	*	*	0.1	0.4	1.6	4.3	13.1	37.8	90.7	179.5	319.7	25.0
1999	24.5	*	*	0.1	0.4	1.4	4.3	12.9	38.3	91.8	178.0	317.2	25.0
Alzheimer's disease													
2005	24.2	*	*	*	*	*	*	0.2	2.1	20.5	177.3	861.6	22.9
2004	22.5	*	*	*	*	*	*	0.2	1.9	19.7	168.7	818.8	21.8
2003	21.8	*	*	*	*	*	*	0.2	2.0	20.9	164.4	802.4	21.4
2002	20.4	*	*	*	*	*	*	0.1	1.9	19.7	158.1	752.3	20.2
2001	18.9	*	*	*	*	*	*	0.2	2.1	18.7	147.5	710.3	19.1
2000	17.6	*	*	*	*	*	*	0.2	2.0	18.7	139.6	667.7	18.1
1999	16.0	*	*	*	*	*	*	0.2	1.9	17.4	129.5	601.3	16.5
Influenza and pneumonia													
2005	21.3	6.5	0.7	0.3	0.4	0.9	2.1	5.1	11.3	35.5	142.2	593.9	20.3
2004	20.3	6.7	0.7	0.2	0.4	0.8	2.0	4.6	10.8	34.6	139.3	582.6	19.8
2003	22.4	8.0	1.0	0.4	0.5	0.9	2.2	5.2	11.2	37.3	151.1	666.1	22.0
2002	22.8	6.5	0.7	0.2	0.4	0.9	2.2	4.8	11.2	37.5	156.9	696.6	22.6
2001	21.8	7.4	0.7	0.2	0.5	0.9	2.2	4.6	10.7	36.3	148.5	685.6	22.0
2000	23.2	7.6	0.7	0.2	0.5	0.9	2.4	4.7	11.9	39.1	160.3	744.1	23.7
1999	22.8	8.4	0.8	0.2	0.5	0.8	2.4	4.6	11.0	37.2	157.0	751.8	23.5
Nephritis, nephrotic syndrome and nephrosis													
2005	14.8	3.9	*	0.1	0.2	0.7	1.7	4.8	13.6	39.3	110.3	288.3	14.3
2004	14.5	4.3	*	0.1	0.2	0.6	1.8	5.0	13.6	38.6	108.4	286.6	14.2
2003	14.6	4.5	*	0.1	0.2	0.7	1.8	4.9	13.6	40.1	109.5	293.1	14.4
2002	14.2	4.3	*	0.0	0.2	0.7	1.7	4.7	13.0	39.2	109.1	288.6	14.2
2001	13.9	3.3	*	0.0	0.2	0.6	1.7	4.6	13.0	40.2	104.2	287.7	14.0
2000	13.2	4.3	*	0.1	0.2	0.6	1.6	4.4	12.8	38.0	100.8	277.8	13.5
1999	12.7	4.4	*	0.1	0.2	0.6	1.6	4.0	12.0	37.1	97.6	268.9	13.0

TABLE 4.2

Death rates, by age, for the 15 leading causes of death, 1999–2005 [CONTINUED]

[Rates on an annual basis per 100,000 population in specified group; age-adjusted rates per 100,000 U.S. standard population. Rates are based on populations enumerated as of April 1 for 2000 and estimated as of July 1 for all other years.]

Cause of death and year	All ages[a]						Age						Age-adjusted rate
		Under 1 year[b]	1–4 years	5–14 years	15–24 years	25–34 years	35–44 years	45–54 years	55–64 years	65–74 years	75–84 years	85 years and over	
Septicemia													
2005	11.5	7.4	0.5	0.2	0.4	0.8	1.9	5.2	12.9	32.6	81.4	187.3	11.2
2004	11.4	6.6	0.5	0.2	0.3	0.8	1.9	5.4	12.9	32.4	81.6	186.7	11.2
2003	11.7	6.9	0.5	0.2	0.4	0.8	2.1	5.3	13.1	32.6	85.0	202.5	11.6
2002	11.7	7.3	0.5	0.2	0.3	0.8	1.9	5.2	12.6	34.7	86.5	203.0	11.7
2001	11.3	7.7	0.7	0.2	0.3	0.7	1.8	5.0	12.3	32.8	82.3	205.9	11.4
2000	11.1	7.2	0.6	0.2	0.3	0.7	1.9	4.9	11.9	31.0	80.4	215.7	11.3
1999	11.0	7.5	0.6	0.2	0.3	0.7	1.8	4.6	11.4	31.2	79.4	220.7	11.3
Intentional self-harm (suicide)													
2005	11.0	—	—	0.7	10.0	12.4	14.9	16.5	13.9	12.6	16.9	16.9	10.9
2004	11.0	—	—	0.7	10.3	12.7	15.0	16.6	13.8	12.3	16.3	16.4	10.9
2003	10.8	—	—	0.6	9.7	12.7	14.9	15.9	13.8	12.7	16.4	16.9	10.8
2002	11.0	—	—	0.6	9.9	12.6	15.3	15.7	13.6	13.5	17.7	18.0	10.9
2001[c]	10.8	—	—	0.7	9.9	12.8	14.7	15.2	13.1	13.3	17.4	17.5	10.7
2000	10.4	—	—	0.7	10.2	12.0	14.5	14.4	12.1	12.5	17.6	19.6	10.4
1999	10.5	—	—	0.6	10.1	12.7	14.3	13.9	12.2	13.4	18.1	19.3	10.5
Chronic liver disease and cirrhosis													
2005	9.3	*	*	*	0.1	0.8	6.1	17.7	23.5	27.2	29.0	19.7	9.0
2004	9.2	*	*	*	*	0.8	6.3	18.0	22.6	27.7	28.8	19.7	9.0
2003	9.5	*	*	*	*	0.9	6.8	18.3	23.0	29.5	30.0	20.1	9.3
2002	9.5	*	*	*	0.1	0.9	7.0	18.0	22.9	29.4	31.4	21.4	9.4
2001	9.5	*	*	*	0.1	1.0	7.4	18.5	22.7	30.0	30.2	22.2	9.5
2000	9.4	*	*	*	0.1	1.0	7.5	17.7	23.8	29.8	31.0	23.1	9.5
1999	9.4	*	*	*	0.1	1.0	7.3	17.4	23.7	30.6	31.9	23.2	9.6
Essential (primary) hypertension and hypertensive renal disease													
2005	8.4	*	*	*	0.1	0.2	0.9	2.7	6.4	17.7	55.6	210.0	8.0
2004	7.9	*	*	*	0.1	0.3	0.8	2.7	6.3	17.1	52.6	198.5	7.7
2003	7.5	*	*	*	0.1	0.2	0.8	2.5	6.3	16.9	51.7	188.9	7.4
2002	7.0	*	*	*	0.1	0.2	0.8	2.3	5.7	16.0	48.2	180.4	7.0
2001	6.8	*	*	*	0.1	0.3	0.7	2.4	5.8	15.5	47.7	171.9	6.8
2000	6.4	*	*	*	*	0.2	0.8	2.3	5.9	15.1	45.5	162.9	6.5
1999	6.1	*	*	*	*	0.2	0.7	2.2	5.5	15.2	43.6	152.1	6.2
Parkinson's disease													
2005	6.6	*	*	*	*	*	*	0.2	1.4	13.0	71.2	143.7	6.4
2004	6.1	*	*	*	*	*	*	0.2	1.2	12.0	67.5	135.8	6.1
2003	6.2	*	*	*	*	*	*	0.2	1.3	12.7	67.8	138.2	6.2
2002	5.9	*	*	*	*	*	*	0.1	1.2	12.2	63.9	135.2	5.9
2001	5.8	*	*	*	*	*	*	0.1	1.2	11.7	64.6	134.2	5.9
2000	5.6	*	*	*	*	*	*	0.1	1.1	11.5	61.9	131.9	5.7
1999	5.2	*	*	*	*	*	*	0.1	1.0	11.0	58.2	124.4	5.4

TABLE 4.2

Death rates, by age, for the 15 leading causes of death, 1999–2005 [CONTINUED]

[Rates on an annual basis per 100,000 population in specified group; age-adjusted rates per 100,000 U.S. standard population. Rates are based on populations enumerated as of April 1 for 2000 and estimated as of July 1 for all other years.]

Cause of death and year	All ages[a]	Under 1 year[b]	1–4 years	5–14 years	15–24 years	25–34 years	35–44 years	45–54 years	55–64 years	65–74 years	75–84 years	85 years and over	Age-adjusted rate
Assault (homicide)													
2005	6.1	7.5	2.3	0.8	13.0	11.8	7.1	4.8	2.8	2.4	2.2	2.1	6.1
2004	5.9	8.0	2.4	0.8	12.2	11.2	6.8	4.8	3.0	2.4	2.2	2.1	5.9
2003	6.1	8.5	2.4	0.8	13.0	11.3	7.0	4.9	2.8	2.4	2.5	2.2	6.0
2002	6.1	7.5	2.7	0.9	12.9	11.2	7.2	4.8	3.2	2.3	2.3	2.1	6.1
2001[c]	7.1	8.2	2.7	0.8	13.3	13.1	9.5	6.3	4.0	2.9	2.5	2.4	7.1
2000	6.0	9.2	2.3	0.9	12.6	10.4	7.1	4.7	3.0	2.4	2.4	2.4	5.9
1999	6.1	8.7	2.5	1.1	12.9	10.5	7.1	4.6	3.0	2.6	2.5	2.4	6.0

* Figure does not meet standards of reliability or precision.

— Category not applicable.

[a]Figures for age not stated included in "all ages" but not distributed among age groups.

[b]Death rates for "under 1 year" (based on population estimates) differ from infant mortality rates (based on live births).

[c]Figures include September 11, 2001 related deaths for which death certificates were filed as of October 24, 2002.

SOURCE: Hsiang-Ching Kung et al., "Table 9. Death Rates by Age and Age-Adjusted Death Rates for the 15 Leading Causes of Death in 2005: United States, 1999–2005," in "Deaths: Final Data for 2005," *National Vital Statistics Reports*, vol. 56, no. 10, January 2008, ftp://ftp.cdc.gov/pub/Health_Statistics/NCHS/Publications/NVSR/56_10/table09.xls (accessed January 30, 2008)

TABLE 4.3

Estimated numbers of deaths of persons with AIDS, by year of death and selected characteristics, 2001–05

	Year of death					
	2001	**2002**	**2003**	**2004**	**2005**	**Cumulative[a]**
Data for 50 states and the District of Columbia						
Age at death (years)						
<13	47	25	23	15	7	4,865
13–14	3	9	7	14	14	271
15–19	44	38	38	38	42	1,061
20–24	206	152	163	188	157	8,555
25–29	612	555	531	509	457	43,157
30–34	1,672	1,451	1,328	1,208	1,102	94,260
35–39	3,145	2,922	2,889	2,604	2,129	114,833
40–44	3,714	3,527	3,682	3,655	3,371	101,420
45–49	3,035	3,231	3,355	3,479	3,261	69,832
50–54	2,082	2,279	2,480	2,634	2,635	41,897
55–59	1,098	1,174	1,371	1,508	1,529	23,600
60–64	624	602	732	755	805	13,497
≥65	698	675	805	845	808	13,511
Race/ethnicity						
White, not Hispanic	5,239	5,153	5,263	5,137	5,006	235,879
Black, not Hispanic	9,085	8,927	9,077	9,302	8,562	211,559
Hispanic	2,436	2,306	2,774	2,664	2,444	77,125
Asian/Pacific Islander	99	93	88	113	97	3,383
American Indian/Alaska Native	79	84	75	85	81	1,657
Transmission category						
Male adult or adolescent						
Male-to-male sexual contact	5,995	5,867	6,111	6,078	5,929	260,749
Injection drug use	3,749	3,662	3,759	3,570	3,159	104,450
Male-to-male sexual contact and injection drug use	1,342	1,273	1,354	1,314	1,364	39,920
High-risk heterosexual contact[b]	1,485	1,434	1,554	1,729	1,584	24,655
Other[c]	169	163	156	136	104	9,824
Subtotal	12,740	12,400	12,934	12,826	12,140	439,598
Female adult or adolescent						
Injection drug use	1,829	1,876	1,916	1,959	1,651	41,529
High-risk heterosexual contact[b]	2,258	2,225	2,400	2,531	2,413	40,233
Other[c]	86	84	94	77	64	4,082
Subtotal	4,172	4,185	4,411	4,567	4,128	85,844
Child (<13 years at diagnosis)						
Perinatal	66	52	53	58	46	4,800
Other[d]	3	4	6	1	1	515
Subtotal	69	56	59	60	48	5,315
Region of residence						
Northeast	5,091	5,047	5,376	4,904	3,948	174,327
Midwest	1,682	1,675	1,655	1,619	1,541	52,933
South	7,469	7,361	7,776	8,353	8,240	191,845
West	2,738	2,559	2,597	2,577	2,588	111,652
Subtotal for 50 states and the District of Columbia	16,980	16,641	17,404	17,453	16,316	530,756
Data for U.S. dependent areas	724	662	598	628	619	19,355
Total[e]	**17,726**	**17,318**	**18,020**	**18,099**	**17,011**	**550,394[f]**

Note: These numbers do not represent reported case counts. Rather, these numbers are point estimates, which result from adjustments of reported case counts. The reported case counts have been adjusted for reporting delays and for redistribution of cases in persons initially reported without an identified risk factor, but not for incomplete reporting.
[a]From the beginning of the epidemic through 2005.
[b]Heterosexual contact with a person known to have, or to be at high risk for, HIV infection.
[c]Includes hemophilia, blood transfusion, perinatal exposure, and risk factor not reported or not identified.
[d]Includes hemophilia, blood transfusion, and risk factor not reported or not identified.
[e]Includes persons of unknown race or multiple races and persons of unknown sex. Because column totals were calculated independently of the values for the subpopulations, the values in each column may not sum to the column total.
[f]Includes 1,162 persons of unknown race or multiple races, 280 persons of unknown state of residence, and 2 persons who were residents of other areas.

SOURCE: "Table 7. Estimated Numbers of Deaths of Persons with AIDS, by Year of Death and Selected Characteristics, 2001–2005 and Cumulative—United States and Dependent Areas," in *HIV/AIDS Surveillance Report: Cases of HIV Infection and AIDS in the United States and Dependent Areas, 2005*, vol. 17, rev. ed., U.S. Department of Health and Human Services, Centers for Disease Control and Prevention, June 2007, http://www.cdc.gov/hiv/topics/surveillance/resources/reports/2005report/pdf/2005SurveillanceReport.pdf (accessed January 30, 2008).

more than nine thousand patients who suffered from life-threatening illnesses. Patients enrolled in the study had about a 50% chance of dying within six months.

The researchers published the results of their study in "A Controlled Trial to Improve Care for Seriously Ill Hospitalized Patients" (*Journal of the American Medical Association,* vol. 274, no. 20, November 22–29, 1995). The SUPPORT investigators hypothesized that increased communication between patients and physicians, better understanding of patients' wishes, and the use of computer-based projections of patient survival would result in "earlier treatment decisions, reductions in time spent in undesirable states before death, and reduced resource use."

Phase I of the study was observational. The researchers reviewed patients' medical records and interviewed patients, surrogates (people who make decisions if patients become incompetent), and physicians. Discussions and decisions about life-sustaining measures were observed.

The researchers interviewed patients, families, and surrogates about the patients' thoughts on cardiopulmonary resuscitation, their perceptions of their quality of life, the frequency and severity of their pain, and their satisfaction with the care provided. The physicians who acknowledged responsibility for the patients' medical decisions were also interviewed to determine their understanding of patients' views on cardiopulmonary resuscitation and how patients' wishes influenced their medical care. The surrogates were again interviewed after the patients' deaths.

Problems with End-of-Life Care

Phase I of SUPPORT found a lack of communication between physicians and patients, showed aggressive treatment of dying patients, and revealed a disturbing picture of hospital death. Of the 4,301 patients who participated in this phase, 31% expressed a desire that CPR be withheld. However, only 47% of physicians reported knowledge of their patients' wishes. About half (49%) of patients who requested not to be resuscitated did not have a do-not-resuscitate (DNR) order in their medical chart. Of the 79% who died with a DNR order, 46% of the orders were written within only two days of death.

The patients' final days in the hospital included an average of eight days in "generally undesirable states"— in an intensive care unit (ICU), receiving artificial respiration, or in a coma. More than a third (38%) stayed ten days in the ICU, and almost half (46%) were mechanically ventilated within three days before death. Surrogates reported that 50% of conscious patients complained of moderate or severe pain at least half the time in their last three days.

Phase II: Intervention to Improve Care

Phase II of SUPPORT was implemented to address the shortcomings documented in Phase I. It tested an intervention delivered by experienced nurses and lasted another two years, involving patient participants with characteristics similar to those in Phase I. This time, however, the doctors were given printed reports about the patients and their wishes regarding life-sustaining treatments. SUPPORT nurses facilitated the flow of information among patients, families, and health-care personnel, and helped manage patients' pain. To determine if the intervention worked in addressing problems in the care of seriously ill hospitalized patients at medical centers, researchers measured outcomes on five quantitative outcomes: incidence and timing of DNR orders; patient-physician agreement on CPR preferences; days in an ICU in a comatose condition or receiving mechanical ventilation; pain; and hospital resource use.

RESULTS OF PHASE II. Patricia A. Murphy et al. indicate in "Under the Radar: Contributions of the SUPPORT Nurses" (*Nursing Outlook*, vol. 49, no. 5, September–October 2001) that the SUPPORT intervention failed to produce changes in the outcomes that were measured. In "Improving Care Near the End of Life: Why Is It So Hard?" (*Journal of the American Medical Association*, vol. 274, no. 20, November 22–29, 1995), Bernard Lo indicates that he believes the results reported in the SUPPORT study raise more questions than answers. Among other issues, Lo claims that while Phase I showed poor doctor-patient communication, Phase II, instead of directly addressing this shortcoming, added a third party, the SUPPORT nurses, to do the physicians' job.

Murphy et al. note that their analysis of SUPPORT nurses' narratives suggests, however, that the nurses made a difference during the intervention in ways that were not acknowledged by the measurement of the five quantitative outcomes. The nurses supported patients and their families, brought them information, and helped them interpret it. They note that many of the nurses' narratives suggest that effective communication is a precondition of patient or family readiness "to hear a grave prognosis, engage in serious decision making, or 'let go' of a loved one."

Betty A. Ditillo suggests in "The Emergence of Palliative Care: A New Specialized Field of Medicine Requiring an Interdisciplinary Approach" (*Critical Care Nursing Clinics of North America*, vol. 14, no. 2, June 2002) that the movement in the United States to improve end-of-life care (the palliative care movement) is a result of the SUPPORT study. Ditillo notes that "the delivery of effective palliative care requires an interdisciplinary team approach in order to meet the complex needs of patients and families." These complex needs include help in understanding various life-sustaining treatments and support to decide whether to accept or refuse such treatments at the end of life.

LIFE-SUSTAINING TREATMENTS

Life-sustaining treatments, also called life support, can take over many functions of an ailing body. Under normal conditions, when a patient suffers from a treatable illness, life support is a temporary measure used only until the body can function on its own. The ongoing debate about prolonging life-sustaining treatments concerns the incurably ill and permanently unconscious.

Cardiopulmonary Resuscitation

Traditional cardiopulmonary resuscitation (CPR) consists of two basic life-support skills administered in the event of cardiac or respiratory arrest: artificial circulation and artificial respiration. Cardiac arrest may be caused by a heart attack, which is an interruption of blood flow to the heart muscle. A coronary artery clogged with an accumulation of fatty deposits is a common cause of interrupted blood flow to the heart. By contrast, respiratory arrest may be the result of an accident (such as drowning) or the final stages of a pulmonary disease (such as emphysema).

In CPR, artificial circulation is accomplished by compressing the chest rhythmically to cause blood to flow sufficiently to give a person a chance for survival. Artificial respiration (rescue breathing) is accomplished by breathing into the victim's nose and mouth. According to the article "Changing the Rules on CPR for Cardiac Arrest" (*Harvard Women's Health Watch*, vol. 14, no. 10, June 2007), recent research indicates that in the case of cardiac arrest, providing chest compressions only is more effective than providing chest compressions and rescue breathing. Medical researchers have determined that taking the time to give rescue breaths to heart attack victims reduces the effectiveness of chest compressions, and effective chest compressions are vital in helping the heart retain its ability to beat on its own after being shocked with a defibrillator. However, if the person experiences respiratory arrest, rescue breathing must be performed to keep the person alive until an ambulance arrives.

The article "Changing the Rules on CPR for Cardiac Arrest" indicates that people who have cardiac arrest away from a hospital have a survival rate of only 1% to 3%. However, among people given CPR for cardiac or respiratory arrest, the survival rate is much higher. Tina I. Horsted et al. find in "Long-Term Prognosis after Out-of-Hospital Cardiac Arrest" (*Resuscitation*, vol. 72 no. 2, 2007) that 12.3% of people who were given CPR because of an out-of-hospital cardiac arrest or a noncardiac cause for respiratory arrest, such as drowning, were alive six months after the CPR and hospitalization.

REFUSAL OF CPR WITH A DNR ORDER. CPR is intended for healthy individuals who unexpectedly suffer a heart attack or other trauma, such as drowning. Generally, following CPR, survivors eventually resume a normal life. The outcome is quite different, however, for patients in the final stages of a terminal illness. In *Ethics on Call: A Medical Ethicist Shows How to Take Charge of Life-and-Death Choices* (1992), Nancy Neveloff Dubler and David Nimmons observe that for people with a terminal disease, dying after being "successfully" resuscitated virtually ensures a slower, harder, more painful death. In addition, patients who are dying, especially those experiencing a painful death, may welcome their demise.

A person not wishing to be resuscitated in case of cardiac or respiratory arrest may ask a physician to write a DNR order on his or her chart. This written order instructs health-care personnel not to initiate CPR, which can be very important because CPR is usually performed in an emergency. Even if a patient's living will includes refusal of CPR, emergency personnel rushing to a patient have no time to check the living will. A DNR order on a patient's chart is more accessible. A living will, also called an advance directive, is a written document stating how an individual wants medical decisions to be made if he or she loses the ability to make those decisions for him- or herself.

NONHOSPITAL DNR ORDERS. Outside the hospital setting, such as at home, people who do not want CPR performed in case of an emergency can request a nonhospital DNR order from their physician. Also called a prehospital DNR order, it instructs emergency medical personnel to withhold CPR. The DNR order may be on a bracelet or necklace or on a wallet card. However, laypeople performing CPR on an individual with a nonhospital DNR order cannot be prosecuted by the law. Caring Connections (http://www.caringinfo.org/stateaddownload), a program of the National Hospice and Palliative Care Organization (NHPCO), provides information about each of the fifty states' advance directives, including information about laws authorizing nonhospital DNR orders.

Mechanical Ventilation

When a patient's lungs are not functioning properly, a ventilator, or respirator, breathes for the patient. Oxygen is supplied to the lungs via a tube inserted through the mouth or nose into the windpipe. Mechanical ventilation is generally used to temporarily maintain normal breathing in those who have been in serious accidents or who suffer from a serious illness, such as pneumonia. In some cases, if the patient needs ventilation indefinitely, the physician might perform a tracheotomy to open a hole in the neck for placement of the breathing tube in the windpipe.

Ventilators are also used on terminally ill patients. In these cases the machine keeps the patient breathing but does nothing to cure the disease. Those preparing a living will are advised to give clear instructions about their desires regarding continued use of an artificial respirator that could prolong the process of dying.

Artificial Nutrition and Hydration

Artificial nutrition and hydration (ANH) is another technology that has further complicated the dying process.

In the twenty-first century, nutrients and fluids supplied intravenously or through a stomach or intestinal tube can indefinitely sustain the nutritional and hydration needs of comatose and terminally ill patients. ANH has a strong emotional impact because it relates to basic sustenance. In addition, the symbolism of feeding can be so powerful that families who know that their loved one would not want to be kept alive may still feel that not feeding is wrong. The NHPCO notes in "Artificial Nutrition (Food) and Hydration (Fluids) at the End of Life" (2006, http://www.caringinfo.org/UserFiles/File/PDFs/ArtificialNutritionAndHydration.pdf) that appetite loss is common in dying patients and is not a significant contributor to their suffering. It also explains that the withdrawal of ANH from a dying patient does not lead to a long and painful death. Moreover, evidence exists that avoiding ANH contributes to a more comfortable death.

ANH has traditionally been used in end-of-life care when patients experience a loss of appetite and difficulty swallowing. Health-care practitioners use ANH to prolong life, prevent aspiration pneumonia (inflammation of the lungs due to inhaling food particles or fluid), maintain independence and physical function, and decrease suffering and discomfort. However, ANH does not always accomplish these goals, as the Hospice and Palliative Nurses Association (HPNA) notes in the position statement "Artificial Nutrition and Hydration in End-of-Life Care" (June 2003, http://www.hpna.org/pdf/PositionStatement_ArtificialNutritionAndHydration.pdf). According to the HPNA, "studies show that tube feeding does not appear to prolong life in most patients with life-limiting, progressive diseases; moreover, complications from tube placement may increase mortality. Furthermore, artificially-delivered nutrition does not protect against aspiration and in some patient populations may actually *increase* the risk of aspiration and its complications."

In "Position of the American Dietetic Association: Ethical and Legal Issues in Nutrition, Hydration, and Feeding" (*Journal of the American Dietetic Association*, vol. 102, no. 5, May 2002), the American Dietetic Association (ADA) takes the formal position that "the development of clinical and ethical criteria for the nutrition and hydration of persons through the life span should be established by members of the health care team. Registered dietitians should work collaboratively to make nutrition, hydration, and feeding recommendations in individual cases." The ADA suggests that the patient should determine the extent of his or her nutrition and hydration and that shared decision making should occur between health-care professionals and the family when the patient cannot make such decisions.

Kidney Dialysis

Kidney dialysis is a medical procedure by which a machine takes over the function of the kidneys in removing waste products from the blood. Dialysis can be used when an illness or injury temporarily impairs kidney function. It may also be used by patients with irreversibly damaged kidneys awaiting organ transplantation.

Kidney failure may also occur as an end-stage of a terminal illness. Even though dialysis may cleanse the body of waste products, it cannot cure the disease. People who wish to let their illness take its course may refuse dialysis. They will eventually lapse into a coma and die.

DISORDERS OF CONSCIOUSNESS

A coma is a deep state of unconsciousness caused by damage to the brain, often from illness or trauma. Most people in a coma recover within a few days, but some do not. Figure 4.1 shows the possible outcomes for those who do not recover from a coma quickly. For some, their brain dies. That is, they irreversibly lose all cerebral and brain stem function. Table 2.1 in Chapter 2 lists the clinical criteria for brain death.

More typically, patients who do not recover quickly from a coma progress to a vegetative state. Those in a vegetative state for one month are then referred to as being in a persistent vegetative state (PVS), and after a longer period are referred to as being in a permanent vegetative state. (See Figure 4.1.) The word *permanent* implies no chance of recovery.

Table 2.2 in Chapter 2 lists the criteria for the diagnosis of a PVS. PVS patients are unaware of themselves or their environment. They do not respond to stimuli, understand language, or have control of bowel and bladder functions. They are intermittently awake but are not

FIGURE 4.1

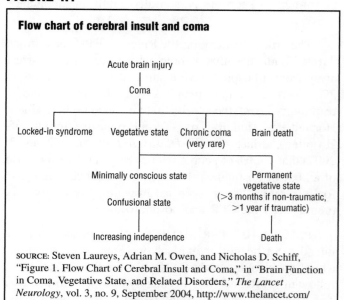

SOURCE: Steven Laureys, Adrian M. Owen, and Nicholas D. Schiff, "Figure 1. Flow Chart of Cerebral Insult and Coma," in "Brain Function in Coma, Vegetative State, and Related Disorders," *The Lancet Neurology*, vol. 3, no. 9, September 2004, http://www.thelancet.com/journals/laneur/full?issue_key=S1474-4422(00)X0030-0 (accessed March 25, 2008). Copyright © 2004 with permission from Elsevier.

conscious—a condition often referred to as "eyes open unconsciousness."

Some PVS patients may recover further to regain partial consciousness. This condition is called a minimally conscious state (MCS). Partial MCS means that perception is severely altered, but that the patient shows an awareness of self or the environment and exhibits behaviors such as following simple commands and smiling or crying at appropriate times. Some patients emerge from an MCS and some remain in an MCS permanently.

Another disorder of consciousness that rarely occurs after a coma is locked-in syndrome. The patient with locked-in syndrome has full consciousness, but all the voluntary muscles of the body are paralyzed except (usually) for those that control vertical eye movement and blinking. People with locked-in syndrome communicate primarily with eye or eyelid movements.

Treatment of PVS Patients

In "The Vegetative and Minimally Conscious States: Consensus-Based Criteria for Establishing Diagnosis and Prognosis" (*Neurorehabilitation*, vol. 19, no. 4, 2004), Joseph T. Giacino discusses implications for treatment of PVS and MCS patients. He notes that early interventions should focus on maintaining the patient's physical health and preventing complications. Standard interventions include stretching exercises, skin care, nutritional supplementation, and pain management. In MCS patients, functional communication systems and interaction should be established. If the patient does not improve and the criteria for permanence of the condition are met, decisions must be made concerning changes in the level of care and whether life-sustaining treatment should be withdrawn. At this time professionals having expertise in the evaluation and management of patients with disorders of consciousness should be consulted to determine an appropriate course of action.

Takamitsu Yamamoto and Yoichi Katayama report in "Deep Brain Stimulation Therapy for the Vegetative State" (*Neuropsychological Rehabilitation*, vol. 15, nos. 3–4, July–September 2005) that deep brain stimulation (DBS) therapy may help PVS and MCS patients. DBS therapy involves implanting electrodes within the brain and stimulating the brain at regular intervals. The exact treatment course depends on the patient and his or her reaction to DBS. Yamamoto and Katayama report that eight of twenty-one PVS patients emerged from that state and were able to communicate but remained bedridden. After long-term rehabilitation, one of the eight patients was able to move to a wheelchair. Four of five MCS patients who were treated with DBS were eventually able to resume their life at home, whereas one patient remained bedridden. The researchers suggest that along with physical therapy and specialized rehabilitation programs to help restore nervous system function (neurorehabilitation programs), DBS may be a useful treatment for PVS and MCS patients.

Chances of Recovery

Giacino summarizes the consensus opinion of the major professional organizations in neurorehabilitation and neurology concerning, among other things, the prognosis of (prospects for) patients in a vegetative state (VS). He notes that the probability of recovery of consciousness from a VS depends on the length of time a patient has been in this condition and whether it was brought on by traumatic or nontraumatic causes.

After three months in a VS, the probability of recovering from a trauma-induced VS is approximately 35% and from a nontrauma-induced VS is 10%. Of the 35% who will recover from a trauma-induced VS, about 20% will still have severe disabilities at one year postinjury, whereas the remaining 15% will have moderate to good outcomes.

Of those with trauma-induced VS who do not begin recovery by three months, 35% will die and the other 30% will remain in a VS at one year postinjury. Of those who are alive at six months, approximately 30% will die, 50% will remain in a VS, and 15% will recover consciousness by twelve months.

Of those with nontrauma-induced VS who do not begin recovery by three months, approximately half will die during the next nine months and the other half will remain in a VS. No cases of recovery after six months in a nontrauma-induced VS have been documented.

ORGAN TRANSPLANTATION

Most organ and tissue donations are from people who have died as a result of brain injury and subsequent brain death. Once death is pronounced, the body is kept on mechanical support (if possible) to maintain the organs until it is determined whether the person will be a donor.

There are some organ and tissue donations that can come from living people. For example, it is possible to lead a healthy life with only one of the two kidneys that humans are born with, so people with two healthy kidneys will sometimes donate one to someone in need. Portions of the liver, lungs, and pancreas have also been transplanted out of a living donor, but this is less common. In most cases, living donors make their donations to help a family member or close friend.

Organ transplantation has come a long way since the first kidney was transplanted from one identical twin to another in 1954. The introduction in 1983 of cyclosporine, an immunosuppressant drug that helps prevent the body's immune system from rejecting a donated organ,

FIGURE 4.2

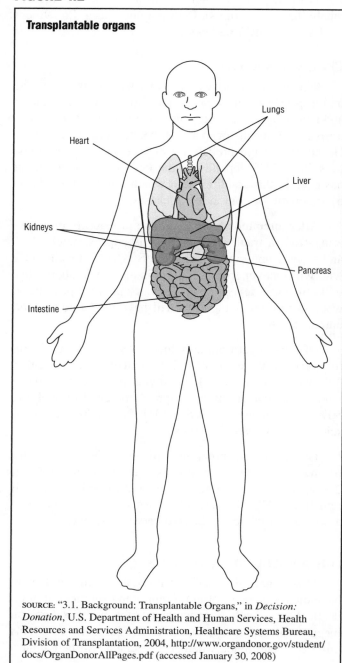

Transplantable organs

Lungs

Heart

Liver

Kidneys

Pancreas

Intestine

SOURCE: "3.1. Background: Transplantable Organs," in *Decision: Donation*, U.S. Department of Health and Human Services, Health Resources and Services Administration, Healthcare Systems Bureau, Division of Transplantation, 2004, http://www.organdonor.gov/student/docs/OrganDonorAllPages.pdf (accessed January 30, 2008)

made it possible to successfully transplant a variety of organs and tissues.

Figure 4.2 and Figure 4.3 show the organs and tissues transplantable with twenty-first-century immunosuppressant drugs and technologies. The organs that may be transplanted from people who have died are the heart, intestines, kidneys, liver, lungs, and pancreas. Tissues that may be transplanted from people who have died include bone, cartilage, cornea, heart valves, pancreas islet cells, skin, tendons, and veins. Living people may donate a kidney, parts of a lung or liver, or bone marrow.

Typically, donated organs must be transplanted within six to forty-eight hours of harvest, whereas some tissue may be stored for future use.

Soon after organ transplantation began, the demand for donor organs exceeded the supply. In 1984 Congress passed the National Organ Transplant Act to create "a centralized network to match scarce donated organs with critically ill patients." (For the process of matching organ donors and recipients, see Figure 4.4.) In the twenty-first century organ transplant is an accepted medical treatment for end-stage illnesses.

The United Network for Organ Sharing (UNOS), a private company under contract with the Division of Transplantation of the U.S. Department of Health and Human Services, manages the national transplant waiting list. It maintains data on all clinical organ transplants and distributes organ donor cards. (See Figure 4.5.) It assists in placing donated organs for transplantation by running the donor-recipient computer matching process. It also helps with the transportation of donated organs for transplantation. As of May 1, 2008, UNOS (http://www.unos.org/) reported that 99,147 people were waiting for a transplant in the United States. Between January and April 2008, 2,197 transplants had been performed in the United States.

Table 4.4 shows the waiting list for organs between 1996 and 2005. "Total registrations" refers to all the registrations from all transplant centers for all organs. Therefore, this figure is larger than "total patients," which is the number of patients waiting for a transplant. An individual may show up as more than one registration in the "registrations" category because that individual may be registered at more than one transplant center or for more than one organ. However, individuals waiting for transplants are counted only once in the "total patients" category, but they may show up more than once in the listing of organ types under that heading if they need more than one organ.

The total number of patients waiting for an organ transplant nearly doubled in just nine years, from 47,397 in 1996 to 89,884 in 2005. (See Table 4.4.) The total number of registrations nearly doubled as well, from 49,283 in 1996 to 94,086 in 2005. Nonetheless, the organ transplants during that same time period grew by only 40.7%, from 19,566 in 1996 to 27,527 in 2005. (See Table 4.5.)

The kidney is the organ most frequently transplanted. In 2005 there were 16,072 (58.4%) kidney transplants out of a total of 27,527 organ transplants. (See Table 4.5.) There were also 6,000 (21.7%) liver, 2,063 (7.5%) heart, and 1,405 (5.1%) lung transplants.

The number of all donors rose 57.3% between 1996 and 2005, from 9,208 to 14,488. The number of deceased donors increased 40.1%, from 5,418 to 7,593, whereas

FIGURE 4.3

Transplantable tissues

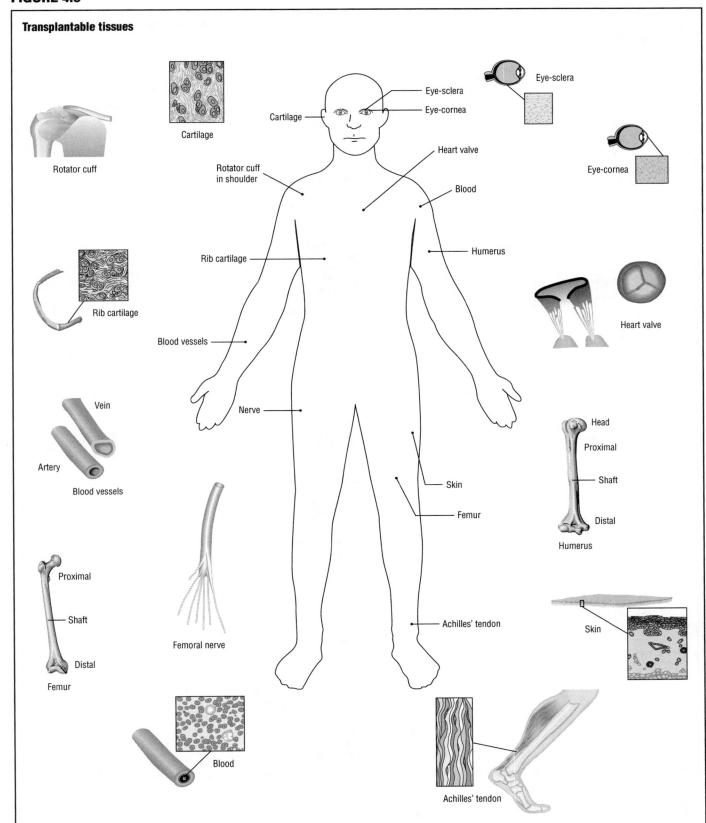

SOURCE: "3.2. Background: Transplantable Tissues," in *Decision: Donation*, U.S. Department of Health and Human Services, Health Resources and Services Administration, Healthcare Systems Bureau, Division of Transplantation, 2004, http://www.organdonor.gov/student/docs/OrganDonorAllPages.pdf (accessed January 30, 2008)

FIGURE 4.4

Matching donors and recipients: The Organ Procurement & Transplantation Network (OPTN) and the Scientific Registry of Transplant Recipients (SRTR)

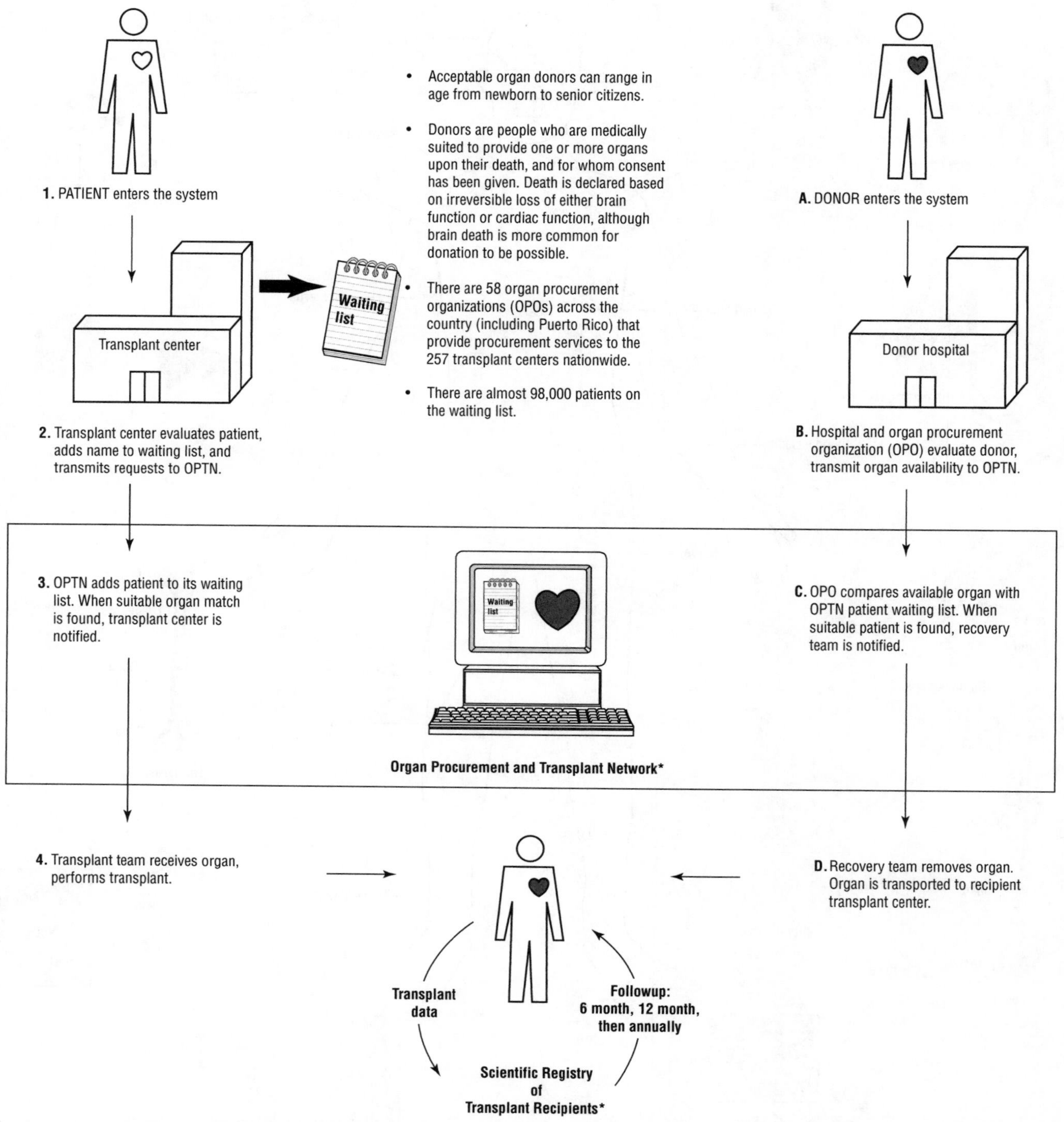

1. PATIENT enters the system

Transplant center

Waiting list

2. Transplant center evaluates patient, adds name to waiting list, and transmits requests to OPTN.

- Acceptable organ donors can range in age from newborn to senior citizens.

- Donors are people who are medically suited to provide one or more organs upon their death, and for whom consent has been given. Death is declared based on irreversible loss of either brain function or cardiac function, although brain death is more common for donation to be possible.

- There are 58 organ procurement organizations (OPOs) across the country (including Puerto Rico) that provide procurement services to the 257 transplant centers nationwide.

- There are almost 98,000 patients on the waiting list.

A. DONOR enters the system

Donor hospital

B. Hospital and organ procurement organization (OPO) evaluate donor, transmit organ availability to OPTN.

3. OPTN adds patient to its waiting list. When suitable organ match is found, transplant center is notified.

Waiting list

Organ Procurement and Transplant Network*

C. OPO compares available organ with OPTN patient waiting list. When suitable patient is found, recovery team is notified.

4. Transplant team receives organ, performs transplant.

D. Recovery team removes organ. Organ is transported to recipient transplant center.

Transplant data

Followup: 6 month, 12 month, then annually

Scientific Registry of Transplant Recipients*

*Operated by the United Network for Organ Sharing (UNOS), Richmond, VA, under contract with the U.S. Department of Health and Human Services, Health Resources and Services Administration, Division of Transplantation.

SOURCE: *Questions and Answers about Organ Donation*, U.S. Department of Health and Human Services, Health Resources and Services Administration, Division of Transplantation, undated. Updated by UNOS as of February 2008.

FIGURE 4.5

Organ/tissue donor card

Organ/Tissue Donor Card

I wish to donate my organs and tissues. I wish to give:

☐ any needed organs and tissues   ☐ only the following organs and tissues:

_____

Donor
Signature _____ Date _____

Witness _____

Witness _____

SOURCE: "Organ/Tissue Donor Card," U.S. Department of Health and Human Services, undated, ftp://ftp.hrsa.gov/osp/newdonorcard.pdf (accessed January 30, 2008)

living donors showed an increase of slightly more than twice that—81.9%—from 3,790 to 6,895. (See Table 4.6.) Most living donors provide kidneys. The donation of kidneys by living donors increased by 78.5% from 1996 to 2005—from 3,679 to 6,566. Living donors may also contribute a portion of their liver; the donation by living donors of liver tissue increased fivefold from 62 in 1996 to 321 in 2005. Living donors of pancreas, intestine, and lung tissue are few, with living donors of lung tissue dropping precipitously to only two donors in 2005 from the mid-twenties between 2002 and 2004, and from even higher numbers of donors before that. Edward R. Garrity et al. suggest in "Heart and Lung Transplantation in the United States, 1996–2005" (*American Journal of Transplantation*, vol. 7, suppl. 1, May 2007) that the reason for this decrease in the demand for living donor lung transplantation is a system change in May 2005 for allocating lungs from deceased donors. This change resulted in a decrease in the number of people on lung transplant waiting lists and an increase in the ability to get patients transplanted sooner.

Organ Donation

The Uniform Anatomical Gift Act of 1968 gives a person the opportunity to sign a donor card indicating a desire to donate organs or tissue after death. People who wish to be donors should complete a donor card, which should be carried at all times. Alternatively, the wish to be a donor can be indicated on a driver's license or in a living will. Prospective donors should inform their family and physician of their decision. At the time of death, hospitals always ask for the family's consent, even if a donor has already indicated his or her wish to donate organs. Should the family refuse, the doctors will not take the organs, despite the deceased's wish. In 2005 most organ donors whose cause of death was known died of a stroke (43.7%) or head trauma (38%), as might happen in a motor vehicle accident. (See Table 4.7.) Anoxia (lack of oxygen, as in drowning or choking) was the cause of death of 15% of organ donors.

TABLE 4.4

United Network for Organ Sharing (UNOS) and Scientific Registry of Transplant Recipients (SRTR) national patient waiting list for organ transplant, end of year, 1996–2005

	Year									
	1996	**1997**	**1998**	**1999**	**2000**	**2001**	**2002**	**2003**	**2004**	**2005**
Total registrations	**49,283**	**55,508**	**62,328**	**68,151**	**74,800**	**80,209**	**81,913**	**85,489**	**90,090**	**94,086**
Organ type										
Kidney	33,961	37,385	40,844	43,659	47,265	50,385	53,254	56,670	61,283	65,859
Pancreas transplant alone	213	229	282	251	313	394	412	456	507	529
Pancreas after kidney	149	152	181	279	459	679	787	928	983	987
Kidney-pancreas	1,378	1,532	1,757	2,136	2,452	2,473	2,509	2,445	2,446	2,544
Liver	7,342	9,433	11,739	14,174	16,440	18,269	17,072	17,310	17,411	17,673
Intestine	81	92	96	106	141	169	183	172	196	203
Heart	3,643	3,823	4,075	3,945	3,960	3,906	3,743	3,477	3,223	2,980
Lung	2,277	2,630	3,101	3,373	3,566	3,725	3,756	3,842	3,870	3,170
Heart-lung	239	232	253	228	204	209	197	189	171	141
Total patients	**47,397**	**53,381**	**59,862**	**65,260**	**71,628**	**76,893**	**78,498**	**81,979**	**85,610**	**89,884**
Organ type										
Kidney	32,262	35,529	38,710	41,204	44,603	47,622	50,372	53,661	57,389	62,294
Pancreas transplant alone	210	225	276	249	312	386	409	453	502	521
Pancreas after kidney	145	148	177	276	455	668	774	917	971	977
Kidney-pancreas	1,352	1,493	1,697	2,049	2,363	2,368	2,407	2,364	2,381	2,474
Liver	7,243	9,278	11,544	13,931	16,102	17,916	16,724	16,957	16,967	17,168
Intestine	79	87	93	101	133	164	180	167	191	202
Heart	3,633	3,809	4,060	3,922	3,942	3,885	3,728	3,468	3,210	2,970
Lung	2,236	2,584	3,056	3,306	3,516	3,675	3,707	3,803	3,828	3,139
Heart-lung	237	228	249	222	202	209	197	189	171	139

SOURCE: "Table 1.3. Waiting List at End of Year, 1996 to 2005," in *2006 Annual Report of the U.S. Organ Procurement and Transplantation Network and the Scientific Registry of Transplant Recipients: Transplant Data 1996–2005*, U.S. Department of Health and Human Services, Health Resources and Services Administration, Healthcare Systems Bureau, Division of Transplantation, 2006, http://www.ustransplant.org/annual_reports/current/103_dh.pdf (accessed January 30, 2008)

TABLE 4.5

United Network for Organ Sharing (UNOS) and Scientific Registry of Transplant Recipients (SRTR) transplants, by organ and donor type, 1996–2005

Organ/donor type		1996	1997	1998	1999	2000	2001	2002	2003	2004	2005
All organs	Total	19,566	20,091	21,318	21,826	23,011	23,945	24,552	25,086	26,541	27,527
	Deceased	15,798	16,049	16,744	16,818	17,095	17,362	17,935	18,273	19,551	20,635
	Living	3,768	4,042	4,544	5,008	5,916	6,583	6,617	6,813	6,990	6,892
Kidney	Total	11,263	11,561	12,317	12,632	13,445	14,101	14,526	14,857	15,674	16,072
	Deceased	7,595	7,634	7,898	7,916	7,957	8,066	8,286	8,387	9,027	9,509
	Living	3,668	3,927	4,419	4,716	5,488	6,035	6,240	6,470	6,647	6,563
Pancreas transplant alone	Total	44	64	73	125	118	130	142	116	130	129
	Deceased	44	64	73	125	117	129	141	116	130	129
	Living	—	—	—	—	1	1	1	—	—	—
Pancreas after kidney transplant	Total	113	130	156	220	304	304	374	344	419	343
	Deceased	112	130	156	220	304	304	374	344	419	342
	Living	1	—	—	—	—	—	—	—	—	1
Kidney-pancreas	Total	858	847	969	938	914	889	902	869	880	896
	Deceased	848	841	967	930	908	886	902	866	880	895
	Living	10	6	2	8	6	3	—	3	—	1
Liver	Total	3,932	4,012	4,369	4,606	4,807	4,984	5,059	5,364	5,779	6,000
	Deceased	3,870	3,926	4,277	4,353	4,407	4,465	4,697	5,043	5,457	5,679
	Living	62	86	92	253	400	519	362	321	322	321
Intestine	Total	15	23	28	31	30	42	42	52	52	68
	Deceased	13	21	26	29	27	42	41	48	46	63
	Living	2	2	2	2	3	—	1	4	6	5
Heart	Total	2,319	2,266	2,310	2,157	2,167	2,171	2,112	2,026	1,961	2,063
	Deceased	2,318	2,266	2,310	2,157	2,167	2,171	2,112	2,026	1,961	2,063
	Living	1	—	—	—	—	—	—	—	—	—
Lung	Total	812	929	866	892	958	1,059	1,041	1,080	1,168	1,405
	Deceased	788	908	837	863	940	1,034	1,028	1,065	1,153	1,404
	Living	24	21	29	29	18	25	13	15	15	1
Heart-lung	Total	38	62	46	51	46	27	32	28	37	32
	Deceased	38	62	46	51	46	27	32	28	37	32
	Living	—	—	—	—	—	—	—	—	—	—
Multi-organ	Total	172	197	184	174	222	238	322	350	441	519
	Deceased	172	197	184	174	222	238	322	350	441	519
	Living	—	—	—	—	—	—	—	—	—	—

Notes: (—) = None in category.
An organ that is divided into segments (liver, lung, pancreas, intestine) is counted once per transplant.
Kidney-pancreas and heart-lung transplants are counted as one transplant. Other multiple organ transplants are counted only in the multiple organ row.

SOURCE: "Table 1.7. Transplants by Organ and Donor Type, 1996 to 2005," in *2006 Annual Report of the U.S. Organ Procurement and Transplantation Network and the Scientific Registry of Transplant Recipients: Transplant Data 1996–2005*, U.S. Department of Health and Human Services, Health Resources and Services Administration, Healthcare Systems Bureau, Division of Transplantation, 2006, http://www.ustransplant.org/annual_reports/current/107_dh.pdf (accessed January 30, 2008)

TABLE 4.6

United Network for Organ Sharing (UNOS) and Scientific Registry of Transplant Recipients (SRTR) organ donors, by organ and donor type, 1996–2005

Organ/donor type		Year									
		1996	1997	1998	1999	2000	2001	2002	2003	2004	2005
All organs	Total	9,208	9,538	10,361	10,861	11,918	12,687	12,819	13,284	14,153	14,488
	Deceased	5,418	5,479	5,793	5,824	5,985	6,080	6,190	6,457	7,150	7,593
	Living	3,790	4,059	4,568	5,037	5,933	6,607	6,629	6,827	7,003	6,895
Kidney	Total	8,717	9,017	9,760	10,110	10,982	11,566	11,878	12,226	12,972	13,266
	Deceased	5,038	5,084	5,339	5,386	5,489	5,528	5,638	5,753	6,325	6,700
	Living	3,679	3,933	4,421	4,724	5,493	6,038	6,240	6,473	6,647	6,566
Pancreas	Total	1,303	1,328	1,464	1,636	1,707	1,820	1,873	1,773	2,010	2,035
	Deceased	1,292	1,322	1,462	1,628	1,700	1,816	1,872	1,770	2,010	2,033
	Living	11	6	2	8	7	4	1	3	—	2
Liver	Total	4,525	4,686	4,935	5,200	5,397	5,625	5,656	6,003	6,642	7,011
	Deceased	4,463	4,600	4,843	4,947	4,997	5,106	5,294	5,682	6,320	6,690
	Living	62	86	92	253	400	519	362	321	322	321
Intestine	Total	50	74	80	97	90	115	113	126	172	189
	Deceased	48	72	78	95	87	115	112	122	166	184
	Living	2	2	2	2	3	—	1	4	6	5
Heart	Total	2,463	2,426	2,447	2,316	2,284	2,276	2,223	2,120	2,096	2,220
	Deceased	2,462	2,426	2,447	2,316	2,284	2,276	2,223	2,120	2,096	2,220
	Living	1	—	—	—	—	—	—	—	—	—
Lung	Total	801	874	817	835	861	936	945	990	1,093	1,287
	Deceased	756	836	764	777	825	887	920	961	1,065	1,285
	Living	45	38	53	58	36	49	25	29	28	2
Donation after cardiac arrest	Total	71	78	75	87	118	169	189	269	391	561
	Deceased	71	78	75	87	118	169	189	269	391	561

Notes: (—) = None in category.
Includes only organs recovered for transplant.
The number of transplants using living donors may be different from the number of living donors. This is because there is a small number of multi-organ living donors and multiple donors for one transplant. For example, a living donor might donate a kidney and pancreas segment; or two living donors might each donate a lung lobe for one transplant procedure.
A donor of an organ divided into segments (liver, lung, pancreas, intestine) is counted only once for that organ.
A donor of multiple organs is counted once for each organ recovered.
Donors after cardiac death are included in the deceased donor counts as well and are counted separately on the last line.

SOURCE: "Table 1.1. U.S. Organ Donors by Organ and Donor Type, 1996 to 2005," in *2006 Annual Report of the U.S. Organ Procurement and Transplantation Network and the Scientific Registry of Transplant Recipients: Transplant Data 1996–2005*, U.S. Department of Health and Human Services, Health Resources and Services Administration, Healthcare Systems Bureau, Division of Transplantation, 2006, http://www.ustransplant.org/annual_reports/current/101_dh.pdf (accessed January 30, 2008)

TABLE 4.7

Causes of death of donors of any organ, 1996–2005

					Year					
	1996	**1997**	**1998**	**1999**	**2000**	**2001**	**2002**	**2003**	**2004**	**2005**
Total	**5,418**	**5,479**	**5,793**	**5,824**	**5,985**	**6,080**	**6,190**	**6,457**	**7,150**	**7,593**
Cause of death										
Anoxia	526	562	638	640	619	697	741	855	1,025	1,138
Cerebrovascular/stroke	2,270	2,236	2,478	2,508	2,612	2,631	2,630	2,761	3,126	3,317
Head trauma	2,456	2,489	2,497	2,430	2,520	2,545	2,610	2,617	2,793	2,889
Central nervous system (CNS) tumor	50	63	57	61	62	52	56	49	60	57
Other	86	109	88	171	171	154	153	175	144	144
Unknown	30	20	35	14	1	1	—	—	2	48
Cause of Death (%)										
Anoxia	9.7%	10.3%	11.0%	11.0%	10.3%	11.5%	12.0%	13.2%	14.3%	15.0%
Cerebrovascular/stroke	41.9%	40.8%	42.8%	43.1%	43.6%	43.3%	42.5%	42.8%	43.7%	43.7%
Head trauma	45.3%	45.4%	43.1%	41.7%	42.1%	41.9%	42.2%	40.5%	39.1%	38.0%
Central nervous system (CNS) tumor	0.9%	1.1%	1.0%	1.0%	1.0%	0.9%	0.9%	0.8%	0.8%	0.8%
Other	1.6%	2.0%	1.5%	2.9%	2.9%	2.5%	2.5%	2.7%	2.0%	1.9%
Unknown	0.6%	0.4%	0.6%	0.2%	0.0%	0.0%	—	—	0.0%	0.6%

(%) = Percentages are calculated based on totals including missing and unknown cases.
(—) = None in category.
Includes donors of organs recovered for transplant and not used, as well as those transplanted. Not all recovered organs are actually transplanted.

SOURCE: Adapted from "Table 2.1. Deceased Donor Characteristics, 1996 to 2005 Deceased Donors of Any Organ," in *2006 Annual Report of the U.S. Organ Procurement and Transplantation Network and the Scientific Registry of Transplant Recipients: Transplant Data 1996–2005*, U.S. Department of Health and Human Services, Health Resources and Services Administration, Healthcare Systems Bureau, Division of Transplantation, 2006, http://www.ustransplant.org/annual_reports/current/201_dc.pdf (accessed January 30, 2008)

CHAPTER 5
SERIOUSLY ILL CHILDREN

What greater pain could mortals have than this:
To see their children dead before their eyes?

—Euripides

To a parent, the death of a child is an affront to the proper order of things. Children are supposed to outlive their parents, not the other way around. When a child comes into the world irreparably ill, what is a parent to do: insist on continuous medical intervention, hoping against hope that the child survives, or let nature take its course and allow the newborn to die? When a five-year-old child has painful, life-threatening disabilities, the parent is faced with a similar agonizing decision. That decision is the parent's to make, preferably with the advice of a sensitive physician. However, what if the ailing child is an adolescent who refuses further treatment for a terminal illness? Does a parent honor that wish? This chapter focuses on infant and child death, the conditions that often cause mortality at young ages, and medical decision making for seriously ill children.

INFANT MORTALITY AND LIFE EXPECTANCY AT BIRTH

Kenneth D. Kochanek and Joyce A. Martin of the Centers for Disease Control and Prevention (CDC) indicate in "Supplemental Analysis of Recent Trends in Infant Mortality" (January 11, 2007, http://www.cdc.gov/nchs/products/pubs/pubd/hestats/infantmort/infantmort.htm) that from 1933 through 2001 the U.S. infant mortality rate declined dramatically. In 1933 the infant mortality rate was 58.1 deaths per 1,000 live births. With each decade, infant mortality declined significantly, to 47 deaths per 1,000 live births in 1940, to 29.2 deaths per 1,000 live births in 1950, to eventually 6.8 deaths per 1,000 live births in 2001. This rate remained relatively steady through 2005. (See Table 5.1 and Table 5.2.)

Table 5.1 shows the decline in infant mortality rates from 1983 to 2004, and Table 5.2 shows figures for 2004

and preliminary figures for 2005. The data in these two tables differ slightly in some cases due to the use of somewhat different data sets.

Advances in neonatology (the medical subspecialty concerned with the care of newborns, especially those at risk), which date back to the 1960s, have contributed to the huge drop in infant death rates. Infants born prematurely or with low birth weights, who were once likely to die, now can survive life-threatening conditions because of the development of neonatal intensive care units. However, the improvements are not consistent for newborns of all races.

African-American infants are more than twice as likely as white and Hispanic infants to die before their first birthday. In 2004 the national death rate for African-American infants was 13.8 per 1,000 live births, compared to 5.7 for non-Hispanic white infants and 5.6 for Hispanic infants. (See Table 5.2.) In 2005 the national death rate for African-American infants was slightly lower than in 2004: 13.7 per 1,000 live births, compared to 5.7 for non-Hispanic white infants and 5.9 for Hispanic infants.

Native American or Alaskan Native infants are about one and half times as likely as white and Hispanic infants to die before their first birthday. In 2004 the national death rate for Native American or Alaskan Native infants was 8.4 per 1,000 live births, compared to 5.7 for white infants and 5.5 for Hispanic infants. (See Table 5.1.)

When are infants dying? Table 5.1 shows death rates during the neonatal period (under twenty-eight days after birth) and the postneonatal period (from twenty-eight days after birth to eleven months of age). The neonatal and postneonatal deaths together comprise the infant death rate. Of all infant deaths in 2004, two-thirds occurred during the neonatal period. For example, 4.5

TABLE 5.1

Infant, neonatal, and postneonatal mortality rates, by race and Hispanic origin of mother, selected years, 1983–2004

[Data are based on linked birth and death certificates for infants]

Race and Hispanic origin of mother	1983[a]	1985[a]	1990[a]	1995[b]	2000[b]	2002[b]	2003[b]	2004[b]
				Infant[c] deaths per 1,000 live births				
All mothers	10.9	10.4	8.9	7.6	6.9	7.0	6.8	6.8
White	9.3	8.9	7.3	6.3	5.7	5.8	5.7	5.7
Black or African American	19.2	18.6	16.9	14.6	13.5	13.8	13.5	13.2
American Indian or Alaska Native	15.2	13.1	13.1	9.0	8.3	8.6	8.7	8.4
Asian or Pacific Islander[d]	8.3	7.8	6.6	5.3	4.9	4.8	4.8	4.7
Chinese	9.5	5.8	4.3	3.8	3.5	3.0	—	—
Japanese	*5.6	*6.0	*5.5	*5.3	*4.5	*4.9	—	—
Filipino	8.4	7.7	6.0	5.6	5.7	5.7	—	—
Hawaiian	11.2	*9.9	*8.0	*6.5	9.0	9.6	—	—
Other Asian or Pacific Islander	8.1	8.5	7.4	5.5	4.8	4.7	—	—
Hispanic or Latino[e,f]	9.5	8.8	7.5	6.3	5.6	5.6	5.6	5.5
Mexican	9.1	8.5	7.2	6.0	5.4	5.4	5.5	5.5
Puerto Rican	12.9	11.2	9.9	8.9	8.2	8.2	8.2	7.8
Cuban	7.5	8.5	7.2	5.3	4.6	3.7	4.6	4.6
Central and South American	8.5	8.0	6.8	5.5	4.6	5.1	5.0	4.6
Other and unknown Hispanic or Latino	10.6	9.5	8.0	7.4	6.9	7.1	6.7	6.7
Not Hispanic or Latino:								
White[f]	9.2	8.6	7.2	6.3	5.7	5.8	5.7	5.7
Black or African American[f]	19.1	18.3	16.9	14.7	13.6	13.9	13.6	13.6
				Neonatal[c] deaths per 1,000 live births				
All mothers	7.1	6.8	5.7	4.9	4.6	4.7	4.6	4.5
White	6.1	5.8	4.6	4.1	3.8	3.9	3.9	3.8
Black or African American	12.5	12.3	11.1	9.6	9.1	9.3	9.2	8.9
American Indian or Alaska Native	7.5	6.1	6.1	4.0	4.4	4.6	4.5	4.3
Asian or Pacific Islander[d]	5.2	4.8	3.9	3.4	3.4	3.4	3.4	3.2
Chinese	5.5	3.3	2.3	2.3	2.5	2.4	—	—
Japanese	*3.7	*3.1	*3.5	*3.3	*2.6	*3.7	—	—
Filipino	5.6	5.1	3.5	3.4	4.1	4.1	—	—
Hawaiian	*7.0	*5.7	*4.3	*4.0	*6.2	*5.6	—	—
Other Asian or Pacific Islander	5.0	5.4	4.4	3.7	3.4	3.3	—	—
Hispanic or Latino[e,f]	6.2	5.7	4.8	4.1	3.8	3.8	3.9	3.8
Mexican	5.9	5.4	4.5	3.9	3.6	3.6	3.8	3.7
Puerto Rican	8.7	7.6	6.9	6.1	5.8	5.8	5.7	5.3
Cuban	*5.0	6.2	5.3	*3.6	*3.2	*3.2	3.4	*2.8
Central and South American	5.8	5.6	4.4	3.7	3.3	3.5	3.6	3.4
Other and unknown Hispanic or Latino	6.4	5.6	5.0	4.8	4.6	5.1	4.7	4.7
Not Hispanic or Latino:								
White[f]	5.9	5.6	4.5	4.0	3.8	3.9	3.8	3.7
Black or African American[f]	12.0	11.9	11.0	9.6	9.2	9.3	9.3	9.1
				Postneonatal[c] deaths per 1,000 live births				
All mothers	3.8	3.6	3.2	2.6	2.3	2.3	2.2	2.3
White	3.2	3.1	2.7	2.2	1.9	1.9	1.9	1.9
Black or African American	6.7	6.3	5.9	5.0	4.3	4.5	4.3	4.3
American Indian or Alaska Native	7.7	7.0	7.0	5.1	3.9	4.0	4.2	4.2
Asian or Pacific Islander[d]	3.1	2.9	2.7	1.9	1.4	1.4	1.4	1.5
Chinese	4.0	*2.5	*2.0	*1.5	*1.0	*0.7	—	—
Japanese	*	*2.9	*	*	*	*	—	—
Filipino	*2.8	2.7	2.5	2.2	1.6	1.7	—	—
Hawaiian	*4.2	*4.3	*3.8	*	*	*4.0	—	—
Other Asian or Pacific Islander	3.0	3.0	3.0	1.9	1.4	1.4	—	—
Hispanic or Latino[e,f]	3.3	3.2	2.7	2.1	1.8	1.8	1.7	1.7
Mexican	3.2	3.2	2.7	2.1	1.8	1.8	1.7	1.7
Puerto Rican	4.2	3.5	3.0	2.8	2.4	2.4	2.5	2.5
Cuban	*2.5	*2.3	*1.9	*1.7	*	*	*	*1.7
Central and South American	2.6	2.4	2.4	1.9	1.4	1.6	1.4	1.2
Other and unknown Hispanic or Latino	4.2	3.9	3.0	2.6	2.3	2.0	1.9	2.0
Not Hispanic or Latino:								
White[f]	3.2	3.0	2.7	2.2	1.9	1.9	1.9	2.0
Black or African American[f]	7.0	6.4	5.9	5.0	4.4	4.6	4.3	4.5

infants died per 1,000 live births of all mothers in 2004 during the neonatal period, compared to a total of 6.8 infant deaths per 1,000 live births of all mothers. This proportion of deaths occurring during the neonatal period was relatively consistent across race and Hispanic origin of the mother in 2004.

TABLE 5.1

Infant, neonatal, and postneonatal mortality rates, by race and Hispanic origin of mother, selected years, 1983–2004 [CONTINUED]

[Data are based on linked birth and death certificates for infants]

— Data not available.
*Estimates are considered unreliable. Rates preceded by an asterisk are based on fewer than 50 deaths in the numerator. Rates not shown are based on fewer than 20 deaths in the numerator.
[a]Rates based on unweighted birth cohort data.
[b]Rates based on a period file using weighted data.
[c]Infant (under 1 year of age), neonatal (under 28 days), and postneonatal (28 days–11 months).
[d]Starting with 2003 data, estimates are not shown for Asian or Pacific Islander subgroups during the transition from single race to multiple race reporting.
[e]Persons of Hispanic origin may be of any race.
[f]Prior to 1995, data shown only for states with an Hispanic-origin item on their birth certificates.
Notes: The race groups white, black, American Indian or Alaska Native, and Asian or Pacific Islander include persons of Hispanic and non-Hispanic origin. Starting with 2003 data, some states reported multiple-race data. The multiple-race data for these states were bridged to the single-race categories of the 1977 Office of Management and Budget standards for comparability with other states. National linked files do not exist for 1992–1994. Data for additional years are available.

SOURCE: Adapted from "Table 19. Infant, Neonatal, and Postneonatal Mortality Rates, by Detailed Race and Hispanic Origin of Mother: United States, Selected Years 1983–2004," in *Health, United States, 2007. With Chartbook on Trends in the Health of Americans*, Centers for Disease Control and Prevention, National Center for Health Statistics, November 2007, http://www.cdc.gov/nchs/data/hus/hus07.pdf (accessed January 30, 2008)

TABLE 5.2

Infant deaths and infant mortality rates, by age, race, and Hispanic origin, 2004 and 2005

[Data are based on the continuous file of records received from the states. Rates per 1,000 live births.]

Age, race, and Hispanic origin	2005		2004	
	Number	Rate	Number	Rate
All races[a]				
Under 1 year	28,534	6.89	27,936	6.79
Under 28 days	18,834	4.55	18,593	4.52
28 days–11 months	9,699	2.34	9,343	2.27
Total white				
Under 1 year	18,623	5.76	18,231	5.66
Under 28 days	12,317	3.81	12,198	3.78
28 days–11 months	6,307	1.95	6,033	1.87
Non-Hispanic white				
Under 1 year	13,092	5.73	13,046	5.68
Under 28 days	8,563	3.75	8,638	3.76
28 days–11 months	4,529	1.98	4,408	1.92
Total black				
Under 1 year	8,663	13.69	8,494	13.79
Under 28 days	5,717	9.04	5,622	9.13
28 days–11 months	2,946	4.66	2,872	4.66
Hispanic[b]				
Under 1 year	5,782	5.88	5,321	5.62
Under 28 days	3,897	3.96	3,633	3.84
28 days–11 months	1,885	1.92	1,688	1.78

[a]Includes races other than white or black.
[b]Includes all persons of Hispanic origin of any race.
Notes: Data are subject to sampling or random variation. Figures for 2005 are based on weighted data rounded to the nearest individual, so categories may not add to totals. Race and Hispanic origin are reported separately on both the birth and death certificate. Rates for Hispanic origin should be interpreted with caution because of the inconsistencies between reporting Hispanic origin on birth and death certificates. Race categories are consistent with the 1977 Office of Management and Budget (OMB) standards. Multiple-race data were reported for deaths by 21 states and the District of Columbia in 2005 and by 15 states in 2004, and for births, by 19 states in 2005 and by 15 states in 2004. The multiple-race data for these states were bridged to the single-race categories of the 1977 OMB standards for comparability with other states.

SOURCE: Hsiang-Ching Kung et al., "Table 4. Infant Deaths and Infant Mortality Rates, by Age, Race, and Hispanic Origin: United States, Final 2004 and Preliminary 2005," in *Deaths: Preliminary Data for 2005*, Centers for Disease Control and Prevention, National Center for Health Statistics, September 2007, http://www.cdc.gov/nchs/data/hestat/preliminarydeaths05_tables.pdf#1 (accessed February 1, 2008)

Life expectancy is the age to which people born in a particular year in a particular location can anticipate living. Infants born in the United States in 2005 are expected to live an average of 77.9 years, up from 77.8 years in 2004. (See Table 5.3.) However, those in certain groups have slightly different life expectancies. Females have a longer life expectancy than males. Female infants born in 2005 are expected to live for 80.4 years, whereas

TABLE 5.3

Deaths and life expectancy at birth, by race and sex; infant deaths and mortality rates, by race, 2004 and 2005

[Data are based on a continuous file of records received from the states. Figures for 2005 are based on weighted data rounded to the nearest individual, so categories may not add to totals]

	All races[a]		White[b]		Black[c]	
	2005	2004	2005	2004	2005	2004
All deaths	2,447,903	2,397,615	2,099,812	2,056,643	291,287	287,315
Male	1,207,548	1,181,668	1,029,025	1,007,266	148,270	145,970
Female	1,240,355	1,215,947	1,070,787	1,049,377	143,017	141,345
Age-adjusted death rate[c]	798.8	800.8	786.0	786.3	1,011.3	1,027.3
Male	951.0	955.7	933.9	936.9	1,245.8	1,269.4
Female	677.6	679.2	667.1	666.9	841.7	855.3
Life expectancy at birth[d]	77.9	77.8	78.3	78.3	73.2	73.1
Male	75.2	75.2	75.7	75.7	69.6	69.5
Female	80.4	80.4	80.8	80.8	76.5	76.3
All infant deaths	28,534	27,936	18,623	18,231	8,663	8,494
Infant mortality rate[e]	6.89	6.79	5.76	5.66	13.69	13.79

[a]Includes races other than white and black.
[b]Race categories are consistent with the 1977 Office of Management and Budget (OMB) standards. Multiple-race data were reported in 2005 for California, Connecticut, the District of Columbia, Florida, Hawaii, Idaho, Kansas, Maine, Michigan, Minnesota, Montana, Nebraska, New Hampshire, New Jersey, New York, Oklahoma, South Carolina, South Dakota, Utah, Washington, Wisconsin, and Wyoming; and in 2004, for California, Hawaii, Idaho, Maine, Michigan, Minnesota, Montana, New Hampshire, New Jersey, New York, Oklahoma, South Dakota, Washington, Wisconsin, and Wyoming. The multiple-race data for these reporting areas were bridged to the single-race categories of the 1977 OMB standards for comparability with other reporting areas.
[c]Age-adjusted death rates are per 100,000 U.S. standard population, based on the year 2000 standard.
[d]Life expectancy at birth stated in years.
[e]Infant mortality rates are deaths under 1 year of age per 1,000 live births in specified group.

SOURCE: Hsiang-Ching Kung et al., "Table A. Deaths, Age-Adjusted Death Rates, and Life Expectancy at Birth, by Race and Sex; and Infant Deaths and Mortality Rates, by Race: United States, Final 2004 and Preliminary 2005," in *Deaths: Preliminary Data for 2005*, Centers for Disease Control and Prevention, National Center for Health Statistics, September 2007, http://www.cdc.gov/nchs/data/hestat/preliminarydeaths05_tables.pdf#1 (accessed February 1, 2008)

males born in that same year are expected to live for 75.2 years. White infants born in 2005 are expected to live 78.3 years, whereas African-American infants are expected to live 73.2 years. The male-female life expectancy differences exist among these groups as well.

CAUSES OF INFANT MORTALITY

Birth defects are the leading cause of infant mortality in the United States. Birth defects are abnormalities of structure, function, or metabolism present at birth. In 2005 these congenital problems accounted for 5,562 (19.5%) out of 28,534 total causes of infant deaths. (See Table 5.4.) Birth defects are listed in Table 5.4 as congenital malformations, deformations, and chromosomal abnormalities.

Some of the more serious birth defects are anencephaly (absence of the majority of the brain) and spina bifida (incomplete development of the back and spine). Down syndrome, a condition in which babies are born with an extra copy of chromosome 21 in their cells, results in anatomical and developmental problems along with cognitive deficits. Down syndrome children may be born with birth defects that are fatal, including defects of the heart, lungs, and gastrointestinal tract. However, many Down syndrome children live well into adulthood.

According to the CDC, in "Birth Defects" (2008, http://www.cdc.gov/ncbddd/bd/default.htm), one out of

every thirty-three babies born in the United States each year have birth defects. The CDC notes that babies born with birth defects are more likely to have poor health and long-term disabilities than babies born without birth defects.

Disorders related to short gestation (premature birth) and low birth weight accounted for the second-leading cause of infant mortality in 2005—out of a total of 28,534 infant deaths, 4,709 babies died from these disorders. (See Table 5.4.) Among African-American infants, these disorders were the leading cause of infant death (1,881 out of 8,655 infant deaths from all causes). Other causes of infant deaths were sudden infant death syndrome, maternal complications of pregnancy, and complications of the placenta, cord, and membranes. These five leading causes of infant mortality accounted for more than half (53.5%) of the total infant deaths in all races in 2005.

BIRTH DEFECTS

The March of Dimes Birth Defects Foundation, a national volunteer organization that seeks to improve infant health by preventing birth defects and lowering infant mortality rates, reports in "Birth Defects" (April 2006, http://www.marchofdimes.com/pnhec/4439_1206 .asp) that about 120,000 babies are born annually in the United States with birth defects. Some birth defects have genetic causes—inherited abnormalities such as Tay-Sachs

TABLE 5.4

Ten leading causes of infant deaths and infant mortality rates, by race and Hispanic origin, 2005

[Data are based on a continuous file of records received from the states. Rates are per 100,000 live births.]

Rank[a]	Cause of death, race, and Hispanic origin	Number	Rate
	All races[b]		
—	All causes	28,534	689.2
1	Congenital malformations, deformations and chromosomal abnormalities	5,562	134.3
2	Disorders related to short gestation and low birth weight, not elsewhere classified	4,709	113.7
3	Sudden infant death syndrome	2,107	50.9
4	Newborn affected by maternal complications of pregnancy	1,786	43.1
5	Newborn affected by complications of placenta, cord and membranes	1,111	26.8
6	Accidents (unintentional injuries)	1,069	25.8
7	Respiratory distress of newborn	861	20.8
8	Bacterial sepsis of newborn	834	20.1
9	Neonatal hemorrhage	664	16.0
10	Necrotizing enterocolitis of newborn	549	13.3
—	All other causes (residual)	9,282	224.2
	Total white		
—	All causes	18,634	576.6
1	Congenital malformations, deformations and chromosomal abnormalities	4,194	129.8
2	Disorders related to short gestation and low birth weight, not elsewhere classified	2,628	81.3
3	Sudden infant death syndrome	1,404	43.4
4	Newborn affected by maternal complications of pregnancy	1,060	32.8
5	Newborn affected by complications of placenta, cord and membranes	761	23.5
6	Accidents (unintentional injuries)	721	22.3
7	Respiratory distress of newborn	539	16.7
8	Bacterial sepsis of newborn	525	16.2
9	Neonatal hemorrhage	463	14.3
10	Intrauterine hypoxia and birth asphyxia	384	11.9
—	All other causes (residual)	5,955	184.3
	Non-Hispanic white		
—	All causes	13,103	573.6
1	Congenital malformations, deformations and chromosomal abnormalities	2,855	125.0
2	Disorders related to short gestation and low birth weight, not elsewhere classified	1,790	78.4
3	Sudden infant death syndrome	1,152	50.4
4	Newborn affected by maternal complications of pregnancy	755	33.0
5	Accidents (unintentional injuries)	561	24.6
6	Newborn affected by complications of placenta, cord and membranes	545	23.9
7	Respiratory distress of newborn	387	16.9
8	Bacterial sepsis of newborn	357	15.6
9	Neonatal hemorrhage	332	14.5
10	Intrauterine hypoxia and birth asphyxia	288	12.6
—	All other causes (residual)	4,081	178.6
	Total black		
—	All causes	8,655	1,368.1
1	Disorders related to short gestation and low birth weight, not elsewhere classified	1,881	297.3
2	Congenital malformations, deformations and chromosomal abnormalities	1,080	170.7
3	Newborn affected by maternal complications of pregnancy	658	104.0
4	Sudden infant death syndrome	633	100.1
5	Newborn affected by complications of placenta, cord and membranes	321	50.7
6	Accidents (unintentional injuries)	312	49.3
7	Respiratory distress of newborn	293	46.3
8	Bacterial sepsis of newborn	270	42.7
9	Necrotizing enterocolitis of newborn	208	32.9
10	Neonatal hemorrhage	170	26.9
—	All other causes (residual)	2,829	447.2

disease (a fatal disease that generally affects children of east European Jewish ancestry) or chromosomal irregularities such as Down syndrome. Other birth defects result from environmental factors—infections during pregnancy, such as rubella (German measles), or drugs used by the pregnant woman. The specific causes of many birth defects are unknown, but scientists think that many result from a combination of genetic and environmental factors. Even though many birth defects are impossible to prevent, some can be avoided, such as those caused by maternal alcohol and drug consumption during pregnancy.

Two types of birth defects that have been the subject of considerable ethical debate are neural tube defects and permanent disabilities coupled with operable but life-threatening factors. An example of the latter is Down syndrome.

Neural Tube Defects

Neural tube defects (NTDs) are abnormalities of the brain and spinal cord resulting from the failure of the neural tube to develop properly during early pregnancy. The neural tube is the embryonic nerve tissue that develops into

TABLE 5.4

Ten leading causes of infant deaths and infant mortality rates, by race and Hispanic origin, 2005 [CONTINUED]

[Data are based on a continuous file of records received from the states. Rates are per 100,000 live births.]

Rank[a]	Cause of death, race, and Hispanic origin	Number	Rate
	Hispanic[c]		
—	All causes	5,784	588.5
1	Congenital malformations, deformations and chromosomal abnormalities	1,385	140.9
2	Disorders related to short gestation and low birth weight, not elsewhere classified	890	90.6
3	Newborn affected by maternal complications of pregnancy	322	32.8
4	Sudden infant death syndrome	257	26.1
5	Newborn affected by complications of placenta, cord and membranes	224	22.8
6	Bacterial sepsis of newborn	173	17.6
7	Respiratory distress of newborn	166	16.9
8	Accidents (unintentional injuries)	164	16.7
9	Neonatal hemorrhage	138	14.0
10	Necrotizing enterocolitis of newborn	110	11.2
—	All other causes (residual)	1,955	198.9

— Category not applicable.

[a]Rank based on number of deaths.

[b]Includes races other than white and black.

[c]Includes all persons of Hispanic origin of any race.

Notes: Figures are based on weighted data rounded to the nearest individual, so categories may not add to totals or subtotals. Race and Hispanic origin are reported separately on both the birth and death certificate. Rates for Hispanic origin should be interpreted withcaution because of inconsistencies between reporting Hispanic origin on birth and death certificates. Race categories are consistent with the 1977 Office of Management and Budget(OMB) standards. Multiple-race data were reported for deaths by 21 states and the District of Columbia and for births by 19 states. The multiple-race data for these states were bridged to the single-race categories of the 1977 OMB standards for comparability with other states. Data for persons of Hispanic origin are included in the data for each race group, according to the decedent's reported race. For certain causes of death such as unintentional injuries, homicides, suicides, and respiratory diseases, preliminary and final data differ because of the truncated nature of thepreliminary file. Data are subject to sampling or random variation.

SOURCE: Hsiang-Ching Kung et al., "Table 8. Infant Deaths and Infant Mortality Rates for the 10 Leading Causes of Infant Death, by Race and Hispanic Origin: United States, Preliminary 2005," in *Deaths: Preliminary Data for 2005*, Centers for Disease Control and Prevention, National Center for Health Statistics, September 2007, http://www.cdc.gov/nchs/data/hestat/preliminarydeaths05_tables.pdf#1 (accessed February 1, 2008)

the brain and the spinal cord. The CDC states in "Spina Bifida and Anencephaly before and after Folic Acid Mandate—United States, 1995–1996 and 1999–2000" (*Morbidity and Mortality Weekly Report*, vol. 53, no. 17, May 7, 2004) that between 1995 and 1996 four thousand pregnancies were affected with NTDs. This number dropped to three thousand between 1999 and 2000. The CDC suggests that this decline was due to an increase in folic acid consumption by pregnant women during these years.

The CDC notes that folic acid can prevent 50% to 70% of NTDs if women contemplating pregnancy consume sufficient folic acid before conception and then throughout the first trimester of pregnancy. Thus, in 1992 the U.S. Public Health Service recommended that all women capable of becoming pregnant consume four hundred micrograms of folic acid daily. In addition, the U.S. Food and Drug Administration mandated that as of January 1998 all enriched cereal grain products be fortified with folic acid.

The two most common NTDs are anencephaly and spina bifida.

ANENCEPHALY. Anencephalic infants die before birth (in utero or stillborn) or shortly thereafter. The incidence of anencephaly decreased significantly from 18.4 cases per 100,000 live births in 1991 to 9.4 cases per 100,000 live births in 2001. (See Figure 5.1 and Table 5.5.) The largest drop during this period was from 1991 to 1992.

Between 1993 and 2001 the general trend was downward. In 2002 the rates began to rise a bit, from 9.6 cases per 100,000 live births in 2002 to 11.1 cases per 100,000 live births in 2005. Nonetheless, the CDC explains in "Trends in Spina Bifida and Anencephalus in the United States" that this slight increase is statistically insignificant, meaning that the differences are unimportant and could have occurred by chance alone.

Issues of brain death and organ donation sometimes surround anencephalic infants. One case that gained national attention was that of Theresa Ann Campo in 1992. Before their daughter's birth, Theresa's parents discovered through prenatal testing that their baby would be born without a fully developed brain. They decided to carry the fetus to term and donate her organs for transplantation. When baby Theresa was born, her parents asked for her to be declared brain dead. However, Theresa's brain stem was still functioning, so the court ruled against the parents' request. Baby Theresa died ten days later and her organs were not usable for transplant because they had deteriorated as a result of oxygen deprivation.

Some physicians and ethicists agree that even if anencephalic babies have a brain stem, they should be considered brain dead. Lacking a functioning higher brain, these babies can feel nothing and have no consciousness. Others fear that declaring anencephalic babies dead could be the start of a "slippery slope" that

FIGURE 5.1

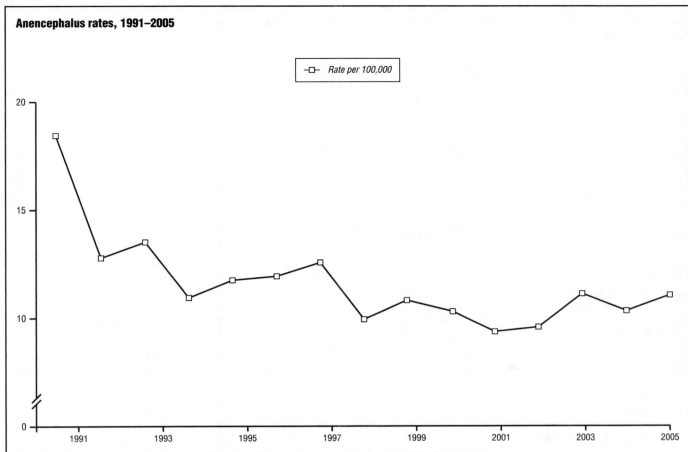

Anencephalus rates, 1991–2005

Rate per 100,000

Notes: Excludes data for Maryland, New Mexico, and New York, which did not require reporting for anencephalus for some years.

SOURCE: Adapted from T.J. Mathews, "Figure 2. Anencephalus Rates, 1991–2005," in *Trends in Spina Bifida and Anencephalus in the United States, 1991–2005*, Centers for Disease Control and Prevention, National Center for Health Statistics, December 2007, http://www.cdc.gov/nchs/products/pubs/pubd/hestats/spine_anen_fig_2.png (accessed February 1, 2008)

might eventually include babies with other birth defects in the same category. Other people are concerned that anencephalic babies may be kept alive for the purpose of harvesting their organs for transplant at a later date.

SPINA BIFIDA. Spina bifida, which literally means "divided spine," is caused by the failure of the vertebrae (backbone) to completely cover the spinal cord early in fetal development, leaving the spinal cord exposed. Depending on the amount of nerve tissue exposed, spina bifida defects range from minor developmental disabilities to paralysis.

Before the advent of antibiotics in the 1950s, most babies with severe spina bifida died soon after birth. With antibiotics and many medical advances, some of these newborns can be saved.

The treatment of newborns with spina bifida can pose serious ethical problems. Should an infant with a milder form of the disease be treated actively and another with severe defects be left untreated? In severe cases, should the newborn be sedated and not be given nutrition and

hydration until death occurs? Or should this seriously disabled infant be cared for while suffering from bladder and bowel malfunctions, infections, and paralysis? What if infants who have been left to die unexpectedly survive? Would they be more disabled than if they had been treated right away?

The development of fetal surgery to correct spina bifida before birth added another dimension to the debate. There are risks for both the mother and the fetus during and after fetal surgery, but techniques have improved since the first successful surgery of this type in 1997. In 2003 the National Institute of Child Health and Human Development began funding the Management of Myelomeningocele Study (http://www.spinabifidamoms.com/english/index.html) to compare the progress between babies who have prenatal (prebirth) surgery and those who have postnatal (after birth) surgery. The study was ongoing as of May 2008.

Figure 5.2 and Table 5.6 show that spina bifida rates increased from 22.8 cases per 100,000 live births in 1992

TABLE 5.5

Number of live births, anencephalus cases, and anencephalus rates, 1991–2005

Year	Anencephalus cases	Total live births	Rate
2005	432	3,887,109	11.11
2004	401	3,860,720	10.39
2003	441	3,715,577	11.14
2002	348	3,645,770	9.55
2001	343	3,640,555	9.42
2000	376	3,640,376	10.33
1999	382	3,533,565	10.81
1998	349	3,519,240	9.92
1997	434	3,469,667	12.51
1996	416	3,478,723	11.96
1995	408	3,484,539	11.71
1994	387	3,527,482	10.97
1993	481	3,562,723	13.50
1992	457	3,572,890	12.79
1991	655	3,564,453	18.38

Note: Excludes data for Maryland, New Mexico, and New York, which did not require reporting for anencephalus for some years.

SOURCE: Adapted from T.J. Mathews, "Table 2. Number of Live Births and Anencephalus Cases and Rates per 100,000 Live Births for the United States, 1991–2005," in *Trends in Spina Bifida and Anencephalus in the United States, 1991–2005*, Centers for Disease Control and Prevention, National Center for Health Statistics, December 2007, http://www.cdc.gov/nchs/data/hestat/spine_anen_tables.pdf#2 (accessed February 1, 2008)

TABLE 5.6

Number of live births, spina bifida cases, and spina bifida rates, 1991–2005

Year	Spina bifida cases	Total live births	Rate
2005	698	3,887,109	17.96
2004	755	3,860,720	19.56
2003	702	3,715,577	18.89
2002	734	3,645,770	20.13
2001	730	3,640,555	20.05
2000	759	3,640,376	20.85
1999	732	3,533,565	20.72
1998	790	3,519,240	22.45
1997	857	3,469,667	24.70
1996	917	3,478,723	26.36
1995	975	3,484,539	27.98
1994	900	3,527,482	25.51
1993	896	3,562,723	25.15
1992	816	3,572,890	22.84
1991	887	3,564,453	24.88

Note: Excludes data for Maryland, New Mexico, and New York, which did not require reporting for spina bifida for some years.

SOURCE: Adapted from T.J. Mathews, "Table 1. Number of Live Births and Spina Bifida Cases and Rates per 100,000 Live Births for the United States, 1991–2005," in *Trends in Spina Bifida and Anencephalus in the United States, 1991–2005*, Centers for Disease Control and Prevention, National Center for Health Statistics, December 2007, http://www.cdc.gov/nchs/data/hestat/spine_anen_tables.pdf#1 (accessed February 1, 2008)

FIGURE 5.2

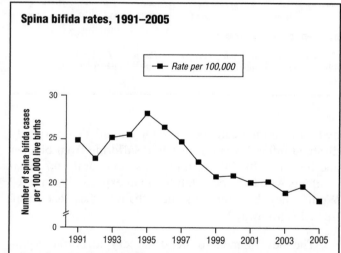

Spina bifida rates, 1991–2005

Notes: Excludes data for Maryland, New Mexico, and New York, which did not require reporting for spina bifida for some years.

SOURCE: Adapted from T.J. Mathews, "Figure 1. Spina Bifida Rates, 1991–2005," in *Trends in Spina Bifida and Anencephalus in the United States, 1991–2005*, Centers for Disease Control and Prevention, National Center for Health Statistics, December 2007, http://www.cdc.gov/nchs/products/pubs/pubd/hestats/spine_anen_fig_1.png (accessed February 1, 2008)

cally insignificant, the rate for 2005 (eighteen cases per one hundred thousand live births) was the lowest ever reported. As mentioned earlier, the decline in spina bifida rates is an indicator of successful efforts to prevent this defect by increasing folic acid consumption among women of childbearing age.

Down Syndrome

Down syndrome is a condition caused by chromosomal irregularities that occur during cell division of either the egg or the sperm before conception. Instead of the normal forty-six chromosomes, Down syndrome newborns have an extra copy of chromosome 21, giving them a total of forty-seven chromosomes. Along with having certain anatomical differences from non–Down syndrome children, Down children have varying degrees of mental retardation and approximately 40% have congenital heart diseases.

In "Risk Factors for Down Syndrome (Trisomy 21): Maternal Cigarette Smoking and Oral Contraceptive Use in a Population-Based Case-Control Study" (October 5, 2005, http://www.cdc.gov/ncbddd/bd/ds.htm), the CDC estimates the prevalence of Down syndrome as approximately one out of eight hundred live births. The occurrence of this genetic condition rises with increasing maternal age, with a marked increase seen in children of women over thirty-five years of age.

Robert Barnhart and Barbara Connolly report in "Aging and Down Syndrome: Implications for Physical

to 28 cases per 100,000 live births in 1995, but after 1995 the rates declined significantly to 20.7 cases per 100,000 live births in 1999. Even though the CDC explains in "Trends in Spina Bifida and Anencephalus in the United States" that the decline from 1999 to 2005 was statisti-

Therapy" (*Physical Therapy*, vol. 87, no. 10, October 2007) that the life expectancy of people with Down syndrome has increased over the decades, from an average of nine years of age in 1929 to fifty-five years in 2007. Except for the most severe heart defects, many other problems accompanying Down syndrome may be corrected by surgery and helped with exercise, strength training, and a healthy diet. Depending on the degree of mental retardation, many people with Down syndrome are able to hold jobs and live independently.

Birth Defects and National Laws

In April 1998 President Bill Clinton (1946–) signed into law the Birth Defects Prevention Act, which authorized a nationwide network of birth defects research and prevention programs and called for a nationwide information clearinghouse on birth defects.

The Children's Health Act of 2000 authorized expanded research and services for a variety of childhood health problems. In addition, it created the National Center on Birth Defects and Developmental Disabilities (NCBDDD) at the CDC. Developmental disabilities are conditions that impair day-to-day functioning, such as difficulties with communication, learning, behavior, and motor skills. They are chronic conditions that initially appear in people aged eighteen years and younger.

The Birth Defects and Developmental Disabilities Prevention Act of 2003 revised and extended the Birth Defects Prevention Act of 1998. It also reauthorized the NCBDDD from 2004 to 2008. The NCBDDD works with state health departments, academic institutions, and other public health partners to monitor birth defects and developmental disabilities, as well as to support research to identify their causes or risk factors. In addition, the center develops strategies and promotes programs to prevent birth defects and developmental disabilities.

The Economic Cost of Long-Term Care for Birth Defects and Developmental Disabilities

In "Increased Risk for Developmental Disabilities in Children Who Have Major Birth Defects: A Population-Based Study" (*Pediatrics*, vol. 108, no. 3, September 2001), Pierre Decouflé et al. examine selected developmental disabilities associated with major birth defects. The investigators combined data from two independent population-based surveillance systems to determine if major birth defects were associated with serious developmental disabilities.

When compared to children who had no major birth defects, the prevalence of developmental disabilities among children with major birth defects was extremely high. Decouflé et al. observe that conditions such as mental retardation, cerebral palsy (a disorder marked by muscular impairment usually caused by brain damage),

epilepsy (a disorder of the brain that results in seizures), autism (a brain disorder that affects communication, social interaction, and imaginative play), profound hearing loss, and legal blindness "prove costly in terms of special education services, medical and supportive care, demands on caregivers, and economic loss to society." They conclude, "Our data suggest that birth defects pose a greater burden on society than previously recognized."

In a similar study, Beverly Petterson et al. investigated the degree to which intellectual disabilities and birth defects occurred together and published their results in "Co-occurrence of Birth Defects and Intellectual Disability" (*Paediatric and Perinatal Epidemiology*, vol. 21, no. 1, January 2007). The researchers determine that birth defects were present in nearly one-third of children with intellectual disabilities. Looking at the statistics from a birth defects standpoint, children with chromosomal abnormalities, such as Down syndrome, were more likely to have intellectual disabilities than children with non-chromosomal birth defects, such as spina bifida. Petterson et al. show that 97% of Down syndrome children have intellectual disabilities, whereas 18.8% of children with spina bifida do. Children with birth defects of the nervous system, although not chromosomal in origin, also had a high incidence of intellectual disabilities (38.6%).

Most people with birth defects and/or developmental disabilities require long-term care or services. Table 5.7 shows the economic costs of mental retardation, cerebral palsy, hearing loss, and vision impairment in 2003. Of these four developmental disabilities, mental retardation had the highest rate of occurrence, at twelve affected children per one thousand children aged five to ten years, and the highest cost, at over $1 million per person.

LOW BIRTH WEIGHT AND PREMATURITY
Low Birth Weight

In "Births: Final Data for 2005" (*National Vital Statistics Reports*, vol. 56, no. 6, December 5, 2007), Joyce A. Martin et al. of the CDC indicate that infants who weigh less than twenty-five hundred grams (five pounds, eight ounces) at birth are considered to be of low birth weight. Those born weighing less than fifteen hundred grams (three pounds, four ounces) have very low birth weight. Babies born with low birth weights are more likely to die within their first year or have long-term disabilities than babies not born with low birth weight.

Low birth weight may result from various causes, including premature birth, poor maternal nutrition, teen pregnancy, drug and alcohol use, smoking, or sexually transmitted diseases. Martin et al. note that in 2005 teens had a higher percentage of low-birth-weight babies than women between the ages of twenty and thirty-nine years. (See Table 5.8.) According to the CDC, from 1990 through 2004 cigarette smokers consistently had a higher

TABLE 5.7

Estimated prevalence and lifetime economic costs for certain developmental disabilities, by cost category, 2003

Developmental disability	Rate[a]	Direct medical costs[b] (millions)	Direct nonmedical costs[c] (millions)	Indirect costs[d] (millions)	Total costs (millions)	Average costs per person
Mental retardation	12.0	$7,061	$5,249	$38,927	**$51,237**	$1,014,000
Cerebral palsy	3.0	1,175	1,054	9,241	**11,470**	921,000
Hearing loss	1.2	132	469	1,931	**2,102**	383,000
Vision impairment	1.1	159	652	2,636	**2,484**	601,000

Note: Lifetime economic costs are present value estimates, in 2003 dollars, of lifetime costs for persons born in 2000, based on a 3% discount rate.
[a]Per 1,000 children aged 5–10 years, on the basis of Metropolitan Atlanta Developmental Disabilities Surveillance Program data for 1991–1994.
[b]Includes physician visits, prescription medications, hospital inpatient stays, assistive devices, therapy and rehabilitation (for persons aged <18 years), and long-term care (for persons aged 18–76 years), adjusted for age-specific survival.
[c]Includes costs of home and vehicle modifications for persons aged < 76 years and costs of special education for persons aged 3–17 years.
[d]Includes productivity losses from increased morbidity (i.e., inability to work or limitation in the amount or type of work performed) and premature mortality for persons ≤ 35 years with mental retardation, aged ≤ 25 years with cerebral palsy, and aged ≤ 17 years with hearing loss and vision impairment.

SOURCE: A. Honeycutt et al., "Table. Estimated Prevalence and Lifetime Economic Costs for Mental Retardation, Cerebral Palsy, Hearing Loss,and Vision Impairment, by Cost Category—United States, 2003," in "Economic Costs Associated with Mental Retardation, Cerebral Palsy, Hearing Loss, and Vision Impairment—United States, 2003," *Morbidity and Mortality Weekly Report*, vol. 53, no. 3, January 30, 2004, http://www.cdc.gov/mmwr/PDF/wk/mm5303.pdf (accessed February 28, 2008), and "Errata: Vol. 53, No. 3," *Morbidity and Mortality Weekly Report*, vol. 55, no. 32, August 18, 2006, http://www.cdc.gov/mmwr/PDF/wk/mm5532.pdf (accessed February 28, 2008)

percentage of low-birth-weight babies than nonsmokers (12.5% versus 7.8% in 2004) and a higher percentage of very-low-birth-weight babies (1.9% versus 1.5% in 2004). (See Table 5.9.)

According to Martin et al., 338,565 (8.2%) of the 4.1 million live births in 2005 were low-birth-weight infants, matching highs reported in the late 1960s and early 1970s. (See Table 5.8.) African-American (14%) mothers were about twice as likely as non-Hispanic white (7.3%) and Hispanic (6.9%) mothers to have low-birth-weight babies.

Martin et al. indicate that 1.5% of the babies born in 2005 were very-low-birth-weight infants. (See Table 5.10.) The proportion of very-low-birth-weight babies has been increasing since the 1980s, although rates stabilized from the late 1990s through 2004. (See Table 5.9.) Martin et al. report that the birth weight distribution in general has shifted toward lower birth weights since the early 1990s. The researchers explain that the shift is likely influenced by a variety of factors, including "increases in the multiple birth rate, obstetric interventions such as induction of labor and cesarean delivery, older maternal age at childbearing and increased use of infertility therapies." In 2005 the highest percentage of low-birth-weight babies (21.1%) was with women between the ages of forty-five to fifty-four years. (See Table 5.8.)

Prematurity

The usual length of human pregnancy is forty weeks. Infants born before thirty-seven weeks of pregnancy are considered premature. A premature infant does not have fully formed organ systems. If the premature infant is born with a birth weight comparable to a full-term baby and has organ systems only slightly underdeveloped, the chances of survival are great. Conversely, premature infants of very low birth weight are susceptible to many risks and are less likely to survive. If they survive, they may suffer from mental retardation and other abnormalities of the nervous system.

A severe medical condition called respiratory distress syndrome (RDS) commonly affects premature infants born before thirty-five weeks of pregnancy. In RDS immature lungs do not function properly and may cause infant death within hours after birth. Intensive care includes the use of a mechanical ventilator to facilitate breathing. Premature infants also commonly have immature gastrointestinal systems, which preclude them from taking in nourishment properly. Unable to suck and swallow, they must be fed through a stomach tube.

WHO MAKES MEDICAL DECISIONS FOR INFANTS?

Before the 1980s in the United States, the courts were supportive of biological parents making decisions regarding the medical care of their newborns. Parents often made these decisions in consultation with pediatricians. Beginning in the 1970s medical advancements allowed for the survival of infants who would have not had a chance for survival before that time. Parents' and physicians' decisions became more challenging and complex.

The history of federal and state laws pertaining to the medical care of infants began in 1982 with the Baby Doe regulations. These regulations created a standard of medical care for infants: the possibility of future handicaps in a child should play no role in his or her medical treatment decisions.

The Baby Doe Rules

In April 1982 an infant with Down syndrome was born at Bloomington Hospital in Indiana. The infant also

TABLE 5.8

Number and percent of low birthweight and number of live births by age, race, and Hispanic origin of mother, 2005

Age and race and Hispanic origin of mother	Low birthweight[a] Number	Low birthweight[a] Percent	Birthweight Total	Less than 500 grams	500–999 grams	1,000–1,499 grams	1,500–1,999 grams	2,000–2,499 grams	2,500–2,999 grams	3,000–3,499 grams	3,500–3,999 grams	4,000–4,499 grams	4,500–4,999 grams	5,000 grams or more	Not stated
All races[b]															
All ages	338,565	8.2	4,138,349	6,599	23,864	31,325	66,453	210,324	748,042	1,596,944	1,114,887	289,098	42,119	4,715	3,979
Under 15 years	892	13.3	6,722	25	92	103	178	494	1,866	2,592	1,162	174	19	1	16
15–19 years	41,525	10.0	414,593	867	3,209	3,707	7,710	26,032	94,910	169,715	89,144	16,745	1,876	186	492
15 years	2,100	11.5	18,249	61	190	215	401	1,233	4,528	7,441	3,538	563	44	5	30
16 years	4,484	10.9	41,064	75	406	412	849	2,742	9,911	16,837	8,218	1,405	141	14	54
17 years	7,597	10.3	73,878	146	586	656	1,435	4,774	17,218	30,472	15,420	2,786	266	32	87
18 years	11,814	10.1	116,476	275	861	1,065	2,155	7,458	26,370	47,978	25,003	4,623	501	50	137
19 years	15,530	9.4	164,926	310	1,166	1,359	2,870	9,825	36,883	66,987	36,965	7,368	924	85	184
20–24 years	86,321	8.3	1,040,388	1,679	5,924	7,641	16,006	55,071	208,845	418,820	258,493	58,625	7,510	791	983
25–29 years	83,247	7.4	1,131,596	1,674	5,745	7,430	16,036	52,362	194,306	438,676	318,052	83,072	11,888	1,299	1,056
30–34 years	71,707	7.5	950,691	1,397	4,996	6,919	14,743	43,652	150,671	354,909	279,330	79,465	12,364	1,374	871
35–39 years	42,140	8.7	483,156	776	3,017	4,241	8,961	25,145	77,876	173,727	139,211	42,023	6,891	848	440
40–44 years	11,354	10.8	104,667	169	813	1,143	2,441	6,788	18,217	36,525	28,150	8,603	1,503	206	109
45–54 years	1,379	21.1	6,536	12	68	141	378	780	1,351	1,980	1,345	391	68	10	12
Non Hispanic white[c]															
All ages	166,101	7.3	2,279,768	2,497	10,015	14,967	33,687	104,935	364,726	857,136	672,270	187,269	27,541	2,840	1,885
Under 15 years	147	11.0	1,331	3	12	17	29	86	302	546	280	48	6	1	1
15–19 years	14,950	9.1	165,005	288	1,056	1,335	2,839	9,432	33,650	66,161	40,392	8,589	996	97	170
15 years	491	10.4	4,702	13	56	46	108	268	1,001	1,908	1,078	190	22	2	10
16 years	1,238	9.8	12,675	23	104	126	243	742	2,692	5,078	2,996	595	51	7	18
17 years	2,573	9.7	26,487	48	183	225	516	1,601	5,400	10,618	6,437	1,286	137	13	23
18 years	4,419	9.3	47,329	104	292	399	828	2,796	9,552	19,125	11,493	2,396	274	25	45
19 years	6,229	8.4	73,812	100	421	539	1,144	4,025	15,005	29,432	18,388	4,122	512	50	74
20–24 years	38,062	7.4	515,518	554	2,329	3,269	7,244	24,666	93,832	203,953	140,105	34,184	4,491	456	435
25–29 years	42,408	6.6	642,553	681	2,533	3,716	8,356	27,122	98,844	243,625	195,010	53,749	7,654	778	485
30–34 years	39,512	6.8	581,645	563	2,299	3,683	8,471	24,496	82,092	211,959	183,371	54,916	8,464	834	497
35–39 years	23,812	7.8	305,142	327	1,357	2,288	5,180	14,660	44,818	107,484	93,825	29,617	4,826	526	234
40–44 years	6,320	9.8	64,352	75	388	582	1,315	3,960	10,345	22,154	18,386	5,900	1,055	139	53
45–54 years	890	21.1	4,222	6	41	77	253	513	843	1,254	901	266	49	9	10
Non Hispanic black[c]															
All ages	81,674	14.0	583,759	2,477	8,014	8,573	15,764	46,846	144,803	221,819	108,698	22,149	3,203	405	1,008
Under 15 years	463	17.2	2,697	15	54	50	95	249	862	960	358	43	1	—	—
15–19 years	14,165	14.6	96,813	376	1,301	1,355	2,655	8,478	27,382	37,832	14,867	2,151	205	24	187
15 years	836	14.9	5,602	29	77	87	162	481	1,664	2,157	811	114	5	5	14
16 years	1,636	15.1	10,829	35	158	149	310	984	3,156	4,193	1,605	200	19	1	19
17 years	2,597	14.6	17,747	67	244	244	454	1,588	5,024	7,035	2,634	387	32	4	34
18 years	3,950	14.8	26,627	101	336	391	742	2,380	7,494	10,413	4,065	592	55	6	52
19 years	5,146	14.3	36,008	144	486	484	987	3,045	10,044	14,034	5,752	858	94	12	68
20–24 years	25,779	13.7	188,673	724	2,280	2,595	4,788	15,392	49,573	73,820	32,629	5,736	749	78	309
25–29 years	18,740	13.1	142,885	602	1,820	1,939	3,603	10,776	33,955	54,436	28,316	6,178	897	117	246
30–34 years	12,643	13.7	92,336	454	1,423	1,442	2,541	6,783	19,954	33,948	20,012	4,729	786	108	156
35–39 years	7,507	15.8	47,411	254	906	901	1,527	3,919	10,226	16,513	9,940	2,618	461	67	79
40–44 years	2,212	18.0	12,256	50	217	272	513	1,160	2,693	4,092	2,464	662	103	10	20
45–54 years	165	24.0	688	2	13	19	42	89	158	218	112	32	1	1	1

TABLE 5.8

Number and percent of low birthweight and number of live births by age, race, and Hispanic origin of mother, 2005 [CONTINUED]

Age and race and Hispanic origin of mother	Low birthweight[a] Number	Low birthweight[a] Percent	Total	Birthweight Less than 500 grams	500–999 grams	1,000–1,499 grams	1,500–1,999 grams	2,000–2,499 grams	2,500–2,999 grams	3,000–3,499 grams	3,500–3,999 grams	4,000–4,499 grams	4,500–4,999 grams	5,000 grams or more	Not stated
Hispanic[d]															
All ages	67,796	6.9	985,505	1,212	4,586	5,988	12,710	43,300	176,438	399,295	266,338	64,704	9,167	1,174	593
Under 15 years	252	10.2	2,466	6	22	34	48	142	642	1,000	483	75	11	—	—
15–19 years	10,980	8.0	136,906	177	752	908	1,950	7,193	30,356	59,319	30,279	5,246	570	50	106
15 years	714	9.9	7,241	17	53	73	118	453	1,714	3,072	1,499	223	14	1	4
16 years	1,453	9.1	15,928	17	136	125	275	900	3,705	6,895	3,257	540	63	5	10
17 years	2,154	8.0	26,877	29	136	168	401	1,420	6,133	11,744	5,741	988	80	12	25
18 years	3,045	8.0	38,090	60	210	249	515	2,011	8,373	16,618	8,443	1,425	140	14	32
19 years	3,614	7.4	48,770	54	217	293	641	2,409	10,431	20,990	11,339	2,070	273	18	35
20–24 years	18,731	6.5	287,896	319	1,095	1,494	3,377	12,446	54,868	121,320	74,552	16,127	1,910	220	168
25–29 years	16,305	6.1	266,590	291	1,133	1,365	3,060	10,456	44,209	107,357	76,211	19,248	2,770	330	160
30–34 years	12,624	6.8	186,398	267	922	1,262	2,386	7,787	29,198	71,610	54,816	15,260	2,460	333	97
35–39 years	6,967	8.1	85,739	121	521	719	1,464	4,142	13,733	31,697	24,717	7,194	1,185	199	47
40–44 years	1,799	9.7	18,597	29	131	188	388	1,063	3,250	6,678	5,070	1,497	249	42	12
45–54 years	138	15.1	913	2	10	18	37	71	182	314	210	57	12	—	—

—Quantity zero.

[a]Less than 2,500 grams (5 lb 8 oz).

[b]Includes races other than white and black and origin not stated.

[c]Race and Hispanic origin are reported separately on birth certificates. Persons of Hispanic origin may be of any race. Race categories are consistent with the 1977 Office of Management and Budget (OMB) standards. Nineteen states reported multiple-race data for 2005. Multiple-race data for these states were bridged to the single-race categories of the 1977 OMB standards for comparability with other states.

[d]Includes all persons of Hispanic origin of any race.

SOURCE: Joyce A. Martin et al., "Table 35. Number and Percentage Low Birthweight and Number of Live Births by Birthweight, by Age and Race and Hispanic Origin of Mother: United States, 2005," in "Births: Final Data for 2005," *National Vital Statistics Reports*, vol. 56, no. 6, December 5, 2007, http://www.cdc.gov/nchs/data/nvsr56/nvsr56_06.pdf (accessed February 2, 2008)

TABLE 5.9

Low-birthweight live births, by mother's race, Hispanic origin, and smoking status, selected years, 1970–2004

[Data are based on birth certificates]

Birthweight, race and Hispanic origin of mother, and smoking status of mother	1970	1975	1980	1985	1990	1995	1999	2000	2002	2003	2004
Low birthweight (less than 2,500 grams)					**Percent of live births**[a]						
All races	7.93	7.38	6.84	6.75	6.97	7.32	7.62	7.57	7.82	7.93	8.08
White	6.85	6.27	5.72	5.65	5.70	6.22	6.57	6.55	6.80	6.94	7.07
Black or African American	13.90	13.19	12.69	12.65	13.25	13.13	13.11	12.99	13.29	13.37	13.44
American Indian or Alaska Native	7.97	6.41	6.44	5.86	6.11	6.61	7.15	6.76	7.23	7.37	7.45
Asian or Pacific Islander[b]	—	—	6.68	6.16	6.45	6.90	7.45	7.31	7.78	7.78	7.89
Chinese	6.67	5.29	5.21	4.98	4.69	5.29	5.19	5.10	5.52	—	—
Japanese	9.03	7.47	6.60	6.21	6.16	7.26	7.95	7.14	7.57	—	—
Filipino	10.02	8.08	7.40	6.95	7.30	7.83	8.30	8.46	8.61	—	—
Hawaiian	—	—	7.23	6.49	7.24	6.84	7.69	6.76	8.14	—	—
Other Asian or Pacific Islander	—	—	6.83	6.19	6.65	7.05	7.76	7.67	8.16	—	—
Hispanic or Latino[c]	—	—	6.12	6.16	6.06	6.29	6.38	6.41	6.55	6.69	6.79
Mexican	—	—	5.62	5.77	5.55	5.81	5.94	6.01	6.16	6.28	6.44
Puerto Rican	—	—	8.95	8.69	8.99	9.41	9.30	9.30	9.68	10.01	9.82
Cuban	—	—	5.62	6.02	5.67	6.50	6.80	6.49	6.50	7.04	7.72
Central and South American	—	—	5.76	5.68	5.84	6.20	6.38	6.34	6.53	6.70	6.70
Other and unknown Hispanic or Latino	—	—	6.96	6.83	6.87	7.55	7.63	7.84	7.87	8.01	7.78
Not Hispanic or Latino[c]											
White	—	—	5.69	5.61	5.61	6.20	6.64	6.60	6.91	7.04	7.20
Black or African American	—	—	12.71	12.62	13.32	13.21	13.23	13.13	13.39	13.55	13.74
Cigarette smoker[d]	—	—	—	—	1 1.25	12.18	12.06	11.88	12.15	12.40	12.54
Nonsmoker[d]	—	—	—	—	6.14	6.79	7.21	7.19	7.48	7.66	7.79
Very low birthweight (less than 1,500 grams)											
All races	1.17	1.16	1.15	1.21	1.27	1.35	1.45	1.43	1.46	1.45	1.48
White	0.95	0.92	0.90	0.94	0.95	1.06	1.15	1.14	1.17	1.17	1.20
Black or African American	2.40	2.40	2.48	2.71	2.92	2.97	3.14	3.07	3.13	3.07	3.07
American Indian or Alaska Native	0.98	0.95	0.92	1.01	1.01	1.10	1.26	1.16	1.28	1.30	1.28
Asian or Pacific Islander[b]	—	—	0.92	0.85	0.87	0.91	1.08	1.05	1.12	1.09	1.14
Chinese	0.80	0.52	0.66	0.57	0.51	0.67	0.68	0.77	0.74	—	—
Japanese	1.48	0.89	0.94	0.84	0.73	0.87	0.86	0.75	0.97	—	—
Filipino	1.08	0.93	0.99	0.86	1.05	1.13	1.41	1.38	1.31	—	—
Hawaiian	—	—	1.05	1.03	0.97	0.94	1.41	1.39	1.55	—	—
Other Asian or Pacific Islander	—	—	0.96	0.91	0.92	0.91	1.09	1.04	1.17	—	—
Hispanic or Latino[c]	—	—	0.98	1.01	1.03	1.11	1.14	1.14	1.17	1.16	1.20
Mexican	—	—	0.92	0.97	0.92	1.01	1.04	1.03	1.06	1.06	1.13
Puerto Rican	—	—	1.29	1.30	1.62	1.79	1.86	1.93	1.96	2.01	1.96
Cuban	—	—	1.02	1.18	1.20	1.19	1.49	1.21	1.15	1.37	1.30
Central and South American	—	—	0.99	1.01	1.05	1.13	1.15	1.20	1.20	1.17	1.19
Other and unknown Hispanic or Latino	—	—	1.01	0.96	1.09	1.28	1.32	1.42	1.44	1.28	1.27
Not Hispanic or Latino[c]											
White	—	—	0.87	0.91	0.93	1.04	1.15	1.14	1.17	1.18	1.20
Black or African American	—	—	2.47	2.67	2.93	2.98	3.18	3.10	3.15	3.12	3.15
Cigarette smoker[d]	—	—	—	—	1.73	1.85	1.91	1.91	1.88	1.92	1.88
Nonsmoker[d]	—	—	—	—	1.18	1.31	1.43	1.40	1.45	1.44	1.47

— Data not available.

[a]Excludes live births with unknown birthweight. Percent based on live births with known birthweight.

[b]Starting with 2003 data, estimates are not shown for Asian or Pacific Islander subgroups during the transition from single race to multiple race reporting.

[c]Prior to 1993, data from states lacking an Hispanic-origin item on the birth certificate were excluded. Data for non-Hispanic white and non-Hispanic black women for years prior to 1989 are not nationally representative and are provided for comparison with Hispanic data.

[d]Percent based on live births with known smoking status of mother and known birthweight. Data from states that did not require the reporting of mother's tobacco use during pregnancy on the birth certificate are not included. Reporting area for tobacco use increased from 43 states and the District of Columbia (DC) in 1989 to 49 states and DC in 2000–2002. Data for 2003 and 2004 exclude states that implemented the 2003 revision of the U.S. Standard Certificate of Live Birth: Pennsylvania and Washington (in 2003), Florida, Idaho, Kentucky, New Hampshire, New York state (excluding New York City), Pennsylvania, South Carolina, Tennessee, and Washington (in 2004). Tobacco use data based on the 2003 revision are not comparable with data based on the 1989 revision of the U.S. Standard Certificate of Live Birth. California has never required reporting of tobacco use during pregnancy.

Notes: The race groups, white, black, American Indian or Alaska Native, and Asian or Pacific Islander, include persons of Hispanic and non-Hispanic origin. Persons of Hispanic origin may be of any race. Starting with 2003 data, some states reported multiple-race data. The multiple-race data for these states were bridged to the single-race categories of the 1977 Office of Management and Budget standards for comparability with other states. Interpretation of trend data should take into consideration expansion of reporting areas and immigration. Data for additional years are available.

SOURCE: "Table 13. Low-Birthweight Live Births, by Detailed Race, Hispanic Origin, and Smoking Status of Mother: United States, Selected Years 1970–2004," in *Health, United States, 2007. With Chartbook on Trends in the Health of Americans*, Centers for Disease Control and Prevention, National Center for Health Statistics, November 2007, http://www.cdc.gov/nchs/data/hus/hus07.pdf (accessed January 30, 2008)

had esophageal atresia, an obstruction in the esophagus that prevents the passage of food from the mouth to the stomach. Following their obstetrician's recommendation, the parents decided to forgo surgery to repair the baby's esophagus. The baby would be kept pain-free with medication and allowed to die.

TABLE 5.10

Percent of births with selected medical or health characteristics, by race, Hispanic origin, and birthplace of mother, 2005

| | | Origin of mother | | | | | | | | |
| | | Hispanic | | | | | | Non-Hispanic | | |
Characteristic	All origins[a]	Total	Mexican	Puerto Rican	Cuban	Central and South American	Other and unknown Hispanic	Total[b]	White	Black
All births Mother										
Diabetes during pregancy	3.8	3.8	3.8	4.7	3.9	3.6	3.7	3.9	3.7	3.5
Weight gain of less than 16 lbs[c]	13.0	15.8	17.0	13.6	9.2	13.6	14.9	12.3	10.8	18.9
CNM delivery[d]	7.4	8.3	8.0	10.2	4.2	9.5	8.4	7.1	7.1	6.9
Cesarean delivery	30.3	29.0	28.0	31.1	45.0	30.9	29.6	30.7	30.4	32.6
Infant										
Gestational age										
Very preterm[e]	2.0	1.8	1.7	2.5	2.1	1.7	2.0	2.1	1.6	4.2
Preterm[f]	12.7	12.1	11.8	14.3	13.2	12.0	13.6	12.9	11.7	18.4
Birthweight										
Very low birth weight[g]	1.5	1.2	1.1	1.9	1.5	1.2	1.4	1.6	1.2	3.3
Low birth weight[h]	8.2	6.9	6.5	9.9	7.6	6.8	8.3	8.6	7.3	14.0
4,000 grams or more[i]	8.1	7.6	8.0	6.1	8.0	7.3	6.1	8.3	9.6	4.4
Twin births[j]	32.2	22.0	20.3	31.1	32.2	23.4	26.1	35.3	36.1	36.4
Triplet or higher births[k]	161.8	77.2	64.1	124.7	180.5	100.5	92.4	187.7	217.8	105.5

[a]Includes origin not stated.
[b]Includes races other than white and black.
[c]Excludes data for California, which did not report weight gain on the birth certificate.
[d]Births delivered by certified nurse midwives (CNM).
[e]Born prior to 32 completed weeks of gestation.
[f]Born prior to 37 completed weeks of gestation.
[g]Birthweight of less than 1,500 grams (3 lb 4 oz).
[h]Birthweight of less than 2,500 grams (5 lb 8 oz).
[i]Equivalent to 8 lb 14 oz.
[j]Live births in twin deliveries per 1,000 births.
[k]Live births in triplets and other higher order multiple deliveries per 100,000 live births.
Notes: Race and Hispanic origin are reported separately on birth certificates. Race categories are consistent with the 1977 Office of Management and Budget (OMB) standards. Persons of Hispanic origin may be of any race. In this table Hispanic women are classified only by place of origin; non-Hispanic women are classified by race. Nineteen states reported multiple-race data for 2005. The multiple-race data for these states were bridged to the single-race categories of the 1977 OMB standards for comparability with other states.

SOURCE: Joyce A. Martin et al., "Table 24. Percentage of Births with Selected Medical or Health Characteristics, by Hispanic Origin of Mother and by Race for Mothers of Non-Hispanic Origin: United States, 2005," in "Births: Final Data for 2005," *National Vital Statistics Reports*, vol. 56, no. 6, December 5, 2007, http://www.cdc.gov/nchs/data/nvsr/nvsr56/nvsr56_06.pdf (accessed February 2, 2008)

Disagreeing with the parents' decision, the hospital took them to the county court. The judge ruled that the parents had the legal right to their decision, which was based on a valid medical recommendation. The Indiana Supreme Court refused to hear the appeal. Before the county prosecutor could present the case to the U.S. Supreme Court, the six-day-old baby died.

The public outcry following the death of "Baby Doe" (the infant's court-designated name) brought immediate reaction from the administration of President Ronald Reagan (1911–2004). The U.S. Department of Health and Human Services (HHS) informed all hospitals receiving federal funding that discrimination against handicapped newborns would violate section 504 of the Rehabilitation Act of 1973. This section (nondiscrimination under federal grants and programs) states: "No otherwise qualified individual with a disability in the United States . . . shall, solely by reason of her or his disability, be excluded from participation in, be denied the benefits of, or be subjected to discrimination under any program, service or activity receiving Federal financial assistance."

Furthermore, all hospitals receiving federal aid were required to post signs that read: "Discriminatory failure to feed and care for handicapped infants in this facility is prohibited by Federal law." The posters listed a toll-free hotline for anonymous reports of failure to comply.

Even though government investigators (called Baby Doe squads) were summoned to many hospitals to verify claims of mistreatment (the hotline had five hundred calls in its first three weeks alone), no violation of the law could be found. On the contrary, the investigators found doctors resuscitating babies who were beyond treatment because they feared legal actions. Finally, a group led by the American Academy of Pediatrics filed suit in March 1983 to have the Baby Doe rules overturned because they believed them to be harsh, unreasonably intrusive, and not necessarily in the best interests of the child. After various legal battles, in 1986 the U.S. Supreme Court ruled that the HHS did not have the authority to require such regulations and invalidated them.

Child Abuse Amendments of 1984 and Their Legacy

As the Baby Doe regulations were being fought in the courts, Congress enacted and President Reagan signed the Child Abuse Amendments of 1984 (CAA).

The CAA extended and improved the provisions of the Child Abuse Prevention and Treatment Act and the Child Abuse Prevention and Treatment and Adoption Reform Act of 1978. The CAA established that states' child protection services systems would respond to complaints of medical neglect of children, including instances of withholding medically indicated treatment from disabled infants with life-threatening conditions. It noted that parents were the ones to make medical decisions for their disabled infants based on the advice of their physicians. These laws have been amended many times over the years, most recently by the Keeping Children and Families Safe Act of 2003, without voiding the states' and parents' responsibilities to disabled infants.

Born-Alive Infants Protection Act of 2001

The Born-Alive Infants Protection Act of 2001 was signed by President George W. Bush (1946–) in August 2002. The purpose of the law is to ensure that all infants born alive, whether developmentally able to survive long term, are given legal protection as people under federal law. The law neither prohibits nor requires medical care for newly born infants who are below a certain weight or developmental age.

David Boyle et al. of the American Academy of Pediatrics Neonatal Resuscitation Program (NRP) Steering Committee state in "Born-Alive Infants Protection Act of 2001, Public Law No. 107-207" (*Pediatrics*, vol. 111, no. 3, 2003) that the law:

> Should not in any way affect the approach that physicians currently follow with respect to the extremely premature infant. ... At the time of delivery, and regardless of the circumstances of the delivery, the medical condition and prognosis of the newly born infant should be assessed. At that point decisions about withholding or discontinuing medical treatment that is considered futile may be considered by the medical care providers in conjunction with the parents acting in the best interest of their child. Those newly born infants who are deemed appropriate to not resuscitate or to have medical support withdrawn should be treated with dignity and respect, and provided with "comfort care" measures.

MEDICAL DECISION MAKING FOR OLDER CHILDREN

Under U.S. law, children under the age of eighteen cannot provide legally binding consent regarding their health care. Parents or guardians legally provide that consent, and, in most situations, physicians and the courts give parents wide latitude in the medical decisions they make for their children.

Religious Beliefs and Medical Treatment

When a parent's decisions are not in the best interests of the child, the state may intervene. In "Child Welfare versus Parental Autonomy: Medical Ethics, the Law, and Faith-Based Healing" (*Theoretical Medicine and Bioethics*, vol. 25, no. 4, July 2004), Kenneth S. Hickey and Laurie Lyckholm explain that forty-six states exempt parents from child abuse and neglect laws if they rely on spiritual healing rather than on having their minor children receive medical treatment. The states without these laws are Hawaii, Massachusetts, Nebraska, and North Carolina. Confusing this issue, however, is the agreement of the courts that religious exemption laws are no defense against criminal neglect. The legal distinction between practicing one's religion and criminal conduct in the treatment of one's children remains unclear.

Adolescents

The United Nations defines adolescents as people between the ages of ten and nineteen. Early adolescence is from ten to fourteen years, whereas late adolescence is from fifteen to nineteen years.

David R. Freyer of Michigan State University indicates in "Care of the Dying Adolescent: Special Considerations" (*Pediatrics*, vol. 113, no. 2, February 2004) that over three thousand U.S. adolescents die each year from chronic illnesses such as cancer, heart disease, acquired immunodeficiency syndrome, and metabolic disorders. Even though many laws concerning minors have changed, such as allowing minors to seek medical treatment for reproductive health and birth control services without parental consent, most states have no laws for end-of-life decisions by minors who are adolescents.

Freyer notes that even though U.S. laws do not consider adolescents under the age of eighteen to be competent to make their own health-care decisions, health-care practitioners often do. A broad consensus has developed among pediatric health-care practitioners, developmental psychologists, ethicists, and lawyers that by the age of fourteen years terminally ill adolescents (unless they demonstrate otherwise) "have the functional competence to make binding medical decisions for themselves, including decisions relating to the discontinuance of life-sustaining therapy and other end-of-life issues." According to Freyer, some experienced health-care practitioners think that terminally ill children as young as ten years "often meet the criteria for having functional competence and should have substantial, if not decisive, input on major end-of-life care decisions, including the discontinuation of active therapy."

CHAPTER 6
SUICIDE, EUTHANASIA, AND PHYSICIAN-ASSISTED SUICIDE

BACKGROUND

The eleventh edition of *Merriam-Webster's Collegiate Dictionary* defines the term *euthanasia*, which derives from the Greek for "easy death," as "the act or practice of killing or permitting the death of hopelessly sick or injured individuals ... in a relatively painless way for reasons of mercy." This present-day definition differs from that of the classical Greeks, who considered euthanasia simply "one mode of dying." To the Greeks, euthanasia was a rational act by people who deemed their life no longer useful. That these individuals sought the help of others to end their life was considered morally acceptable.

The movement to legalize euthanasia in England began in 1935 with the founding of the Voluntary Euthanasia Society by well-known figures such as George Bernard Shaw (1856–1950), Bertrand Russell (1872–1970), and H. G. Wells (1866–1946). In 1936 the House of Lords (one of the houses of the English Parliament) defeated a bill that would have permitted euthanasia in cases of terminal illness. Nonetheless, it was common knowledge that physicians practiced euthanasia. The same year, it was rumored that King George V (1865–1936), who had been seriously ill for several years, was "relieved of his sufferings" by his physician, with the approval of his wife, Queen Mary (1867–1953).

The Euthanasia Society of America was established in 1938. In 1967 this group prepared the first living will. Renamed the Society for the Right to Die in 1974, it merged in 1991 with another organization called Concern for Dying, and the two became Choice in Dying (CID). Even though the CID took no position on physician-assisted suicide, it "advocated for the rights of dying patients." It also educated the public about the importance of advance directives and end-of-life issues. In 2000 the CID dissolved, although many of its staff remained to found Partnership for Caring, which continued its programs. The organization's goal was to guarantee that Americans have access to quality end-of-life care. In early

2004 Partnership for Caring merged with Last Acts, a coalition of professional and consumer organizations that work to improve end-of-life care. The merged organization was named Last Acts Partnership, and its mission was to provide education, service, and counseling to people who needed accurate and reliable information about end-of-life care. Last Acts Partnership was also an advocate for policy reform in end-of-life issues. In 2005 Last Acts Partnership ceased its activities and all rights and copyrights to material produced by Partnership for Caring, Last Acts, and Last Acts Partnership were legally obtained by the National Hospice and Palliative Care Organization (NHPCO; http://www.nhpco.org/templates/1/homepage.cfm). As of May 2008, the NHPCO was still operating.

Euthanasia and the Nazis

The Nazis' version of euthanasia was a bizarre interpretation of an idea espoused by two German professors, Alfred Hoche (1865–1943) and Karl Binding (1841–1920), in their 1920 book *Die Freigabe der Vernichtung lebensunwerten Lebens* (*The Permission to Destroy Life Unworthy of Life*). While initially advocating that it was ethical for physicians to assist in the death of those who requested an end to their suffering, the authors later argued that it was also permissible to end the lives of the mentally retarded and the mentally ill.

Some contemporary opponents of euthanasia fear that a society that allows physician-assisted suicide may eventually follow the path of the Nazi dictator Adolf Hitler's (1889–1945) euthanasia program, which began with the killing of physically and mentally impaired individuals and culminated in the annihilation of entire religious and ethnic groups considered by the Nazis to be unworthy of life. However, those supporting euthanasia argue that unlike the murderous Nazi euthanasia program designed by Hitler and his followers, twenty-first-century proposals are based on voluntary requests by individuals in situations of physical suffering and would be sanctioned by laws passed by democratic governments.

Distinguishing between Euthanasia and Physician-Assisted Suicide

In the United States the debate over euthanasia distinguishes between active and passive euthanasia. Active euthanasia, also called voluntary active euthanasia by those who distinguish it from the kind of euthanasia practiced by the Nazis, involves the hastening of death through the administration of lethal drugs, as requested by the patient or another competent individual who represents the patient's wishes.

By contrast, passive euthanasia involves forgoing medical treatment, knowing that such a decision will result in death. This action is not considered illegal because the underlying illness, which is permitted to run its natural course, will ultimately cause death. It is generally accepted in the United States that terminally ill individuals have a right to refuse medical treatment, as do those who are sick but not terminally so. However, some people think that allowing patients to forgo medical treatment is a practice tantamount to enabling suicide and is therefore morally reprehensible.

The debate about euthanasia in the United States has been expanded to include the question of whether a competent, terminally ill patient has the right to physician-assisted suicide, in which a physician provides the means (such as lethal drugs) for the patient to self-administer and commit suicide. The distinction between the two actions, euthanasia and physician-assisted suicide, is at times difficult to define: for example, a patient in the latter stages of amyotrophic lateral sclerosis (also known as Lou Gehrig's disease) is physically unable to kill him- or herself; therefore, a physician who aids in such a person's suicide would technically be performing euthanasia.

SUICIDE

Different Cultures and Religions

Different religions and cultures have viewed suicide in different ways. Ancient Romans who dishonored themselves or their families were expected to commit suicide to maintain their dignity and, frequently, the family property. Early Christians were quick to embrace martyrdom as a guarantee of eternal salvation, but during the fourth century St. Augustine of Hippo (354–430) discouraged the practice. He and later theologians were concerned that many Christians who were suffering in this world would see suicide as a reasonable and legitimate way to depart to a better place in the hereafter. The view of the Christian theologian St. Thomas Aquinas (1225?–1274) is reflected in *Catechism of the Catholic Church* (2003) by the Catholic Church, which states that "suicide contradicts the natural inclination of the human being to preserve and perpetuate his life ... [and] is contrary to love for the living God."

Even though Islam and Judaism also condemn the taking of one's own life, Buddhist monks and nuns have been known to commit suicide by self-immolation (burning themselves alive) as a form of social protest. In a ritual called suttee, which is now outlawed, widows in India showed devotion to their deceased husbands by being cremated with them, sometimes throwing themselves on the funeral pyres, although it was not always voluntary. Widowers (men whose wives had died), however, did not follow this custom.

Quasi-religious reasons sometimes motivate mass suicide. In 1978 more than nine hundred members of a group known as the People's Temple killed themselves in Jonestown, Guyana. In 1997 a group called Heaven's Gate also committed mass suicide in California. The devastating terrorist attacks of September 11, 2001, were the result of a suicidal plot enacted by religious extremist groups. Suicide bombings in other parts of the world have also been attributed to extremist groups that have twisted or misinterpreted the fundamental tenets of Islam to further their political objectives.

The Japanese people have traditionally associated a certain idealism with suicide. During the twelfth century samurai warriors practiced voluntary *seppuku* (ritual self-disembowelment) to avoid dishonor at the hands of their enemies. Some samurai committed this form of slow suicide to atone for wrongdoing or to express devotion to a superior who had died. Even as recently as 1970, the famed author Yukio Mishima (1925–1970) publicly committed *seppuku*. During World War II (1939–1945) Japanese kamikaze pilots inflicted serious casualties with suicidal assaults in which they would purposely crash their planes into enemy ships, killing themselves along with enemy troops.

Suicide is still practiced in modern Japan. For example, in 1998 several government officials and businessmen hanged themselves in separate incidents involving scandals that attracted public attention. The reasons given for the suicides ranged from proclaiming innocence to assuming responsibility for wrongdoing. However, Japan's high level of suicides goes beyond such practices. According to the article "A Suicide Every 15 Minutes" (*New Zealand Herald*, February 25, 2008), in 2008 Japanese government statistics revealed that more than thirty thousand suicides had occurred in that country each year from 1998 to 2006. Reasons proposed for the high number of Japanese suicides include bullying at school, online suicide pacts, unemployment, and old age, with the root cause being depression. Eric Prideaux reports in "World's Suicide Capital—Tough Image to Shake" (*Japan Times*, November 20, 2007) that among the Group of Eight countries (Canada, France, Germany, Italy, Japan, Russia, the United Kingdom, and the United States) Japan ranks first in the number of female suicides annually and second in male suicides annually after Russia. Both Japan and the United States have about the same number of suicides each year, but Japan has half the population.

TABLE 6.1

Death rates for suicide, by sex, race, Hispanic origin, and age, selected years, 1950–2004

[Data are based on death certificates]

Sex, race, Hispanic origin, and age	1950[a]	1960[a]	1970	1980	1990	2000	2003	2004
All persons				Deaths per 100,000 resident population				
All ages, age-adjusted[b]	13.2	12.5	13.1	12.2	12.5	10.4	10.8	10.9
All ages, crude	11.4	10.6	11.6	11.9	12.4	10.4	10.8	11.0
Under 1 year	...	...	...	...	...	...	*	*
1–4 years	...	...	...	...	...	...	*	*
5–14 years	0.2	0.3	0.3	0.4	0.8	0.7	0.6	0.7
15–24 years	4.5	5.2	8.8	12.3	13.2	10.2	9.7	10.3
15–19 years	2.7	3.6	5.9	8.5	11.1	8.0	7.3	8.2
20–24 years	6.2	7.1	12.2	16.1	15.1	12.5	12.1	12.5
25–44 years	11.6	12.2	15.4	15.6	15.2	13.4	13.8	13.9
25–34 years	9.1	10.0	14.1	16.0	15.2	12.0	12.7	12.7
35–44 years	14.3	14.2	16.9	15.4	15.3	14.5	14.9	15.0
45–64 years	23.5	22.0	20.6	15.9	15.3	13.5	15.0	15.4
45–54 years	20.9	20.7	20.0	15.9	14.8	14.4	15.9	16.6
55–64 years	26.8	23.7	21.4	15.9	16.0	12.1	13.8	13.8
65 years and over	30.0	24.5	20.8	17.6	20.5	15.2	14.6	14.3
65–74 years	29.6	23.0	20.8	16.9	17.9	12.5	12.7	12.3
75–84 years	31.1	27.9	21.2	19.1	24.9	17.6	16.4	16.3
85 years and over	28.8	26.0	19.0	19.2	22.2	19.6	16.9	16.4
Male								
All ages, age-adjusted[b]	21.2	20.0	19.8	19.9	21.5	17.7	18.0	18.0
All ages, crude	17.8	16.5	16.8	18.6	20.4	17.1	17.6	17.7
Under 1 year	...	...	...	...	...	...	*	*
1–4 years	...	...	...	...	...	...	*	*
5–14 years	0.3	0.4	0.5	0.6	1.1	1.2	0.9	0.9
15–24 years	6.5	8.2	13.5	20.2	22.0	17.1	16.0	16.8
15–19 years	3.5	5.6	8.8	13.8	18.1	13.0	11.6	12.6
20–24 years	9.3	11.5	19.3	26.8	25.7	21.4	20.2	20.8
25–44 years	17.2	17.9	20.9	24.0	24.4	21.3	21.9	21.7
25–34 years	13.4	14.7	19.8	25.0	24.8	19.6	20.6	20.4
35–44 years	21.3	21.0	22.1	22.5	23.9	22.8	23.2	23.0
45–64 years	37.1	34.4	30.0	23.7	24.3	21.3	23.5	23.7
45–54 years	32.0	31.6	27.9	22.9	23.2	22.4	24.4	24.8
55–64 years	43.6	38.1	32.7	24.5	25.7	19.4	22.3	22.1
65 years and over	52.8	44.0	38.4	35.0	41.6	31.1	29.8	29.0
65–74 years	50.5	39.6	36.0	30.4	32.2	22.7	23.4	22.6
75–84 years	58.3	52.5	42.8	42.3	56.1	38.6	35.1	34.8
85 years and over	58.3	57.4	42.4	50.6	65.9	57.5	47.8	45.0
Female								
All ages, age-adjusted[b]	5.6	5.6	7.4	5.7	4.8	4.0	4.2	4.5
All ages, crude	5.1	4.9	6.6	5.5	4.8	4.0	4.3	4.6
Under 1 year	...	...	...	...	...	...	*	*
1–4 years	...	...	...	...	...	...	*	*
5–14 years	0.1	0.1	0.2	0.2	0.4	0.3	0.3	0.5
15–24 years	2.6	2.2	4.2	4.3	3.9	3.0	3.0	3.6
15–19 years	1.8	1.6	2.9	3.0	3.7	2.7	2.7	3.5
20–24 years	3.3	2.9	5.7	5.5	4.1	3.2	3.4	3.6
25–44 years	6.2	6.6	10.2	7.7	6.2	5.4	5.7	6.0
25–34 years	4.9	5.5	8.6	7.1	5.6	4.3	4.6	4.7
35–44 years	7.5	7.7	11.9	8.5	6.8	6.4	6.6	7.1
45–64 years	9.9	10.2	12.0	8.9	7.1	6.2	7.0	7.6
45–54 years	9.9	10.2	12.6	9.4	6.9	6.7	7.7	8.6
55–64 years	9.9	10.2	11.4	8.4	7.3	5.4	5.9	6.1
65 years and over	9.4	8.4	8.1	6.1	6.4	4.0	3.8	3.8
65–74 years	10.1	8.4	9.0	6.5	6.7	4.0	3.8	3.8
75–84 years	8.1	8.9	7.0	5.5	6.3	4.0	4.0	3.9
85 years and over	8.2	6.0	5.9	5.5	5.4	4.2	3.3	3.6

Suicide in the United States

Except for certain desperate medical situations, suicide in the United States is generally considered an unacceptable act, the result of irrationality or severe depression. It is often referred to as a permanent solution to a short-term problem.

In spite of this generally held belief, suicide was the eleventh-leading cause of death in the United States in 2005. (See Table 4.1 in Chapter 4.) There were nearly 1.9 times as many suicides as homicides that year. Nevertheless, since 1950 the national suicide rate has dropped from 13.2 suicides per 100,000 people to 10.9 per 100,000 in 2004. (See Table 6.1.) However, the 2004 rate is up from a low of 10.4 suicides per 100,000 in 2000.

GENDER AND RACIAL DIFFERENCES. In 2004 the suicide rate for men (18 people per 100,000) was four times that for women (4.5 people per 100,000). (See Table 6.1.) Over the decades, the male suicide rate has ranged from

TABLE 6.1

Death rates for suicide, by sex, race, Hispanic origin, and age, selected years, 1950–2004 [CONTINUED]

[Data are based on death certificates]

Sex, race, Hispanic origin, and age	1950[a]	1960[a]	1970	1980	1990	2000	2003	2004
				Deaths per 100,000 resident population				
White male[c]								
All ages, age-adjusted[b]	22.3	21.1	20.8	20.9	22.8	19.1	19.6	19.6
All ages, crude	19.0	17.6	18.0	19.9	22.0	18.8	19.5	19.6
15–24 years	6.6	8.6	13.9	21.4	23.2	17.9	16.9	17.9
25–44 years	17.9	18.5	21.5	24.6	25.4	22.9	23.9	23.8
45–64 years	39.3	36.5	31.9	25.0	26.0	23.2	26.1	26.1
65 years and over	55.8	46.7	41.1	37.2	44.2	33.3	32.1	31.2
65–74 years	53.2	42.0	38.7	32.5	34.2	24.3	25.2	24.2
75–84 years	61.9	55.7	45.5	45.5	60.2	41.1	37.5	37.1
85 years and over	61.9	61.3	45.8	52.8	70.3	61.6	51.4	48.4
Black or African American male[c]								
All ages, age-adjusted[b]	7.5	8.4	10.0	11.4	12.8	10.0	9.2	9.6
All ages, crude	6.3	6.4	8.0	10.3	12.0	9.4	8.8	9.0
15–24 years	4.9	4.1	10.5	12.3	15.1	14.2	12.1	12.2
25–44 years	9.8	12.6	16.1	19.2	19.6	14.3	14.3	13.7
45–64 years	12.7	13.0	12.4	11.8	13.1	9.9	9.0	10.1
65 years and over	9.0	9.9	8.7	11.4	14.9	11.5	9.2	11.3
65–74 years	10.0	11.3	8.7	11.1	14.7	11.1	8.3	9.8
75–84 years[d]	*	*	*	10.5	14.4	12.1	11.3	15.0
85 years and over	—	*	*	*	*	*	*	*
American Indian or Alaska Native male[c]								
All ages, age-adjusted[b]	—	—	—	19.3	20.1	16.0	16.6	18.7
All ages, crude	—	—	—	20.9	20.9	15.9	17.1	19.5
15–24 years	—	—	—	45.3	49.1	26.2	27.2	30.7
25–44 years	—	—	—	31.2	27.8	24.5	30.1	30.8
45–64 years	—	—	—	*	*	15.4	9.5	16.0
65 years and over	—	—	—	*	*	*	*	*
Asian or Pacific Islander male[c]								
All ages, age-adjusted[b]	—	—	—	10.7	9.6	8.6	8.5	8.4
All ages, crude	—	—	—	8.8	8.7	7.9	8.0	7.9
15–24 years	—	—	—	10.8	13.5	9.1	9.0	9.3
25–44 years	—	—	—	11.0	10.6	9.9	9.2	8.4
45–64 years	—	—	—	13.0	9.7	9.7	10.0	11.1
65 years and over	—	—	—	18.6	16.8	15.4	17.5	15.1
Hispanic or Latino male[c,e]								
All ages, age-adjusted[b]	—	—	—	—	13.7	10.3	9.7	9.8
All ages, crude	—	—	—	—	11.4	8.4	8.3	8.6
15–24 years	—	—	—	—	14.7	10.9	11.2	12.8
25–44 years	—	—	—	—	16.2	11.2	10.9	11.0
45–64 years	—	—	—	—	16.1	12.0	12.0	11.8
65 years and over	—	—	—	—	23.4	19.5	15.6	15.9
White, not Hispanic or Latino male[e]								
All ages, age-adjusted[b]	—	—	—	—	23.5	20.2	21.0	21.0
All ages, crude	—	—	—	—	23.1	20.4	21.6	21.6
15–24 years	—	—	—	—	24.4	19.5	18.2	19.0
25–44 years	—	—	—	—	26.4	25.1	26.8	26.8
45–64 years	—	—	—	—	26.8	24.0	27.4	27.4
65 years and over	—	—	—	—	45.4	33.9	33.1	32.1
White female[c]								
All ages, age-adjusted[b]	6.0	5.9	7.9	6.1	5.2	4.3	4.6	5.0
All ages, crude	5.5	5.3	7.1	5.9	5.3	4.4	4.7	5.1
15–24 years	2.7	2.3	4.2	4.6	4.2	3.1	3.1	3.8
25–44 years	6.6	7.0	11.0	8.1	6.6	6.0	6.4	6.6
45–64 years	10.6	10.9	13.0	9.6	7.7	6.9	7.8	8.5
65 years and over	9.9	8.8	8.5	6.4	6.8	4.3	4.0	4.0

3.5 to 4.5 times as high as the female suicide rate, except for 1970. In that year the female suicide rate was up, resulting in the male suicide rate being only 2.7 times that of the female suicide rate.

The racial group with the lowest suicide rate in 2004 was African-American females (1.8 per 100,000), followed closely by Hispanic females (2 per 100,000). (See Table 6.1.) In addition, adults aged seventy-five to eighty-four years had the lowest suicide rate of all age groups.

CIRCUMSTANCES OF SUICIDE. The National Vital Statistics System, which is a part of the Centers for Disease Control and Prevention (CDC), collects data from the fifty states, two cities (New York City and Washington, D.C.), and five territories (Puerto Rico, the Virgin Islands, Guam, American Samoa, and the Common-

TABLE 6.1

Death rates for suicide, by sex, race, Hispanic origin, and age, selected years, 1950–2004 [CONTINUED]

[Data are based on death certificates]

Sex, race, Hispanic origin, and age	1950[a]	1960[a]	1970	1980	1990	2000	2003	2004
Black or African American female[c]				Deaths per 100,000 resident population				
All ages, age-adjusted[b]	1.8	2.0	2.9	2.4	2.4	1.8	1.9	1.8
All ages, crude	1.5	1.6	2.6	2.2	2.3	1.7	1.8	1.8
15–24 years	1.8	*	3.8	2.3	2.3	2.2	2.0	2.2
25–44 years	2.3	3.0	4.8	4.3	3.8	2.6	2.8	2.9
45–64 years	2.7	3.1	2.9	2.5	2.9	2.1	2.4	2.2
65 years and over	*	*	2.6	*	1.9	1.3	1.4	*
American Indian or Alaska Native female[c]								
All ages, age-adjusted[b]	—	—	—	4.7	3.6	3.8	3.5	5.9
All ages, crude	—	—	—	4.7	3.7	4.0	3.7	6.2
15–24 years	—	—	—	*	*	*	8.3	10.5
25–44 years	—	—	—	10.7	*	7.2	4.6	9.8
45–64 years	—	—	—	*	*	*	*	*
65 years and over	—	—	—	*	*	*	*	*
Asian or Pacific Islander female[c]								
All ages, age-adjusted[b]	—	—	—	5.5	4.1	2.8	3.1	3.5
All ages, crude	—	—	—	4.7	3.4	2.7	3.1	3.4
15–24 years	—	—	—	*	3.9	2.7	3.4	2.8
25–44 years	—	—	—	5.4	3.8	3.3	3.4	4.1
45–64 years	—	—	—	7.9	5.0	3.2	4.3	4.5
65 years and over	—	—	—	*	8.5	5.2	4.6	6.4
Hispanic or Latino female[c,e]								
All ages, age-adjusted[b]	—	—	—	—	2.3	1.7	1.7	2.0
All ages, crude	—	—	—	—	2.2	1.5	1.5	1.8
15–24 years	—	—	—	—	3.1	2.0	2.2	2.5
25–44 years	—	—	—	—	3.1	2.1	2.0	2.3
45–64 years	—	—	—	—	2.5	2.5	2.4	3.1
65 years and over	—	—	—	—	*	*	*	1.8
White, not Hispanic or Latino female[e]								
All ages, age-adjusted[b]	—	—	—	—	5.4	4.7	5.0	5.4
All ages, crude	—	—	—	—	5.6	4.9	5.3	5.7
15–24 years	—	—	—	—	4.3	3.3	3.3	4.0
25–44 years	—	—	—	—	7.0	6.7	7.2	7.5
45–64 years	—	—	—	—	8.0	7.3	8.3	9.1
65 years and over	—	—	—	—	7.0	4.4	4.2	4.1

...Category not applicable.

*Rates based on fewer than 20 deaths are considered unreliable and are not shown.

—Data not available.

[a]Includes deaths of persons who were not residents of the 50 states and the District of Columbia.

[b]Age-adjusted rates are calculated using the year 2000 standard population. Prior to 2003, age-adjusted rates were calculated using standard million proportions based on rounded population numbers. Starting with 2003 data, unrounded population numbers are used to calculate age-adjusted rates.

[c]The race groups, white, black, Asian or Pacific Islander, and American Indian or Alaska Native, include persons of Hispanic and non-Hispanic origin. Persons of Hispanic origin may be of any race. Death rates for the American Indian or Alaska Native and Asian or Pacific Islander populations are known to be underestimated.

[d]In 1950, rate is for the age group 75 years and over.

[e]Prior to 1997, excludes data from states lacking an Hispanic-origin item on the death certificate.

Notes: Starting with Health, United States, 2003, rates for 1991–1999 were revised using intercensal population estimates based on the 2000 census. Rates for 2000 were revised based on 2000 census counts. Rates for 2001 and later years were computed using 2000-based postcensal estimates. Figures for 2001 include September 11-related deaths for which death certificates were filed as of October 24, 2002. Age groups were selected to minimize the presentation of unstable age-specific death rates based on small numbers of deaths and for consistency among comparison groups. In 2003, seven states reported multiple-race data. In 2004, 15 states reported multiple-race data. The multiple-race data for these states were bridged to the single-race categories of the 1977 Office of Management and Budget standards for comparability with other states. Data for additional years are available.

SOURCE: "Table 46. Death Rates for Suicide, by Sex, Race, Hispanic Origin, and Age: United States, Selected Years 1950–2004," in *Health, United States, 2007. With Chartbook on Trends in the Health of Americans*, Centers for Disease Control and Prevention, National Center for Health Statistics, November 2007, http://www.cdc.gov/nchs/data/hus/hus07.pdf (accessed January 30, 2008)

wealth of the Northern Mariana Islands). Each is responsible for registering vital events: births, deaths, marriages, divorces, and fetal deaths. Suicide data are compiled as part of the death data.

To add more specificity to violent death data, the CDC instituted the National Violent Death Reporting System (NVDRS) in 2002. In "National Violent Death Reporting System State Profiles" (August 9, 2007, http://www.cdc.gov/ncipc/profiles/nvdrs/state_profiles.htm),

the CDC states that the NVDRS is a state-based system that collects information on the numbers and kinds of violent deaths along with details regarding those deaths. Six states joined the NVDRS initially and by 2004 seven states were members. The CDC received funding in 2006 to expand the system to seventeen states. Eventually, the system will include the fifty states, all U.S. territories, and the District of Columbia.

Figure 6.1 shows the percentage of suicide cases by selected circumstances as reported by the NVDRS in

FIGURE 6.1

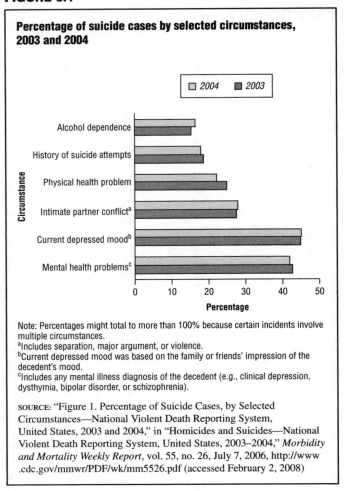

Percentage of suicide cases by selected circumstances, 2003 and 2004

Note: Percentages might total to more than 100% because certain incidents involve multiple circumstances.

[a]Includes separation, major argument, or violence.

[b]Current depressed mood was based on the family or friends' impression of the decedent's mood.

[c]Includes any mental illness diagnosis of the decedent (e.g., clinical depression, dysthymia, bipolar disorder, or schizophrenia).

SOURCE: "Figure 1. Percentage of Suicide Cases, by Selected Circumstances—National Violent Death Reporting System, United States, 2003 and 2004," in "Homicides and Suicides—National Violent Death Reporting System, United States, 2003–2004," *Morbidity and Mortality Weekly Report*, vol. 55, no. 26, July 7, 2006, http://www .cdc.gov/mmwr/PDF/wk/mm5526.pdf (accessed February 2, 2008)

2003 and 2004. These data are collected from a variety of sources, including death certificates, police reports, medical examiner and coroner reports, and crime laboratories. Because people may have more than one reason for committing suicide, the figures for each year do not total 100%. The two most common reasons found for suicide in 2003 and 2004 were depression and other mental health problems.

RURAL VERSUS URBAN SUICIDE RATES. Gopal K. Singh and Mohammad Siahpush compare in "Increasing Rural-Urban Gradients in U.S. Suicide Mortality, 1970–1997" (*American Journal of Public Health*, vol. 92, no. 7, July 2002) the suicide rates in rural and urban populations in the United States. The researchers report that the rate of suicide in rural populations of males increased between 1970 and 1997, whereas the rate of suicide in urban populations of males decreased over the same period. Even though the rates are lower for females and the changes are not as dramatic, a decrease was also noted in the suicide rate for urban females, whereas the suicide rate among rural females remained relatively stable.

In explaining these differences, Singh and Siahpush suggest that both rural and urban areas have experienced

profound social and demographic changes during the past three decades. However, they contend that change has affected life in rural areas more than in urban areas. They note that high levels of social isolation, as often occurs in rural areas, are correlated with high suicide rates.

In "A Review of the Literature on Rural Suicide" (*Crisis*, vol. 27, no. 4, 2006), Jameson K. Hirsch agrees with Singh and Siahpush's observations and suggests that high rates of suicide in rural areas are not only a U.S. phenomenon but also a global phenomenon. Hirsch concludes that "a better understanding of the relationships between rural life and culture, geographic and interpersonal isolation, economic and sociopolitical distress, and suicide may inform improved treatments for rural individuals."

Suicide among Young People

Suicide rates among young people aged fifteen to twenty-four years nearly tripled between 1950 and 1990, from 4.5 deaths per 100,000 to 13.2 deaths per 100,000. (See Table 6.1.) Rates among young adults aged twenty-five to thirty-four years increased as well, but not as dramatically; they increased 1.7 times from 9.1 deaths per 100,000 to 15.2 deaths per 100,000. However, the young adult rates were higher than the suicide rates among young people. Suicide rates dropped from 1990 to 2000 and then remained relatively stable through 2004. In 2005 suicide was the third-leading cause of death among people aged fifteen to twenty-four and the second-leading cause of death among people aged twenty-five to thirty-four. (See Table 4.2 in Chapter 4.)

Differences exist among racial groups in suicide rates. For example, the overall suicide rate among African-American males is lower than that of white males. In the fifteen- to twenty-four-year-old age group, suicide rates for white males ranged from 1.3 to 2.1 times as high as those for African-American males from 1950 through 2004. (See Table 6.1.) In 2004 the suicide rate for white males aged fifteen to twenty-four years was 1.5 times as high as that of African-American males of the same age group (17.9 deaths per 100,000 versus 12.2 deaths per 100,000). The suicide rates for both groups of young men rose from 1950 to 1990 and decreased by 2000. The rate for white males of this age group remained relatively stable through 2004, but decreased further for African-American males in 2003 and 2004.

In 1990 the highest suicide death rate among youths aged fifteen to twenty-four was 49.1 suicides per 100,000 people among Native American or Alaskan Native males. (See Table 6.1.) By 2000 this rate fell to 26.2 per 100,000 but rose to 27.2 in 2003 and to 30.7 in 2004.

ATTEMPTED SUICIDE AMONG YOUNG PEOPLE. Males of all races and ages are more likely to die from suicide attempts than are females of the same race and age. (See Table 6.1.) However, among high school students, females

TABLE 6.2

Suicidal ideation and suicide attempts and injuries among students in grades 9–12, by sex, grade level, race, and Hispanic origin, selected years, 1991–2005

[Data are based on a national sample of high school students, grades 9–12]

Sex, grade level, race, and Hispanic origin	1991	1993	1995	1997	1999	2001	2003	2005
				Percent of students who seriously considered suicide[a]				
Total	29.0	24.1	24.1	20.5	19.3	19.0	16.9	16.9
Male								
Total	20.8	18.8	18.3	15.1	13.7	14.2	12.8	12.0
9th grade	17.6	17.7	18.2	16.1	11.9	14.7	11.9	12.2
10th grade	19.5	18.0	16.7	14.5	13.7	13.8	13.2	11.9
11th grade	25.3	20.6	21.7	16.6	13.7	14.1	12.9	11.9
12th grade	20.7	18.3	16.3	13.5	15.6	13.7	13.2	11.6
Not Hispanic or Latino								
White	21.7	19.1	19.1	14.4	12.5	14.9	12.0	12.4
Black or African American	13.3	15.4	16.7	10.6	11.7	9.2	10.3	7.0
Hispanic or Latino	18.0	17.9	15.7	17.1	13.6	12.2	12.9	11.9
Female								
Total	37.2	29.6	30.4	27.1	24.9	23.6	21.3	21.8
9th grade	40.3	30.9	34.4	28.9	24.4	26.2	22.2	23.9
10th grade	39.7	31.6	32.8	30.0	30.1	24.1	23.8	23.0
11th grade	38.4	28.9	31.1	26.2	23.0	23.6	20.0	21.6
12th grade	30.7	27.3	23.9	23.6	21.2	18.9	18.0	18.0
Not Hispanic or Latino								
White	38.6	29.7	31.6	26.1	23.2	24.2	21.2	21.5
Black or African American	29.4	24.5	22.2	22.0	18.8	17.2	14.7	17.1
Hispanic or Latino	34.6	34.1	34.1	30.3	26.1	26.5	23.4	24.2
				Percent of students who attempted suicide[a]				
Total	7.3	8.6	8.7	7.7	8.3	8.8	8.5	8.4
Male								
Total	3.9	5.0	5.6	4.5	5.7	6.2	5.4	6.0
9th grade	4.5	5.8	6.8	6.3	6.1	8.2	5.8	6.8
10th grade	3.3	5.9	5.4	3.8	6.2	6.7	5.5	7.6
11th grade	4.1	3.4	5.8	4.4	4.8	4.9	4.6	4.5
12th grade	3.8	4.5	4.7	3.7	5.4	4.4	5.2	4.3
Not Hispanic or Latino								
White	3.3	4.4	5.2	3.2	4.5	5.3	3.7	5.2
Black or African American	3.3	5.4	7.0	5.6	7.1	7.5	7.7	5.2
Hispanic or Latino	3.7	7.4	5.8	7.2	6.6	8.0	6.1	7.8
Female								
Total	10.7	12.5	11.9	11.6	10.9	11.2	11.5	10.8
9th grade	13.8	14.4	14.9	15.1	14.0	13.2	14.7	14.1
10th grade	12.2	13.1	15.1	14.3	14.8	12.2	12.7	10.8
11th grade	8.7	13.6	11.4	11.3	7.5	11.5	10.0	11.0
12th grade	7.8	9.1	6.6	6.2	5.8	6.5	6.9	6.5
Not Hispanic or Latino								
White	10.4	11.3	10.4	10.3	9.0	10.3	10.3	9.3
Black or African American	9.4	11.2	10.8	9.0	7.5	9.8	9.0	9.8
Hispanic or Latino	11.6	19.7	21.0	14.9	18.9	15.9	15.0	14.9
				Percent of students with an injurious suicide attempt[a,b]				
Total	1.7	2.7	2.8	2.6	2.6	2.6	2.9	2.3
Male								
Total	1.0	1.6	2.2	2.0	2.1	2.1	2.4	1.8
9th grade	1.0	2.1	2.3	3.2	2.6	2.6	3.1	2.1
10th grade	0.5	1.3	2.4	1.4	1.8	2.5	2.1	2.2
11th grade	1.5	1.1	2.0	2.6	2.1	1.6	2.0	1.4
12th grade	0.9	1.5	2.2	1.0	1.7	1.5	1.8	1.0
Not Hispanic or Latino								
White	1.0	1.4	2.1	1.5	1.6	1.7	1.1	1.5
Black or African American	0.4	2.0	2.8	1.8	3.4	3.6	5.2	1.4
Hispanic or Latino	0.5	2.0	2.9	2.1	1.4	2.5	4.2	2.8

are more likely than males to attempt suicide. As shown in Table 6.2, 10.8% of female high school students attempted suicide in 2005, compared to 6% of male high school stu-

dents. More female (21.8%) than male (12%) high school students seriously considered suicide. Also, more female (2.9%) than male (1.8%) high school students injured

TABLE 6.2

Suicidal ideation and suicide attempts and injuries among students in grades 9–12, by sex, grade level, race, and Hispanic origin, selected years, 1991–2005 [CONTINUED]

[Data are based on a national sample of high school students, grades 9–12]

Sex, grade level, race, and Hispanic origin	1991	1993	1995	1997	1999	2001	2003	2005
Female								
Total	**2.5**	**3.8**	**3.4**	**3.3**	**3.1**	**3.1**	**3.2**	**2.9**
9th grade	2.8	3.5	6.3	5.0	3.8	3.8	3.9	4.0
10th grade	2.6	5.1	3.8	3.7	4.0	3.6	3.2	2.4
11th grade	2.1	3.9	2.9	2.8	2.8	2.8	2.9	2.9
12th grade	2.4	2.9	1.3	2.0	1.3	1.7	2.2	2.2
Not Hispanic or Latino								
White	2.3	3.6	2.9	2.6	2.3	2.9	2.4	2.7
Black or African American	2.9	4.0	3.6	3.0	2.4	3.1	2.2	2.6
Hispanic or Latino	2.7	5.5	6.6	3.8	4.6	4.2	5.7	3.7

[a]Response is for the 12 months preceding the survey.
[b]A suicide attempt that required medical attention.
Notes: Only youths attending school participated in the survey. Persons of Hispanic origin may be of any race.

SOURCE: "Table 62. Suicidal Ideation, Suicide Attempts, and Injurious Suicide Attempts among Students in Grades 9–12, by Sex, Grade Level, Race, and Hispanic Origin: United States, Selected Years 1991–2005," in *Health, United States, 2007. With Chartbook on Trends in the Health of Americans*, Centers for Disease Control and Prevention, National Center for Health Statistics, November 2007, http://www.cdc.gov/nchs/data/hus/hus07.pdf (accessed January 30, 2008)

TABLE 6.3

Percentage of high school students who attempted suicide and whose suicide attempt required medical attention, by sex, race/ethnicity, and grade, 2005

	Attempted suicide[a,b]			Suicide attempt treated by a doctor or nurse[a,b]		
	Female	Male	Total	Female	Male	Total
Category	%	%	%	%	%	%
Race/ethnicity						
White[c]	9.3	5.2	7.3	2.7	1.5	2.1
Black[c]	9.8	5.2	7.6	2.6	1.4	2.0
Hispanic	14.9	7.8	11.3	3.7	2.8	3.2
Grade						
9	14.1	6.8	10.4	4.0	2.1	3.0
10	10.8	7.6	9.1	2.4	2.2	2.3
11	11.0	4.5	7.8	2.9	1.4	2.2
12	6.5	4.3	5.4	2.2	1.0	1.6
Total	**10.8**	**6.0**	**8.4**	**2.9**	**1.8**	**2.3**

[a]During the 12 months preceding the survey.
[b]One or more times.
[c]Non-Hispanic.

SOURCE: Adapted from Danice K. Eaton et al., "Table 18. Percentage of High School Students Who Actually Attempted Suicide and Whose Suicide Attempt Resulted in an Injury, Poisoning, or Overdose That Had to Be Treated by a Doctor or Nurse, by Sex, Race/Ethnicity, and Grade—United States, Youth Risk Behavior Survey, 2005," in "Youth Risk Behavior Surveillance—United States, 2005," *Morbidity and Mortality Weekly Report*, vol. 55, no. SS-5, June 9, 2006, http://www.cdc.gov/mmwr/PDF/SS/SS5505.pdf (accessed February 2, 2008)

themselves in their suicide attempts. However, in 2004 only 3.5% of females aged fifteen to nineteen years died from their suicide attempts, whereas 12.6% of males of the same age group died. (See Table 6.1.)

Even though death rates from suicide declined among young adults aged fifteen to nineteen between 1990 and 2004, the percentage of high school students who attempted suicide increased from 7.3% in 1991 to 8.4% in 2005, peaking at 8.8% in 2001. (See Table 6.1 and Table 6.2.) The percentage of students injured during a suicide attempt

also rose from 1.7% in 1991 to 2.9% in 2003, with a decline to 2.3% in 2005.

The percentage of high school students who attempted suicide in 2005 was highest among ninth graders and decreased with increasing grade level. (See Table 6.3.) The percentage of suicide attempts requiring medical attention followed the same pattern: a higher percentage of the suicide attempts of ninth graders required medical attention than did those of older students, and this percentage decreased as the grade level increased. Hispanic students

TABLE 6.4

Percentage of high school students who attempted suicide and whose suicide attempt required medical attention, by sex and selected U.S. sites, 2005

Site	Attempted suicide[a,b]			Suicide attempt treated by a doctor or nurse[b]		
	Female	Male	Total	Female	Male	Total
	%	%	%	%	%	%
State surveys						
Alabama	8.2	11.3	9.7	2.9	5.6	4.2
Arizona	13.9	9.2	11.6	3.3	2.9	3.1
Arkansas	14.3	9.5	12.1	4.7	3.7	4.4
Colorado	9.9	3.4	6.7	1.4	0.6	1.0
Connecticut	11.8	12.0	12.1	—[c]	—	—
Delaware	8.7	5.7	7.1	1.9	2.6	2.3
Florida	10.6	6.0	8.5	2.9	2.4	2.7
Georgia	10.0	5.4	7.8	2.5	2.0	2.2
Hawaii	16.6	9.0	12.9	3.7	3.7	3.7
Idaho	11.5	6.2	8.9	3.6	2.1	2.8
Indiana	11.4	7.9	9.6	3.4	3.6	3.5
Iowa	10.4	4.0	7.2	2.2	1.8	2.0
Kansas	8.8	4.0	6.5	2.3	0.9	1.6
Kentucky	11.2	7.0	9.2	3.1	2.2	2.7
Maine	6.6	6.0	6.4	1.1	2.7	1.9
Maryland	12.4	6.1	9.3	3.3	2.2	2.7
Massachusetts	7.2	5.6	6.4	2.4	2.5	2.4
Michigan	11.0	7.3	9.3	3.5	3.1	3.3
Missouri	9.3	4.9	7.1	2.3	1.4	1.8
Montana	13.3	6.7	10.3	4.1	1.8	3.1
Nebraska	11.1	7.7	9.4	3.1	3.2	3.2
Nevada	11.2	5.9	8.7	3.8	2.8	3.4
New Hampshire	10.8	2.8	7.1	2.5	0.5	1.6
New Jersey	—	—	—	—	—	—
New Mexico	14.7	10.0	12.5	5.8	4.4	5.1
New York	8.7	5.3	7.1	1.7	1.9	1.8
North Carolina	13.3	12.7	13.1	—	—	—
North Dakota	8.3	4.5	6.4	2.2	1.1	1.7
Ohio	11.3	6.9	9.1	4.1	2.0	3.1
Oklahoma	9.0	6.7	7.9	2.3	1.4	1.8
Rhode Island	10.9	5.6	8.4	3.2	2.8	3.1
South Carolina	11.1	10.8	11.1	3.1	4.1	3.6
South Dakota	14.3	7.6	11.1	3.6	3.0	3.4
Tennessee	13.1	5.6	9.4	3.0	1.9	2.4
Texas	12.5	6.1	9.4	3.2	1.6	2.5
Utah	11.5	5.3	8.4	3.3	2.8	3.0
Vermont	8.7	3.6	6.2	2.7	1.3	2.1
West Virginia	12.3	5.2	8.8	3.8	1.2	2.5
Wisconsin	11.0	6.5	8.8	3.0	1.9	2.4
Wyoming	10.9	6.6	8.7	2.9	2.5	2.7
Median	11.1	6.1	8.8	3.1	2.2	2.7
Range	6.6–16.6	2.8–12.7	6.2–13.1	1.1–5.8	0.5–5.6	1.0–5.1

were the most likely to attempt suicide and white students were the least likely. In addition, suicide attempts were the highest among high school students living in North Carolina (13.1%), Hawaii (12.9%), Arkansas (12.1%), and Connecticut (12.1%). (See Table 6.4.)

In its collection of suicide-related statistics, the CDC has data on the percentage of high school students who feel sad or hopeless, who seriously consider attempting suicide, and who make a suicide plan. In 2005, 28.5% of high school students in all grades felt sad or hopeless. (See Table 6.5.) Approximately 16.9% seriously considered attempting suicide and 13% made a suicide plan. In 2005 the states in which more than 30% of high school students felt sad or hopeless were Arizona (34.3%), Arkansas (32.4%), Hawaii (31.8%), Texas (31.4%), and Tennessee (31%). (See Table 6.6.)

Table 6.7 shows the annual suicide rates among young people by method. The use of firearms was the method most frequently used by ten- to fourteen-year-olds from 1990 to 1996 for both males and females. In 1997 and from 2000 to 2004 hanging/suffocation overtook firearms as the most frequently used method of suicide in this age group for both sexes. In addition, the use of hanging/suffocation to commit suicide more than doubled from 2003 to 2004 for females. Poisoning was generally the third most widely used method of suicide for ten- to fourteen-year-olds, but it was used much less frequently than firearms or hanging/suffocation by adolescent males. In 1990 and 1993, however, poisoning was used more frequently than hanging/suffocation by adolescent females.

In the fifteen- to nineteen-year-old age group, hanging/suffocation overtook the use of firearms as the primary

TABLE 6.4

Percentage of high school students who attempted suicide and whose suicide attempt required medical attention, by sex and selected U.S. sites, 2005 [CONTINUED]

	Attempted suicide[a,b]			Suicide attempt treated by a doctor or nurse[b]		
	Female	Male	Total	Female	Male	Total
Site	%	%	%	%	%	%
Local surveys						
Baltimore, MD	11.4	10.4	11.0	3.7	3.6	3.6
Boston, MA	10.8	7.8	9.4	2.7	3.9	3.3
Broward County, FL	11.2	6.1	8.8	3.6	3.0	3.5
Charlotte-Mecklenburg, NC	11.5	12.6	12.1	—	—	—
Chicago, IL	9.3	7.8	8.6	3.9	2.8	3.4
Dallas, TX	12.8	6.2	9.7	3.8	1.2	2.6
DeKalb County, GA	11.1	8.4	9.9	2.8	2.8	2.8
Detroit, MI	10.0	6.4	8.6	3.9	2.7	3.4
District of Columbia	15.1	9.0	12.3	3.9	2.4	3.3
Hillsborough County, FL	10.3	9.1	10.0	3.9	3.6	3.9
Los Angeles, CA	17.4	2.1	9.9	4.0	1.2	2.6
Memphis, TN	13.3	8.6	11.1	3.8	4.9	4.3
Miami-Dade County, FL	11.1	4.7	8.1	2.7	1.7	2.2
Milwaukee, WI	9.9	11.7	10.9	3.8	5.1	4.4
New Orleans, LA	11.1	14.2	13.0	4.2	6.5	5.5
New York City, NY	11.8	7.3	9.6	2.0	3.3	2.6
Orange County, FL	11.6	6.0	8.8	2.9	3.0	2.9
Palm Beach County, FL	7.6	6.6	7.2	2.3	2.4	2.3
San Bernardino, CA	16.1	10.8	13.8	5.1	3.8	4.5
San Diego, CA	12.5	6.9	10.0	2.7	2.1	2.6
San Francisco, CA	13.5	8.6	11.0	3.3	3.2	3.3
Median	11.4	7.8	9.9	3.7	3.0	3.3
Range	7.6–17.4	2.1–14.2	7.2–13.8	2.0–5.1	1.2–6.5	2.2–5.5

[a]During the 12 months preceding the survey.
[b]One or more times.
[c]Not available.

SOURCE: Adapted from Danice K. Eaton et al., "Table 19. Percentage of High School Students Who Actually Attempted Suicide and Whose Suicide Attempt Resulted in an Injury, Poisoning, or Overdose That Had to Be Treated by a Doctor or Nurse, by Sex—Selected U.S. Sites, Youth Risk Behavior Survey, 2005," in "Youth Risk Behavior Surveillance—United States, 2005," *Morbidity and Mortality Weekly Report*, vol. 55, no. SS-5, June 9, 2006, http://www.cdc.gov/mmwr/PDF/SS/SS5505.pdf (accessed February 2, 2008)

TABLE 6.5

Percentage of high school students who felt sad or hopeless, who seriously considered attempting suicide, and who made a suicide plan, by sex, race/ethnicity, and grade, 2005

	Felt sad or hopeless[a,b]			Seriously considered attempting suicide[b]			Made a suicide plan[b]		
	Female	Male	Total	Female	Male	Total	Female	Male	Total
Category	%	%	%	%	%	%	%	%	%
Race/ethnicity									
White[c]	33.4	18.4	25.8	21.5	12.4	16.9	15.4	9.7	12.5
Black[c]	36.9	19.5	28.4	17.1	7.0	12.2	13.5	5.5	9.6
Hispanic	46.7	26.0	36.2	24.2	11.9	17.9	18.5	10.7	14.5
Grade									
9	38.5	19.9	29.0	23.9	12.2	17.9	17.6	10.2	13.9
10	37.0	21.3	28.9	23.0	11.9	17.3	18.1	10.3	14.1
11	38.0	19.4	28.8	21.6	11.9	16.8	16.3	9.5	12.9
12	32.6	20.2	26.4	18.0	11.6	14.8	12.0	9.0	10.5
Total	**36.7**	**20.4**	**28.5**	**21.8**	**12.0**	**16.9**	**16.2**	**9.9**	**13.0**

[a]Almost every day for ≥2 weeks in a row so that they stopped doing some usual activities.
[b]During the 12 months preceding the survey.
[c]Non-Hispanic.

SOURCE: Adapted from Danice K. Eaton et al., "Table 16. Percentage of High School Students Who Felt Sad or Hopeless, Who Seriously Considered Attempting Suicide, and Who Made a Plan about How They Would Attempt Suicide, by Sex, Race/Ethnicity, and Grade—Youth Risk Behavior Survey, 2005," in "Youth Risk Behavior Surveillance—United States, 2005," *Morbidity and Mortality Weekly Report*, vol. 55, no. SS-5, June 9, 2006, http://www.cdc.gov/mmwr/PDF/SS/SS5505.pdf (accessed February 2, 2008)

TABLE 6.6

Percentage of high school students who felt sad or hopeless, who seriously considered attempting suicide, and who made a suicide plan, by sex and selected U.S. sites, 2005

Site	Felt sad or hopeless[a, b]			Seriously considered attempting suicide[b]			Made a suicide plan[b]		
	Female	Male	Total	Female	Male	Total	Female	Male	Total
	%	%	%	%	%	%	%	%	%
State surveys									
Alabama	31.2	25.6	28.5	19.5	14.7	17.1	16.4	13.5	15.0
Arizona	43.7	24.9	34.3	25.4	16.0	20.7	19.5	12.7	16.1
Arkansas	38.2	26.3	32.4	24.5	13.7	19.2	19.6	11.8	15.8
Colorado	36.4	14.4	25.0	18.3	9.3	13.6	14.1	7.3	10.6
Connecticut	31.4	18.3	24.8	18.0	12.3	15.1	15.9	11.6	13.8
Delaware	35.3	19.9	27.5	16.2	9.6	12.7	13.4	8.8	11.0
Florida	35.2	19.7	27.3	19.0	10.1	14.5	14.2	8.9	11.6
Georgia	36.1	22.2	29.1	23.4	11.5	17.4	17.8	11.9	14.9
Hawaii	40.2	24.0	31.8	26.0	14.1	19.8	22.0	12.9	17.2
Idaho	36.0	20.1	28.0	20.9	11.0	15.9	18.4	10.7	14.5
Indiana	33.6	21.2	27.3	22.0	14.3	18.0	17.0	12.6	14.8
Iowa	31.5	19.1	25.3	20.5	12.1	16.2	16.5	9.7	13.0
Kansas	26.6	16.5	21.4	17.1	9.2	13.0	12.6	6.5	9.6
Kentucky	35.0	21.8	28.2	18.3	12.6	15.4	13.4	9.9	11.6
Maine	25.7	15.8	20.6	15.7	11.1	13.3	10.1	10.5	10.3
Maryland	38.1	21.5	29.7	22.0	12.9	17.4	15.6	9.0	12.2
Massachusetts	33.4	20.2	26.7	15.2	10.2	12.7	13.5	9.8	11.7
Michigan	32.9	19.7	26.3	19.6	12.0	15.8	14.1	10.3	12.2
Missouri	31.6	19.8	25.5	19.9	10.9	15.3	14.0	8.1	11.0
Montana	34.0	17.6	25.6	25.0	10.2	17.5	19.2	9.9	14.6
Nebraska	31.5	19.0	25.1	21.5	11.8	16.5	17.7	11.1	14.3
Nevada	33.6	22.2	27.8	21.5	10.9	16.1	18.5	11.5	15.0
New Hampshire	32.7	17.6	24.9	18.6	9.1	14.0	14.8	8.8	11.8
New Jersey	—[c]	—	—	—	—	—	—	—	—
New Mexico	36.2	21.0	28.7	22.4	14.6	18.5	18.7	12.8	15.7
New York	35.3	19.3	27.3	18.9	9.8	14.4	12.5	7.9	10.2
North Carolina	32.3	20.7	26.5	18.7	12.5	15.6	15.4	10.8	13.1
North Dakota	25.3	15.5	20.3	18.9	11.9	15.4	14.6	9.9	12.2
Ohio	33.9	20.5	27.0	21.5	14.6	17.9	16.0	11.4	13.6
Oklahoma	34.6	21.4	27.9	20.0	10.9	15.4	14.9	9.8	12.4
Rhode Island	34.1	17.2	25.7	17.4	10.7	14.0	13.3	8.8	11.0
South Carolina	33.9	23.2	28.6	16.9	12.8	14.9	15.1	12.1	13.6
South Dakota	29.3	23.6	26.4	24.6	13.6	19.1	17.8	15.0	16.5
Tennessee	40.5	21.7	31.0	24.6	13.2	18.9	17.8	10.3	14.0
Texas	39.4	23.6	31.4	21.0	10.8	15.9	15.1	9.4	12.2
Utah	35.5	21.2	28.2	20.8	11.9	16.2	16.8	11.6	14.1
Vermont	29.9	14.9	22.2	—	—	—	14.9	8.0	11.4
West Virginia	34.4	24.7	29.6	21.0	12.7	16.9	15.1	9.8	12.4
Wisconsin	33.3	22.2	27.6	21.8	14.1	17.8	18.3	12.7	15.4
Wyoming	33.4	19.6	26.3	21.8	13.3	17.4	19.3	12.2	15.7
Median	33.9	20.5	27.3	20.6	11.9	16.0	15.6	10.3	13.1
Range	25.3–43.7	14.4–26.3	20.3–34.3	15.2–26.0	9.1–16.0	12.7–20.7	10.1–22.0	6.5–15.0	9.6–17.2

method of committing suicide in 2001 for females, but it remained the most-used method by males in this age group from 1990 through 2004. (See Table 6.7.) The use of firearms by fifteen- to nineteen-year-old males decreased steadily from 1994 to 2003, with a slight increase in 2004. Poisoning ranked low in this age group from 1990 through 2004, as it did in the ten- to fourteen-year-old group. The use of firearms was also the most widely used means of committing suicide in those aged twenty to twenty-four in 1990 to 2004. Hanging/suffocation was generally second, and poisoning third, although in some years poisoning overtook suffocation as a means of suicide for females.

In general, the use of firearms is the method most often used by youths and young adults to commit suicide, with hanging/suffocation second and poisoning third.

This pattern was also seen in the general population in 2005. (See Table 6.8.) The rate of death by firearms (5.7 suicides per 100,000 people) was more than twice that of suffocation (2.4 suicides per 100,000 people), and suffocation was used 1.3 times as much as poisoning (1.9 suicides per 100,000 people). Other methods were used much less frequently.

The statistics in this section underscore the urgent need for prevention, education, and support programs to help teens and young adults at risk. The National Center for Injury Prevention and Control (NCIPC) sponsors initiatives to raise public awareness of suicide and strategies to reduce suicide deaths. Along with supporting research about risk factors for suicide in the general population, the NCIPC develops programs for high-risk populations.

TABLE 6.6

Percentage of high school students who felt sad or hopeless, who seriously considered attempting suicide, and who made a suicide plan, by sex and selected U.S. sites, 2005 [CONTINUED]

Site	Felt sad or hopeless[a,b]			Seriously considered attempting suicide[b]			Made a suicide plan[b]		
	Female	Male	Total	Female	Male	Total	Female	Male	Total
	%	%	%	%	%	%	%	%	%
Local surveys									
Baltimore, MD	34.6	22.6	29.0	16.8	10.3	13.8	13.5	9.9	11.8
Boston, MA	36.8	22.7	30.1	15.6	9.2	12.5	12.7	9.5	11.2
Broward County, FL	40.2	23.9	32.1	19.6	9.0	14.5	13.5	8.3	10.9
Charlotte-Mecklenburg, N	32.5	21.4	27.0	15.7	11.0	13.4	14.7	10.5	12.6
Chicago, IL	31.9	23.8	28.0	15.0	10.5	12.9	13.4	7.4	10.6
Dallas, TX	39.2	20.9	30.2	19.1	10.4	14.8	15.6	10.0	12.8
DeKalb County, GA	33.5	20.6	27.3	18.0	8.5	13.4	14.8	8.4	11.7
Detroit, MI	37.5	20.1	29.7	18.4	8.9	14.2	14.2	5.7	10.4
District of Columbia	26.3	16.9	21.8	14.3	7.3	10.8	11.2	6.3	8.7
Hillsborough County, FL	39.5	24.0	31.9	19.9	11.5	15.8	16.9	11.3	14.2
Los Angeles, CA	43.6	21.6	32.6	25.5	7.6	16.4	19.3	6.8	13.0
Memphis, TN	34.1	19.3	27.1	17.4	8.8	13.3	16.0	7.2	11.7
Miami-Dade County, FL	37.5	21.5	29.5	16.8	7.0	11.9	13.0	7.4	10.2
Milwaukee, WI	39.6	25.3	32.6	15.9	9.0	12.4	13.5	10.8	12.1
New Orleans, LA	31.9	23.2	27.9	10.9	12.9	11.9	8.9	10.2	9.6
New York City, NY	40.3	24.3	32.3	20.0	10.3	15.3	13.6	9.9	11.9
Orange County, FL	37.6	21.6	29.7	17.7	10.2	14.0	12.8	7.1	9.8
Palm Beach County, FL	32.3	23.3	27.8	15.2	11.3	13.3	11.4	8.3	9.9
San Bernardino, CA	47.7	26.5	37.6	23.3	11.8	17.9	19.9	12.0	16.1
San Diego, CA	40.8	26.3	33.8	23.0	12.1	17.5	16.3	9.8	13.0
San Francisco, CA	33.1	21.8	27.3	18.4	10.0	14.1	17.1	11.2	14.0
Median	37.5	22.6	29.7	17.7	10.2	13.8	13.6	9.5	11.7
Range	26.3–47.7	16.9–26.5	21.8–37.6	10.9–25.5	7.0–12.9	10.8–17.9	8.9–19.9	5.7–12.0	8.7–16.1

[a]Almost every day for ≥2 weeks in a row so that they stopped doing some usual activities.
[b]During the 12 months preceding the survey.
[c]Not available.

SOURCE: Adapted from Danice K. Eaton et al., "Table 17. Percentage of High School Students Who Felt Sad or Hopeless, Who Seriously Considered Attempting Suicide, and Who Made a Plan about How They Would Attempt Suicide, by Sex—Selected U.S. Sites, Youth Risk Behavior Survey, 2005," in "Youth Risk Behavior Surveillance—United States, 2005," *Morbidity and Mortality Weekly Report*, vol. 55, no. SS-5, June 9, 2006, http://www.cdc.gov/mmwr/PDF/SS/SS5505.pdf (accessed February 2, 2008)

SUICIDE AMONG GAY AND LESBIAN ADOLESCENTS.
Susan McAndrew and Tony Warne indicate in "Ignoring the Evidence Dictating the Practice: Sexual Orientation, Suicidality, and the Dichotomy of the Mental Health Nurse" (*Journal of Psychiatric and Mental Health Nursing*, vol. 11, no. 4, August 2004) that the suicide rate for gay and lesbian adolescents is dramatically higher than for the general adolescent population. Adolescence (the transition to adulthood) is often a difficult period. For gay and lesbian adolescents, this transition is compounded by having to come to terms with their sexuality in a society generally unaccepting of homosexuality.

At this period in their life, when the need to confide in and gain acceptance from friends and family may be crucial, gay and lesbian adolescents are often torn between choices that do not necessarily meet either of these needs. Those who are open about their sexual orientation risk disappointing or even alienating their families and facing the hostility of their peers. Teens who choose not to disclose their homosexuality may suffer emotional distress because they have nowhere to turn for emotional support. In either scenario, despair, isolation, anger, guilt, and overwhelming depression may promote suicidal thoughts or actual suicide attempts.

In "Sexual Orientation and Risk Factors for Suicidal Ideation and Suicide Attempts among Adolescents and Young Adults" (*American Journal of Public Health*, vol. 97, no. 11, November 2007), Vincent M. B. Silenzio et al. analyze data from the National Longitudinal Study of Adolescent Health and determine that young adults aged eighteen to twenty-six years who identified themselves as lesbian, gay, or bisexual were more likely than young adults of the same age group who were not lesbian, gay, or bisexual to have had thoughts of suicide (17.2% versus 6.3%) and to have attempted suicide (4.9% versus 1.6%). Exact data are not available for suicide deaths of gay, lesbian, and bisexual teenagers because the sexual orientation of suicide victims is often unknown.

EUTHANASIA AND PHYSICIAN-ASSISTED SUICIDE

The U.S. Constitution does not guarantee the right to choose to die. However, the U.S. Supreme Court recognizes that Americans have a fundamental right to privacy, or what is sometimes called the "right to be left alone." Even though the right to privacy is not explicitly mentioned in the Constitution, the Supreme Court has inter-

TABLE 6.7

Annual suicide rates among persons aged 10–24 years, by age group, method, sex, and year, 1990–2004

[Per 100,000 population in sex-age group]

	10–14 years				15–19 years				20–24 years			
Sex/year	All methods[a]	Firearm	Hanging/ suffocation[b]	Poisoning[c]	All methods	Firearm	Hanging/ suffocation	Poisoning	All methods	Firearm	Hanging/ suffocation	Poisoning
Females												
1990	0.80	0.44	0.15**	0.17**	3.73	2.09	0.55	0.89	4.11	2.19	0.43	1.15
1991	0.67	0.36	0.15**	0.10**	3.70	1.83	0.59	1.09	3.88	1.79	0.52	1.11
1992	0.90	0.42	0.24	0.22**	3.42	1.62	0.62	1.03	3.84	1.92	0.58	1.02
1993	0.93	0.45	0.19**	0.20**	3.80	2.00	0.62	0.92	4.36	2.11	0.59	1.24
1994	0.95	0.52	0.28	0.13**	3.44	1.99	0.51	0.74	3.87	2.00	0.61	0.82
1995	0.82	0.50	0.20**	0.09**	3.07	1.64	0.57	0.62	4.21	2.15	0.80	0.97
1996	0.80	0.35	0.33	0.07**	3.49	1.69	1.02	0.51	3.57	1.65	0.71	0.88
1997	0.76	0.29	0.33	0.12**	3.31	1.70	0.95	0.47	3.59	1.63	0.88	0.75
1998	0.86	0.37	0.35	0.07**	2.84	1.43	0.81	0.38	3.70	1.72	0.87	0.65
1999	0.51	0.23	0.22	0.03**	2.75	1.11	0.89	0.48	3.37	1.36	0.84	0.79
2000	0.62	0.20**	0.33	0.07**	2.75	1.06	1.02	0.42	3.23	1.29	0.78	0.70
2001	0.64	0.21	0.32	0.08**	2.70	0.96	0.99	0.52	3.06	1.03	0.87	0.83
2002	0.62	0.17**	0.33	0.11**	2.36	0.75	0.98	0.43	3.48	1.18	0.95	0.92
2003	0.54	0.11**	0.31	0.06**	2.66	0.77	1.24	0.43	3.39	1.18	1.10	0.82
2004	0.95	0.09**	0.68	0.15**	3.52	0.98	1.72	0.54	3.59	1.14	1.23	0.76
Males												
1990	2.17	1.19	0.91	0.02**	18.17	12.63	3.48	1.49	25.69	16.69	5.19	2.41
1991	2.28	1.37	0.78	0.08**	17.92	12.70	3.16	1.26	25.40	16.97	4.52	2.51
1992	2.40	1.44	0.80	0.11**	17.61	12.59	3.17	1.20	25.42	16.79	5.04	2.11
1993	2.40	1.51	0.78	0.04**	17.39	12.29	3.20	1.11	26.47	18.04	4.94	2.23
1994	2.36	1.43	0.79	0.08**	17.95	13.11	3.27	0.74	27.96	18.80	5.21	2.30
1995	2.57	1.38	1.06	0.06**	17.11	11.86	3.39	0.85	27.01	17.27	5.96	1.96
1996	2.23	1.29	0.90	0.01**	15.38	10.20	3.50	0.88	24.47	15.73	5.36	1.79
1997	2.29	0.98	1.21	0.03**	14.94	9.78	3.84	0.51	22.66	14.34	5.02	1.79
1998	2.30	1.15	1.12	0.01**	14.34	9.31	3.57	0.65	22.33	13.71	5.72	1.50
1999	1.85	0.77	0.99	0.03**	13.05	8.40	3.36	0.54	20.85	12.81	4.80	1.61
2000	2.26	0.86	1.28	0.08**	13.00	7.63	3.98	0.67	21.40	12.90	5.66	1.32
2001	1.93	0.64	1.21	0.02**	12.87	7.11	4.33	0.63	20.37	11.76	5.92	1.38
2002	1.81	0.63	1.11	0.00**	12.22	6.38	4.32	0.72	20.62	11.78	6.11	1.11
2003	1.73	0.57	1.11	0.03**	11.61	6.26	4.22	0.57	20.21	11.42	6.26	1.16
2004	1.71	0.46	1.24	0.00**	12.65	6.47	4.71	0.66	20.84	11.12	6.63	1.49

[a]Includes cutting, jumping, burning, drowning, and other or unspecified methods.
[b]Includes self-inflicted asphyxiation and ligature strangulation.
[c]Includes intentional drug overdose and carbon monoxide exposure.
**Unstable rate based on 20 or fewer deaths.

SOURCE: "Table. Suicide Rates for Youths and Young Adults Aged 10–24 Years, by Age Group, Method,Sex, and Year—National Vital Statistics System, United States, 1990–2004," in "Suicide Trends among Youths and Young Adults Aged 10–24 Years—United States, 1990–2004," *Morbidity and Mortality Weekly Report*, vol. 56, no. 35, September 7, 2007, http://www.cdc.gov/mmwr/PDF/wk/mm5635.pdf (accessed February 2, 2008)

preted several amendments as encompassing this right. For example, in *Roe v. Wade* (410 U.S. 113, 1973), the Court ruled that the Fourteenth Amendment protects the right to privacy against state action, specifically a woman's right to abortion. In another example in the landmark Karen Ann Quinlan case, which was based on right-to-privacy rulings by the U.S. Supreme Court, the New Jersey Supreme Court held that the right to privacy included the right to refuse unwanted medical treatment and, as a consequence, the right to die (see Chapter 8).

The Acceptability of Euthanasia and Physician-Assisted Suicide

In "When Is Physician Assisted Suicide or Euthanasia Acceptable?" (*Journal of Medical Ethics*, vol. 29, no. 6, December 2003), Stéphanie Frileux et al. examine the opinion of the general public on euthanasia and physician-assisted suicide. The researchers define these terms as follows: "In physician-assisted suicide, the physician provides the patient with the means to end his or her own life. In euthanasia, the physician deliberately and directly intervenes to end the patient's life; this is sometimes called 'active euthanasia' to distinguish it from withholding or withdrawing treatment needed to sustain life." Their study posed the questions: "Should a terminally ill patient be allowed to die? Should the medical profession have the option of helping such a patient to die?" Frileux et al. find that acceptability of euthanasia or physician-assisted suicide by the general public appears to depend on four factors: the level of patient suffering, the extent to which the patient requested death, the age of the patient, and the degree of curability of the illness. In general, people judged euthanasia as less acceptable than physician-assisted suicide.

Lauris C. Kaldjian et al. study in "Internists' Attitudes toward Terminal Sedation in End of Life Care" (*Journal of*

TABLE 6.8

Number of suicide deaths and suicide death rates, 2005

Mechanism of suicide	Number of deaths	Rate of death (per 100,000 population)
All mechanisms	32,637	11.0
Firearm	17,002	5.7
Suffocation	7,248	2.4
Poisoning	5,744	1.9
Fall	683	0.2
Cut/pierce	590	0.2
Drowning	375	0.1
Other specified, classifiable	328	0.1
Other specified, not elsewhere classified	228	0.1
Unspecified	166	0.1
Fire/flame	160	0.1
All transport	113	0.0

SOURCE: Adapted from Hsiang-Ching Kung et al., "Table 18. Number of Deaths, Death Rates, and Age-Adjusted Death Rates for Injury Deaths According to Mechanism and Intent of Death: United States, 2005," in "Deaths: Final Data for 2005," *National Vital Statistics Reports*, vol. 56, no. 10, January 2008, ftp://ftp.cdc.gov/pub/Health_Statistics/NCHS/Publications/NVSR/56_10/table18.xls (accessed January 30, 2008)

Medical Ethics, vol. 30, no. 5, October 2004) the attitudes of internists (doctors specializing in internal medicine) toward physician-assisted suicide and other end-of-life care issues. Most physicians in the study (96%) agreed that it is appropriate to increase pain-reducing medication when needed in end-of-life care. More than three-quarters (78%) also agreed that if a terminally ill patient has pain that cannot be managed well, terminal sedation is appropriate. (Terminal sedation means alleviating the pain and discomfort of dying people by sedating them or by providing medication that alleviates their painful or uncomfortable symptoms but that has complete sedation as a side effect. These patients are not usually given nutrition or fluids. Terminal sedation is controversial because some feel it is tantamount to euthanasia, only slower, while still being perfectly legal.) One-third (33%) agreed that physician-assisted suicide is acceptable in some circumstances.

Kaldjian et al. also note that those who reported more experience with terminally ill patients were relatively more likely to support terminal sedation but not physician-assisted suicide than those who reported less or no experience with terminally ill patients. Those most likely to support both terminal sedation and physician-assisted suicide were those with no experience with terminally ill patients. In addition, the data show that those who did not attend religious services or attended less than monthly were the most likely to support both terminal sedation and physician-assisted suicide, whereas those who attended weekly were the least likely to support both. No matter the number of terminal patients physicians cared for in the preceding year or the frequency with which they attended religious services, a large proportion supported terminal sedation but not physician-assisted suicide.

Patients Requesting Assisted Suicide and Euthanasia

Diane E. Meier et al. studied various characteristics of patients requesting and receiving euthanasia and physician-assisted suicide and reported their results in "Characteristics of Patients Requesting and Receiving Physician-Assisted Death" (*Archives of Internal Medicine*, vol. 163, no. 13, July 14, 2003). The 1,902 physicians who responded to the researchers' survey reported 415 recent requests for aid in dying. Of these requests, 361 (89%) came from patients alone or in conjunction with their families. Only forty-six (11%) requests came from the family alone. Of the requests, 52% were for a lethal prescription, 25% for a lethal injection, and 23% for either a prescription or an injection.

Meier et al. find that the patients requesting euthanasia or physician-assisted suicide were predominantly male (61%), forty-six to seventy-five years old (56%), and of white European descent (89%). Almost half (47%) were college graduates and had a primary diagnosis of cancer. A large number were experiencing severe pain (38%) or severe discomfort other than pain (42%). Many were described by their physicians as dependent (53%), bedridden (42%), and expected to live less than one month (28%).

Marijke C. Jansen-van der Weide, Bregje D. Onwuteaka-Philipsen, and Gerrit van der Wal reveal in "Granted, Undecided, Withdrawn, and Refused Requests for Euthanasia and Physician-Assisted Suicide" (*Archives of Internal Medicine*, vol. 165, no. 15, August 8–22, 2005) the characteristics of patients in the Netherlands who explicitly requested euthanasia or physician-assisted suicide from April 2000 to December 2002. As in the Meier et al. study, more than half of the patients requesting euthanasia and assisted suicide were male (54%). Most of the patients were diagnosed with cancer (90%), a greater percentage than in the Meier et al. study. Even though only 9% were diagnosed with depression, 92% were "feeling bad."

Table 6.9 shows the characteristics of patients at the end of life in Oregon, the only state in the Union in which assisted suicide is legal. These results, which are from patients who died between 1998 and 2005 and in 2006, are similar to the results found in the Meier et al. and Jansen-van der Weide, Onwuteaka-Philipsen, and van der Wal studies. The patients who died after ingesting a lethal dose of medication were predominantly male (53% in 1998–2005 and 57% in 2006), fifty-five to eighty-four years old (76% in 1998–2005 and 79% in 2006), and white (97% in 1998–2005 and 98% in 2006). More than 40% were college graduates (42% in 1998–2005 and 41% in 2006) and had a primary diagnosis of cancer (80% in 1998–2005 and 87% in 2006, close to the figures of the Jansen-van der Weide, Onwuteaka-Philipsen, and van der Wal study).

TABLE 6.9

Characteristics and end-of-life care of DWDA (Death with Dignity Act) patients who ingested lethal medication, Oregon, 1998–2006

Characteristics	2006 (N = 46)[a]	1998–2005 (N = 246)[a]	Total (N = 292)[a]
Sex			
Male (%)	26 (57)	131 (53)	157 (54)
Female (%)	20 (43)	115 (47)	135 (46)
Age			
18–34 (%)	0 (0)	3 (1)	3 (1)
35–44 (%)	1 (2)	7 (3)	8 (3)
45–54 (%)	2 (4)	26 (11)	28 (10)
55–64 (%)	10 (22)	45 (18)	55 (19)
65–74 (%)	11 (24)	72 (29)	83 (28)
75–84 (%)	15 (33)	72 (29)	87 (30)
85+ (%)	7 (15)	21 (9)	28 (10)
Median years (range)	74 (36–96)	69 (25–94)	70 (25–96)
Race			
White (%)	45 (98)	239 (97)	284 (97)
Asian (%)	0 (0)	6 (2)	6 (2)
American Indian (%)	0 (0)	1 (<1)	1 (<1)
Hispanic (%)	1 (2)	0-	1 (<1)
Marital status			
Married (%)	23 (50)	110 (45)	133 (46)
Widowed (%)	8 (17)	55 (22)	63 (22)
Divorced (%)	10 (22)	64 (26)	74 (25)
Never married (%)	5 (11)	17 (7)	22 (8)
Education			
Less than high school (%)	4 (9)	21 (9)	25 (9)
High school graduate (%)	11 (24)	71 (29)	82 (28)
Some college (%)	12 (26)	52 (21)	64 (22)
Baccalaureate or higher (%)	19 (41)	102 (42)	121 (41)
Residence			
Metro counties (%)[b]	18 (39)	95 (39)	113 (39)
Coastal counties (%)[c]	2 (4)	19 (8)	21 (7)
Other western counties (%)	19 (41)	117 (48)	136 (47)
East of the Cascades (%)	7 (15)	15 (6)	22 (8)
Underlying illness			
Malignant neoplasms (%)	40 (87)	196 (80)	236 (81)
Lung and bronchus (%)	6 (13)	48 (20)	54 (18)
Pancreas (%)	7 (15)	20 (8)	27 (9)
Breast (%)	2 (4)	23 (9)	25 (9)
Colon (%)	3 (7)	16 (7)	19 (7)
Prostate (%)	2 (4)	13 (5)	15 (5)
Other (%)	20 (43)	76 (31)	96 (33)
Amyotrophic lateral sclerosis (%)	3 (7)	20 (8)	23 (8)
Chronic lower respiratory disease (%)	0 (0)	11 (4)	11 (4)
HIV/AIDS (%)	1 (2)	5 (2)	6 (2)
Illnesses listed below (%)[d]	2 (4)	14 (6)	16 (5)
End of life care			
Hospice			
Enrolled (%)	35 (76)	213 (87)	248 (86)
Not enrolled (%)	11 (24)	31 (13)	42 (14)
Unknown	—	2	2
Insurance			
Private (%)	29 (64)	151 (62)	180 (62)
Medicare or Medicaid (%)	15 (33)	90 (37)	105 (36)
None (%)	1 (2)	2 (1)	3 (1)
Unknown	1	3	4

TABLE 6.9

Characteristics and end-of-life care of DWDA (Death with Dignity Act) patients who ingested lethal medication, Oregon, 1998–2006
[CONTINUED]

Characteristics	2006 (N = 46)[a]	1998–2005 (N = 246)[a]	Total (N = 292)[a]
End-of-life concerns[e]			
Losing autonomy (%)	44 (96)	207 (86)	251 (87)
Less able to engage in activities making life enjoyable (%)	44 (96)	206 (85)	250 (87)
Loss of dignity (%)[f]	35 (76)	96 (82)	131 (80)
Losing control of bodily functions (%)	27 (59)	138 (57)	165 (57)
Burden on family, friends/caregivers (%)	20 (43)	90 (37)	110 (38)
Inadequate pain control or concern about it (%)	22 (48)	54 (22)	76 (26)
Financial implications of treatment (%)	0-	7 (3)	7 (2)
PAS process			
Referred for psychiatric evaluation (%)	2 (4)	34 (14)	36 (13)
Patient died at			
Home (patient, family or friend) (%)	43 (93)	232 (94)	275 (94)
Long term care, assisted living or foster care facility (%)	2 (4)	11 (4)	13 (4)
Hospital (%)	—	1 (1)	1 (<1)
Other (%)	1 (2)	2 (1)	3 (1)
Lethal medication			
Secobarbital (%)	31 (67)	105 (43)	136 (47)
Pentobarbital (%)	15 (33)	137 (56)	152 (52)
Other (%)	—	4 (2)	4 (1)
Health-care provider present when medication ingested[g]			
Prescribing physician (%)	15 (33)	48 (28)	63 (29)
Other provider, prescribing physician not present (%)	23 (51)	92 (54)	115 (53)
No provider (%)	7 (16)	31 (18)	38 (18)
Unknown	1	5	6
Complications			
Regurgitated (%)	4 (9)	12 (5)	16 (6)
Seizures (%)	—	—	—
Awakened after taking prescribed medication (%)	0 ([h])	1 ([h])	1 ([h])
None (%)	40 (91)	229 (95)	269 (94)
Unknown	2	5	7
Emergency medical services			
Called for intervention after lethal medication ingested (%)	—	—	—
Calls for other reasons (%)[i]	1 (2)	3 (1)	4 (1)
Not called after lethal medication ingested (%)	45 (98)	239 (99)	284 (99)
Unknown		4	4

- General weakness (57%)

- Hopeless suffering (52%)

- Meaningless suffering (33%)

- Loss of dignity (19%)

- Physical symptoms, such as pain and nausea (19%)

- Weakness after long medical treatment (14%)

The primary reasons for a request to hasten death were:

- Loss of dignity (75%)

- Hopeless suffering (63%)

- General weakness (63%)

- Loss of control over own life (56%)

- Physical symptoms, such as pain and nausea (56%)

Reasons for Assisted Suicide Requests

In "Requests to Forgo Potentially Life-Prolonging Treatment and to Hasten Death in Terminally Ill Cancer Patients: A Prospective Study" (*Journal of Pain and Symptom Management*, vol. 31, no. 2, February 2006), Jean-Jacques Georges et al. reveal terminal cancer patients' reasons for refusing medical treatment or for requesting that their death be hastened. The primary reasons to forgo treatment were:

TABLE 6.9

Characteristics and end-of-life care of DWDA (Death with Dignity Act) patients who ingested lethal medication, Oregon, 1998–2006 [CONTINUED]

Characteristics	2006 (N = 46)[a]	1998–2005 (N = 246)[a]	Total (N = 292)[a]
Timing of PAS event			
Duration (weeks) of patient-physician relationship			
Median	15	12	12
Range	1–767	0–1065	0–1065
Duration (days) between 1st request and death[i]			
Median	54	39	42
Range	15–747	15–1009	15–1009
Minutes between ingestion and unconsciousness			
Median	5	5	5
Range	1–29	1–38	1–38
Unknown	4	24	28
Minutes between ingestion and death			
Median	29	25	25
Range (minutes - hours)	1 min–16.5 hrs	4 min–48 hrs	1 min–48 hrs
Unknown	3	17	20

N = the number of patients (total sample size).

[a]Unknowns are excluded when calculating percentages.

[b]Clackamas, Multnomah, and Washington counties.

[c]Excluding Douglas and Lane counties.

[d]Includes aortic stenosis, alcoholic hepatic failure, cardiomyopathy, congestive heart failure, corticobasal degeneration, diabetes mellitus with renal complications, digestive organ neoplasm of unknown behavior, emphysema, endocarditis, hepatitis C, myelodysplastic syndrome, organ-limited amyloidosis, pulmonary disease with fibrosis, scleroderma, and Shy-Drager syndrome.

[e]Affirmative answers only ("don't know" included in negative answers). Available for 17 patients in 2001.

[f]First asked in 2003.

[g]The data shown are for 2001–2006. Information about the presence of a health care provider/volunteer, in the absence of the prescribing physician, was first collected in 2001. Attendance by the prescribing physician has been recorded since 1998. During 1998–2006, the prescribing physician was present when 35% of the patients ingested the lethal medication.

[h]Historically, the annual report tables list information on patients who died as a result of ingesting medication prescribed under the provisions of the Death with Dignity Act. Because one patient regained consciousness after ingesting the lethal medication and then died 14 days later from his/her illness rather than from the medication, the complication is recorded here but the patient is not included in the total number of physician assisted suicide (PAS) deaths.

[i]Calls included three to pronounce death and one to help a patient who had fallen.

[j]Note that an extended period of time may elapse from the patient's first request until the attending physician writes a prescription for the lethal medication.

SOURCE: "Table 1. Characteristics and End-of-Life Care of 292 DWDA Patients Who Died after Ingesting a Lethal Dose of Medication, by Year, Oregon, 1998–2006," in *Death with Dignity Act—2006 Report*, Oregon Department of Human Services, March 2007, http://egov.oregon.gov/DHS/ph/pas/docs/yr9-tbl-1.pdf (accessed February 2, 2008)

- Meaningless suffering (38%)
- Dependency (38%)

Even though patients nearing death have concerns about physical pain and suffering, they are also highly focused on loss of dignity, loss of control, and being a burden or dependent on others.

Jansen-van der Weide, Onwuteaka-Philipsen, and van der Wal note some of the same reasons patients requested assistance in dying. The three most often cited reasons for requesting euthanasia or physician-assisted suicide were pointless suffering (75%), deterioration or loss of dignity (69%), and weakness or tiredness (60%). Depression was the reason most likely to have influenced a patient to request assistance in dying and not wanting to burden his or her family was the second-most influential factor.

To gain an additional perspective on why terminally ill people in Oregon pursue assisted suicide, Linda Ganzini, Elizabeth R. Goy, and Steven K. Dobscha conducted a study to determine family members' perceptions of the reasons behind these requests and published their findings in "Why Oregon Patients Request Assisted Death: Family Members' Views" (*Journal of General Internal Medicine*, vol. 23, no. 2, February 2008). Their findings are similar to the results of studies previously cited in this chapter. According to family members, the most important reasons their loved ones requested assisted suicide was to control the circumstances of their death, because they feared not only a loss of dignity but also a poor quality of life with little independence and ability to care for themselves in the future. Conversely, family members reported that the least important reasons their loved ones requested assisted suicide included depression, financial concerns, and poor social support.

SUPPORTERS OF ASSISTED SUICIDE
End-of-Life Choices

On July 21, 2003, the Hemlock Society officially became End-of-Life Choices. The organization advocates for legislation to allow Americans to live with the freedom of choosing a dignified death and informs and educates the public about the right to die.

End-Of-Life Choices was founded as the Hemlock Society in 1980 by Derek Humphry (1930–), a British journalist. In 1975 Humphry helped his wife take her own life to end the pain and suffering caused by her terminal bone cancer. Humphry recounted this incident in *Jean's Way: A Love Story* (1978). The book launched his career in the voluntary euthanasia movement two years later.

In 1991 Humphry published *Final Exit: The Practicalities of Self-Deliverance and Assisted Suicide for the Dying*. The suicide manual, which was on the *New York Times* best-seller list for eighteen weeks, gives explicit instructions on how to commit suicide. Even though Humphry insisted that his how-to book was written only for those who were terminally ill, and not for those suffering from depression, some physicians were concerned about how the book would affect those suffering from depression. In October 1991, while *Final Exit* was selling out at bookstores, Humphry's second wife, Ann Wickett, whom he had divorced the year before, committed suicide. She had been diagnosed with cancer and was reportedly depressed. The third edition of *Final Exit* was published in 2002.

Humphry retired from the Hemlock Society in 1992, but his more recent activities have also sparked controversy. In 1999 he recorded a video depicting a variety of methods for committing suicide. Though it had been available from the Hemlock Society USA for several months, the video drew even more criticism when it aired on public television in Oregon a number of times in 2000. Critics asserted that this airing provided dangerous information, particularly to people who were depressed or mentally ill and to children.

In 2004 Humphry published *The Good Euthanasia Guide 2004: Where, What, and Who in Choices in Dying*. Much of the book describes international suicide laws.

Jack Kevorkian

Jack Kevorkian (1928–) first earned the nickname "Dr. Death" when, as a medical resident, he would photograph patients at the time of death to gather data that would help him differentiate death from coma, shock, and fainting. During his study and residency, he suggested unconventional ideas, such as the harvesting of organs from death-row inmates. His career as a doctor was also "checkered" (Kevorkian's own word) and notable for controversy.

In the late 1980s Kevorkian retired from pathology work and pursued an interest in the concept of physician-assisted suicide, becoming one of its best-known and most passionate advocates. He constructed the Mercitron, a machine that would allow a patient to press a red button and self-administer a lethal dose of poisonous potassium chloride, along with thiopental, a painkiller. Raphael Cohen-Almagor notes in "A Circumscribed Plea for Voluntary Physician-Assisted Suicide" (*Annals of the New York Academy of Sciences*, vol. 913, no. 1, September 2000) that Kevorkian claims to have assisted in over 130 suicides.

The first patient to commit suicide with Kevorkian's assistance and his Mercitron was Janet Adkins. Adkins, a Hemlock Society member, sought Kevorkian's aid because she did not want to wait until she lost her cognitive abilities to Alzheimer's disease. In June 1990 Adkins committed suicide in Kevorkian's van in a public campground.

In 1991 Kevorkian assisted in the deaths of two Michigan women on the same day. Sherry Miller, aged forty-three, had multiple sclerosis, and Marjorie Wantz, aged fifty-eight, complained of a painful pelvic disease. Neither one was terminally ill, but court findings showed that they both suffered from depression. In 1996 Kevorkian was tried for the assisted deaths of Miller and Wantz under the common law that considers assisted suicide illegal. Common law against assisted suicide means there is a precedent of customs, usage, and court decisions that support prosecution of an individual assisting in a suicide. Kevorkian was acquitted.

He continued to draw media attention with increasingly controversial actions. In February 1998 twenty-one-year-old Roosevelt Dawson, a paralyzed university student, became the youngest person to commit suicide with Kevorkian's help. In June 1998 Kevorkian announced that he was donating kidneys from Joseph Tushkowski, a quadriplegic whose death he had assisted. His actions were denounced by transplant program leaders, medical ethicists, and most of the public. The organs were refused by all medical centers and transplant teams.

In October 1998 Kevorkian euthanized fifty-two-year-old Thomas Youk, a man afflicted with Lou Gehrig's disease, at the patient's request. Kevorkian videotaped the death and gave the video to the CBS television show *60 Minutes* for broadcast. The death was televised nationwide in November 1998 during primetime and included an interview with Kevorkian. He taunted Oakland County, Michigan, prosecutors to file charges against him. They did, and Kevorkian was convicted of second-degree murder in March 1999. On April 13, 1999, the seventy-year-old retired pathologist was sentenced to ten to twenty-five years in prison. While in prison, Kevorkian staged three hunger strikes and was subjected to force-feeding by prison officials. Kevorkian was released from prison on June 1, 2007, due to good behavior, and in March 2008 he announced plans to run for Congress in Michigan.

ASSISTED SUICIDE'S DETRACTORS

In general, physician-assisted suicide is seen as being at odds with the work of doctors and nurses. In "Physician-Assisted Suicide" (*Annals of Internal Medicine*, vol. 135, no. 3, August 7, 2001), the American College of Physicians–American Society of Internal Medicine (ACP–ASIM) states its position on physician-assisted suicide. The organization notes that it does not support the legalization of physician-assisted suicide. In addition, the ACP–ASIM explains that not only would the routine practice of physician-assisted suicide raise serious ethical concerns but also it "would undermine the patient-physician relationship and the trust necessary to sustain it."

In 2005 the ACP again officially opposed physician-assisted suicide. The organization's formal position statement on this topic was published within the fifth edition of *Ethics Manual* (http://www.acponline.org/running_practice/ethics/manual/ethicman5th.htm). The statement reads:

> The College does not support legalization of physician-assisted suicide. After much consideration, the College concluded that making physician-assisted suicide legal raised serious ethical, clinical, and social concerns and that the practice might undermine patient trust and distract from reform in end of life care. The College was also concerned with the risks that legalization posed to vulnerable populations, including poor persons, patients with dementia, disabled persons, those

from minority groups that have experienced discrimination, those confronting costly chronic illnesses, or very young children. One state, Oregon, has legalized the practice of physician-assisted suicide, and its experience is being reviewed. Other states might legalize this practice, but the major emphasis of the College and its members, including those who might lawfully participate in the practice, must focus on ensuring that all persons facing serious illness can count on good care through to the end of life, with prevention or relief of suffering, commitment to human dignity, and support for the burdens borne by family and friends. Physicians and patients must continue to search together for answers to the problems posed by the difficulties of living with serious illness before death, without violating the physician's personal and professional values, and without abandoning the patient to struggle alone.

In 1994 the American Nurses Association's (ANA; 2008, http://www.nursingworld.org/MainMenuCategories/HealthcareandPolicyIssues/ANAPositionStatements/EthicsandHumanRights.aspx) position statements on assisted suicide and active euthanasia were adopted by its board of directors. The ANA "believes that the nurse should not participate in assisted suicide. Such an act is in violation of the Code for Nurses with Interpretive Statements (Code for Nurses) and the ethical traditions of the profession. Nurses, individually and collectively, have an obligation to provide comprehensive and compassionate end-of-life care which includes the promotion of comfort and the relief of pain, and at times, forgoing life-sustaining treatments." The ANA also "believes that the nurse should not participate in active euthanasia because such an act is in direct violation of the Code for Nurses with Interpretive Statements (Code for Nurses), the ethical traditions and goals of the profession, and its covenant with society. Nurses have an obligation to provide timely, humane, comprehensive and compassionate end-of-life care."

The American Medical Association (AMA) updated its position statement on physician-assisted suicide in 1996. The AMA (2007, http://www.ama-assn.org/apps/pf_new/pf_online?f_n=browse&doc=policyfiles/HnE/E-2.211.HTM) states: "Allowing physicians to participate in assisted suicide would cause more harm than good. Physician-assisted suicide is fundamentally incompatible with the physician's role as healer, would be difficult or impossible to control, and would pose serious societal risks."

THE BATTLE OVER LEGALIZING PHYSICIAN-ASSISTED SUICIDE

As of May 2008, Oregon was the only state with a law allowing physician-assisted suicide and then only in limited circumstances. Attempts to allow assisted suicide have been defeated in California, Maine, Michigan, Washington, and Wyoming. In addition, an assisted suicide proposal was shelved in the Hawaii legislature.

The Oregon Death with Dignity Act

In November 1994 Oregon voters approved Measure 16 by a vote of 51% to 49%, making Oregon the first state in the Union to legalize physician-assisted suicide. Under the Oregon Death with Dignity Act (ODDA), a mentally competent adult resident of Oregon who is terminally ill (likely to die within six months) may request a prescription for a lethal dose of medication to end his or her life. At least two physicians must concur on the terminal diagnosis, and the patient must request the medication in writing, witnessed by two individuals who are neither related to the patient nor are caregivers of the patient. The patient must take the medication him- or herself.

Between 1994 and 1997 the ODDA was kept on hold due to legal challenges. In November 1997 Oregonians voted to defeat a measure to repeal the 1994 law. Immediately after this voter reaffirmation of the ODDA, the U.S. Drug Enforcement Administration (DEA) warned Oregon doctors that they could be arrested or have their medical licenses revoked for prescribing lethal doses of drugs. The DEA administrator Thomas Constantine (1938–), who was under pressure from some members of Congress, stated that prescribing a drug for suicide would be a violation of the Controlled Substances Act (CSA) of 1970 because assisted suicide was not a "legitimate medical purpose." Janet Reno (1938–), who was then the U.S. attorney general, overruled Constantine and decided that that portion of the CSA would not apply to states that legalize assisted suicide. Those opposed to the practice observed that Reno's ruling was inconsistent with other rulings, citing the government's opposite ruling in states that have legalized marijuana for medical use. (Reno maintained that the prescription of marijuana was still illegal, regardless of its medicinal value.)

In response to the DEA decision, Congress moved toward the passage of the Pain Relief Promotion Act. This law would promote the use of federally controlled drugs for the purpose of palliative care but would prevent their use for euthanasia and assisted suicide. In 2000 the U.S. House of Representatives passed the bill, but the U.S. Senate did not. The act never became law.

On November 6, 2001, John D. Ashcroft (1942–), who succeeded Reno as the U.S. attorney general, overturned Reno's 1998 ruling that prohibited the DEA from acting against physicians who use drugs under the ODDA. Ashcroft said that taking the life of terminally ill patients is not a "legitimate medical purpose" for federally controlled drugs. The Oregon Medical Association and the Washington State Medical Association opposed Ashcroft's ruling, and even physicians opposed to assisted suicide expressed concern that the ruling might compromise patient care and that any DEA investigation might discourage physicians from prescribing pain medication to patients in need.

The state of Oregon disagreed so vehemently with Ashcroft's interpretation of the CSA that on November 7, 2001, Oregon's attorney general filed suit, claiming that Ashcroft was acting unconstitutionally. A November 8, 2001, restraining order allowed the ODDA to remain in effect while the case was tried.

On April 17, 2002, Judge Robert E. Jones (1927–) of the U.S. District Court for the District of Oregon ruled in favor of the ODDA. His decision read, in part:

State statutes, state medical boards, and state regulations control the practice of medicine. The CSA was never intended, and the [U.S. Department of Justice] and DEA were never authorized, to establish a national medical practice or act as a national medical board. To allow an attorney general—an appointed executive whose tenure depends entirely on whatever administration occupies the White House—to determine the legitimacy of a particular medical practice without a specific congressional grant of such authority would be unprecedented and extraordinary.... Without doubt there is tremendous disagreement among highly respected medical practitioners as to whether assisted suicide or hastened death is a legitimate medical practice, but opponents have been heard and, absent a specific prohibitive federal statute, the Oregon voters have made the legal, albeit controversial, decision that such a practice is legitimate in this sovereign state.

The Justice Department appealed the ruling to the Ninth Circuit Court of Appeals. On May 26, 2004, the court stopped Ashcroft's attempts to override the Oregon law. The divided three-judge panel ruled that Ashcroft overstepped his authority when he declared that physicians who prescribe lethal drug doses are in violation of the CSA and when he instructed the DEA to prosecute the physicians. In addition, the court noted that Ashcroft's interpretation of the CSA violated Congress's intent.

In February 2005 the U.S. Supreme Court agreed to hear the Bush administration's challenge of the ODDA. On January 17, 2006, the Court let stand Oregon's physician-assisted suicide law. The High Court held that the CSA "does not allow the Attorney General to prohibit doctors from prescribing regulated drugs for use in physician-assisted suicide under state law permitting the procedure." Writing for the majority, Justice Anthony M. Kennedy (1936–) stated that both Ashcroft and Alberto Gonzales (1955–), who replaced Ashcroft as the U.S. attorney general, did not have the power to override the Oregon physician-assisted suicide law. Kennedy also added that it should not be the attorney general who determines what is a "legitimate medical purpose" for the administration of drugs, because the job description for the attorney general does not include making health and medical policy.

ANALYSIS OF THE EFFECTS OF THE ODDA. In March 1998 an Oregon woman in her mid-eighties who had terminal breast cancer ended her life with a lethal dose of barbiturates. Hers was the first known death under the ODDA. By the end of 2006, a total of 292 people had reportedly committed suicide with a doctor's assistance under the ODDA. According to the Oregon Department of Human Services, in *Summary of Oregon's Death with Dignity Act—2006* (March 2007, http://egov.oregon.gov/DHS/ph/pas/docs/year9.pdf), sixty-five Oregon patients requested and received lethal medications in 2006. Of these patients, thirty-five took the medications and died in 2006. In addition, eleven patients with prescriptions from an earlier year took their medications and died, bringing the total of DWDA deaths to forty-six in 2006. (See Figure 6.2.) Prescriptions for lethal medication increased every year from 1998 to 2003 and have since leveled off.

Table 6.9 shows that over 90% of patients who died under the ODDA did so at home. A small percentage died in long-term care or other similar facilities. Other than a few instances in which the lethal medication was regurgitated, medical complications have been few.

EUTHANASIA AND PHYSICIAN-ASSISTED SUICIDE IN EUROPE

The Netherlands

Euthanasia became legal in the Netherlands on April 10, 2001. Before that date, active euthanasia was a criminal offense under article 293 of the Dutch Penal Code, which read, "He who takes the life of another person on this person's explicit and serious request will be punished with imprisonment of up to twelve years or a fine of the fifth category." At the same time, however, section 40 of the same penal code stated that an individual was not punishable if he or she was driven by "an irresistible force" (legally known as force majeure) to put another person's welfare above the law. This might include a circumstance in which a physician is confronted with the conflict between the legal duty of not taking a life and the humane duty to end a patient's intolerable suffering.

ORIGIN OF OPEN PRACTICE. In 1971 Geertruida Postma granted an elderly nursing home patient's request to die by injecting the patient with morphine and ending her life. The patient was her seventy-eight-year-old mother, who was partially paralyzed and was tied to a chair to keep her from falling. Postma was found guilty of murder, but her penalty consisted of a one-week suspended jail sentence and one-year probation. This light sentence encouraged other physicians to come forward, admitting that they had also assisted in patients' suicides.

Two years later the Royal Dutch Medical Association announced that, should a physician assist in the death of a terminally ill patient, it was up to the court to decide if the physician's action could be justified by "a conflict of duties." In Alkmaar, Netherlands, Piet Schoonheim helped the ninety-five-year-old Marie Barendregt to die in 1982 by using a lethal injection. Barendregt, who was severely

FIGURE 6.2

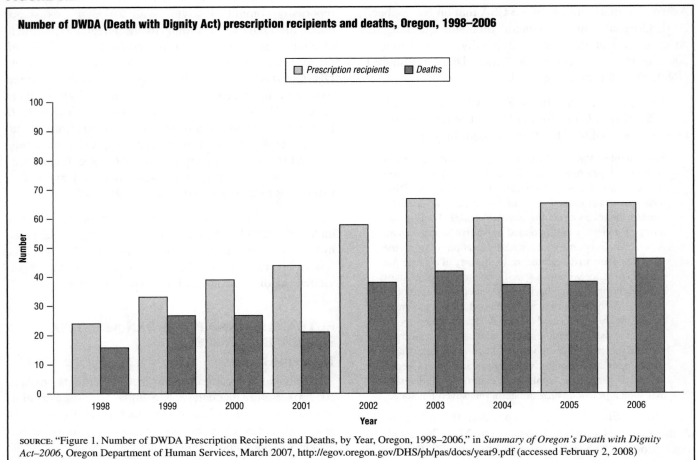

Number of DWDA (Death with Dignity Act) prescription recipients and deaths, Oregon, 1998–2006

SOURCE: "Figure 1. Number of DWDA Prescription Recipients and Deaths, by Year, Oregon, 1998–2006," in *Summary of Oregon's Death with Dignity Act–2006*, Oregon Department of Human Services, March 2007, http://egov.oregon.gov/DHS/ph/pas/docs/year9.pdf (accessed February 2, 2008)

disabled, had initially signed an advance directive refusing artificial (life-prolonging) treatment. Schoonheim assisted in Barendregt's death with the knowledge of the patient's son and after consultation with two independent physicians. In 1984 the Dutch Supreme Court, ruling on this well-known Alkmaar case (the court case is referred to by the name of the city where the trial took place), found Schoonheim not guilty of murder.

Since then, until euthanasia was legalized, each euthanasia case brought under prosecution was judged on its individual circumstances. The force majeure defense ensured acquittal, while compliance with certain guidelines for performing euthanasia laid down by the Royal Dutch Medical Association and the Dutch courts in 1984 protected physicians from prosecution.

On April 10, 2001, the Dutch Parliament voted forty-six to twenty-eight to legalize physician-assisted suicide by passing the Termination of Life on Request and Assisted Suicide (Review Procedures) Act. Arguments in favor of the bill included public approval ratings of 90%. In May 2001 the results of a Dutch public opinion poll revealed that nearly half of respondents favored making lethal drugs available to older adults who no longer wanted to live.

MONITORING OF EUTHANASIA AND PHYSICIAN-ASSISTED SUICIDE. Bregje D. Onwuteaka-Philipsen et al. explain in "Dutch Experience of Monitoring Euthanasia" (*British Medical Journal*, vol. 331, no. 7518, September 24, 2005) that euthanasia and physician-assisted suicide have been monitored in the Netherlands since 1994, with the first review procedure given approval by the Dutch government in 1991. Even though euthanasia and physician-assisted suicide were not yet legal in that country, physicians were required to report cases and would not be prosecuted if they met the requirements for prudent practice that had been developed. The substantive requirements asserted that "the patient's request must be voluntary and well considered," "the patient's condition must be unbearable and hopeless," "no acceptable alternatives for treatment are available," and "the method is medically and technically appropriate." The procedural requirements asserted that "another doctor is consulted before proceeding" and that "the case is reported as an unnatural death." The procedure was evaluated in 1996, and a new system was introduced in 1998, but euthanasia and physician-assisted suicide remained illegal.

In 2001, along with legalizing euthanasia and physician-assisted suicide, the Termination of Life on Request and

Assisted Suicide (Review Procedures) Act established a revised review procedure. Throughout the review changes, the requirements for prudent practice did not change and were the main focus of review. The purpose of the review process was to have physicians report on euthanasia and physician-assisted suicide and to follow prudent practice.

Euthanasia in Belgium

The Belgian Act on Euthanasia passed in 2002 after the Dutch law, making Belgium the second country to legalize euthanasia. The law applies to competent adults who have an incurable illness causing unbearable, constant suffering and to patients in a persistent vegetative state who made their wishes known within the previous five years in front of two witnesses. It allows someone to terminate the life of another at his or her "voluntary, well-considered, and repeated" request, but does not allow physician-assisted suicide. All acts of euthanasia must be reported.

Switzerland Allows Assisted Suicide but Not Euthanasia

Euthanasia is not legal medical treatment in Switzerland as it is in Oregon, Belgium, and the Netherlands, but the country does not punish suicide assisted by physicians or people with no medical training if they conducted the act for altruistic reasons. Assisted suicide is a crime if motivated by financial gain or by selfish or negative reasons.

Assisted suicide is not considered an appropriate part of medical practice by the Swiss Academy of Medical Sciences, so physicians generally do not assist in suicides of the terminally ill. Members of EXIT (the Swiss Society for Humane Dying) are allowed to help terminally ill Swiss residents commit suicide in their home. In January 2006 the Vaud University Hospital Center in Lausanne began allowing EXIT to help patients already admitted to the hospital and who could no longer go home to take their own life.

CHAPTER 7

ADVANCE DIRECTIVES

The movement toward greater patient participation in health care that began in the 1960s and 1970s focused increasing attention on patients' desire for control over nearly all aspects of medical care, including critical care. Dramatic medical and technological advances further underscored the importance of planning ahead for end-of-life care. Baby boomers (the generation of people born between 1946 and 1964), on the threshold of aging and faced with caring for elderly parents, became increasingly aware of the need to make provisions for their own future medical treatment. Advance directives filled this need.

ADVANCE DIRECTIVES
What Are Advance Directives?

Advance directives are legal documents that help protect patients' rights of self-determination (the right to make one's own medical decisions, including the right to accept or refuse treatment). These documents are a person's requests concerning health care, should he or she be unable to do so when the need arises due to physical or mental disabilities. There are two main documents in an advance directive: a living will and a durable power of attorney for health care.

A living will is a legal document stating a person's wishes for dealing with life-sustaining medical procedures in case he or she is debilitated and cannot speak for him- or herself. A living will is different from a last will and testament. A last will and testament deals with property and comes into effect after a person has died. A living will deals with health and personal care and is in effect when a person is alive. A durable power of attorney, the other part of an advance directive, is a legal document in which one person gives another (called the agent or proxy) legal authority to act or speak on his or her behalf should he or she become debilitated and not able to make decisions on his or her own.

A Brief History of Advance Directives

In 1967 the Euthanasia Society of America and the attorney Luis Kutner (1908–1993), the cofounder of Amnesty International, devised the first living will. California was the first state to recognize the legality of living wills (1976) and the durable power of attorney for health care (1984). The California Natural Death Act of 1976 states that to preserve "dignity and privacy ... any adult person may execute a directive directing the withholding or withdrawal of life-sustaining procedures in a terminal condition." As of October 2007, all fifty states and the District of Columbia had laws recognizing the use of living wills and durable powers of attorney for health care, although the provisions of these laws varied from state to state. (See Table 7.1.)

LIVING WILLS

As mentioned previously, a living will is one part of an advance directive. It is a document that outlines a patient's preferences about end-of-life medical treatments in the event that he or she is unable to communicate or make his or her own decisions. Laws regulating living wills vary from state to state. For example, Abigail Petersen explains in "Survey of States' Health Care Decision-Making Standards" (*BIFOCAL: Bar Associations in Focus on Aging and the Law*, vol. 28, no. 4, April 2007) that in 2007 twenty-seven states placed limits on allowing the withdrawal of life support from pregnant patients. In the most restrictive states a living will request to withhold or withdraw life support would not be honored if the patient was a pregnant woman. In some states, however, pregnancy limitations were less restrictive. They might state, for example, that life support could be withdrawn from a pregnant patient, but only if she had made her wishes explicit in her living will to withdraw life support even if she were pregnant.

TABLE 7.1

Health care power of attorney and combined advance directive legislation, October 2007

State	Type	Form	Limits on agent's powers	Prohibited agents	Formalities of execution	Prohibited witnesses	Authority over autopsy, organ donation or remains	Comity provision
1. ALABAMA ALA. STAT. §22–8A-2 to -14 (West 2007). "Natural Death Act" *See also* Durable Power of Attorney Act, §26–1–2 *Separate living will statute:* NO	Combined advance directive *[modeled on UHCDA]**	YES Must be substantially followed	• Mental health facility admission and treatments • Psycho-surgery • Sterilization • Abortion • Pregnancy limitation • Nutrition & hydration — refusal permitted if expressly authorized	• Indiv. provider* * Exception for relatives employed by the provider	• 2 or more witnesses age 19 or older	• Minor = 18 • Agent • Proxy signor • Relative • Heir • Person responsible for care costs	NO	YES
2. ALASKA ALASKA STAT. §13.52.010 to -.395 (West 2007) "Health Care Decisions Act" *Separate living will statute:* NO	Combined advance directive *[modeled on UHCDA]* plus incorporates mental health directive	YES Optional	• Psycho-surgery* • Sterilization* • Abortion • Removal of bodily organs* • Temporary admission to mental health facility* • Electro-convulsive therapy* • Psychotropic medication* • Life-sustaining procedures* • Pregnancy limitation * • Consent/refusal permitted only if expressly authorized.	• Facility provider* * Exception for relatives	• 2 witnesses or notarized	• Agent • Facility provider One may not be: • Relative • Heir	Organ donation	YES
3. ARIZONA Ariz. Rev. Stat. Ann. §36–3201 to -3262 (West 2007)	Combined advance directive	YES Optional	None specified	None specified	• 1 witness or notarized	• Agent • Provider • If only one witness, person may not be: • Relative • Heir	Autopsy Organ donation	YES
4. ARKANSAS Ark. Code. Ann. §20–13–104 (2007) "Durable Power of Attorney for Health Care Act" *See also* Ark. Code Ann. §20–17–201 to -218 (proxy appointment in living will declaration)	Special DPA	NO (But proxy appointment in living will declaration does have optional form)	• Life-sustaining treatment— unless the DPA incorporates a proxy authorization from statute, §20-17-202 the living will declaration • Pregnancy limitation	None specified	• 2 witnesses	None specified	NO	YES, if part of a (living will) declaration
5. CALIFORNIA Cal. Probate Code §4600 to -4948 806 (West 2007) *Separate living will statute: NO*	Combined advance directive	YES Optional	• Civil commitment • Electro-convulsive therapy • Psycho-surgery • Sterilization • Abortion	• Supervising indiv. provider* • Facility provider* • Conservator - unless conditions are met. * Exception for relatives who are employees of	• 2 witnesses or notarized • Special institutional requirements	• Agent • Indiv. provider • Facility provider One may not be: • Relative • Heir	Autopsy Organ donation Disposition of remains	YES

TABLE 7.1

Health care power of attorney and combined advance directive legislation, October 2007 [CONTINUED]

State	Type	Form	Limits on agent's powers	Prohibited agents	Formalities of execution	Prohibited witnesses	Authority over autopsy, organ donation or remains	Comity provision
6. COLORADO Colo. Rev. Stat. §15–14–503 to –509 (West 2007) "Colorado Patient Autonomy Act" See also §§15–14–501 to –502 and §15–14–601 to –611 re DPA *Separate living will statute: NO* Rev.Stat. §15–18–101 to –113	Special DPA	NO	None specified	None specified	None specified	N/A	NO	YES
7. CONNECTICUT Conn. Gen. Stat. §19a–570 to –580d (West 2007) See also Conn. Gen. Stat. §1–43 et seq. (2007) (statutory short form DPA) and § 1–56r (designation of person for decision-making) *Separate living will statute: NO*	Combined advance directive	YES Optional	• None specified (but authority is described as authority to "convey" principal's wishes, rather than to make decisions for principal.) • Pregnancy limitation	• Facility provider* • Attending physician • Administrator or employee of gov't agency financially responsible for care* * Exception for relatives	• 2 witnesses • Special institutional requirements	• Agent	NO	NO
8. DELAWARE Del. Code Ann. tit. 16, §§2501 to 2518 (2007) *Separate living will statute: NO*	Combined advance directive *[modeled on UHCDA]**	YES Optional	• Pregnancy limitation	• Residential LTC facility provider* * Exception for relatives	• 2 witnesses • Special institutional requirements	• Facility provider* • Relative • Heir • Creditor • Person responsible for care costs	NO	YES
9. DISTRICT OF COLUMBIA D.C. Code Ann. §21–2201 to –2213 (2007) *Separate living will statute:* D.C. Code Ann. §7–621 to –630 (2007)	Special DPA	YES Optional	• Decision to medicate defendant to render him/her competent to stand trial	• Indiv. provider • Facility provider	• 2 witnesses	• Principal • Individual provider • Facility provider • One may not be relative or heir	NO	NO
10. FLORIDA Fla. Stat. Ann. §765.101 to –.404 (West 2007) *Separate living will statute: NO*	Combined advance directive	YES Optional	• Mental health facility admission* • Electro-convulsive therapy* • Psycho-surgery* • Sterilization* • Abortion • Experimental treatments not approved by IRB* • Life-sustaining procedures while pregnant* • Preganancy limitation* * Consent/refusal permissible if expressly authorized	None specified	• 2 witnesses	• Agent • One may not be spouse or relative	Autopsy (see F.S.A. §872.04) -Organ donation	YES
11. GEORGIA Ga. Code Ann. §31–36–1 to –13 (West 2007) *Separate living will statute:* §31–32–1–12 (West 2007)	Special DPA	YES Optional	• Mental health facility admission or treatment under Title 37 of code • Psycho-surgery • Sterilization	• Indiv. provider directly or indirectly involved	• 2 witnesses • Special institutional requirements	None	Autopsy Organ donation -Disposition of remains	NO
12. HAWAII Hawaii Rev. Stat. §327E-1 to -16 (2007) *See also* Hawaii Rev. Stat. §551D-2.5 re DPA for health care *Separate living will statute: NO*	Combined advance directive *[modeled on UHCDA]**	YES Optional	None specified	• Facility provider* * Exception for relatives	• 2 witnesses or notarized	• Indiv. provider • Facility provider • Agent One may not be • Relative • Heir	No	YES

TABLE 7.1

Health care power of attorney and combined advance directive legislation, October 2007 [CONTINUED]

State	Type	Form	Limits on agent's powers	Prohibited agents	Formalities of execution	Prohibited witnesses	Authority over autopsy, organ donation or remains	Comity provision
13. IDAHO Idaho Code §39–4501 to –4509 (West 2007), specifically §39-4505. *Separate living will statute: NO*	Combined advance directive	YES Optional	Pregnancy limitation	• Indiv. provider* • Community care facility provider* * Exception for relatives who are employees of	2 witnesses or notarized	• Agent • Indiv. provider • Community care facility One may not be relative or heir	No	No
14. ILLINOIS 755 ILCS 45/4–1 through 4–12 (West 2007) *Separate LW statute:* 755 ILCS 35/1 to 35/10	Special DPA	YES Optional	None specified	• Indiv. provider	None specified	None specified	Autopsy Organ donation Disposition of remains	Yes
15. INDIANA Ind. Code §§30–5–1–1 to 30 –5–5–19 (West 2007), specifically §30-5–5–16 and -17, AND Ind. Code §§16-36–1–1 thru -19, specifically §16-36 –1–6 and -7 *Separate LW statute:* Ind. Code Ann. §16–36–4–1 to-21 Ind. Code Ann. §16–36–1–1 to -14 (West 2007)	General DPA with health powers Health care consent statute including appointment of health care representative	NO but mandatory language for authority re life-sustaining treatment (§30–5–5–17) NO but mandatory language above is incorporated by reference at §16-36–1–14	None specified None specified	None specified None specified	• Notarized or one witness • 1 witness	Agent • Agent	Autopsy Organ donation Disposition of remains (but powers terminate upon death of principal) NO	Yes NO
16. IOWA Iowa Code Ann. § 144B. 1 to .12 (West 2007) *Separate LW statute:* Iowa Code Ann. §144A.1 to .12	Special DPA	YES Optional	None specified	• Indiv. provider* * Exception for relatives	2 witnesses or notarized	• Agent • Indiv. provider One may not be relative	NO	YES
17. KANSAS Kan. Stat. Ann. §58–625 to 632 (2003) *Separate LW statute:* Kan. Stat. Ann. §65–28,101 to 28,109	Special DPA	YES Must be substantially followed	• Cannot revoke previous living will	• Indiv. provider* • Facility provider* * Exception for relatives & religious community members	2 witnesses or notarized	• Agent • Relative • Heir • Person responsible for care costs	Autopsy Organ donation Disposition of remains	YES
18. KENTUCKY Ky. Rev. Stat. §311.621 to .643 (Baldwin 2007) *Separate LW statute: NO*	Combined advanced directive (but called "Living Will Directive")	YES Must be substantially followed	• Nutrition & hydration* • Pregnancy limitation • Refusal permissible if specified conditions are met	• Facility provider* * Exception for relatives	• 2 witnesses or notarized	• Relative • Facility provider • Attg. physician • Heir • Person responsible for care costs	NO	NO
19. LOUISIANA La. Rev. Stat. Ann 40:1299 .58.1 to .10 (West 2007) See also DPA ("Procuration") statute: La. Civ. Code Ann. Art 2985 to 3034 (West 2007), specifically art. 2997 *Separate LW statute: NO*	Proxy contained in living will statute	YES Optional	• Powers implicitly limited to executing a living will declaration on behalf of principal. However, a DPA (a "procuration") may confer health decision powers generally on an agent (a "mandatory")	None specified	2 witnesses	• Relative • Heir	NO	YES

TABLE 7.1

Health care power of attorney and combined advance directive legislation, October 2007 [CONTINUED]

State	Type	Form	Limits on agent's powers	Prohibited agents	Formalities of execution	Prohibited witnesses	Authority over autopsy, organ donation or remains	Comity provision
20. MAINE Me. Rev. Stat. Ann. tit. 18A, §5–801 to §5–817 (West 2007) *Separate LW statute: NO*	Combined advance directive *[modeled on UHCDA]**	YES Optional	• Mental health facility admission, consent permissible if expressly authorized	• LTC facility provider* * Exception for relatives	• 2 witnesses	None specified	NO	YES
21. MARYLAND Md. Code Ann. [Health-Gen.] §5–601 to -618 (2007) *Separate LW statute: NO*	Combined advance directive	YES Optional	None specified	• Facility provider* * Exception for relatives	• 2 witnesses • Also recognizes oral directive to a physician with one witness	• Agent • One must not be: heir, or have any other financial interest in person's death	NO	YES
22. MASSACHUSETTS Mass. Gen. Laws Ann. Ch. 201D (West 2007) *Separate LW statute: None*	Special DPA	NO	None specified	• Facility provider* * Exception for relatives	• 2 witnesses	• Agent	NO	YES
23. MICHIGAN Mich. Comp. Laws Ann. §700.5506 to 5512 (West 2007) *Separate LW statute: None*	Special DPA	Only for agent's acceptance	• Pregnancy limitation • Life-sustaining procedures • Refusal permissible if expressly authorized	None specified	• 2 witnesses Agent must accept in writing before acting as agent ("patient advocate")	• Agent • Heir • Relative • Indiv. provider • Facility provider • Employee of life/health insurance provider for patient	Organ donation	NO
24. MINNESOTA Minn. Stat. Ann. §145C.01 to .16 (West 2007) *Separate LW statute: Minn. Stat. §145B.01 to .17 (West 2007)*	Combined advance directive	YES Optional	None specified	• Indiv. provider* • Facility provider* * Exception for relatives	• 2 witnesses or notarized	• Agent • One may not be provider	Organ donation Disposition of remains	YES
25. MISSISSIPPI Miss. Code Ann. §41–41–201 to -229 (West 2007) *Separate LW statute: NO*	Combined advance directive *[modeled on UHCDA]*	YES Optional	• Mental health facility admission, consent permissible if expressly authorized	• LTC facility * Exception for relatives	• 2 witnesses or notarized	• Agent • Indiv. provider • Facility provider • One may not be relative or heir	NO	YES, but only if directive complies with this act
26. MISSOURI Mo. Ann. Stat. §404.800 - .872 (West 2007) and cross-referenced parts of §404.700 to .735 (DPA statute) *Separate LW statute: Mo. Ann. Stat. §459.010 to 459.055 (West 2007)*	Special DPA	NO	• Nutrition & hydration* * Refusal permissible if expressly authorized	• Att. physician* • Facility provider* * Exception for relatives and members of same religious community	• Must contain language of durability and be acknowledged as conveyance of real estate (§404.705)	None specified	NO	YES
27. MONTANA Mont. Code Ann. §50–9–101 to -206 (2007). Also incorporates by reference §72–5–501 and -502 (DPA statute) *Separate LW statute: NO* contained in living will statute: No	Proxy contained in living will statute	YES Optional	• Pregnancy limitation	None specified	• 2 witnesses under LW statute • DPA statute: none, although customarily notarized	None specified	NO	YES

TABLE 7.1

Health care power of attorney and combined advance directive legislation, October 2007 [CONTINUED]

State	Type	Form	Limits on agent's powers	Prohibited agents	Formalities of execution	Prohibited witnesses	Authority over autopsy, organ donation or remains	Comity provision
28. NEBRASKA Neb. Rev. Stat. §30-3401 to -3432 (2007) *Separate LW statute:* Neb. Rev. Stat. §20-401 to -416 (2007)	Special DPA	YES Optional	• Life-sustaining procedures* • Nutrition & hydration* • Pregnancy limitation * Refusal permissible if expressly authorized	• Att. physician* • Facility* • Any agent serving 10 or more principals* * Exception for relatives who are employees of.	• 2 witnesses or notarized	• Agent • Spouse • Relative • Heir • Att. physician • Insurer One may not be facility provider	NO	YES
29. NEVADA Nev. Rev. Stat. §449.800 to .860 (2007) *Separate LW statute:* Nev. Rev. Stat.449 .535 to 690 (2007) with proxy designation. NB. LW statute recognizes an agent under a regular DPA with authority to w/h or w/d life-sustaining treatment.	Special DPA	YES Form with disclosure statement must be substantially followed	• Mental health facility admission • Electro-convulsive therapy • Aversive intervention • Psycho-surgery • Sterilization • Abortion	• Indiv. provider* • Facility provider* * Exception for relatives	• 2 witnesses or notarized	• Agent • Indiv. provider • Facility provider • One may not be relative or heir	NO	NO
30. NEW HAMPSHIRE N.H. Rev. Stat. Ann. §137-J:1 to -J:16 (2007) *LW statute: Repealed*	Combined advanced directive	Form and disclosure statement must be substantially followed	• Mental health facility admission • Sterilization • Pregnancy limitation • Nutrition & hydration* * Refusal permissible if expressly authorized	• Facility provider* * Exception for relatives who are employees of	• 2 witnesses or notarized • Principal must acknowledge receipt of mandatory notice	• Agent • Spouse • Heir • AH physician • One may not be residential care provider	NO	YES
31. NEW JERSEY N.J. Stat. Ann. §26:2H-53 to -81 (West 2007) *Separate LW statute: NO*	Combined advance directive	NO	• None specified	• Att. physician • Facility provider * Exception for relatives	• 2 witnesses or notarized	• Agent	NO	YES
32. NEW MEXICO N.M. Stat. Ann. §24-7A -1 to -18 (West 2007) *Separate LW statute: NO*	Combined advance directive *[modeled on UHCDA]**	YES Optional	• Mental health facility admission	• LTC facility provider* * Exception for relatives	• 2 witnesses recommended, but not required	• None specified	NO	YES, but only if directive complies with this act
33. NEW YORK N.Y. Pub. Health Law §2980 to 2994 (McKinney 2007) *Separate LW statute: None*	Special DPA	YES Optional	• Nutrition & hydration* * Principal must make his/her wishes "reasonably known"	• Att. physician* • Facility provider* • Any agent serving 10 or more principals* * Exception for relatives who are employees of	• 2 witnesses • Special institutional requirements	• Agent	NO	YES
34. NORTH CAROLINA N.C. Gen. Stat. §32A-15 to -26 (2007) *Separate LW statute:* N.C. Gen. Stat. §90-320 to -322 (2007)	Special DPA	YES Optional	None specified	• Indiv. provider*	• 2 witnesses and notarized	• Relative • Heir • Att. physician • Facility provider • Creditor	YES (but authority terminates on death of principal)	NO

TABLE 7.1

Health care power of attorney and combined advance directive legislation, October 2007 (CONTINUED)

State	Type	Form	Limits on agent's powers	Prohibited agents	Formalities of execution	Prohibited witnesses	Authority over autopsy, organ donation or remains	Comity provision
35. NORTH DAKOTA N.D. Cent. Code §23–06.5–01 to –18 (2007)	Special DPA	YES Optional	• Mental health facility admission >45 days • Psycho-surgery • Abortion • Sterilization	• Indiv. provider* • Facility provider* * Exception for relatives who are employees of	• 2 witnesses or notarized • Agent must accept in writing	• Agent* • Spouse* • Heir* • Relative* • Creditor* One may not be: • Indiv. provider • Facility provider * Also disqualifies notary	NO	YES
36. OHIO Ohio Rev. Code §1337.11 to 17 (West 2007) *Separate LW statute:* Ohio Rev. Code §2133.01 to .15 (West 2007)	Special DPA	Only for mandatory disclosure statement	• Life-sustaining procedures* • Nutrition & hydration* • Pregnancy limitation* • Refusal permissible if specified conditions are met	• Att. physician* • Nursing home administrator* *Exception for relatives who are employees of	• 2 witnesses or notarized	• Agent • Relative • Att. physician • Nursing home administrator	NO	YES
37. OKLAHOMA Okla. Stat. Ann. tit. 63, §3101.1 to .16 (West 2007) *Separate LW statute: NO*	Combined advance directive	YES Must be substantially followed	• Nutrition & hydration* • Pregnancy limitation *Refusal permissible if expressly authorized	None specified	• 2 witnesses	• Heir	NO	YES
38. OREGON Or. Rev. Stat. §127.505 to .660 and 127.995 (2007) *Separate LW statute: NO*	Combined advance directive	YES Must be followed. But recognizes that any other form "constitutes evidence of the patient's desires and interests"	• Mental health facility admission • Electro-convulsive therapy • Psycho-surgery • Sterilization • Abortion • Life-sustaining procedures* • Nutrition & hydration* *Refusal permissible if expressly authorized or if specified conditions are met	• Attending physician* • Facility provider* * Exception for relatives	• 2 witnesses • Agent must accept in writing • Special institutional requirements	• Agent • Att. physician • One may not be relative, heir, or facility provider	NO	YES
39. PENNSYLVANIA Pa. Stat. Ann. tit. 20, §5421 to §5488 (West 2007)	Combined advance directive	YES Optional	• Nutrition & hydration • Pregnancy limitation *Refusal permissible if expressly authorized or specified conditions are met	• Indiv. provider* • Facility provider* * Exception for relatives	• 2 witnesses	• Person who signs AD on principal's behalf	Autopsy Organ donation Disposition of remains	YES
40. RHODE ISLAND R.I. Gen. Laws §23–4. 10–1 to –12 (2007) *Separate LW statute:* R.I. Gen Laws §23–4.11–1 to –15 (2007)	Special DPA	YES Not clear whether optional or mandatory	None specified	• Indiv. provider* • Community care facility* * Exception for relatives who are employees of	• 2 witnesses • Principal must be Rhode Island resident	• Agent • Indiv. provider • Community care facility • One may not be relative or heir	NO	YES

TABLE 7.1

Health care power of attorney and combined advance directive legislation, October 2007 [CONTINUED]

State	Type	Form	Limits on agent's powers	Prohibited agents	Formalities of execution	Prohibited witnesses	Authority over autopsy, organ donation or remains	Comity provision
41. SOUTH CAROLINA S.C. Code §62–5–501 to -505 (2007), particularly §62–5–504. *Separate LW statute:* S. C. Code §44–77–10 to -160 (also permits appointment of agent)	Special DPA (within general DPA statute)	YES Must be substantially followed (but conventional DPAs may also contain health powers)	• Nutrition & hydration "necessary for comfort care or alleviation of pain"* • Pregnancy limitation * Refusal permissible if expressly authorized	• Indiv. provider* • Facility provider* • Spouse of a provider* * Exception for relatives	• 2 witnesses	• Agent • Spouse • Relative • Heir • Attending physician • Creditor • Life insurance beneficiary • Person responsible for care costs • One may not be facility provider	Organ donation	YES
42. SOUTH DAKOTA S.D. Codified Laws §59–7–1 -9 (2007) See also §34–12C-1 to -8 (health care consent procedures) *Separate LW statute:* S.D. Codified Laws §34–12D-1 to -22 (2007)	General DPA that permits health decisions authority	NO permissible if	• Pregnancy limitation • Nutrition & hydration* * Refusal permissible if expressly authorized or other conditions are met	None specified	None specified	None specified	NO	YES
43. TENNESSEE Term. Code Ann §68–11–1801 to -1815 (2007) *Separate LW statute: NO*	Combined advance directive	NO	None specified	None specified	• 2 witnesses or notarized	• Agent • Provider • Facility • One may not be relative or heir	NO	YES
44. TEXAS Tex. [Health & Safety] Code Ann. §166.001 to -.166 (Vernon 2007) *Separate LW statute: NO*	(1) Special DPA (2) Proxy contained in LW	(1) Special DPA: (medical PoA): YES. Must be substantially followed plus mandatory disclosure statement (2) LW: YES Optional	• Mental health facility admission • Electro-convulsive therapy • Psycho-surgery • Abortion • Comfort care	• Indiv. provider* • Facility provider* * Exception for relatives who are employees of	• 2 witnesses	One may not be: • Agent • Att. physician • Relative • Facility • Heir • Creditor	NO	YES
45. UTAH Utah Code Ann. §75–2–1101 to -1119 (2007) *Separate LW statute: NO*	Special DPA	YES Must be substantially followed	• Life-sustaining procedures* • Pregnancy limitation * Agent makes health care decisions by executing a medical directive	None specified	• Notarized	None specified	NO	YES
46. VERMONT Vt. Stat. Ann. tit. 18, §5263 to 5278 (2007)	Combined advance directive	YES Disclosure statement must be substantially followed Form optional	• Mental health facility admission	• Indiv. provider* • Residential care provider* Funeral/crematory/ cemetery representative (if authorized to dispose of remains or donate organs) * Exception for relatives who are employees of	• Warning disclosure • 2 witnesses • Special institutional requirements	• Agent • Indiv. provider • Residential care provider • Spouse • Heir • Creditor • Funeral/crematory/ cemetery representative	Organ donation Disposition of remains	YES

TABLE 7.1
Health care power of attorney and combined advance directive legislation, October 2007 [CONTINUED]

State	Type	Form	Limits on agent's powers	Prohibited agents	Formalities of execution	Prohibited witnesses	Authority over autopsy, organ donation or remains	Comity provision
47. VIRGINIA Va. Code §54.1–2981 to -2993 (West 2007) *Separate LW statute: NO*	Combined advance directive	YES Optional	• Mental health facility • Psycho-surgery • Sterilization • Abortion • Decisions about "visitation" unless expressly authorized	None specified	• 2 witnesses	• Spouse • Relative	Organ donation	YES
48. WASHINGTON Wash. Rev. Code Ann. §11.94.010 to .900 (West 2007) *Separate LW statute:* Wash. Rev. Code Ann. § 70.122.010 to -.920 (West 2007)	General DPA	NO	Cross reference to guardianship law [RCWA 11.92.043(5)]: • Electro-convulsive therapy • Psycho-surgery • Other psychiatric • Amputation	• Indiv. provider* • Facility provider* * Exception for relatives	None specified	N/A	NO	YES
49. WEST VIRGINIA W. VA. Code Ann. §16–30–1 to -25 (West 2007) *Separate LW statute: No*	Combined advance directive (but maintains separate living will and medical power of attorney documents)	YES Optional	• Limit on agent's authority to revoke a pre-need funeral contract	• Indiv. provider* • Facility provider* * Exception for relatives who are employees of	• 2 witnesses and notarized	• Agent • Att. physician • Principal's signatory • Relative • Heir • Person responsible for care costs	Autopsy Organ donation Disposition of remains	YES
50. WISCONSIN Wis. Stat. Ann. §155.01 to .80 (West 2007) See DPA cross reference §243.07(6m) (West 2007) *Separate LW statute:* Wisc. Stat. Ann. §§l54.0l to -.l5 (West 2007)	Special DPA	YES Optional, but but discloser statement is mandatory	• Admission to facility for mental health/retardation or other listed conditions • Electro-convulsive therapy • Drastic mental health treatment • Admission to nursing home or residential facility— very limited unless expressly authorized in the document • Nutrition & hydradation* • Pregnancy limitation * Refusal permissible only if specified conditions are met	• Indiv. provider* • Facility provider* * Exception for relatives	• 2 witnesses	• Agent • Indiv. provider • Facility provider* • Relative • Heir • Person responsible for care costs * Exception for chaplains & social workers	Organ donation	YES
51. WYOMING Wyo. Stat. §35–22–401 to -416 (2004) *Separate LW statute:* Wyo. Stat §§35–22–101 to -109 (2004)	Combined advance directive	YES Optional	None specified	• Residential or community care provider* * Exception for relatives who are employees of	• 2 witnesses or notarized	• Agent • Indiv. provider • Facility provider	NO	NO
UNIFORM HEALTH-CARE DECISIONS ACT Separate LW statute: NO	Combined advance directive	YES Optional	• Mental health facility admission, consent permissible if expressly authorized	• LTC facility provider	• 2 witnesses recommended, but not required	None	NO	YES, but only if directive complies with this act

Abbreviations: LW = Living Will. DPA = Durable Power of Attorney. UHCDA = Uniform Health Care Decisions Act.

Note: The descriptions and limitations listed in this chart are broad characterizations for comparison purposes and not as precise quotations from legislative language.

SOURCE: "Health Care Power of Attorney and Combined Advance Directive Legislation—October 2007," American Bar Association, Commission on Legal Problems of the Elderly, 2007, http://www.abanet.org/aging/legislativeupdates/docs/HCPA-CHT_08.pdf (accessed March 10, 2008). Copyright © 2007 by the American Bar Association. Reprinted with permission.

Living wills enable people to list the types of medical treatments they want or do not want. It is therefore important for an individual contemplating a living will to know what these treatments involve. Some examples of life-prolonging treatments patients should consider when preparing a living will include cardiopulmonary resuscitation, mechanical ventilation, artificial nutrition and hydration, and kidney dialysis.

An advance directive form is included in the model Uniform Health Care Decisions Act (UHCDA). This model law was approved by the National Conference of Commissioners on Uniform State Laws in 1993 to provide some consistency among state advance directives and remained a model law as of October 2007. Its advance directive form offers several options that include treatments to prolong life. (See Table 7.2.) The states whose advance directives were modeled on the UHCDA are noted in the column "type" in Table 7.1.

Another form, called "Five Wishes," was developed in Florida by the nonprofit organization Aging with Dignity and is now distributed nationwide. The document probes legal and medical issues as well as spiritual and emotional ones. It even outlines small details, such as requests for favorite music to be played and poems to be read, and provides space for individuals to record their wishes for funeral arrangements. The document is relatively easy to complete because it uses simplified language rather than legal or medical jargon.

The 2007 edition of "Five Wishes" met living will or advance directive criteria in forty states and the District of Columbia. (See Figure 7.1.) It did not meet advance directive criteria in ten states: Alabama, Indiana, Kansas, Kentucky, Nevada, New Hampshire, Ohio, Oregon, Texas, and Utah. Other forms were necessary in these states, although the "Five Wishes" document could still serve as a guide for family and physicians.

Pro-Life Alternative to Living Wills

The National Right to Life Committee (NRLC) opposes active and passive euthanasia and offers an alternative to the standard living will. Called the "Will to Live" (http://www.nrlc.org/euthanasia/willtolive/index .html), it does not consider artificial nutrition and hydration as forms of medical treatment, but as basic necessities for the preservation of life.

DURABLE POWER OF ATTORNEY FOR HEALTH CARE

Even though living wills provide specific directions about medical treatment, most apply only to limited circumstances, such as terminal illness or permanent coma. Living wills cannot address every possible future medical situation. Many medical treatments require decision making, such as surgical procedures, diagnostic tests, blood transfusion, the use of antibiotics, radiation therapy, and chemotherapy.

A durable power of attorney for health care, also called a medical power of attorney, addresses this need. It is the other part of an advance directive and is generally more flexible than a living will. It allows individuals to appoint proxies (agents) who will use their judgment to respond to unforeseen situations based on their knowledge of the patient and the patient's values and beliefs. (See Table 7.2.) The role of this agent or proxy begins as soon as the physician certifies that a patient is incompetent to make his or her own decisions.

Because there is no uniform advance directive statute nationally, the rights of health-care agents vary across states. Limits on agents' powers in each state and the District of Columbia as of October 2007 are shown in Table 7.1.

In the Absence of a Durable Power of Attorney for Health Care

Physicians usually involve family members in medical decisions when the patient has not designated a health-care proxy in advance. This person is called a surrogate. Many states have surrogate consent laws for this purpose. Some have laws that designate the order in which family members may assume the role of surrogate decision maker. For example, the spouse may be the prime surrogate, followed by an adult child, then the patient's parent, and so on.

Petersen indicates that in 2007 thirty-one states specified a decision-making standard for surrogates: either a substituted judgment standard, a best interests standard, or a combination of the two. A substituted judgment standard requires the surrogate to do what the patient would do in the situation were the patient competent. A best interests standard requires the surrogate to weigh health-care options for the patient and then decide what is in the patient's best interest.

ADDITIONAL INSTRUCTIONS IN ADVANCE DIRECTIVES

Artificial Nutrition and Hydration

Some living wills contain a provision for the withdrawal of nutrition and hydration. (See Table 7.2.) Artificial nutrition and hydration (ANH) are legally considered medical treatments and may, therefore, be refused. However, this form of treatment remains controversial in the right-to-die issue because food and liquid are the most basic forms of life sustenance, yet they are not usually needed by dying people and may even make them less comfortable. The unresolved problem is mirrored by the fact that not all states' advance directive statutes (laws) address this issue, and the ones that do show no consensus.

TABLE 7.2

Advance health-care directive

Optional Form

The following form may, but need not, be used to create an advance health-care directive. The other sections of this [Act] govern the effect of this or any other writing used to create an advance health-care directive. An individual may complete or modify all or any part of the following form:

ADVANCE HEALTH-CARE DIRECTIVE

Explanation

You have the right to give instructions about your own health care. You also have the right to name someone else to make health-care decisions for you. This form lets you do either or both of these things. It also lets you express your wishes regarding donation of organs and the designation of your primary physician. If you use this form, you may complete or modify all or any part of it. You are free to use a different form.

Part 1 of this form is a power of attorney for health care. Part 1 lets you name another individual as agent to make health-care decisions for you if you become incapable of making your own decisions or if you want someone else to make those decisions for you now even though you are still capable. You may also name an alternate agent to act for you if your first choice is not willing, able, or reasonably available to make decisions for you. Unless related to you, your agent may not be an owner, operator, or employee of [a residential long-term health-care institution] at which you are receiving care.

Unless the form you sign limits the authority of your agent, your agent may make all health-care decisions for you. This form has a place for you to limit the authority of your agent. You need not limit the authority of your agent if you wish to rely on your agent for all health-care decisions that may have to be made. If you choose not to limit the authority of your agent, your agent will have the right to:

(a) consent or refuse consent to any care, treatment, service, or procedure to maintain, diagnose, or otherwise affect a physical or mental condition;

(b) select or discharge health-care providers and institution;

(c) approve or disapprove diagnostic tests, surgical procedures, programs of medication, and orders not to resuscitate; and

(d) direct the provision, withholding, or withdrawal of artificial nutrition and hydration and all other forms of health care.

Part 2 of this form lets you give specific instructions about any aspect of your health care. Choices are provided for you to express your wishes regarding the provision, withholding, or withdrawal of treatment to keep you alive, including the provision of artificial nutrition and hydration, as well as the provision of pain relief. Space is also provided for you to add to the choices you have made or for you to write out any additional wishes.

Part 3 of this form lets you express an intention to donate your bodily organs and tissues following your death.

Part 4 of this form lets you designate a physician to have primary responsibility for your health care.

After completing this form, sign and date the form at the end. It is recommended but not required that you request two other individuals to sign as witnesses. Give a copy of the signed and completed form to your physician, to any other health-care providers you may have, to any health-care institution at which you are receiving care, and to any health-care agents you have named. You should talk to the person you have named as agent to make sure that he or she understands your wishes and is willing to take the responsibility.

You have the right to revoke this advance health-care directive or replace this form at any time.

* * * * * * * * *

PART 1

POWER OF ATTORNEY FOR HEALTH CARE

1. DESIGNATION OF AGENT: I designate the following individual as my agent to make health-care decisions for me:

_____

(name of individual you choose as agent)

(address)	(city)	(state)	(zip code)

_____

(home phone)   (work phone)

OPTIONAL: If I revoke my agent's authority or if my agent is not willing, able, or reasonably available to make a health-care decision for me, I designate as my first alternate agent:

_____

(name of individual you choose as first alternate agent)

(address)	(city)	(state)	(zip code)

_____

(home phone)   (work phone)

OPTIONAL: If I revoke the authority of my agent and first alternate agent or if neither is willing, able, or reasonably available to make a health-care decision for me, I designate as my second alternate agent:

_____

(name of individual you choose as first alternate agent)

(address)	(city)	(state)	(zip code)

_____

(home phone)   (work phone)

(Add additional sheets if needed.)

Petersen explains that one crux of the ANH controversy is the comfort care–pain relief mandate. She notes that in 2007 thirty-one states addressed comfort care and pain relief associated with life-sustaining procedures, including ANH. Thus, if ANH is seen as a procedure that comforts the dying patient or helps relieve pain, then it must be given regardless of what a health-care proxy or surrogate wants. Two states, however, prohibit ANH if it is expected to cause pain. Again, the proxy or surrogate would have no say. Complicating

TABLE 7.2

Advance health-care directive [CONTINUED]

2. AGENT'S AUTHORITY: My agent is authorized to make all health-care decisions for me, including decisions to provide, withhold, or withdraw artificial nutrition and hydration and other forms of health care to keep me alive, except as I state here:

_____

_____

_____

3. WHEN AGENT'S AUTHORITY BECOMES EFFECTIVE: My agent's authority becomes effective when my primary physician determines that I am unable to make my own health-care decisions unless I mark the following box. If I mark this box [ ], my agent's authority to make health-care decisions for me takes effect immediately.

4. AGENT'S OBLIGATION: My agent shall make health-care decisions for me in accordance with this power of attorney for health care, any instructions I give in Part 2 of this form, and my other wishes to the extent known to my agent. To the extent my wishes are unknown, my agent shall make health-care decisions for me in accordance with what my agent determines to be in my best interest. In determining my best interest, my agent shall consider my personal values to the extent known to my agent.

NOMINATION OF GUARDIAN: If a guardian of my person needs to be appointed for me by a court, I nominate the agent designated in this form. If that agent is not willing, able, or reasonably available to act as guardian, I nominate the alternate agents whom I have named, in the order designated.

PART 2

INSTRUCTIONS FOR HEALTH CARE

If you are satisfied to allow your agent to determine what is best for you in making end-of-life decisions, you need not fill out this part of the form. If you do fill out this part of the form, you may strike any wording you do not want.

6. END-OF-LIFE DECISIONS: I direct that my health-care providers and others involved in my care provide, withhold, or withdraw treatment in accordance with the choice I have marked below:

[   ] (a) Choice Not To Prolong Life
I do not want my life to be prolonged if (i) I have an incurable and irreversible condition that will result in my death within a relatively short time, (ii) I become unconscious and, to a reasonable degree of medical certainty, I will not regain consciousness, or (iii) the likely risks and burdens of treatment would outweigh the expected benefits, OR

[   ] (b) Choice To Prolong Life
I want my life to be prolonged as long as possible within the limits of generally accepted health-care standards.

7. ARTIFICIAL NUTRITION AND HYDRATION: Artificial nutrition and hydration must be provided, withheld, or withdrawn in accordance with the choice I have made in paragraph (6) unless I mark the following box. If I mark this box [   ], artificial nutrition and hydration must be provided regardless of my condition and regardless of the choice I have made in paragraph (6).

8. RELIEF FROM PAIN: Except as I state in the following space, I direct that treatment for alleviation of pain or discomfort be provided at all times, even if it hastens my death:

_____

_____

9. OTHER WISHES: (If you do not agree with any of the optional choices above and wish to write your own, or if you wish to add to the instructions you have given above, you may do so here.) I direct that:

_____

_____

(Add additional sheets if needed.)

PART 3

DONATION OF ORGANS AT DEATH (OPTIONAL)

10. Upon my death (mark applicable box)

[   ] (a) I give any needed organs, tissues, or parts, OR
[   ] (b) I give the following organs, tissues, or parts only

_____

[   ] (c) My gift is for the following purposes (strike any of the following you do not want)
(i) Transplant
(ii) Therapy
(iii) Research
(iv) Education

the matter even more, Petersen reports that six states require that ANH would have to be deemed to have no impact on the patient's illness or to potentially harm the patient before the agent or surrogate would be allowed to forgo ANH.

Relief from Pain

Some living wills also enable an individual to give instructions about the management of pain. Even though a number of studies show that pain is not the primary motivation for assisted suicide requests, many people

TABLE 7.2

Advance health-care directive [CONTINUED]

PART 4

PRIMARY PHYSICIAN (OPTIONAL)

11. I designate the following physician as my primary physician:

_____

(name of physician)

_____

(address)   (city)   (state)   (zip code)

_____

(phone)

OPTIONAL: If the physician I have designated above is not willing, able, or reasonably available to act as my primary physician, I designate the following physician as my primary physician:

_____

(name of physician)

_____

(address)   (city)   (state)   (zip code)

_____

(phone)

* * * * * * * * * *

EFFECT OF COPY: A copy of this form has the same effect as the original.

12. SIGNATURES: Sign and date the form here:

_____   _____

(date)   (sign your name)

_____   _____

(address)   (print name)

_____

(city)   (state)

Optional SIGNATURES OF WITNESSES:

_____   _____

(First witness)   (Second witness)

_____   _____

(print name)   (print name)

_____   _____

(address)   (address)

_____   _____

(city)   (state)   (city)   (state)

_____   _____

(signature of witness)   (signature of witness)

_____   _____

(date)   (date)

SOURCE: "Advance Health-Care Directive," in *Patient Self-Determination Act: Providers Offer Information on Advance Directives but Effectiveness Uncertain,* U.S. General Accounting Office, August 1995, http://www.gao.gov/archive/1995/he95135.pdf (accessed March 10, 2008)

have seen family and friends suffer painful deaths, and they fear the same fate. Experts advise that advance directives should expressly indicate desires for pain control and comfort care, even when individuals have chosen to forgo life-sustaining treatments.

In the past, patient pain may not have been adequately treated because medical professionals lacked training or feared overprescribing pain medications. A variety of legislative and education initiatives by states and medical professional societies have dramatically improved pain management. The Federation of State Medical Boards has developed guidelines to help physi-

cians use medication to manage pain safely and effectively. Special instruction in pain management for patients with life-limiting illnesses is now offered in many medical and nursing schools.

COMBINED ADVANCE DIRECTIVE LAWS

Some states have separate laws that govern living wills and durable powers of attorney for health care. The National Conference of State Legislatures (NCSL) and the Center to Improve Care of the Dying (CICD) believe that rather than having separate laws for these two documents, states should combine right-to-die laws into a single

FIGURE 7.1

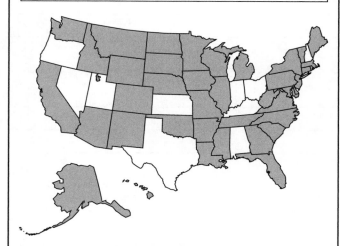

States in which "Five Wishes" is legally valid, 2007

☐ (grey) State in which Five Wishes *meets current legal requirements (including the District of Columbia)*

☐ State in which Five Wishes *does not meet current legal requirements, but can still be useful as an attachment*

Note: Some states have additional requirements associated with Five Wishes. These include CA, CT, DE, DC, MI, NY, ND, SC, VT, WI.

SOURCE: "Five Wishes States," Aging with Dignity, 2007, http://www.agingwithdignity.org/states.html (accessed March 10, 2008)

statute. By October 2007 twenty-five states had done just that. (See Table 7.1.) Of these states, Alabama, Alaska, Delaware, Hawaii, Maine, Mississippi, and New Mexico had also adopted the UHCDA as a model.

The UHCDA has been recommended by the NCSL and the CICD as a model law because it is simple and comprehensive. It contains provisions governing living wills and durable powers of attorney, as well as limits on an agent's powers. The law permits instructions regarding one's future health care to be either written or oral. States using the law as a model may adopt the optional combined directive, which does not require witnesses to the document. It further enables individuals to express their preferences about organ donation and to designate a primary physician. (See Table 7.2.)

Along with showing the type of health-care power of attorney and combined advance directive legislation in each state, Table 7.1 shows other related information, including the comity provision. If a state has a comity provision, that means it has legislation specifically requiring that another state's living will, health-care power of attorney, or both, be honored within its borders.

IMPORTANCE OF COMMUNICATION FOR END-OF-LIFE CARE

The consideration of an advance directive should be the start of an ongoing discussion among the individual,

family members, and the family doctor about end-of-life health care. Discussions about one's advance directive do not have to be limited to treatment preferences and medical circumstances. Sometimes knowing things such as the patient's religious beliefs and values can be important for the proxy when speaking for the patient's interests. The Center for Health Law and Ethics at the University of New Mexico has devised a values history form (http://hsc.unm.edu/ethics/pdf/Values_History.doc) to help people examine their attitudes about issues related to illness, health care, and dying. It may serve as a valuable tool to guide discussions between the patient and the proxy, as well as among family members.

When preparing an advance directive, it is vitally important for the family and proxy to fully understand the care and measures that are wanted. Even when a patient has a living will calling for no "heroic measures," if the family demands such medical intervention, it is likely that the hospital or doctor will comply with the family's wishes rather than risk a lawsuit.

In "Discussions by Elders and Adult Children about End-of-Life Preparation and Preferences" (*Preventing Chronic Disease: Public Health Research, Practice, and Policy*, vol. 5, no. 1, January 2008, www.cdc.gov/pcd/issues/2008/jan/07_0141.htm), Anne P. Glass and Lusine Nahapetyan conducted in-depth interviews with older adults about their end-of-life decisions and with younger adults about their parents' end-of-life decisions to determine factors that helped and hindered discussions among family members regarding end-of-life preparation and preferences. Of the older adult participants in the study, just over half had discussed these topics with their adult children. Of the younger participants, two-thirds had discussed these topics with their parents.

Glass and Nahapetyan determine that fear of death, avoiding talking about death, trust in others to make decisions, family dynamics, and uncertainty about preferences were factors that impeded family discussions about end-of-life preparation and preferences. Factors that facilitated discussion were an acceptance of death, experience with death, religion, or spirituality, and a desire to help the family. The researchers also explain that approaching the topic in a casual manner helped families. An indispensable strategy to avoid confusion and argument over what parents said or wanted, and to avoid the need to get the family together in one place at one time, was for parents to write down their end-of-life preferences.

THE PATIENT SELF-DETERMINATION ACT

In 1990 Congress enacted the Patient Self-Determination Act (PSDA) as part of the Omnibus Budget Reconciliation Act of 1990. This legislation was intended to "reinforce individuals' constitutional right to determine their final health care."

The PSDA took effect on December 1, 1991. It requires most health-care institutions, on admission, to provide patients with a summary of their health-care decision-making rights and to ask them if they have an advance directive. Health-care institutions must also inform the patient of their facility's policies with respect to honoring advance directives. The PSDA requires health-care providers to educate their staff and the community about advance directives. It also prohibits hospital personnel from discriminating against patients based on whether they have an advance directive, and patients are informed that having an advance directive is not a prerequisite to receiving medical care.

CHAPTER 8
COURTS AND THE END OF LIFE

Traditionally, death was said to have occurred when circulation and respiration stopped. However, in 1968 the Ad Hoc Committee of the Harvard Medical School defined irreversible coma, or brain death, as the new criterion for death. As medical technology has become increasingly able to maintain patients who would otherwise die from severe injuries or illnesses, the debate about defining death, and about whether patients have the right to choose to die, has intensified.

THE RIGHT TO PRIVACY: KAREN ANN QUINLAN

The landmark case of Karen Ann Quinlan was the first to deal with the dilemma of withdrawing life-sustaining treatment from a patient who was not terminally ill but who was not really "alive." The decision to terminate life support, which was once a private matter between the patient's family and doctor, became an issue to be decided by the courts. The New Jersey Supreme Court ruling on this case became the precedent for nearly all right-to-die cases nationwide.

In 1975 twenty-one-year-old Karen Ann Quinlan suffered cardiopulmonary arrest after ingesting a combination of alcohol and drugs. She subsequently went into a persistent vegetative state (PVS). Fred Plum, a neurologist, described her as no longer having any cognitive function but retaining the capacity to maintain the vegetative parts of neurological function. She grimaced, made chewing movements, uttered sounds, and maintained a normal blood pressure, but she was entirely unaware of anyone or anything. The medical opinion was that Quinlan had some brain stem function, but that it could not support breathing. She had been on a respirator since her admission to the hospital.

Quinlan's parents asked that her respirator be removed and that she be allowed to die. Quinlan's doctor refused, claiming that his patient did not meet the Harvard Criteria for brain death. Based on the existing medical standards and practices, a doctor could not terminate a patient's life support if that patient did not meet the legal definitions for brain death. According to the Harvard Criteria, Quinlan could not be declared legally dead, and medical experts believed she would die if the respirator were removed.

Joseph Quinlan, Quinlan's father, went to court to seek appointment as his daughter's guardian (because she was of legal age) and to gain the power to authorize "the discontinuance of all extraordinary medical procedures now allegedly sustaining Karen's vital processes." The court refused to grant him guardianship over his daughter and denied his petition to have Quinlan's respirator turned off.

First and Eighth Amendments Are Irrelevant to the Case

Joseph Quinlan subsequently appealed to the New Jersey Supreme Court. He requested, as a parent, to have Quinlan's life support removed based on the U.S. Constitution's First Amendment (the right to religious freedom). In *In re Quinlan* (70 N.J. 10, 355 A.2d 647, 1976), the court rejected his request. It also considered the Eighth Amendment (protection against cruel and unusual punishment) inapplicable in Quinlan's case, stating that this amendment applied to protection from excessive criminal punishment. The court considered Quinlan's cruel and unusual circumstances not punishment inflicted by the law or state, but as the result of "an accident of fate and nature."

The Right to Privacy

However, the New Jersey Supreme Court stated that an individual's right to privacy was most relevant to the case. Even though the Constitution does not expressly indicate a right to privacy, U.S. Supreme Court rulings in past cases had not only recognized this right but had also determined that some areas of the right to privacy are guaranteed by the Constitution. For example, the Supreme Court had upheld the right to privacy in *Griswold v. Connecticut* (381 U.S. 479, 1965; the right to marital privacy, or the right to use contraception) and in *Roe v. Wade* (410 U.S. 113, 1973; the right to abortion). The Court had further presumed that the right to privacy included a patient's right to refuse medical treatment in some situations.

Based on these U.S. Supreme Court rulings, the New Jersey Supreme Court ruled that "Karen's right of privacy may be asserted on her behalf by her guardian under the peculiar circumstances here present," and further noted, "We have no doubt ... that if Karen were herself miraculously lucid for an interval (not altering the existing prognosis of the condition to which she would soon return) and perceptive of her irreversible condition, she could effectively decide upon discontinuance of the life-support apparatus, even if it meant the prospect of natural death."

The State's Interest

Balanced against Quinlan's constitutional right to privacy was the state's interest in preserving life. Judge Richard J. Hughes (1909–1992) of the New Jersey Supreme Court noted that in many cases the court had ordered medical treatment continued because the minimal bodily invasion (usually blood transfusion) resulted in recovery. He indicated that in Quinlan's case bodily invasion was far greater than minimal, consisting of twenty-four-hour nursing care, antibiotics, respirator, catheter, and feeding tube. Judge Hughes further noted, "We think that the State's interest ... weakens and the individual's right to privacy grows as the degree of bodily invasion increases and the prognosis dims. Ultimately there comes a point at which the individual's rights overcome the State's interest."

Prevailing Medical Standards and Practices

Quinlan's physicians had refused to remove the respirator because they did not want to violate the prevailing medical standards and practices. Even though Quinlan's physicians assured the court that the possibility of lawsuits and criminal sanctions did not influence their decision in this specific case, the court believed that the threat of legal ramifications strongly influenced the existing medical standards and practices of health-care providers.

The court also observed that life-prolongation advances had rendered the existing medical standards ambiguous (unclear), leaving doctors in a quandary. Moreover, modern devices used for prolonging life, such as respirators, had confused the issue of "ordinary" and "extraordinary" measures. Therefore, the court suggested that respirators could be considered "ordinary" care for a curable patient, but "extraordinary" care for irreversibly unconscious patients.

The court also suggested that hospitals form ethics committees to assist physicians with difficult cases such as Quinlan's. These committees would be similar to a multijudge panel exploring different solutions to an appeal. The committees would not only diffuse professional responsibility but also eliminate any possibly unscrupulous motives of physicians or families. The justices considered the court's intervention on medical decisions an infringement on the physicians' field of competence.

Is It Homicide?

The state had promised to prosecute anyone who terminated Quinlan's life support because such an act would constitute homicide. However, the New Jersey Supreme Court rejected this consequence because the resulting death would be from natural causes. The court stated that "the exercise of a constitutional right such as we have here found is protected from criminal prosecution.... The constitutional protection extends to third parties whose action is necessary to effectuate the exercise of that right."

After the Respirator Was Removed

In March 1976 the New Jersey Supreme Court ruled that, if the hospital ethics committee agreed that Quinlan would not recover from irreversible coma, her respirator could be removed. Furthermore, all parties involved would be legally immune from criminal and civil prosecution. However, after Quinlan's respirator was removed, she continued to breathe on her own and remained in a PVS until she died of multiple infections in 1985.

Some people wondered why the Quinlans did not request permission to discontinue Karen's artificial nutrition and hydration. In *Karen Ann: The Quinlans Tell Their Story* (1977), the Quinlans stated that they would have had moral problems with depriving their daughter of food and antibiotics.

SUBSTITUTED JUDGMENT
Superintendent of Belchertown State School et al. v. Joseph Saikewicz

Joseph Saikewicz was a mentally incompetent resident of the Belchertown State School of the Massachusetts Department of Mental Health. In April 1976 Saikewicz was diagnosed with acute myeloblastic monocytic leukemia (cancer of the blood). He was sixty-seven years old but had the mental age of about two years and eight months. The superintendent of the mental institution petitioned the court for a guardian ad litem (a temporary guardian for the duration of the trial). The court-appointed guardian recommended that it would be in the patient's best interests that he not undergo chemotherapy.

In May 1976 the probate judge ordered nontreatment of the disease based in part on findings of medical experts, who indicated that chemotherapy might produce remission of leukemia in 30% to 50% of the cases. If remission occurred, it would last between two and thirteen months. Chemotherapy, however, would make Saikewicz suffer adverse side effects that he would not understand. Without chemotherapy, the patient might live for several weeks or months, but would die without the pain or discomfort associated with chemotherapy.

In fact, Saikewicz died on September 4, 1976, from pneumonia, a complication of the leukemia. Nevertheless, his case, *Superintendent of Belchertown State School et al. v. Joseph Saikewicz* (Mass., 370 N.E.2d 417, 1977), was heard by the Massachusetts Supreme Court to establish a precedent on the question of substituted judgment—letting another entity, such as a court, ethics committee, surrogate, or guardian, determine what the patient would do in the situation were the patient competent.

The court agreed that extraordinary measures should not be used if the patient would not recover from the disease. The court also ruled that a person has a right to the preservation of his or her bodily integrity and can refuse medical invasion. The Massachusetts Supreme Court turned to *In re Quinlan* for support of its right of privacy argument.

THE RIGHTS OF AN INCOMPETENT PATIENT. Once the right to refuse treatment had been established, the court declared that everyone, including an incompetent person, has the right of choice, "To presume that the incompetent person must always be subjected to what many rational and intelligent people may decline is to downgrade the status of the incompetent person by placing a lesser value on his intrinsic human worth and vitality."

Referring to *Quinlan*, the court recommended that the patient not receive the treatment most people with leukemia would choose. (Unlike some later courts, the *Quinlan* court accepted the premise that a vegetative patient would not want to remain "alive.") The *Saikewicz* court believed that the "substituted judgment" standard would best preserve respect for the integrity and autonomy of the patient. In other words, the decision maker—in this case, the court—would put itself in Saikewicz's position and make the treatment decision the patient most likely would make were he competent. The court believed Saikewicz would have refused treatment.

In evaluating the role of the hospital and the guardian in the decision-making process, the *Saikewicz* court rejected the *Quinlan* court's recommendation that an ethics committee should be the source of the decision. The court instead concluded, "We do not view the judicial resolution of this most difficult and awesome question— whether potentially life-prolonging treatment should be withheld from a person incapable of making his own

decision—as constituting a 'gratuitous encroachment' on the domain of medical expertise. Rather, such questions of life and death seem to us to require the process of detached but passionate investigation and decision that forms the ideal on which the judicial branch of government was created."

Charles S. Soper, as Director of Newark Developmental Center et al. v. Dorothy Storar

John Storar, a fifty-two-year-old mentally retarded man with a mental age of about eighteen months, was diagnosed with terminal cancer. His mother, Dorothy Storar, petitioned the court to discontinue blood transfusions that were delaying her son's death, which would probably occur within three to six months.

At the time of the hearing, Storar required two units of blood about every one to two weeks. He found the transfusions disagreeable and had to be given a sedative before the procedure. He also had to be restrained during the transfusions. However, without the blood transfusions there would be insufficient oxygen in his blood, causing his heart to beat faster and his respiratory rate to increase. However, the doctor reported that after transfusions Storar had more energy and was able to resume most of his normal activities.

The probate court granted Dorothy Storar the right to terminate the treatments, but the order was stayed and treatment continued pending the appeal to the New York Appellate Division (or appellate court). Storar died before the case, *Charles S. Soper, as Director of Newark Developmental Center et al. v. Dorothy Storar* (N.Y., 420 N.E.2d 64, 1981), could be heard, rendering the decision moot, but because the issue was considered to be of public importance, the appellate court proceeded to hear the case.

The appellate court agreed with the probate court that a guardian can make medical decisions for an incompetent patient. However, the parent/guardian "may not deprive a child of life-saving treatment." In this case there were two threats to Storar's life: the incurable cancer and the loss of blood that could be remedied with transfusions. Because the transfusions did not, in the eyes of the majority opinion written by Judge Sol Wachtler (1930–), cause much pain, the appellate court overturned the probate court's ruling.

Dissenting from this determination, Judge Hugh R. Jones (1914–2001) believed the treatments did not serve Storar's best interests. They did not relieve his pain and, in fact, caused him additional pain. Because the blood transfusions would not cure his cancer, they could be considered extraordinary treatments. Finally, Judge Jones reasoned that Storar's mother had cared for him for a long time and knew best how he felt, and therefore the court should respect her decision.

COMPETENT PATIENTS' WISHES
Michael J. Satz etc. v. Abe Perlmutter

Not all the cases of patients seeking to terminate life support concern incompetent people. Abe Perlmutter, aged seventy-three, was suffering from amyotrophic lateral sclerosis (ALS; sometimes called Lou Gehrig's disease). ALS is always fatal after prolonged physical degeneration, but it does not affect mental function.

Perlmutter's 1978 request to have his respirator removed was approved by the Circuit Court of Broward County, Florida. At a bedside hearing, the court questioned whether the patient truly understood the consequences of his request. Perlmutter told the judge that, if the respirator were removed, "It can't be worse than what I'm going through now."

The state appealed the case before the Florida District Court of Appeals (appellate court), citing the state's duty to preserve life and to prevent the unlawful killing of a human being. The state also noted the hospital's and the doctors' fear of criminal prosecution and civil liability. In *Michael J. Satz, State Attorney for Broward County, Florida v. Abe Perlmutter* (Fla. App., 362 So.2d, 160, 1978), the appellate court concluded that Perlmutter's right to refuse treatment overrode the state's interests and found in Perlmutter's favor.

THE STATE'S INTERESTS. An individual's right to refuse medical treatment is generally honored as long as it is consistent with the state's interests, which include:

- Interest in the preservation of life

- Need to protect innocent third parties

- Duty to prevent suicide

- Requirement that it help maintain the ethical integrity of medical practice

In the *Perlmutter* case, the Florida District Court of Appeals found that the preservation of life is an important goal, but not when the disease is incurable and causes the patient to suffer. The need to protect innocent third parties refers to cases in which a parent refuses treatment and a third party suffers, such as the abandonment of a minor child. Perlmutter's children were all adults and Perlmutter was not committing suicide. Were it not for the respirator, he would be dead; therefore, disconnecting it would not cause his death but would result in the disease running its natural course. Finally, the court turned to *Quinlan* and *Saikewicz* to support its finding that there are times when medical ethics dictates that a dying person needs comfort more than treatment. The court concluded:

> Abe Perlmutter should be allowed to make his choice to die with dignity.... It is all very convenient to insist on continuing Mr. Perlmutter's life so that there can be no question of foul play, no resulting civil liability and no

possible trespass on medical ethics. However, it is quite another matter to do so at the patient's sole expense and against his competent will, thus inflicting never-ending physical torture on his body until the inevitable, but artificially suspended, moment of death. Such a course of conduct invades the patient's constitutional right of privacy, removes his freedom of choice and invades his right to self-determine.

The state again appealed the case, this time to the Supreme Court of Florida, which, in *Michael J. Satz etc. v. Abe Perlmutter* (Fla., 379 So.2d 359, 1980), supported the decision by the Florida District Court of Appeals. Shortly after this ruling, Perlmutter' respirator was disconnected, and he died of his disease on October 6, 1980.

THE SUBJECTIVE, LIMITED-OBJECTIVE, AND PURE-OBJECTIVE TESTS
In the Matter of Claire C. Conroy

Claire Conroy was an eighty-four-year-old nursing-home patient suffering from "serious and irreversible mental and physical impairments with a limited life expectancy." In March 1984 her nephew (her guardian and only living relative) petitioned the Superior Court of Essex County, New Jersey, for removal of her nasogastric feeding tube. Conroy's court-appointed guardian ad litem opposed the petition. The superior court approved the nephew's request, and the guardian ad litem appealed. Claire Conroy died with the nasogastric tube in place while the appeal was pending. Nonetheless, the appellate court chose to hear the case, *In the Matter of Claire C. Conroy* (486 A.2d 1209, [N.J. 1985]). The court reasoned that this was an important case and that its ruling could influence future cases with comparable circumstances.

Conroy suffered from heart disease, hypertension, and diabetes. She also had a gangrenous leg, bedsores, and an eye problem that required irrigation. She lacked bowel control, could not speak, and had a limited swallowing ability. In the appeals trial one medical expert testified that Conroy, although awake, was seriously demented. Another doctor testified that "although she was confused and unaware, 'she responds somehow.'"

Both experts were not sure if the patient could feel pain, although she had moaned when subjected to painful stimuli. However, they agreed that if the nasogastric tube were removed, Conroy would die a painful death.

Conroy's nephew testified that his aunt would never have wanted to be maintained in this manner. She feared doctors and had avoided them all her life. Because she was Roman Catholic, a priest was brought in to testify. In his judgment the removal of the tube would be ethical and moral even though her death might be painful.

The appeals court held that "the right to terminate life-sustaining treatment based on a guardian's judgment was limited to incurable and terminally ill patients who are brain dead, irreversibly comatose, or vegetative, and who would gain no medical benefit from continued treatment."

Furthermore, a guardian's decision did not apply to food withdrawal, which hastens death. The court considered this active euthanasia, which it did not consider ethically permissible.

THE THREE TESTS. The court proposed three tests to determine if Conroy's feeding tube should have been removed. The subjective test served to clarify what Conroy would have decided about her tube feeding if she were able to do so. The court listed acceptable expressions of intent that should be considered by surrogates or by the court—spoken expressions, living wills, durable power of attorney, oral directives, prior behavior, and religious beliefs.

If the court determines that patients in Conroy's circumstance have not explicitly expressed their wishes, two other "best interests" tests may be used: the limited-objective and the pure-objective tests. The limited-objective test permits discontinuing life-sustaining treatment if medical evidence shows that the patient would reject treatment that would only prolong suffering and that medication would not alleviate pain. Under this test, the court requires the additional evidence from the subjective test.

The pure-objective test applies when there is no trustworthy evidence, or any evidence at all, to help guide a decision. The burden imposed on the patient's life by the treatment should outweigh whatever benefit would result from the treatment. "Further, the recurring, unavoidable and severe pain of the patient's life with the treatment should be such that the effect of administering life-sustaining treatment would be inhumane."

In January 1985 the court concluded that Conroy failed the tests. Her intentions, while perhaps clear enough to help support a limited-objective test (she had shown some evidence of a desire to reject treatment) were not strong enough for the subjective test (clear expressions of her intent). In addition, the information on her possible pain versus benefits of remaining alive was not sufficient for either the limited-objective test (her pain might outweigh her pleasure in life) or the pure-objective test (her pain would be so great it would be inhumane to continue treatment). Had Conroy survived the appellate court's decision, the court would have required her guardian to investigate these matters further before reaching a decision.

Justice Alan B. Handler (1931–), dissenting in part, disagreed with the majority's decision to measure Conroy's "best interests" in terms of the possible pain she could have been experiencing. First, in many cases pain can be controlled through medication. Second, pain levels cannot always be determined, as was shown in Con-

roy's case. Finally, not all patients decide based on pain. Some fear being dependent on others, especially when their bodily functions deteriorate; others value personal privacy and dignity. Bodily integrity may be more important than simply prolonging life. Justice Handler supported reliance on knowledgeable, responsible surrogates as opposed to standards set in a series of tests.

CAN DOCTORS BE HELD LIABLE?
Barber v. Superior Court of the State of California

Historically, physicians have been free from prosecution for terminating life support. However, a precedent was set in 1983, when two doctors (Neil Barber and Robert Nejdl) were charged with murder and conspiracy to commit murder after agreeing to requests from a patient's family to discontinue life support.

Clarence Herbert suffered cardio-respiratory arrest following surgery. He was revived and placed on a respirator. Three days later his doctors diagnosed him as deeply comatose. The prognosis was that he would likely never recover. The family requested in writing that Herbert's respirator and other life-sustaining equipment be removed. The doctors complied, but Herbert continued to breathe on his own. After two days the family asked the doctors to remove the intravenous tubes that provided nutrition and hydration. The request was honored. From that point until his death, Herbert received care that provided a clean and hygienic environment and allowed for the preservation of his dignity.

A superior court judge ruled that because the doctors' behavior intentionally shortened the patient's life, they had committed murder. However, the Court of Appeals found in *Barber v. Superior Court of the State of California* (195 Cal.Rptr. 484 [Cal.App. 2 Dist. 1983]) that a patient's right to refuse treatment, and a surrogate's right to refuse treatment for an incompetent, superseded any liability that could be attributed to the physicians.

In ruling that the physicians' compliance with the request of Herbert's family did not constitute murder, the Court of Appeals stated that "cessation of 'heroic' life support measures is not an affirmative act but a withdrawal or omission of further treatment." In addition, artificial nutrition and hydration also constituted a medical treatment.

WHAT ARE THE HOSPITAL'S RIGHTS?
Patricia E. Brophy v. New England Sinai Hospital

In 1983 Paul E. Brophy Sr. suffered the rupture of an aneurysm (a part of an artery wall that weakens, causing it to balloon outward with blood) that left him in a PVS. He was not brain dead, nor was he terminal. He had been a fireman and an emergency medical technician and often expressed the opinion that he never wanted to be kept alive artificially.

Patricia Brophy brought suit when physicians refused to remove or clamp a gastrostomy tube (g-tube) that supplied nutrition and hydration to her husband. The Massachusetts Appeals Court ruled against Brophy, but in *Patricia E. Brophy v. New England Sinai Hospital* (497 N.E.2d 626, [Mass. 1986]) the Massachusetts Supreme Court allowed substituted judgment for a comatose patient who had previously made his intentions clear.

The Massachusetts Supreme Court, however, did agree with the Massachusetts Appeals Court ruling that the hospital could not be forced to withhold food and water, which went against the hospital's ethical beliefs. Consequently, the Massachusetts Supreme Court ordered New England Sinai Hospital to facilitate Brophy's transfer to another facility or to his home, where his wife could carry out his wishes.

In October 1986 Brody was moved to Emerson Hospital in Concord, Massachusetts. He died there on October 23 after eight days with no food. The official cause of death was pneumonia.

VITALIST DISSENSIONS. Justices Joseph R. Nolan and Neil L. Lynch (1930–) of the Massachusetts Supreme Court strongly disagreed with the majority opinion to allow removal of the g-tube. Justice Nolan argued that food and water were not medical treatments that could be refused. In his view, food and water are basic human needs, and by permitting the removal of the g-tube, the court gave its stamp of approval to euthanasia and suicide.

Justice Lynch believed the Massachusetts Supreme Court majority had ignored what he considered valid findings by the Massachusetts Appeals Court, which found that Brophy's wishes, as expressed in his wife's substituted-judgment decision of withholding food and water, did not concern intrusive medical treatment. Rather, Brophy's decision, if he were competent to make it, was to knowingly terminate his life by declining food and water. This was suicide and the state was, therefore, condoning suicide.

In the Matter of Beverly Requena

Beverly Requena was a competent fifty-five-year-old woman with ALS. She informed St. Clare's/Riverside Medical Center—a Roman Catholic hospital—that when she lost the ability to swallow, she would refuse artificial feeding. The hospital filed a suit to force Requena to leave the hospital, citing its policy against withholding food or fluids from a patient.

Time was running out for Requena. She was paralyzed from the neck down and was unable to make sounds, although she could form words with her lips. At the time of the hearing, she could not eat but could suck some nutrient liquids through a straw. Soon, she would not even be able to do that.

The court did not question Requena's right to refuse nutrition, nor did the hospital question that right. That was a right that had been upheld in many previous cases. However, reasserting its policy of refusing to participate in the withholding or withdrawal of artificial nutrition and hydration, the hospital offered to help transfer Requena to another facility that was willing to fulfill her wishes.

Requena did not want to transfer to another hospital. In the last seventeen months, she had formed a relationship of trust in, and affection for, the staff. She also liked the familiar surroundings. The court found that being forced to leave would upset her emotionally and psychologically. The hospital staff was feeling stress as well. They were fond of Requena and did not want to see her die a presumably painful death from dehydration.

Judge Reginald Stanton ruled in *In the Matter of Beverly Requena* (517 A.2d 869 [N.J.Super.A.D. 1986]) that Requena could not be removed from the hospital without her consent and that the hospital would have to comply with her wishes. He stressed the importance of preserving the personal worth, dignity, and integrity of the patient. The hospital may provide her information about her prognosis and treatment options, but Requena alone had the right to decide what was best for her.

WHAT ARE THE NURSING HOME'S RIGHTS?
In the Matter of Nancy Ellen Jobes

In 1980 twenty-four-year-old Nancy Ellen Jobes was in a car accident. At the time, she was four-and-a-half months pregnant. Doctors who treated her determined that her fetus was dead. During the surgery to remove the fetus, Jobes suffered the loss of oxygen and blood flow to the brain. Never regaining consciousness, she was moved to the Lincoln Park Nursing Home several months later.

The nursing home provided nourishment to Jobes through a jejunostomy tube (j-tube) inserted into the jejunum (midsection) of her small intestine. Five years later, Jobes's husband, John Jobes, asked the nursing home to stop his wife's artificial feeding. The nursing home refused, citing moral considerations.

The trial court appointed a guardian ad litem, who, after reviewing the case, filed in favor of John Jobes. The nursing home moved to appoint a life advocate (a person who would support retaining the feeding tube), which was turned down by the trial court. The New Jersey Supreme Court heard the case *In the Matter of Nancy Ellen Jobes* (529 A.2d 434 [N.J. 1987]).

DIFFERING INTERPRETATIONS OF PVS. Whether Jobes was in a PVS was hotly debated, revealing how different medical interpretations of the same patient's condition can produce different conclusions. After Jobes initiated the suit, his wife was transferred to Cornell Medical Center for four days of observation and testing. Fred Plum, a world-renowned neurologist who had coined the term *persistent vegetative state*, and his associate David Levy concluded, after extensive examination and testing, that Jobes was indeed in a PVS and would never recover.

On the contrary, Maurice Victor and Allan Ropper testified for the nursing home. Having examined Jobes for about one-and-a-half hours, Victor reported that even though the patient was severely brain damaged, he did not believe she was in a PVS. She had responded to his commands, such as to pick up her head or to stick out her tongue. However, he could not back up his testimony with any written record of his examination.

Ropper had also examined Jobes for about an hour and a half. He testified that some of the patient's motions, such as lifting an arm off the bed, excluded her from his definition of PVS. (His definition of PVS differed from Plum's in that it excluded patients who made reflexive responses to outside stimuli—a definition that would have also excluded Quinlan.) Testimony from the nurses who had cared for Jobes over the past years was also contradictory, with some asserting she smiled or responded to their care and others saying they saw no cognitive responses.

The New Jersey Supreme Court concluded that the neurological experts, especially Plum and Levy, "offered sufficiently clear and convincing evidence to support the trial court's finding that Jobes is in an irreversibly vegetative state." However, the court could find no "clear and convincing" evidence that Jobes, if she were competent, would want the j-tube removed. Jobes's family and friends, including her minister, had testified that in general conversation she had mentioned that she would not want to be kept alive with artificial life support measures. The court did not accept these past remarks as clear evidence of the patient's intent.

With no clear and convincing evidence of Jobes's beliefs about artificial feeding, the New Jersey Supreme Court turned to *In re Quinlan* for guidance. The court stated, "Our review of these cases and medical authorities confirms our conclusion that we should continue to defer, as we did in *Quinlan*, to family members' substituted judgments about medical treatment for irreversibly vegetative patients who did not clearly express their medical preferences while they were competent. Those decisions are best made because the family is best able to decide what the patient would want."

THE NURSING HOME'S RESPONSIBILITY. The New Jersey Supreme Court reversed the trial court decision that had allowed the nursing home to refuse to participate in the withdrawal of the feeding tube. The court noted, "Mrs. Jobes's family had no reason to believe that they were surrendering the right to choose among medical alternatives when they placed her in the nursing home." The court pointed out that it was not until 1985, five years after Jobes's admission to the Lincoln Park Nursing Home, and only after her family requested the removal of her feeding tube, that her family learned of the policy. The court ordered the nursing home to comply with the family's request.

Justice Daniel J. O'Hern (1930–) dissented on both issues. He claimed that not all families may be as loving as Jobes's. He was concerned for other individuals whose family might not be so caring, but who would still have the authority to order the withdrawal of life-sustaining treatments. He also disagreed with the order given the nursing home to comply with the family's request to discontinue Jobes's feeding. "I believe a proper balance could be obtained by adhering to the procedure adopted [in] *In re Quinlan*, that would have allowed the nonconsenting physician not to participate in the life-terminating process."

CLEAR AND CONVINCING EVIDENCE

Throughout the history of right-to-die cases, there has been considerable debate about how to determine a patient's wishes. How clearly must a patient have expressed his or her wishes before becoming incompetent? Does a parent or other family member best represent the patient? Are casual conversations sufficient to reveal intentions, or must there be written instructions?

In the Matter of Philip K. Eichner, on Behalf of Joseph C. Fox v. Denis Dillon, as District Attorney of Nassau County

Eighty-three-year-old Joseph C. Fox went into a PVS after a hernia operation. He was a member of a Roman Catholic religious order, the Society of Mary. The local director of the society, Philip K. Eichner, filed suit, asking for permission to have Fox's respirator removed.

In *In the Matter of Philip K. Eichner, on Behalf of Joseph C. Fox v. Denis Dillon, as District Attorney of Nassau County* (N.Y., 420 N.E.2d 64, 1981), the court reasoned that "the highest burden of proof beyond a reasonable doubt should be required when granting the relief that may result in the patient's death." The need for high standards "forbids relief whenever the evidence is loose, equivocal, or contradictory." Fox, however, had discussed his feelings in the context of formal religious discussions. Only two months before his final hospitalization, he had stated he would not want his life prolonged if his condition were hopeless. The court argued, "These were obviously solemn pronouncements and not casual remarks made at some social gathering, nor can it be said that he was too young to realize or feel the consequences of his statements."

Fox's case was the first where the reported attitudes of an incompetent patient were accepted as "clear and convincing."

In the Matter of Westchester County Medical Center, on Behalf of Mary O'Connor

Not all patients express their attitudes about the use of life-sustaining treatments in serious religious discussions as did Fox. Nonetheless, courts have accepted evidence of "best interests" or "substituted judgments" in allowing the termination of life-sustaining treatments.

In 1985 Mary O'Connor had a stroke that rendered her mentally and physically incompetent. More than two years later she suffered a second major stroke, after which she had additional disabilities and difficulty swallowing. O'Connor's two daughters moved her to a long-term geriatric facility associated with the Westchester County Medical Center. During her hospital admission, her daughters submitted a signed statement to be added to their mother's medical records. The document stated that O'Connor had indicated in many conversations that "no artificial life support be started or maintained to continue to sustain her life."

In June 1988, when O'Connor's condition deteriorated, she was admitted to Westchester County Medical Center. Because she was unable to swallow, her physician prescribed a nasogastric tube. The daughters objected to the procedure, citing their mother's expressed wish. The hospital petitioned the court for permission to provide artificial feeding, without which O'Connor would starve to death within seven to ten days. The lower court found in favor of O'Connor's daughters. The hospital subsequently brought the case, *In the Matter of Westchester County Medical Center, on Behalf of Mary O'Connor* (531 N.E.2d 607 [N.Y. 1988]), before the New York Court of Appeals.

O'Connor's physician testified that she was not in a coma. Even though he anticipated that O'Connor's awareness might improve in the future, he believed she would never regain the mental ability to understand complex matters. This included the issue of her medical condition and treatment. The physician further indicated that, if his patient were allowed to starve to death, she would experience pain and "extreme, intense discomfort."

A neurologist testifying for the daughters reported that O'Connor's brain damage would keep her from experiencing pain. If she did have pain in the process of

starving to death, she could be given medication. However, the doctor admitted he could not be "medically certain" because he had never had a patient die under the same circumstances.

The New York Court of Appeals majority concluded that, even though family and friends testified that O'Connor "felt that nature should take its course and not use artificial means" and that it is "monstrous" to keep someone alive by "machinery," these expressions did not constitute clear and convincing evidence of her present desire to die. Also, she had never specifically discussed the issue of artificial nutrition and hydration. Nor had she ever expressed her wish to refuse artificial medical treatment should such refusal result in a painful death.

The court further noted that O'Connor's statements about refusing artificial treatments had generally been made in situations involving terminal illness, specifically cancer—her husband had died of cancer and so did two of her brothers, her stepmother, and a close friend. Speaking for the Court of Appeals majority, Judge Wachtler stressed that O'Connor was not terminally ill, was conscious, and could interact with others, albeit minimally. Her main problem was that she could not eat on her own, and her physician could help her with that. Writing for the majority, Judge Wachtler stated, "Every person has a right to life, and no one should be denied essential medical care unless the evidence clearly and convincingly shows that the patient intended to decline the treatment under some particular circumstances. This is a demanding standard, the most rigorous burden of proof in civil cases. It is appropriate here because if an error occurs it should be made on the side of life."

THIS IS TOO RESTRICTIVE. Judge Richard D. Simons (1927–) of the New York Court of Appeals differed from the majority in his opinion of O'Connor's condition. O'Connor's "conversations" were actually limited to saying her name and words such as "okay," "all right," and "yes." Neither the hospital doctor nor the neurologist who testified for her daughters could say for sure that she understood their questions. The court majority mentioned the patient squeezing her doctor's hand in response to some questions, but failed to add that she did not respond to most questions.

Even though it was true the patient was not terminally ill, her severe mental and physical injuries—should nature take its course—would result in her death. Judge Simons believed the artificial feeding would not cure or improve her deteriorating condition.

Judge Wachtler had noted that O'Connor talked about refusing artificial treatment in the aftermath of the deaths of loved ones from cancer. He claimed this had no bearing on her present condition, which was not terminal. Judge Simons pointed out that O'Connor had worked for twenty years in a hospital emergency room and pathology laboratory. She was no casual observer of death, and her "remarks" about not wanting artificial treatment for herself carried a lot of weight. Her expressed wishes to her daughters, who were nurses and coworkers in the same hospital, could not be considered "casual," as the majority observed. Judge Simons stated:

> Until today, under New York law, decisions concerning medical treatment remained the right of the patient. Today's opinion narrowly circumscribes our rule to a degree that makes it all but useless. Few, if any, patients can meet the demanding standard the majority has adopted.... The majority, disguising its action as an application of the rule on self-determination, has made its own substituted judgment by improperly finding facts and drawing inferences contrary to the facts found by the courts below. Judges, the persons least qualified by training, experience or affinity to reject the patient's instructions, have overridden Mrs. O'Connor's wishes, negated her long held values on life and death, and imposed on her and her family their ideas of what her best interests require.

THE CASE OF NANCY CRUZAN

Even though *O'Connor* set a rigorous standard of proof for the state of New York, *Cruzan* was the first right-to-die case heard by the U.S. Supreme Court. It confirmed the legality of such strict standards for the entire country.

Nancy Beth Cruzan, by Co-guardians, Lester L. Cruzan Jr. and Joyce Cruzan v. Robert Harmon

In January 1983 twenty-five-year-old Nancy Beth Cruzan lost control of her car. A state trooper found her lying facedown in a ditch. She was in cardiac and respiratory arrest. Paramedics were able to revive her, but a neurosurgeon diagnosed "a probable cerebral contusion compounded by significant anoxia." The final diagnosis estimated she suffered anoxia (deprivation of oxygen) for twelve to fourteen minutes. At the trial the judge stated that after six minutes of oxygen deprivation, the brain generally suffers permanent damage.

At the time of the U.S. Supreme Court hearing in 1990, Cruzan was able to breathe on her own but was being nourished with a g-tube. Doctors had surgically implanted the feeding tube about a month after the accident, following the consent of her husband. Medical experts diagnosed the thirty-three-year-old patient to be in a PVS and capable of living another thirty years. Cruzan had been a ward of the state of Missouri since January 1986.

Cruzan's case was first heard by a Missouri trial court, which gave her parents, Joyce and Lester Cruzan Jr., the right to terminate artificial nutrition and hydration. The state and the court-appointed guardian ad litem appealed to the Missouri Supreme Court. The guardian ad litem believed it was in Cruzan's best interests to have the artificial feeding tube removed. However, he felt it was his duty as her attorney to take the case to the state supreme court because "this is a case of first impression in the state of Missouri." (A case of first impression is one without a precedent.)

THE RIGHT TO PRIVACY. In *Nancy Beth Cruzan, by Co-guardians, Lester L. Cruzan Jr. and Joyce Cruzan v. Robert Harmon* (760 S.W.2d 408 [Mo.banc 1988]), the Missouri Supreme Court stressed that the state constitution did not expressly provide for the right of privacy, which would support an individual's right to refuse medical treatment. Even though the U.S. Supreme Court had recognized the right of privacy in cases such as *Roe v. Wade* and *Griswold v. Connecticut*, this right did not extend to the withdrawal of food and water. In fact, the U.S. Supreme Court, in *Roe v. Wade*, stressed that it "has refused to recognize an unlimited right of this kind in the past."

THE STATE'S INTEREST IN LIFE. In Cruzan's case the Missouri Supreme Court majority confirmed that the state's interest in life encompassed the sanctity of life and the prolongation of life. The state's interest in the prolongation of life was especially valid in Cruzan's case. She was not terminally ill and, based on medical evidence, would "continue a life of relatively normal duration if allowed basic sustenance." Furthermore, the state was not interested in the quality of life. The court was mindful that its decision would apply not only to Cruzan and feared treading a slippery slope. "Were the quality of life at issue, persons with all manner of handicaps might find the state seeking to terminate their lives. Instead, the state's interest is in life; that interest is unqualified."

THE GUARDIANS' RIGHTS. The Missouri Supreme Court ruled that Cruzan had no constitutional right to die and that there was no clear and convincing evidence that she would not wish to continue her vegetative existence. The majority further found that her parents, or guardians, had no right to exercise substituted judgment on their daughter's behalf. The court concluded, "We find no principled legal basis which permits the co-guardians in this case to choose the death of their ward. In the absence of such a legal basis for that decision and in the face of this State's strongly stated policy in favor of life, we choose to err on the side of life, respecting the rights of incompetent persons who may wish to live despite a severely diminished quality of life."

Therefore, the Missouri Supreme Court reversed the judgment of the Missouri trial court that had allowed discontinuance of Cruzan's artificial feeding.

THE STATE DOES NOT HAVE AN OVERRIDING INTEREST. In his dissent, Judge Charles B. Blackmar (1922–2007) indicated that the state should not be involved in cases such as Cruzan's. He was not convinced that the state had spoken better for Cruzan's interests than did her parents. He also questioned the state's interest in life in the context of espousing capital punishment, which clearly establishes "the proposition that some lives are not worth preserving."

Judge Blackmar did not share the majority's opinion that yielding to the guardians' request would lead to the mass euthanasia of handicapped people whose conditions did not come close to Cruzan's. He stressed that a court ruling is precedent only for the facts of that specific case. Besides, one of the purposes of courts is to protect incompetent people against abuse. He claimed, "The principal opinion attempts to establish absolutes, but does so at the expense of human factors. In so doing, it unnecessarily subjects Nancy and those close to her to continuous torture which no family should be forced to endure."

"ERRONEOUS DECLARATION OF LAW." Judge Andrew J. Higgins (1921–), also dissenting, mainly disagreed with the majority's basic premise that the more than fifty precedent-setting cases from sixteen other states were based on an "erroneous declaration of law." Yet, he noted that all cases cited by the majority upheld an individual's right to refuse life-sustaining treatment, either personally or through the substituted judgment of a guardian. He could not understand the majority's contradiction of its own argument.

Nancy Beth Cruzan, by Her Parents and Co-guardians, Lester L. Cruzan et ux v. Director, Missouri Department of Health et al.

Cruzan's father appealed the Missouri Supreme Court's decision and, in December 1989, the U.S. Supreme Court heard arguments in *Nancy Beth Cruzan, by Her Parents and Co-guardians, Lester L. Cruzan et ux v. Director, Missouri Department of Health et al.* (497 U.S. 261, 1990). This was the first time the right-to-die issue had been brought before the U.S. Supreme Court, which chose not to rule on whether Cruzan's parents could have her feeding tube removed. Instead, it considered whether the U.S. Constitution prohibited the state of Missouri from requiring clear and convincing evidence that an incompetent person desires withdrawal of life-sustaining treatment. In a five-to-four decision the Court held that the Constitution did not prohibit the state of Missouri from requiring convincing evidence that an incompetent person wants life-sustaining treatment withdrawn.

Chief Justice William H. Rehnquist (1924–2005) wrote the opinion, with Justices Byron R. White (1917–2002), Sandra Day O'Connor (1930–), Antonin Scalia (1936–), and Anthony M. Kennedy (1936–) joining. The court majority believed that its rigorous requirement of clear and convincing evidence that Cruzan had refused

termination of life-sustaining treatment was justified. An erroneous decision not to withdraw the patient's feeding tube meant that the patient would continue to be sustained artificially. Possible medical advances or new evidence of the patient's intent could correct the error. An erroneous decision to terminate the artificial feeding could not be corrected, because the result of that decision—death—is irrevocable. The chief justice concluded, "No doubt is engendered by anything in this record but that Nancy Cruzan's mother and father are loving and caring parents. If the State were required by the United States Constitution to repose a right of 'substituted judgment' with anyone, the Cruzans would surely qualify. But we do not think the Due Process Clause requires the State to repose judgment on these matters with anyone but the patient herself." The Due Process Clause of the Fourteenth Amendment provides that no state shall "deprive any person of life, liberty, or property without due process of law."

STATE INTEREST SHOULD NOT OUTWEIGH THE FREEDOM OF CHOICE. Dissenting, Justice William J. Brennan Jr. (1906–1997) pointed out that the state of Missouri's general interest in the preservation of Cruzan's life in no way outweighed her freedom of choice—in this case the choice to refuse medical treatment. He stated, "The regulation of constitutionally protected decisions . . . must be predicated on legitimate state concerns other than disagreement with the choice the individual has made. . . . Otherwise, the interest in liberty protected by the Due Process Clause would be a nullity."

Justice Brennan believed the state of Missouri had imposed an uneven burden of proof. The state would only accept clear and convincing evidence that the patient had made explicit statements refusing artificial nutrition and hydration. However, it did not require any proof that she had made specific statements desiring continuance of such treatment. Hence, it could not be said that the state had accurately determined Cruzan's wishes.

Justice Brennan disagreed that it is better to err on the side of life than death. He argued that, to the patient, erring from either side is "irrevocable." He explained, "An erroneous decision to terminate artificial nutrition and hydration, to be sure, will lead to failure of that last remnant of physiological life, the brain stem, and result in complete brain death. An erroneous decision not to terminate life-support, however, robs a patient of the very qualities protected by the right to avoid unwanted medical treatment. His own degraded existence is perpetuated; his family's suffering is protracted; the memory he leaves behind becomes more and more distorted."

STATE USES NANCY CRUZAN FOR "SYMBOLIC EFFECT." Justice John Paul Stevens (1920–), in a separate dissenting opinion, believed the state of Missouri was using Cruzan for the "symbolic effect" of defining life. The state sought to equate Cruzan's physical existence with life.

However, Justice Stevens pointed out that life is more than physiological functions. In fact, life connotes a person's experiences that make up his or her whole history, as well as "the practical manifestation of the human spirit."

Justice Stevens viewed the state's refusal to let Cruzan's guardians terminate her artificial feeding as ignoring their daughter's interests, and therefore, "unconscionable":

> Insofar as Nancy Cruzan has an interest in being remembered for how she lived rather than how she died, the damage done to those memories by the prolongation of her death is irreversible. Insofar as Nancy Cruzan has an interest in the cessation of any pain, the continuation of her pain is irreversible. Insofar as Nancy Cruzan has an interest in a closure to her life consistent with her own beliefs rather than those of the Missouri legislature, the State's imposition of its contrary view is irreversible. To deny the importance of these consequences is in effect to deny that Nancy Cruzan has interests at all, and thereby to deny her personhood in the name of preserving the sanctity of her life.

CRUZAN CASE FINALLY RESOLVED. On December 14, 1990, nearly eight years after Cruzan's car accident, a Missouri circuit court ruled that new evidence presented by three more friends constituted "clear and convincing" evidence that she would not want to continue existing in a PVS. The court allowed the removal of her artificial feeding. Within two hours of the ruling, Cruzan's doctor removed the tube. Cruzan's family kept a twenty-four-hour vigil with her, until she died on December 26, 1990. Cruzan's family, however, believed she had left them many years earlier.

THE TERRI SCHIAVO CASE

Like Cruzan, the case of Terri Schiavo involved a young woman in a PVS and the question of whether her nutrition and hydration could be discontinued.

In 1990 Schiavo suffered a loss of potassium in her body due to an eating disorder. This physiological imbalance caused her heart to stop beating, which deprived her brain of oxygen and resulted in a coma. She underwent surgery to implant a stimulator in her brain, an experimental treatment. The brain stimulator implant appeared to be a success, and the young woman appeared to be slowly emerging from her coma.

Nonetheless, even though Schiavo was continually provided with appropriate stimulation to recover, she remained in a PVS years later. Her husband, Michael Schiavo, believing that she would never recover and saying that his wife did not want to be kept alive by artificial means, petitioned a Florida court to remove her feeding tube. Her parents, however, believed that she could feel, understand, and respond. They opposed the idea of removing the feeding tube.

In 2000 a Florida trial court determined that Schiavo did not wish to be kept alive by artificial means based on her clear and direct statement to that effect to her husband. However, Schiavo's parents appealed the ruling, based on their belief that their daughter responded to their voices and could improve with therapy. They also contested the assertion that their daughter did not want to be kept alive by artificial means. Schiavo had left no living will to clarify her position, but under Florida's Health Care Advance Directives Law (http://www.flsenate.gov/Statutes/index.cfm?App_mode=Display_Statute&URL=Ch0765/ch0765.htm), a patient's spouse is second in line to decide about whether life support should be suspended (after a previously appointed guardian), adult children are third, and parents are fourth.

Constitutional Breach?

By October 2003 Schiavo's parents had exhausted their appeals, and the Florida appellate courts upheld the ruling of the trial court. At that time, a Florida judge ruled that removal of the tube take place. However, Schiavo's parents requested that the Florida governor Jeb Bush (1953–) intervene. In response, the Florida legislature developed House Bill 35-E (Terri's Law) and passed this bill on October 21, 2003. The law gave Governor Bush the authority to order Schiavo's feeding tube reinserted, and he did that by issuing Executive Order No. 03-201 that same day, six days after the feeding tube had been removed.

Legal experts noted that the Florida legislature, in passing Terri's Law, appeared to have taken judicial powers away from the judicial branch of the Florida government and had given them to the executive branch. If this were the case, then the law was unconstitutional under article 2, section III of the Florida constitution, which states, "No person belonging to one branch shall exercise any powers appertaining to either of the other branches unless expressly provided herein." Thus, Michael Schiavo challenged the law's constitutionality in Pinellas County Circuit Court. Governor Bush requested that the Pinellas County Circuit Court judge dismiss Schiavo's lawsuit arguing against Terri's Law. On April 30, 2004, Judge Charles A. Davis Jr. (1948–) rejected the governor's technical challenges, thereby denying the governor's motion to dismiss. In May 2004 the law that allowed Governor Bush to intervene in the case was ruled unconstitutional by a Florida appeals court.

Continued Appeals

Schiavo's parents then appealed the case to the Florida Supreme Court, which heard the case in September 2004. The court upheld the ruling of the lower court, with the seven justices ruling unanimously and writing that Terri's Law was "an unconstitutional encroachment on the power that has been reserved for the independent judiciary." Nonetheless, Schiavo's parents continued their legal fight to keep her alive, so a stay on the tube's removal was put in place while their appeals were pending. In October 2004 Governor Bush asked the Florida Supreme Court to reconsider its decision. The court refused the request.

Attorneys for the Florida governor then asked the U.S. Supreme Court to hear the Schiavo case. The Supreme Court rejected the request, which essentially affirmed lower court rulings that the governor had no legal right to intervene in the matter. In February 2005 a Florida judge ruled that Michael Schiavo could remove his wife's feeding tube in March of that year. On March 18, 2005, the tube was removed. Days later, in an unprecedented action, the U.S. House of Representatives and the U.S. Senate approved legislation, which was quickly signed by President George W. Bush (1946–), granting Terri Schiavo's parents the right to sue in federal court. In effect, this legislation allowed the court to intervene in the case and restore Terri's feeding tube. However, when Schiavo's parents appealed to the court, a federal judge refused to order the feeding tube reinserted. They then filed an appeal with the U.S. Supreme Court. Once again, the High Court refused to hear the case.

The Effect of the Schiavo Situation on End-of-Life Decision Making

Terri Schiavo died on March 31, 2005. Her death and the events leading up to her death resulted in an intense debate among Americans over end-of-life decisions and brought new attention to the question of who should make the decision to stop life support.

The medical examiners who conducted Schiavo's autopsy found her brain "profoundly atrophied," only half the normal size, and noted that "no amount of therapy or treatment would have regenerated the massive loss of neurons." An autopsy cannot definitively establish a PVS, but the Schiavo findings were seen as "very consistent" with a PVS.

THE CONSTITUTIONALITY OF ASSISTED SUICIDE

Washington et al. v. Harold Glucksberg et al.

In January 1994 four state of Washington doctors, three terminally ill patients, and the organization Compassion in Dying filed a suit in the U.S. District Court. The plaintiffs sought to have the Washington Revised Code 9A.36.060(1) (1994) declared unconstitutional. This Washington law states, "A person is guilty of promoting a suicide attempt when he knowingly causes or aids another person to attempt suicide."

According to the plaintiffs, mentally competent terminally ill adults have the right, under the Equal Protection Clause of the Fourteenth Amendment, to a physi-

cian's assistance in determining the time and manner of their death. In *Compassion in Dying v. Washington* (850 F. Supp. 1454, 1459 [WD Wash. 1994]), the U.S. District Court agreed, stating that the Washington Revised Code violated the Equal Protection Clause's provision that "all persons similarly situated should be treated alike."

In its decision, the district court relied on *Planned Parenthood of Southeastern Pennsylvania v. Casey* (505 U.S. 833, 1992; a reaffirmation of *Roe v. Wade*'s holding of the right to abortion) and *Cruzan v. Director, Missouri Department of Health* (the right to refuse unwanted life-sustaining treatment). The court found Washington's statute against assisted suicide unconstitutional because the law "places an undue burden on the exercise of [that] constitutionally protected liberty interest."

In *Compassion in Dying v. State of Washington* (49 F. 3d 586, 591, 1995), a panel (three or more judges but not the full court) of the Court of Appeals for the Ninth Circuit Court reversed the district court's decision, stressing that in the 205 years of U.S. history, no court had ever recognized the right to assisted suicide. However, in *Compassion in Dying v. State of Washington* (79 F. 3d 790, 798, 1996), the Ninth Circuit Court reheard the case en banc (by the full court), reversed the panel's decision, and affirmed the district court's ruling.

The en banc Court of Appeals for the Ninth Circuit Court did not mention the Equal Protection Clause violation as indicated by the district court. However, it referred to *Casey* and *Cruzan*, adding that the U.S. Constitution recognizes the right to die. Quoting from *Casey*, Judge Stephen R. Reinhardt (1931–) wrote, "Like the decision of whether or not to have an abortion, the decision how and when to die is one of 'the most intimate and personal choices a person may make in a lifetime, . . . central to personal dignity and autonomy.'"

THE U.S. SUPREME COURT DECIDES. The state of Washington and its attorney general appealed the case *Washington et al. v. Harold Glucksberg et al.* (117 S.Ct. 2258, 1997) to the U.S. Supreme Court. Instead of addressing the plaintiffs' initial question of whether mentally competent terminally ill adults have the right to physician-assisted suicide, Chief Justice Rehnquist reframed the issue, focusing on "whether Washington's prohibition against 'caus[ing]' or 'aid[ing]' a suicide offends the Fourteenth Amendment to the United States Constitution."

Chief Justice Rehnquist recalled the more than seven hundred years of Anglo-American common-law tradition disapproving of suicide and assisted suicide. He added that assisted suicide is considered a crime in almost every state, with no exceptions granted to mentally competent terminally ill adults.

PREVIOUS SUBSTANTIVE DUE-PROCESS CASES. The plaintiffs argued that in previous substantive due-process cases, such as *Cruzan*, the U.S. Supreme Court had acknowledged the principle of self-autonomy by ruling "that competent dying persons have the right to direct the removal of life-sustaining medical treatment and thus hasten death." Chief Justice Rehnquist claimed that, although committing suicide with another's help is just as personal as refusing life-sustaining treatment, it is not similar to refusing unwanted medical treatment. In fact, according to the chief justice, the *Cruzan* court specifically stressed that most states ban assisted suicide.

STATE'S INTEREST. The Court pointed out that the state of Washington's interest in preserving human life includes the entire spectrum of that life, from birth to death, regardless of a person's physical or mental condition. The Court agreed with the state that allowing assisted suicide might imperil the lives of vulnerable populations such as the poor, the elderly, and the disabled. The state included the terminally ill in this group.

Furthermore, the Court agreed with the state of Washington that legalizing physician-assisted suicide would eventually lead to voluntary and involuntary euthanasia. Because a health-care proxy's decision is legally accepted as an incompetent patient's decision, what if the patient cannot self-administer the lethal medication? In such a case a physician or a family member would have to administer the drug, thus committing euthanasia.

The Court unanimously ruled that:

> [The Washington Revised] Code ... does not violate the Fourteenth Amendment, either on its face (in all or most cases in which it might be applied) or "as applied to competent terminally ill adults who wish to hasten their deaths by obtaining medication prescribed by their doctors." Throughout the Nation, Americans are engaged in an earnest and profound debate about the morality, legality, and practicality of physician assisted suicide. Our holding permits this debate to continue, as it should in a democratic society. The decision of the en banc Court of Appeals is reversed, and the case is remanded [sent back] for further proceedings consistent with this opinion.

PROVISION OF PALLIATIVE CARE. Concurring, Justices O'Connor and Stephen G. Breyer (1938–) wrote that "terminally ill patients in New York and Washington ... can obtain palliative care (care that relieves pain, but does not cure the illness), even potentially lethal doses of drugs that are foreseen to result in death." Hence, the justices did not see the need to address a dying person's constitutional right to obtain relief from pain. Justice O'Connor believed the Court was justified in banning assisted suicide for two reasons, "The difficulty of defining terminal illness and the risk that a dying patient's request for assistance in ending his or her life might not be truly voluntary."

Dennis C. Vacco, Attorney General of New York et al. v. Timothy E. Quill et al.

REFUSING LIFE-SUSTAINING TREATMENT IS ESSENTIALLY THE SAME AS ASSISTED SUICIDE. In 1994 three New York physicians and three terminally ill patients sued the New York attorney general. In *Quill v. Koppell* (870 F. Supp. 78, 84–85 [SDNY 1994]), they claimed before the U.S. District Court that New York violated the Equal Protection Clause by prohibiting physician-assisted suicide. The state permits a competent patient to refuse life-sustaining treatment, but not to obtain physician-assisted suicide. The plaintiffs claimed that these are "essentially the same thing." The court disagreed, stating that withdrawing life support to let nature run its course differs from intentionally using lethal drugs to cause death.

The plaintiffs brought their case *Quill v. Vacco* (80 F. 3d 716, 1996) to the Court of Appeals for the Second Circuit (appellate court), which reversed the district court's ruling. The appellate court found that the New York statute does not treat equally all competent terminally ill patients wishing to hasten their death. The court stated, "The ending of life by [the withdrawal of life-support systems] is *nothing more or less* than assisted suicide."

REFUSING LIFE-SUSTAINING TREATMENT DIFFERS FROM ASSISTED SUICIDE. New York's attorney general appealed the case to the U.S. Supreme Court. In *Dennis C. Vacco, Attorney General of New York et al. v. Timothy E. Quill et al.* (117 S.Ct. 2293, 1997), the Court distinguished between withdrawing life-sustaining medical treatment and assisted suicide. The Court contended that when a patient refuses life support, he or she dies because the disease has run its natural course. By contrast, if a patient self-administers lethal drugs, death results from that medication.

The Court also distinguished between the physician's role in both scenarios. A physician who complies with a patient's request to withdraw life support does so to honor a patient's wish because the treatment no longer benefits the patient. Likewise, when a physician prescribes painkilling drugs, the needed drug dosage might hasten death, although the physician's only intent is to ease pain. However, when a physician assists in suicide, his or her prime intention is to hasten death. Therefore, the Court reversed the ruling made by the Court of Appeals for the Second Circuit.

STATE LEGISLATURES REJECT PHYSICIAN-ASSISTED SUICIDE

Justices Stevens and David H. Souter (1939–) issued opinions encouraging individual states to enact legislation to permit physician-assisted suicide in selected cases. At the state level, more than thirty bills to legalize physician-assisted suicide had been introduced. As of May 2008, Oregon was the only state with a law that legalizes the practice. The Oregon legislation was approved in 1994 and reaffirmed by voters in 1997. Nonetheless, state ballot initiatives in other states failed to garner enough votes to legalize physician-assisted suicide.

Steve Geissinger reports in "Assisted Suicide Legislation Shelved" (*Oakland Tribune*, June 8, 2007) that voters in California in 1988 and again in 1992 rejected the initiative. The California Compassionate Choices Act (AB374), modeled after the Oregon Death with Dignity Act, was shelved in June 2007 due to a lack of sufficient votes. The bill was expected to be revisited during the 2008 legislative session.

Washington state voters rejected a physician-assisted initiative in 1991, Michigan in 1998, Maine in 2000, and Wyoming in 2004. In addition, an assisted suicide proposal was shelved in the Hawaii legislature in 2004 and was unsuccessful in another try in 2005. The Vermont House of Representatives voted down an assisted suicide initiative in 2007.

In March 2008 Jack Kevorkian (1928–) announced his plans to run for Congress in Michigan. Kevorkian was released from prison in 2007 after serving a sentence for assisting in the death of Thomas Youk, a fifty-two-year-old man with ALS.

THE SUPREME COURT RULING ON PHYSICIAN-ASSISTED SUICIDE IN OREGON

In late 2001 the U.S. attorney general John D. Ashcroft (1942–) reversed a decision made by his predecessor, Janet Reno (1938–), by asserting that the Controlled Substances Act of 1970 could be used against Oregon physicians who helped patients commit suicide by prescribing lethal drugs. If that were the case, then the U.S. Drug Enforcement Administration (DEA) could disallow the prescription-writing privileges of any Oregon physician who prescribed drugs commonly used for assisted suicide. The possibility would also exist for those physicians to be criminally prosecuted as well. In response, the state of Oregon filed a lawsuit against Ashcroft's decision.

In May 2004 a federal appeals court upheld the Oregon Death with Dignity Act. The decision, by a divided three-judge panel of the U.S. Court of Appeals for the Ninth Circuit in San Francisco, said the U.S. Department of Justice did not have the power to punish physicians for prescribing medication for the purpose of assisted suicide. The majority opinion stated that Ashcroft overstepped his authority in trying to block enforcement of Oregon's law.

In February 2005 the U.S. Supreme Court agreed to hear the Bush administration's challenge of Oregon's physician-assisted suicide law. On January 17, 2006, the Court let stand Oregon's physician-assisted suicide law. The High Court held that the Controlled Substances Act "does not allow the Attorney General to prohibit doctors from prescribing regulated drugs for use in physician-assisted suicide under state law permitting the procedure." Writing for the majority, Justice Kennedy explained that both Ashcroft and Alberto Gonzales (1955–), who succeeded Ashcroft as the U.S. attorney general, did not have the power to override the Oregon physician-assisted suicide law. Furthermore, Justice Kennedy added that the attorney general does not have the authority to make health and medical policy.

CHAPTER 9

THE COST OF HEALTH CARE

INCREASING COSTS

Americans want a quality health-care system despite its increasingly high cost. Table 9.1 shows the progression of medical costs in the United States from 1960 to 2006. The table compares the growth in national health-care expenditures and in gross domestic product (GDP; the total value of all the goods and services produced by a nation in a given year) over those years, and presents the national health expenditures as a percentage of the GDP.

In 1960 the United States spent 5.2% of its GDP on health care. (See Table 9.1.) In 1970 this percentage had risen to 7.2%, and by 1980 it had risen to 9.1%. The rise continued, and by 1990 health care consumed 12.3% of the GDP. Growth of the cost of health care slowed somewhat during the 1990s, so that by 2000 heath care was 13.8% of the nation's GDP. Since 2000, health-care costs have continued their upward climb at a significant pace. In 2006 health-care costs consumed 16% of the GDP.

The Consumer Price Index (CPI) is a measure of the average change in prices paid by consumers. For many years the medical component of the CPI increased at a greater rate than any other component, even food and housing. Between 1960 and 2006 the average annual percent of change from the previous year shown in the overall CPI was well below the average annual percent of change for medical care. (See Table 9.2.) In 2006 the overall CPI increased by 3.2%, whereas medical care increased by 4%. (Energy, however, had the highest percent of change from 2004 to 2006).

The upper portion of Table 9.2 shows the change in prices in a different way—it provides the CPI figure (price level) for each year shown rather than the average annual percent of change from the previous year given in the table. The CPI figure is computed by the Bureau of Labor Statistics (BLS). It is based on the average price of goods and services for the thirty-six-month period covering 1982, 1983, and 1984, which the BLS set to equal 100. (These years are not shown in the top portion of Table 9.2.) Each year, the BLS measures changes in prices in relation to that figure of 100. The resultant figures show the change in relation to the reference years of 1982 to 1984. Thus, the years before the 1982–84 period have price levels below 100, and the years after this period have price levels above 100. For example, an index of 110 means there has been a 10% increase in price since the reference period. An index of 90 means a 10% decrease. "All items" cost slightly more than twice as much in 2006 than they did during the 1982–84 period (201.6 versus 100), whereas medical care cost well over three times as much (336.2 versus 100).

So where did all the money spent on health care in 2006 come from? Fifty-three percent came from private funds, including private health insurance (34%), out-of-pocket expenses (12%), and other private sources (7%). (See Figure 9.1.) The remaining 46% came from federal or state government sources.

Where did all the money spent on health care in 2006 go? Hospital and physician costs, traditionally composing the greater part of health-care expenses, were 31% and 21%, respectively, whereas prescription drug costs were 10% of all health-care expenses. (See Figure 9.2.)

GOVERNMENT HEALTH-CARE PROGRAMS

Unlike most developed countries, the United States does not have universal health care. Two government entitlement programs that provide health-care coverage for older adults (aged sixty-five and older), the poor, and the disabled are Medicare and Medicaid. Enacted in 1965 as amendments to the Social Security Act of 1935, these programs went into effect in 1966. In 1972 amendments to Medicare extended medical insurance coverage to those disabled long term and those with chronic kidney disease or end-stage renal disease. In 2006, 43.2 million older adults and people with disabilities were enrolled in Medicare, with total expenditures of $408.3 billion. (See Table 9.3.)

TABLE 9.1

National health expenditures, selected years 1960–2006

Item	1960	1970	1980	1990	2000	2001	2002	2003	2004	2005	2006
					Billions of dollars						
National health expenditures	$27.5	$74.9	$253.4	$714.0	$1,353.6	$1,469.6	$1,603.4	$1,732.4	$1,852.3	$1,973.3	$2,105.5
Private	20.7	46.8	147.0	427.3	757.0	807.6	882.3	955.1	1,014.8	1,076.6	1,135.2
Public	6.8	28.1	106.3	286.7	596.6	662.0	721.1	777.3	837.5	896.8	970.3
Federal	2.9	17.7	71.6	193.9	417.6	464.1	508.6	550.7	597.1	639.1	704.9
State and local	3.9	10.4	34.8	92.8	179.0	197.9	212.5	226.6	240.4	257.7	265.4
					Millions						
U.S. population	186	210	230	254	283	285	288	291	294	297	300
					Billions of dollars						
Gross domestic product	$526	$1,039	$2,790	$5,803	$9,817	$10,128	$10,470	$10,961	$11,686	$12,434	$13,195
					Per capita amount in dollars						
National health expenditures	$148	$356	$1,100	$2,813	$4,790	$5,148	$5,560	$5,952	$6,301	$6,649	$7,026
Private	111	222	638	1,684	2,679	2,829	3,059	3,281	3,452	3,627	3,788
Public	36	134	462	1,130	2,111	2,319	2,500	2,670	2,849	3,022	3,238
Federal	15	84	311	764	1,478	1,626	1,763	1,892	2,031	2,153	2,352
State and local	21	49	151	366	634	693	737	779	818	868	886
					Percent distribution						
National health expenditures	100.0	100.0	100.0	100.0	100.0	100.0	100.0	100.0	100.0	100.0	100.0
Private	75.3	62.4	58.0	59.8	55.9	55.0	55.0	55.1	54.8	54.6	53.9
Public	24.7	37.6	42.0	40.2	44.1	45.0	45.0	44.9	45.2	45.4	46.1
Federal	10.4	23.7	28.2	27.1	30.8	31.6	31.7	31.8	32.2	32.4	33.5
State and local	14.3	13.9	13.7	13.0	13.2	13.5	13.3	13.1	13.0	13.1	12.6
					Percent of gross domestic product						
National health expenditures	5.2	7.2	9.1	12.3	13.8	14.5	15.3	15.8	15.9	15.9	16.0
					Average annual percent growth from previous year shown						
National health expenditures		10.5	13.0	10.9	7.0	8.6	9.1	8.0	6.9	6.5	6.7
Private		8.5	12.1	11.3	6.7	6.7	9.3	8.3	6.2	6.1	5.4
Public		15.3	14.2	10.4	7.3	11.0	8.9	7.8	7.7	7.1	8.2
Federal		20.0	15.0	10.5	7.2	11.2	9.6	8.3	8.4	7.0	10.3
State and local		10.2	12.8	10.3	7.7	10.5	7.4	6.6	6.1	7.2	3.0
U.S. population		1.2	0.9	1.0	1.0	1.0	1.0	0.9	1.0	1.0	1.0
Gross domestic product		7.0	10.4	7.6	5.9	3.2	3.4	4.7	6.6	6.4	6.1

*Census resident-based population less armed forces overseas and population of outlying areas.
Note: Numbers and percents may not add to totals because of rounding. Dollar amounts shown are in current dollars.

SOURCE: Adapted from "Table 1. National Health Expenditures Aggregate, per Capita Amounts, Percent Distribution, and Average Annual Percent Growth, by Source of Funds: Selected Calendar Years 1960–2006," in *National Health Expenditure Data: Historical—NHE Web Tables*, Centers for Medicare and Medicaid Services, Office of the Actuary, National Health Statistics Group, January 2008, http://www.cms.hhs.gov/NationalHealthExpendData/downloads/tables.pdf (accessed February 2, 2008)

The Original Medicare Plan

The Original Medicare Plan, enacted under Title XVIII of the Social Security Act, comprises two health-related insurance plans:

- Part A (hospital insurance) is funded by Social Security payroll taxes. It pays for inpatient hospital care, which includes physicians' fees, nursing services, meals, a semiprivate room, special care units, operating room costs, laboratory tests, and some drugs and supplies. It also pays for skilled nursing facility care after hospitalization, home health-care visits by nurses or medical technicians, and hospice care for the terminally ill. Table 9.3 shows that in 2006, 42.9 million Americans were enrolled in Part A, hospital insurance. Of the $408.3 billion in total Medicare expenditures, $191.9 billion (47%) was spent on hospital insurance.

- Part B (medical insurance) is an elective medical insurance. Because Part A does not pay all health-care costs

and other expenses associated with hospitalization, many beneficiaries enroll in the Part B plan. Most people pay a monthly premium for this coverage. Those monthly premiums and general federal revenues finance Part B. Coverage includes physicians' and surgeons' services, diagnostic and laboratory tests, outpatient hospital services, outpatient physical therapy, speech pathology services, home health-care services, and medical equipment and supplies. Table 9.3 shows that in 2006, 40.3 million Americans were enrolled in Part B. Of the $408.3 billion in total Medicare expenditures, $169 billion (41%) was spent on medical insurance.

Medicare Supplement Insurance (Medigap)

The Original Medicare Plan coverage (Part A and Part B) has gaps, which means that it does not cover all medical costs and services. Medigap insurance is supplemental Medicare insurance that pays these expenses. Medigap is not a way to get Medicare benefits; rather, it is

TABLE 9.2

Consumer price index and average annual percent change for general items and medical care components, selected years, 1960–2006

[Data are based on reporting by samples of providers and other retail outlets]

Items and medical care components	1960	1970	1980	1990	1995	2000	2003	2004	2005	2006
	Consumer price index (CPI)									
All items	29.6	38.8	82.4	130.7	152.4	172.2	184.0	188.9	195.3	201.6
All items less medical care	30.2	39.2	82.8	128.8	148.6	167.3	178.1	182.7	188.7	194.7
Services	24.1	35.0	77.9	139.2	168.7	195.3	216.5	222.8	230.1	238.9
Food	30.0	39.2	86.8	132.4	148.4	167.8	180.0	186.2	190.7	195.2
Apparel	45.7	59.2	90.9	124.1	132.0	129.6	120.9	120.4	119.5	119.5
Housing	—	36.4	81.1	128.5	148.5	169.6	184.8	189.5	195.7	203.2
Energy	22.4	25.5	86.0	102.1	105.2	124.6	136.5	151.4	177.1	196.9
Medical care	22.3	34.0	74.9	162.8	220.5	260.8	297.1	310.1	323.2	336.2
Components of medical care										
Medical care services	19.5	32.3	74.8	162.7	224.2	266.0	306.0	321.3	336.7	350.6
Professional services	—	37.0	77.9	156.1	201.0	237.7	261.2	271.5	281.7	289.3
Physicians' services	21.9	34.5	76.5	160.8	208.8	244.7	267.7	278.3	287.5	291.9
Dental services	27.0	39.2	78.9	155.8	206.8	258.5	292.5	306.9	324.0	340.9
Eye glasses and eye care[a]	—	—	—	117.3	137.0	149.7	155.9	159.3	163.2	168.1
Services by other medical professionals[a]	—	—	—	120.2	143.9	161.9	177.1	181.9	186.8	192.2
Hospital and related services	—	—	69.2	178.0	257.8	317.3	394.8	417.9	439.9	468.1
Hospital services[b]	—	—	—	—	—	115.9	144.7	153.4	161.6	172.1
Inpatient hospital services[b,c]	—	—	—	—	—	113.8	140.1	148.1	156.6	167.5
Outpatient hospital services[a,c]	—	—	—	138.7	204.6	263.8	337.9	356.3	373.0	395.0
Hospital rooms	9.3	23.6	68.0	175.4	251.2	—	—	—	—	—
Other inpatient services[a]	—	—	—	142.7	206.8	—	—	—	—	—
Nursing homes and adult day care[b]	—	—	—	—	—	117.0	135.2	140.4	145.0	151.0
Health insurance[d]	—	—	—	—	—	—	—	—	—	103.1
Medical care commodities	46.9	46.5	75.4	163.4	204.5	238.1	262.8	269.3	276.0	285.9
Prescription drugs and medical supplies	54.0	47.4	72.5	181.7	235.0	285.4	326.3	337.1	349.0	363.9
Nonprescription drugs and medical supplies[a]	—	—	—	120.6	140.5	149.5	152.0	152.3	151.7	154.6
Internal and respiratory over-the-counter drugs	—	42.3	74.9	145.9	167.0	176.9	181.2	180.9	179.7	183.4
Nonprescription medical equipment and supplies	—	—	79.2	138.0	166.3	178.1	178.1	179.7	180.6	183.2
	Average annual percent change from previous year shown									
All items	...	2.7	7.8	4.7	3.1	2.5	2.2	2.7	3.4	3.2
All items excluding medical care	...	2.6	7.8	4.5	2.9	2.4	2.1	2.6	3.3	3.2
All services	...	3.8	8.3	6.0	3.9	3.0	3.5	2.9	3.3	3.8
Food	...	2.7	8.3	4.3	2.3	2.5	2.4	3.4	2.4	2.4
Apparel	...	2.6	4.4	3.2	1.2	−0.4	−2.3	−0.4	−0.7	0.0
Housing	...	—	8.3	4.7	2.9	2.7	2.9	2.5	3.3	3.8
Energy	...	1.3	12.9	1.7	0.6	3.4	3.1	10.9	17.0	11.2
Medical care	...	4.3	8.2	8.1	6.3	3.4	4.4	4.4	4.2	4.0
Components of medical care										
Medical care services	...	5.2	8.8	8.1	6.6	3.5	4.8	5.0	4.8	4.1
Professional services	...	—	7.7	7.2	5.2	3.4	3.2	3.9	3.8	2.7
Physicians' services	...	4.6	8.3	7.7	5.4	3.2	3.0	4.0	3.3	1.5
Dental services	...	3.8	7.2	7.0	5.8	4.6	4.2	4.9	5.6	5.2
Eye glasses and eye care[a]	...	—	—	—	3.2	1.8	1.4	2.2	2.4	3.0
Services by other medical professionals[a]	...	—	—	—	3.7	2.4	3.0	2.7	2.7	2.9
Hospital and related services	...	—	—	9.9	7.7	4.2	7.6	5.9	5.3	6.4
Hospital services[b]	...	—	—	—	—	—	7.7	6.0	5.3	6.5
Inpatient hospital services[b,c]	...	—	—	—	—	—	7.2	5.7	5.7	7.0
Outpatient hospital services[a,c]	...	—	—	—	8.1	5.2	8.6	5.4	4.7	5.9
Hospital rooms	...	9.8	11.2	9.9	7.4	—	—	—	—	—
Other inpatient services[a]	...	—	—	—	7.7	—	—	—	—	—
Nursing homes and adult day care[b]	...	—	—	—	—	—	4.9	3.8	3.3	4.1
Health insurance[d]	...									

extra insurance sold by private insurance companies to those who have Original Medicare Plan coverage. Except in Massachusetts, Minnesota, and Wisconsin, there are ten standardized plans labeled Plan A through Plan J. Medigap policies only work with the Original Medicare Plan.

Medicare Advantage Plans (Part C)

Medicare Advantage Plans are offered by private companies that have contracts with Medicare to provide Medicare services. Even though there are generally lower copayments (the amounts patients pay for each medical service) and extra benefits with Medicare Advantage Plans versus the Original Medicare Plan, generally patients must see physicians who belong to the plan and go to certain hospitals to get services. Medicare Advantage Plans include Medicare Health Maintenance Organizations, Medicare Preferred Provider Organizations, Medicare Special Needs Plans (designed for specific groups of people), and Medicare Private Fee-for-Service Plans.

TABLE 9.2

Consumer price index and average annual percent change for general items and medical care components, selected years, 1960–2006

[CONTINUED]

[Data are based on reporting by samples of providers and other retail outlets]

Items and medical care components	1960	1970	1980	1990	1995	2000	2003	2004	2005	2006
				Average annual percent change from previous year shown						
Medical care commodities	...	−0.1	5.0	8.0	4.6	3.1	3.3	2.5	2.5	3.6
Prescription drugs and medical supplies	...	−1.3	4.3	9.6	5.3	4.0	4.6	3.3	3.5	4.3
Nonprescription drugs and medical supplies[a]	...	—	—	—	3.1	1.2	0.6	0.2	−0.4	1.9
Internal and respiratory over-the-counter drugs	...	—	5.9	6.9	2.7	1.2	0.8	−0.2	−0.7	2.1
Nonprescription medical equipment and supplies	...	—	—	5.7	3.8	1.4	0.0	0.9	0.5	1.4

—Data not available.
...Category not applicable.
[a]December 1986 = 100.
[b]December 1996 = 100.
[c]Special index based on a substantially smaller sample.
[d]December 2005 = 100.
Notes: Consumer price index for all urban consumers (CPI-U) U.S. city average, detailed expenditure categories. 1982–1984 =100, except where noted. Data are not seasonally adjusted.

SOURCE: "Table 122. Consumer Price Index and Average Annual Percent Change for All Items, Selected Items, and Medical Care Components: United States, Selected Years 1960–2006," in *Health, United States, 2007. With Chartbook on Trends in the Health of Americans*, Centers for Disease Control and Prevention, National Center for Health Statistics, November 2007, http://www.cdc.gov/nchs/data/hus/hus07.pdf (accessed January 30, 2008)

FIGURE 9.1

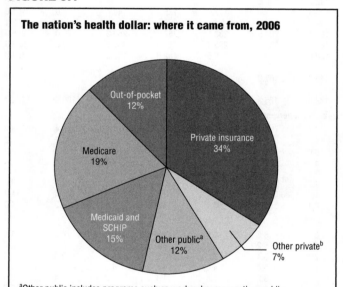

The nation's health dollar: where it came from, 2006

[a]Other public includes programs such as workers' compensation, public health activity, Department of Defense, Department of Veterans Affairs, Indian Health Service, state and local hospital subsidies and school health.
[b]Other private includes industrial in-plant, privately funded construction, and non-patient revenues, including philanthropy.
Note: Numbers shown may not add to 100.0 because of rounding.
SCHIP = State Children's Health Insurance Program, a federal program that gives funds to states to pay for health care insurance for low-income families with children not covered by Medicaid.

SOURCE: "The Nation's Health Dollar, Calendar Year 2006: Where It Came From," in *National Health Expenditure Data: Historical*, Centers for Medicare and Medicaid Services, Office of the Actuary, National Health Statistics Group, January 2008, http://www.cms.hhs.gov/NationalHealthExpendData/downloads/PieChart Sources Expenditures 2006.pdf (accessed February 2, 2008)

FIGURE 9.2

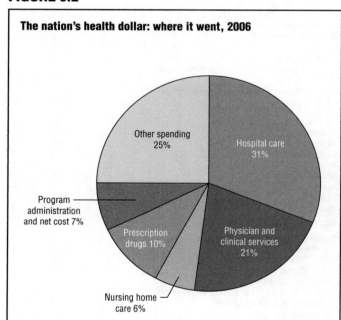

The nation's health dollar: where it went, 2006

Note: Other spending includes dentist services, other professional services, home health, durable medical products, over-the-counter medicines and sundries, public health, other personal health care, research and structures and equipment.

SOURCE: "The Nation's Health Dollar, Calendar Year 2006: Where It Went," in *National Health Expenditure Data: Historical*, Centers for Medicare and Medicaid Services, Office of the Actuary, National Health Statistics Group, January 2008, http://www.cms.hhs.gov/NationalHealth ExpendData/downloads/PieChartSourcesExpenditures2006.pdf (accessed February 2, 2008)

Other Medicare Health Plans

Other types of Medicare Health Plans include Medicare Cost Plans, Demonstrations, and Programs of All-inclusive Care for the Elderly (PACE). Medicare Cost Plans are limited in number and combine features of both Medicare Advantage Plans and the Original Medicare Plan. Demonstrations are special projects that test possible future improvements in Medicare costs, coverage, and quality of care. PACE provides services for frail elderly Americans.

TABLE 9.3

Medicare enrollees and expenditures, by Medicare program and type of service, selected years, 1970–2006

[Data are compiled from various sources by the Centers for Medicare & Medicaid Services]

Medicare program and type of service	1970	1980	1990	1995	2000	2001	2002	2003	2004	2005	2006[a]
Enrollees						Number in millions					
Total Medicare[b]	**20.4**	**28.4**	**34.3**	**37.6**	**39.7**	**40.1**	**40.5**	**41.2**	**41.9**	**42.6**	**43.2**
Hospital insurance	20.1	28.0	33.7	37.2	39.3	39.7	40.1	40.7	41.4	42.2	42.9
Supplementary medical insurance[c]	19.5	27.3	32.6	35.6	37.3	37.7	38.0	38.6	—	—	—
Part B	19.5	27.3	32.6	35.6	37.3	37.7	38.0	38.6	39.1	39.7	40.3
Part D[d]	—	—	—	—	—	—	—	—	1.2	1.8	27.9
Expenditures						Amount in billions					
Total Medicare	**$7.5**	**$36.8**	**$111.0**	**$184.2**	**$221.7**	**$244.8**	**$265.8**	**280.8**	**308.9**	**336.4**	**408.3**
Total hospital insurance (HI)	5.3	25.6	67.0	117.6	131.0	143.4	152.7	154.6	170.6	182.9	191.9
HI payments to managed care organizations[e]	—	0.0	2.7	6.7	21.4	20.8	19.2	19.5	20.8	24.9	32.9
HI payments for fee-for-service utilization	5.1	25.0	63.4	109.5	105.1	117.0	129.3	134.5	146.5	154.7	155.7
Inpatient hospital	4.8	24.1	56.9	82.3	87.1	96.0	104.2	108.7	116.4	121.7	121.0
Skilled nursing facility	0.2	0.4	2.5	9.1	11.1	13.1	15.2	14.7	17.1	18.5	19.9
Home health agency	0.1	0.5	3.7	16.2	4.0	4.1	5.0	4.8	5.4	5.9	6.0
Hospice	—	—	0.3	1.9	2.9	3.7	4.9	6.2	7.6	8.6	8.9
Home health agency transfer[f]	—	—	—	—	1.7	3.1	1.2	−2.2	0.0	0.0	0.0
Administrative expenses[g]	0.2	0.5	0.9	1.4	2.8	2.5	3.0	2.8	3.3	3.3	3.3
Total supplementary medical insurance (SMI)[c]	2.2	11.2	44.0	66.6	90.7	101.4	113.2	126.1	138.3	153.4	216.4
Total Part B	2.2	11.2	44.0	66.6	90.7	101.4	113.2	126.1	137.9	152.4	169.0
Part B payments to managed care organizations[e]	0.0	0.2	2.8	6.6	18.4	17.6	17.5	17.3	18.7	22.1	31.5
Part B payments for fee-for-service											
Part B payments for fee-for-service utilization[h]	1.9	10.4	39.6	58.4	72.2	85.1	94.5	104.3	116.2	126.9	134.1
Physician/supplies[i]	1.8	8.2	29.6	—	—	—	—	—	—	—	—
Outpatient hospital[j]	0.1	1.9	8.5	—	—	—	—	—	—	—	—
Independent laboratory[k]	0.0	0.1	1.5	—	—	—	—	—	—	—	—
Physician fee schedule	—	—	—	31.7	37.0	42.0	44.8	48.3	54.1	57.7	58.4
Durable medical equipment	—	—	—	3.7	4.7	5.4	6.5	7.5	7.8	7.9	8.4
Laboratory[j]	—	—	—	4.3	4.0	4.4	5.0	5.5	6.0	6.5	7.1
Other[m]	—	—	—	9.9	13.6	16.0	19.6	22.6	25.0	27.5	29.3
Hospital[n]	—	—	—	8.7	8.4	12.8	13.6	15.3	17.4	20.2	23.8
Home health agency	0.0	0.2	0.1	0.2	4.5	4.5	5.0	5.1	5.9	7.1	7.2
Home health agency transfer[f]	—	—	—	—	−1.7	−3.1	−1.2	2.2	0.0	0.0	0.0
Administrative expenses[g]	0.2	0.6	1.5	1.6	1.8	1.8	2.3	2.4	2.8	3.2	3.1
Part D transitional assistance and start-up costs[o]	—	—	—	—	—	—	—	—	0.2	0.7	0.0
Total Part D[d]	**—**	**—**	**—**	**—**	**—**	**—**	**—**	**—**	**0.4**	**1.0**	**47.4**
						Percent distribution of expenditures					
Total hospital insurance (HI)	100.0	100.0	100.0	100.0	100.0	100.0	100.0	100.0	100.0	100.0	100.0
HI payments to managed care organizations[e]	—	0.0	4.0	5.7	16.3	14.5	12.6	12.6	12.2	13.6	17.1
HI payments for fee-for-service utilization	97.0	97.9	94.6	93.1	80.2	81.6	84.7	87.0	85.9	84.6	81.1
Inpatient hospital	91.4	94.3	85.0	70.0	66.5	67.0	68.3	70.3	68.2	66.6	63.1
Skilled nursing facility	4.7	1.5	3.7	7.8	8.5	9.1	10.0	9.5	10.0	10.1	10.4
Home health agency	1.0	2.1	5.5	13.8	3.1	2.9	3.3	3.1	3.2	3.2	3.1
Hospice	—	—	0.5	1.6	2.2	2.6	3.2	4.0	4.4	4.7	4.6
Home health agency transfer[f]	—	—	—	—	1.3	2.2	0.8	−1.4	0.0	0.0	0.0
Administrative expenses[g]	3.0	2.1	1.4	1.2	2.1	1.7	2.0	1.8	2.0	1.8	1.7
Total supplementary medical insurance (SMI)[c]	100.0	100.0	100.0	100.0	100.0	100.0	100.0	100.0	100.0	100.0	100.0
Total Part B	100.0	100.0	100.0	100.0	100.0	100.0	100.0	100.0	99.7	99.3	78.1
Part B payments to managed care organizations[d]	1.2	1.8	6.4	9.9	20.2	17.3	15.5	13.7	13.6	14.5	18.6
Part B payments for fee-for-service utilization[h]	88.1	92.8	90.1	87.6	79.6	84.0	83.5	82.7	84.0	82.7	79.3
Physician/supplies[i]	80.9	72.8	67.3	—	—	—	—	—	—	—	—
Outpatient hospital[j]	5.2	16.9	19.3	—	—	—	—	—	—	—	—
Independent laboratory[k]	0.5	1.0	3.4	—	—	—	—	—	—	—	—

Medicare Prescription Drug Plans (Part D)

On January 1, 2006, Medicare began to offer insurance coverage for prescription drugs to everyone with Medicare. Its Medicare Prescription Drug Plans typically pay half a person's prescription drug costs. Most people pay a monthly premium for this coverage. Medicare Prescription Drug Plans are available with the Original Medicare Plan, Medicare Advantage Plans, and the other Medicare health plans. Table 9.3 shows that in 2006, 27.9 million Americans were enrolled in Part D (prescription drug plans). Of the $408.3 billion in total Medicare expenditures, $47.4 billion (12%) was spent on prescription drug plans.

Medicaid

The Medicaid health insurance program, enacted under Title XIX of the Social Security Act, provides medical assistance to low-income people, including those with disabilities and members of families with dependent children. Jointly financed by federal and state governments, Medicaid

TABLE 9.3

Medicare enrollees and expenditures, by Medicare program and type of service, selected years, 1970–2006 [CONTINUED]

[Data are compiled from various sources by the Centers for Medicare & Medicaid Services]

Medicare program and type of service	1970	1980	1990	1995	2000	2001	2002	2003	2004	2005	2006[a]
Physician fee schedule	—	—	—	47.5	40.8	41.5	39.6	38.3	39.2	37.9	34.6
Durable medical equipment	—	—	—	5.5	5.2	5.4	5.8	6.0	5.6	5.3	5.0
Laboratory[j]	—	—	—	6.4	4.4	4.3	4.4	4.3	4.4	4.3	4.2
Other[k]	—	—	—	14.8	15.0	15.8	17.3	17.9	18.1	18.0	17.3
Hospital[l]	—	—	—	13.0	9.3	12.6	12.0	12.1	12.6	13.5	14.1
Home health agency	1.5	2.1	0.2	0.3	4.9	4.5	4.5	4.0	4.3	4.3	4.3
Home health agency transfer[f]	—	—	—	0.0	−1.9	−3.1	−1.0	1.7	0.0	0.0	0.0
Administrative expenses[g]	10.7	5.4	3.5	2.4	2.0	1.8	2.0	1.9	2.0	1.8	1.8
Part D transitional assistance and start-up costs[o]	—	—	—	—	—	—	—	—	0.2	0.4	0.0
Total Part D[d]	—	—	—	—	—	—	—	—	0.3	0.7	21.9

—Data not available.

0.0 Quantity greater than 0 but less than 0.05.

[a]Preliminary figures.

[b]Average number enrolled in the hospital insurance (HI) and/or supplementary medical insurance (SMI) programs for the period.

[c]Starting with 2004 data, the SMI trust fund consists of two separate accounts: Part B (which pays for a portion of the costs of physicians' services, out patient hospital services, and other related medical and health services for voluntarily enrolled aged and disabled individuals) and Part D (Medicare prescription drug account which pays private plans to provide prescription drug coverage).

[d]The Medicare Modernization Act, enacted on December 8, 2003, established within SMI two Part D accounts related to prescription drug benefits: the Medicare prescription drug account and the transitional assistance account. The Medicare prescription drug account is used in conjunction with the broad, voluntary prescription drug benefits that began in 2006. The transitional assistance account was used to provide transitional assistance benefits, beginning in 2004 and extending through 2005, for certain low-income beneficiaries prior to the start of the new prescription drug benefit.

[e]Medicare-approved managed care organizations.

[f]Starting with 1999 data, reflects annual home health HI to SMI transfer amounts.

[g]Includes research, costs of experiments and demonstration projects, fraud and abuse promotion, and peer review activity (changed to Quality Improvement Organization in 2002).

[h]Type-of-service reporting categories for fee-for-service reimbursement differ before and after 1991.

[i]Includes payment for physicians, practitioners, durable medical equipment, and all suppliers other than independent laboratory through 1990. Starting with 1991 data, physician services subject to the physician fee schedule are shown. Payments for laboratory services paid under the laboratory fee schedule and performed in a physician office are included under laboratory beginning in 1991. Payments for durable medical equipment are shown separately beginning in 1991. The remaining services from the physician category are included in other.

[j]Includes payments for hospital outpatient department services, skilled nursing facility outpatient services, Part B services received as an inpatient in a hospital or skilled nursing facility setting, and other types of outpatient facilities. Starting with 1991 data, payments for hospital outpatient departments services, except for laboratory services, are listed under hospital. Hospital outpatient laboratory services are included in the laboratory line.

[k]Starting with 1991 data, those independent laboratory services that were paid under the laboratory fee schedule (most of the independent lab category) are included in the laboratory line; the remaining services are included in the physician fee schedule and other lines.

[l]Payments for laboratory services paid under the laboratory fee schedule performed in a physician office, independent lab, or in a hospital outpatient department.

[m]Includes payments for physician-administered drugs; freestanding ambulatory surgical center facility services; ambulance services; supplies; freestanding end-stage renal disease (ESRD) dialysis facility services; rural health clinics; outpatient rehabilitation facilities; psychiatric hospitals; and federally qualified health centers.

Includes the hospital facility costs for Medicare Part B services that are predominantly in the outpatient department, with the exception of hospital outpatient laboratory services, which are included on the laboratory line. Physician reimbursement is included on the physician fee schedule line.

[o]Part D administrative and transitional start-up costs were funded through the SMI Part B account.

Notes: Percents are calculated using unrounded data. Totals do not necessarily equal the sum of rounded components. Estimates include service disbursements as of February 2006 for Medicare enrollees residing in the United States, Puerto Rico, Virgin Islands, Guam, other outlying areas, foreign countries, and unknown residence. Some numbers in this table have been revised and differ from previous editions of Health, United States.

SOURCE: "Table 141. Medicare Enrollees and Expenditures and Percent Distribution, by Medicare Program and Type of Service: United States and Other Areas, Selected Years 1970–2006," in *Health, United States, 2007. With Chartbook on Trends in the Health of Americans*, Centers for Disease Control and Prevention, National Center for Health Statistics, November 2007, http://www.cdc.gov/nchs/data/hus/hus07.pdf (accessed January 30, 2008)

coverage includes hospitalization, physicians' services, laboratory fees, diagnostic screenings, and long-term nursing home care.

Even though people aged sixty-five and older made up only 7.8% of all Medicaid recipients in 2004, they received 23.1% of all Medicaid benefits. (See Table 9.4.) The average payment was $13,687 per older adult, compared to $13,714 for the blind and disabled, $2,475 for adults in families with dependent children, and $1,664 for children under the age of twenty-one.

WHO PAYS FOR END-OF-LIFE CARE?

Hsiang-Ching Kung et al. state in "Deaths: Final Data for 2005" (*National Vital Statistics Reports*, vol. 56, no. 10, April 24, 2008) that nearly three-fourths (73%) of those who died in 2005 were aged sixty-five

or older. Medicare covers the medical expenses of these older adults during the terminal stage of their life. Medicaid further covers older adults who have exhausted their Medicare benefits, as well as poor and disabled younger patients. Health programs under the U.S. Department of Veterans Affairs and the U.S. Department of Defense also pay for terminal care.

In "Medical Expenditures during the Last Year of Life: Findings from the 1992–1996 Medicare Current Beneficiary Survey" (*Health Services Research*, vol. 37, no. 6, December 2002), the most comprehensive documentation of Medicare end-of-life costs available, Donald Hoover et al. of Rutgers University note that Medicare currently pays most end-of-life medical costs for individuals in this age group but state that the elderly may be expected to pay an increasing proportion of

TABLE 9.4

Medicaid recipients and medical vendor payments, by eligibility, race, and ethnicity, selected fiscal years, 1972–2004

[Data are compiled by the Centers for Medicare & Medicaid Services from the Medicaid Data System]

Basis of eligibility and race and ethnicity	1972	1980	1990	1995	2000	2001	2002	2003	2004
Recipients					**Number in millions**				
All recipients	17.6	21.6	25.3	36.3	42.8	46.0	49.3	52.0	55.6
					Percent of recipients				
Basis of eligibility[a]									
Aged (65 years and over)	18.8	15.9	12.7	11.4	8.7	8.3	7.9	7.8	7.8
Blind and disabled	9.8	13.5	14.7	16.1	16.1	15.4	15.0	14.8	14.6
Adults in families with dependent children[b]	17.8	22.6	23.8	21.0	20.5	21.1	22.6	22.2	22.2
Children under age 21[c]	44.5	43.2	44.4	47.3	46.1	45.7	47.1	47.8	47.8
Other Title XIX[d]	9.0	6.9	3.9	1.7	8.6	9.5	7.4	7.5	7.6
Race and ethnicity[e]									
White	—	—	42.8	45.5	—	40.2	40.9	41.2	41.1
Black or African American	—	—	25.1	24.7	—	23.1	22.8	22.4	22.1
American Indian or Alaska Native	—	—	1.0	0.8	—	1.3	1.3	1.4	1.3
Asian or Pacific Islander	—	—	2.0	2.2	—	3.0	3.4	3.3	3.3
Hispanic or Latino	—	—	15.2	17.2	—	17.9	19.0	19.3	19.4
Multiple race or unknown	—	—	14.0	9.6	—	14.6	12.6	12.5	12.7
Vendor payments[f]					**Amount in billions**				
All payments	$6.3	$23.3	$64.9	$120.1	$168.3	$186.3	$213.5	$233.2	$257.7
					Percent distribution				
Total	100.0	100.0	100.0	100.0	100.0	100.0	100.0	100.0	100.0
Basis of eligibility[a]									
Aged (65 years and over)	30.6	37.5	33.2	30.4	26.4	25.9	24.4	23.7	23.1
Blind and disabled	22.2	32.7	37.6	41.1	43.2	43.1	43.3	43.7	43.3
Adults in families with dependent children[b]	15.3	13.9	13.2	11.2	10.6	10.7	10.9	11.4	11.8
Children under age 21[c]	18.1	13.4	14.0	15.0	15.9	16.3	16.8	17.1	17.2
Other Title XIX[d]	13.9	2.6	1.6	1.2	3.9	3.9	4.6	4.1	4.7
Race and ethnicity[e]									
White	—	—	53.4	54.3	—	54.4	54.1	53.8	53.4
Black or African American	—	—	18.3	19.2	—	19.8	19.6	19.7	19.8
American Indian or Alaska Native	—	—	0.6	0.5	—	1.1	1.1	1.2	1.2
Asian or Pacific Islander	—	—	1.0	1.2	—	2.5	2.8	2.4	2.5
Hispanic or Latino	—	—	5.3	7.3	—	9.4	9.7	10.6	10.7
Multiple race or unknown	—	—	21.3	17.6	—	12.9	12.6	12.2	12.3
Vendor payments per recipient[f]					**Amount**				
All recipients	$358	$1,079	$2,568	$3,311	$3,936	$4,053	$4,328	$4,487	$4,639
Basis of eligibility[a]									
Aged (65 years and over)	580	2,540	6,717	8,868	11,929	12,725	13,370	13,677	13,687
Blind and disabled	807	2,618	6,564	8,435	10,559	11,318	12,470	13,303	13,714
Adults in families with dependent children[b]	307	662	1,429	1,777	2,030	2,059	2,095	2,296	2,475
Children under age 21[c]	145	335	811	1,047	1,358	1,448	1,545	1,606	1,664
Other Title XIX[d]	555	398	1,062	2,380	1,778	1,680	2,692	2,458	2,867
Race and ethnicity[e]									
White	—	—	3,207	3,953	—	5,489	5,721	5,869	6,026
Black or African American	—	—	1,878	2,568	—	3,480	3,733	3,944	4,158
American Indian or Alaska Native	—	—	1,706	2,142	—	3,452	3,774	4,001	4,320
Asian or Pacific Islander	—	—	1,257	1,713	—	3,283	3,562	3,328	3,513
Hispanic or Latino	—	—	903	1,400	—	2,126	2,215	2,463	2,563
Multiple race or unknown	—	—	3,909	6,099	—	3,576	4,338	4,395	4,493

end-of-life costs as the number of elderly individuals in the population increases and end-of-life costs increase as a result.

Hoover et al. show that an average person over age sixty-five who died between 1992 and 1996 created approximately $40,000 of medical expenditures in his or her last year of life. Of this amount, Medicare paid approximately $32,800 (82%), supplemental/private insurance paid about $2,000 (5%), and the individual paid approximately $5,200 (13%). The researchers deter-mine that about 25% of Medicare expenditures and about 20% of all health-care expenditures for the elderly go to those in their last year of life.

According to Hoover et al., several initiatives such as hospice and advanced directives have attempted to reduce end-of-life medical costs. However, the research-ers contend that costs have not decreased notably as a fraction of total Medicare expenditures over the past twenty-five years. Nonetheless, Donald H. Taylor Jr. et al. suggest in "What Length of Hospice Use Maximizes

TABLE 9.4

Medicaid recipients and medical vendor payments, by eligibility, race, and ethnicity, selected fiscal years, 1972–2004 [CONTINUED]

[Data are compiled by the Centers for Medicare & Medicaid Services from the Medicaid Data System]

—Data not available.

[a]In 1980 and 1985, recipients are included in more than one category. In 1990–1996, 0.2%-2.5% of recipients have unknown basis of eligibility. Starting with 1997 data, unknowns are included in other Title XIX.

[b]Includes adults in the Aid to Families with Dependent Children (AFDC) program. Starting with 1997 data, includes adults in the Temporary Assistance for Needy Families (TANF) program. Starting with 2001 data, includes women in the Breast and Cervical Cancer Prevention and Treatment Program.

[c]Includes children in the AFDC program. Starting with 1997 data, includes children (including those in the foster care system) in the TANF program.

[d]Includes some participants in the Supplemental Security Income program and other people deemed medically needy in participating states. Starting with 1997 data, excludes foster care children and includes unknown eligibility.

[e]Race and ethnicity are as determined on initial Medicaid application. Categories are mutually exclusive. Starting with 2001 data, the Hispanic category included Hispanic persons, regardless of race. Persons indicating more than one race were included in the unknown category.

[f]Vendor payments exclude disproportionate share hospital (DSH) payments ($14.3 billion in FY2004) and DSH mental health facility payments ($2.9 billion in FY2004).

Notes: 1972 data are for fiscal year ending June 30. All other years are for fiscal year ending September 30. Starting with 1999 data, a new Medicaid data system was introduced. Prior to 1999, recipient counts exclude those individuals who only received coverage under prepaid health care and for whom no direct vendor payments were made during the year, and vendor payments exclude payments to health maintenance organizations and other prepaid health plans ($19 billion in 1998). Data for additional years are available.

SOURCE: "Table 144. Medicaid Recipients and Medical Vendor Payments, by Basis of Eligibility, and Race and Ethnicity: United States, Selected Fiscal Years 1972–2004," in *Health, United States, 2007. With Chartbook on Trends in the Health of Americans*, Centers for Disease Control and Prevention, National Center for Health Statistics, November 2007, http://www.cdc.gov/nchs/data/hus/hus07.pdf (accessed January 30, 2008)

Reduction in Medical Expenditures Near Death in the U.S. Medicare Program?" (*Social Science and Medicine*, vol. 65, 2007) that research results are mixed on this topic. Results of their research reveal that "hospice use reduced Medicare program expenditures during the last year of life by an average of $2,309 per hospice user." Taylor et al. note that the amount of the reduction varied based on the disease from which the patient was dying. The maximum reduction was seen in terminal cancer patients and was calculated to be approximately $7,000 per patient when hospice was used for the last 50 to 103 days of life.

No specific information about the cost of end-of-life care exists for the one-fourth of those who die every year who are under age sixty-five. Such care is more than likely financed by employer health insurance, personal funds, Medicare, and Medicaid. Nonetheless, aside from funds paid out for hospice services, the government has no other information about this group's terminal health care.

Medicare Hospice Benefits

In 1982 Congress created a Medicare hospice benefit program via the Tax Equity and Fiscal Responsibility Act to provide services to terminally ill patients with six months or less to live. In 1989 the U.S. General Accounting Office (GAO; now called the U.S. Government Accountability Office) reported that only 35% of eligible hospices were Medicare certified, in part due to the Health Care Financing Administration's low rates of reimbursement to hospices. That same year Congress gave hospices a 20% increase in reimbursement rates through a provision in the Omnibus Budget Reconciliation Act.

Under the Balanced Budget Act (BBA) of 1997, Medicare hospice benefits are divided into three benefit periods:

- An initial ninety-day period
- A subsequent ninety-day period
- An unlimited number of subsequent sixty-day periods, based on a patient's satisfying the program eligibility requirements

At the start of each period the Medicare patient must be recertified as terminally ill. After the patient's death, the patient's family receives up to thirteen months of bereavement service.

In 2006 there were 3,078 Medicare-certified hospices, a substantial increase from 31 hospices in 1984. (See Table 9.5.) This growth was stimulated in part by increased reimbursement rates established by Congress in 1989. Of the 3,078 hospices, 650 were with home health agencies (HHA), 563 were affiliated with hospitals (HOSP), 14 were with skilled nursing facilities (SNF), and 1,851 were freestanding hospices. From 2000 to 2006 the number of Medicare-certified freestanding hospices had nearly doubled, whereas other types of hospice facilities decreased slightly in number (HHA and SNF) or remained relatively static (HOSP). Medicare pays most of the cost of hospice care.

Terminally ill Medicare patients who stayed in a hospice incurred less Medicare cost than those who stayed in a hospital or skilled nursing facility. In 2006 a one-day stay in a hospice cost Medicare $136, compared to $535 for a skilled nursing facility and $5,036 for a hospital. (See Table 9.6.)

The Hospice Association of America (HAA) contends that terminally ill patients often wait too long to enter hospice care. The HAA believes the difficulty of predicting when death may occur could account for part of the delay, along with the reticence of caregivers, patients, and family to accept a terminal prognosis.

TABLE 9.5

Number of Medicare-certified hospices, by type, 1984–2004

Year	HHA	HOSP	SNF	FSTG	Total
1984	n/a	n/a	n/a	n/a	31
1985	n/a	n/a	n/a	n/a	158
1986	113	54	10	68	245
1987	155	101	11	122	389
1988	213	138	11	191	553
1989	286	182	13	220	701
1990	313	221	12	260	806
1991	325	282	10	394	1,011
1992	334	291	10	404	1,039
1993	438	341	10	499	1,288
1994	583	401	12	608	1,604
1995	699	460	19	679	1,857
1996	815	526	22	791	2,154
1997	823	561	22	868	2,274
1998	763	553	21	878	2,215
1999	762	562	22	928	2,274
2000	739	554	20	960	2,273
2001	690	552	20	1003	2,265
2002	676	557	17	1,072	2,322
2003	653	561	16	1,214	2,444
2004	656	562	14	1,438	2,670
2005	672	551	13	1,648	2,884
2006	650	563	14	1,851	3,078

Notes: Home health agency-based (HHA) hospices are owned and operated by freestanding proprietary and nonprofit home care agencies. Hospital-based (HOSP) hospices are operating units or departments of a hospital.
SNF = Skilled nursing facility-based.
FSTG = Freestanding.

SOURCE: "Table 1. Number of Medicare-Certified Hospices, by Auspice, 1984–2004, in *Hospice Facts & Statistics*, Hospice Association of America, February 2007, http://www.nahc.org/facts/hospicefx07.pdf (accessed February 5, 2008). Reproduced with the express and limited permission from the National Association for Home Care & Hospice. All rights reserved.

Even though terminal care is often associated with hospice, the hospice Medicare benefit represents a small proportion of the total Medicare dollars spent. In 2006, $8.5 billion (2.5%) of all Medicare benefit payments went to hospice care. (See Table 9.7.) The 2007 projected hospice spending was comparably small, at $9.7 billion (2.6%) of the projected $376.4 billion in total Medicare expenditures.

Medicaid Hospice Benefits

Hospice services also comprise a small portion of Medicaid reimbursements. In 2003 Medicaid reimbursements for hospice accounted for $897.6 million (0.4%) of the $234.1 billion in total expenditures. (See Table 9.8.) Providing hospice care under Medicaid is optional for each state. In 2006 forty-eight states and Washington, D.C., offered hospice benefits. (See Figure 9.3.)

Home Health Care

The concept of home health care began as postacute care after hospitalization, an alternative to longer, costlier hospital stays. The Centers for Medicare and Medicaid Services explains in *Medicare and Home Health Care* (September 2007, http://www.medicare.gov/Publications/Pubs/pdf/10969.pdf) that in the twenty-first century Medicare's home health-care services provide medical help, prescribed by a doctor, to home-bound people who are covered by Medicare. Having been hospitalized is not a prerequisite. There are no limits to the number of professional visits or to the length of coverage. As long as the patient's condition warrants it, the following services are provided:

- Part-time or intermittent skilled nursing and home health aide services

- Speech-language pathology services

- Physical and occupational therapy

- Medical social services

- Medical supplies

- Durable medical equipment (such as walkers and hospital beds, with a 20% co-pay)

Over time, the population receiving home care services has changed. By 2000 much of home health care was associated with rehabilitation from critical illnesses, and fewer users were long-term patients with

TABLE 9.6

Comparison of hospital, skilled nursing facility, and hospice Medicare charges, 1998–2006

	1998	1999	2000	2001	2002	2003	2004	2005*	2006*
Hospital inpatient charges per day	$2,177	$2,583	$2,762	$3,069	$3,574	$4,117	$4,559	$4,773	$5,036
Skilled nursing facility charges per day	482	424	413	422	475	487	493	521	535
Hospice charges per covered day of care	113	113	118	120	125	129	132	134	136

Notes: Hospital data for 2005 and 2006 are updated using the Bureau of Labor Statistics' (BLS) Producer Price Index (PPI) for General Medical and Surgical Hospitals. Skilled nursing facility data for 2005 and 2006 are updated using the PPI for Nursing Care Facilities. Hospice data for 2005 and 2006 are updated using the PPI for Home Health Care Services.

SOURCE: "Table 15. Comparison of Hospital, SNF, and Hospice Medicare Charges, 1998–2006," in *Hospice Facts & Statistics*, Hospice Association of America, February 2007, http://www.nahc.org/facts/hospicefx07.pdf (accessed February 5, 2008). Reproduced with the express and limited permission from the National Association for Home Care & Hospice. All rights reserved.

TABLE 9.7

Medicare benefit payments, fiscal years 2006 and 2007

	2006 (estimated)		2007 (projected)	
	Amount ($millions)	Percent of total	Amount ($millions)	Percent of total
Total Medicare benefit payments*	339,483	100.0	376,441	100.0
Part A				
Hospital care	119,121	35.1	125,510	33.3
Skilled nursing facility	19,236	5.7	20,665	5.5
Home health	5,922	1.7	6,442	1.7
Hospice	8,515	2.5	9,694	2.6
Managed care	28,668	8.4	39,934	10.6
Total	**181,462**	**53.5**	**202,545**	**53.8**
Part B				
Physician	57,984	17.1	59,503	15.8
Durable medical equipment	8,191	2.4	8,563	2.3
Carrier lab	3,682	1.1	3,848	1.0
Other carrier	15,269	4.5	16,809	4.5
Hospital	22,119	6.5	23,626	6.3
Home health	7,096	2.1	7,709	2.0
Intermediary lab	3,182	0.9	3,287	0.9
Other intermediary	13,291	3.9	14,141	3.8
Managed care	27,207	8.0	36,409	9.7
Total	**158,021**	**46.5**	**173,895**	**46.2**

*Figures may not add to totals due to rounding.

SOURCE: "Table 4. Medicare Benefit Payments, FY2006 and FY2007," in *Hospice Facts & Statistics*, Hospice Association of America, February 2007, http://www.nahc.org/facts/hospicefx07.pdf (accessed February 5, 2008). Reproduced with the express and limited permission from the National Association for Home Care & Hospice. All rights reserved.

TABLE 9.8

Medicaid payments, by type of service, fiscal years 2002 and 2003

	2002 ($millions)	Percent of total	2003 ($millions)	Percent of total
Inpatient hospital	29,127.1	13.6	31,549.2	13.5
Nursing home	39,282.2	18.3	40,381.0	17.2
Physician	8,354.6	3.9	9,209.9	3.9
Outpatient hospital	8,470.6	4.0	9,251.9	4.0
Home health[a]	19,287.8	9.0	21,649.3	9.2
Hospice[b]	706.2	0.3	897.6	0.4
Prescription drugs	28,408.2	13.3	33,714.3	14.4
ICF (MR) services[c]	10,681.3	5.0	10,861.2	4.6
Other	69,879.5	32.6	76,589.1	32.7
Total payments[d]	**214,197.5**	**100.0**	**234,103.5**	**100.0**

Notes: Figures may not add to totals due to rounding.
[a]Home health includes both home health and personal support services.
[b]Hospice outlays come from Form CMS-64 and do not include Medicaid the State Children's Health Insurance Program (SCHIP). All other expenditures come from the MSIS. The federal share of Medicaid's hospice spending in 2001 was $314.6 million, or 57.6%of the total. In fiscal year 2002, it was $404.7 million, or 57.3%. Infiscal year 2003, it was $534.7 million, or 59.6% of total Medicaid hospice payments.
[c]ICF is intermediate care facilities.
[d]Total outlays include hospice outlays from the form CMS-64 plus payments for all service types included in the Medicaid Statistical Information System (MSIS), not just the eight service types listed.

SOURCE: "Table 11. Medicaid Payments, by Type of Service, FY 2002 & FY 2003," in *Hospice Facts & Statistics*, Hospice Association of America, February 2007, http://www.nahc.org/facts/hospicefx07.pdf (accessed February5, 2008). Reproduced with the express and limited permission from the National Association for Home Care & Hospice. All rights reserved.

FIGURE 9.3

States and territories that do not provide the Medicaid hospice benefit, 2006

States	Territories
Connecticut New Hampshire	American Samoa Guam Northern Mariana Islands Puerto Rico Virgin Islands

SOURCE: "Table 12. U.S. States and Territories That Do Not Provide the Medicaid Hospice Benefit, 2006," in *Hospice Facts & Statistics*, Hospice Association of America, February 2007, http://www.nahc.org/facts/hospicefx07.pdf (accessed February 5, 2008). Data from the The Henry J. Kaiser Family Foundation. Reproduced with the express and limited permission from the National Association for Home Care & Hospice. All rights reserved.

chronic conditions. In 2000, 1,017,900 (75%) of home health users received medical/skilled nursing services, 600,900 (44%) received personal care, 502,600 (37%) received therapy, and 160,000 (12%) received psychosocial services. (See Table 9.9.)

The percentage of Medicare payments as a portion of total Medicare payments are shown in Figure 9.4. The percentage of home health-care costs of the Medicare budget was 4.3% in 2000, but that percentage dropped to 3.3% by 2007. The number of home care agencies that were Medicare certified declined from a high of 10,444 in 1997 to a low of 6,861 in 2001. (See Table 9.10.) The number has since risen to 8,838 in 2006 but is still far below the 1997

TABLE 9.9

Number of current home health care patients by services received, 2000

Selected services[a]	Number
All patients[b]	1,355,300
Medical/skilled nursing	
Total medical and/or skilled nursing	1,017,900
Physician	32,300
Skilled nursing	1,016,500
Equipment and/or medication	
Total equipment/medication	174,800
Durable medical equipment and supplies	109,500
Medications	88,900
Personal care	
Total personal care	600,900
Continuous home care	53,100
Companion	40,400
Homemaker-household[c]	329,400
Personal care	476,400
Transportation	25,300*
Respite care	17,000*
Therapeutic	
Total therapeutic	502,600
Dietary and/or nutritional	60,200
Enterostomal therapy	17,700*
IV therapy[d]	52,700
Occupational therapy	112,300
Physical therapy	360,700
Respiratory therapy	29,500
Speech therapy and/or audiology	30,600
Other high tech care[e]	11,000*
Psychosocial	
Total psychosocial	160,000
Counseling	22,400
Psychological	14,700*
Social	117,500
Spiritual and/or pastoral care	15,300*
Referral	34,800
Other[e, f]	46,300

*Figure does not meet standard of reliability or precision because the sample size is between 30 and 59.
[a]Numbers will not add to totals because a patient may be included in more than one category.
[b]Total number of home health care patients.
[c]Includes Meals on Wheels.
[d]IV is intravenous.
[e]Includes enteral nutrition and dialysis.
[f]Includes dental, vocational therapy, volunteers, and other services.

SOURCE: Adapted from "Table 6. Number of Current Home Health Care Patients by Services Received, by Sex and Race: United States, 2000," in *Current Home Health Care Patients*, Centers for Disease Control and Prevention, National Center for Health Statistics, February 2004, http://www.cdc.gov/nchs/data/nhhcsd/curhomecare00.pdf (accessed January 28, 2008)

FIGURE 9.4

Percent Medicare payments by benefit, fiscal years 2000–07

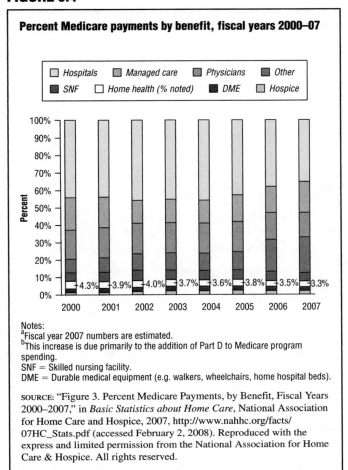

Notes:
[a]Fiscal year 2007 numbers are estimated.
[b]This increase is due primarily to the addition of Part D to Medicare program spending.
SNF = Skilled nursing facility.
DME = Durable medical equipment (e.g. walkers, wheelchairs, home hospital beds).

SOURCE: "Figure 3. Percent Medicare Payments, by Benefit, Fiscal Years 2000–2007," in *Basic Statistics about Home Care*, National Association for Home Care and Hospice, 2007, http://www.nahhc.org/facts/07HC_Stats.pdf (accessed February 2, 2008). Reproduced with the express and limited permission from the National Association for Home Care & Hospice. All rights reserved.

figure. The National Association for Home Care and Hospice believes the decline in agencies since 1997 is the direct result of changes in Medicare home health reimbursement enacted as part of the BBA. However, the recent increase is likely due to relaxed eligibility criteria for home health care, including in 2003 the elimination of the requirement of an acute hospitalization before receiving home care. These relaxed criteria enabled an increased number of beneficiaries to use home health services.

Of the total costs for home health care in 2003, Medicare paid 83.3%. (See Figure 9.5.) Medicaid paid 1.8% of the costs, and individuals paid 8.8%. The remaining 6.1% of home health-care costs in 2003 were paid in other ways, such as by private insurance payments.

MEDICARE LIMITS HOME CARE SERVICES. The GAO indicates in *Medicare Home Health Care: Prospective Payment System Will Need Refinement as Data Become Available* (April 2000, http://www.gao.gov/archive/2000/he00009.pdf) that during the 1990s Medicare's home health care costs increased nearly fivefold, from $3.7 billion in 1990 to $17.8 billion in 1997. In "Length of Stay in Home Care before and after the 1997 Balanced Budget Act" (*Journal of the American Medical Association*, vol. 289, no. 21, 2003), Rachel L. Murkofsky et al. explain that the BBA aimed to cut approximately $16.2 billion from Medicare home care expenditures over a period of five years. The federal government sought to return home health care to its original concept of short-term care plus skilled nursing and therapy services. Medicare beneficiaries who received home health care lost certain personal care services, such as assistance with bathing, dressing, and eating.

The BBA sharply curtailed the growth of home care spending, which greatly affected health-care providers.

TABLE 9.10

Number of Medicare-certified home care agencies, by type, selected years 1967–2006

Year	Freestanding agencies						Facility-based agencies			
	VNA	COMB	PUB	PROP	PNP	OTH	HOSP	REHAB	SNF	Total
1967	549	93	939	0	0	39	133	0	0	1,753
1980	515	63	1,260	186	484	40	359	8	9	2,924
1990	474	47	985	1,884	710	0	1,486	8	101	5,695
1996	576	34	1,177	4,658	695	58	2,634	4	191	10,027
1997	553	33	1,149	5,024	715	65	2.698	3	204	10,444
1998	460	35	968	3,414	610	69	2,356	2	166	8,080
1999	452	35	918	3,192	621	65	2,300	1	163	7,747
2000	436	31	909	2,863	560	56	2,151	1	150	7,152
2001	425	23	867	2,835	543	68	1,976	1	123	6,861
2002	430	27	850	3,027	563	79	1,907	1	119	7,007
2003	439	27	888	3,402	546	74	1,776	0	113	7,265
2004	446	36	932	3,832	558	69	1,695	1	110	7,679
2005	461	36	1,043	4,321	566	74	1,618	2	103	8,224
2006	459	29	1,132	4,919	562	85	1,547	2	103	8,838

VNA: Visiting Nurse Associations are freestanding, voluntary, nonprofit organizations governed by a board of directors and usually financed by tax-deductible contributions as well as by earnings.
COMB: Combination agencies are combined government and voluntary agencies. These agencies are sometimes included with counts for VNAs.
PUB: Public agencies are government agencies operated by a state, county, city, or other unit of local government having a major responsibility for preventing disease and for community health education.
PROP: Proprietary agencies are freestanding, for-profit home care agencies.
PNP: Private not-for-profit agencies are freestanding and privately developed, governed, and owned nonprofit home care agencies. These agencies were not counted separately prior to 1980.
OTH: Other freestanding agencies that do not fit one of the categories for freestanding agencies listed above.
HOSP: Hospital-based agencies are operating units or departments of a hospital. Agencies that have working arrangements with a hospital, or perhaps are even owned by a hospital but operated as separate entities, are classified as freestanding agencies under one of the categories listed above.
REHAB: Refers to agencies based in rehabilitation facilities.
SNF: Refers to agencies based in skilled nursing facilities.

SOURCE: "Table 1. Number of Medicare-Certified Home Care Agencies, by Auspice, for Selected Years, 1967–2006," in *Basic Statistics about Home Care*, National Association for Home Care and Hospice, 2007, http://www.nahhc.org/facts/07HC_Stats.pdf (accessed February 2, 2008). Reproduced with the express and limited permission from the National Association for Home Care & Hospice. All rights reserved.

William D. Spector, Joel W. Cohen, and Irena Pesis-Katx state in "Home Care before and after the Balanced Budget Act of 1997: Shift in Financing and Services" (*Gerontologist*, vol. 44, no. 1, 2004) that after the enactment of the law in 1997, annual Medicare home health-care spending fell 57% from the 1996 level by 1999. The decline was mainly in skilled services, such as skilled nursing care. In addition, the number of current home health-care patients declined, in large part due to decreased funding. (See Figure 9.6.) However, the decline began one year before the BBA, so more factors than decreased Medicare funding were likely to be playing a role in the decline.

LONG-TERM HEALTH CARE

Longer life spans and life-sustaining technologies have created an increasing need for long-term care. For some older people, relatives provide the long-term care; but those who require labor-intensive, round-the-clock care often stay in nursing homes.

Nursing Home Care

Growth of the home health-care industry in the 1980s and early to mid-1990s was only partly responsible for the decline in the rate of Americans entering nursing homes (residents per one thousand population). (See Table 9.11.) Declines also occurred in years when numbers of home health-care patients declined after the implementation of the BBA in 1997. Other factors responsible for the decline in the rate of Americans entering nursing homes are that many elderly people are choosing assisted living and continuing-care retirement communities, which offer alternatives to nursing home care. There is also a trend toward healthy aging—more older adults are living longer with fewer disabilities.

Nonetheless, in 2004 slightly more than 1.3 million adults aged sixty-five and older were nursing home residents. (See Table 9.11.) Most were white (1.1 million; 87%) and female (980,000; 74%), and more than half (674,000; 51%) were eighty-five years and older.

Nursing homes provide terminally ill residents with end-of-life services in a variety of ways:

• Caring for patients in the nursing home

• Transferring patients who request it to hospitals or hospices

• Contracting with hospices to provide palliative care (care that relieves the pain but does not cure the illness) within the nursing home

Medicare does not pay for long-term nursing home services. It pays only for services in a skilled nursing

FIGURE 9.5

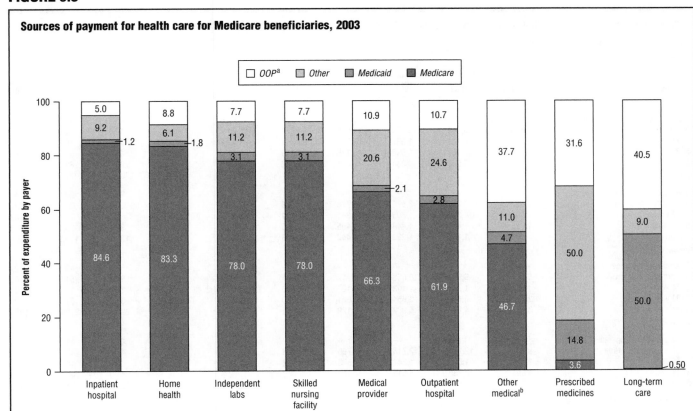

Sources of payment for health care for Medicare beneficiaries, 2003

aOOP is out-of-pocket.
bOther Medical includes things such as hospice and durable medical equipment.
Note: Medicare did not generally cover outpatient prescription drugs in 2003.

SOURCE: "Table 4.13. Sources of Payment for Medicare Beneficiaries by Type of Service, 2003," in *An Overview of the U.S. Health Care System Chartbook*, Centers for Medicare and Medicaid Services and Office of the Assistant Secretary for Planning and Evaluation, January 31, 2007, http://www .cms.hhs.gov/TheChartSeries/downloads/Chartbook_2007_pdf.pdf (accessed February 5, 2008)

FIGURE 9.6

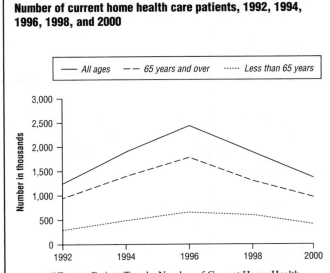

Number of current home health care patients, 1992, 1994, 1996, 1998, and 2000

SOURCE: "Current Patient Trends. Number of Current Home Health Care Patients: United States, 1992, 1994, 1996, 1998, 2000," in *National Home and Hospice Care Data*, Centers for Disease Control and Prevention, National Center for Health Statistics, January 11, 2007, http://www.cdc.gov/nchs/about/major/nhhcsd/nhhcschart.htm (accessed January 28, 2008)

facility for people recovering from medical conditions such as a hip fracture, heart attack, or stroke. Medicaid does pay for nursing home care, but only if the individual meets state income and resource requirements for Medicaid assistance.

Figure 9.5 shows the sources of payment for long-term care for Medicare/Medicaid beneficiaries in 2003. Medicaid pays 50% of long-term care costs for covered individuals. About 40.5% of the costs are paid for by the individuals themselves. The remaining 9% of long-term costs were paid in other ways, such as by long-term care insurance companies for their policyholders.

Patients in a Persistent Vegetative State

The precise number of patients in a persistent vegetative state (PVS) is unknown because no system is in place to count them. Very little information is published in the literature documenting the costs of maintaining patients in a PVS. Melissa C. Bush et al. report in "Pregnancy in a Persistent Vegetative State: Case Report, Comparison to Brain Death, and Review of the Literature" (*Obstetrical and Gynecological Survey*, vol. 58, no.

TABLE 9.11

Nursing home residents 65 years of age and over, by age, sex, and race, selected years, 1973–2004

[Data are based on a sample of nursing home residents]

Age, sex, and race	Number of residents in hundreds					Residents per 1,000 population[a]				
	1973–1974	1985	1995	1999	2004	1973–1974	1985	1995	1999	2004
Age										
65 years and over, age-adjusted[b]	—	—	—	—	—	58.5	54.0	46.4	43.3	34.8
65 years and over, crude	9,615	13,183	14,229	14,695	13,172	44.7	46.2	42.8	42.9	36.3
65–74 years	1,631	2,121	1,897	1,948	1,741	12.3	12.5	10.2	10.8	9.4
75–84 years	3,849	509	5,096	5,176	4,689	57.7	57.7	46.1	43.0	36.1
85 years and over	4,136	5,973	7,235	7,571	6,742	257.3	220.3	200.9	182.5	138.7
Male										
65 years and over, age-adjusted[b]	—	—	—	—	—	42.5	38.8	33.0	30.6	24.1
65 years and over, crude	2,657	3,344	3,571	3,778	3,368	30.0	29.0	26.2	26.5	22.2
65–74 years	651	806	795	841	754	11.3	10.8	9.6	10.3	8.9
75–84 years	1,023	1,413	1,443	1,495	1,408	39.9	43.0	33.5	30.8	27.0
85 years and over	983	1,126	1,333	1,442	1,206	182.7	145.7	131.5	116.5	80.0
Female										
65 years and over, age-adjusted[b]	—	—	—	—	—	67.5	61.5	52.8	49.8	40.4
65 years and over, crude	6,958	9,839	10,658	10,917	9,804	54.9	57.9	54.3	54.6	46.4
65–74 years	980	1,315	1,103	1,107	988	13.1	13.8	10.7	11.2	9.8
75–84 years	2,826	3,677	3,654	3,681	3,280	68.9	66.4	54.3	51.2	42.3
85 years and over	3,153	4,847	5,902	6,129	5,536	294.9	250.1	228.1	210.5	165.2
White[c]										
65 years and over, age-adjusted[b]	—	—	—	—	—	61.2	55.5	45.8	41.9	34.0
65 years and over, crude	9,206	12,274	12,715	12,796	11,488	46.9	47.7	42.7	42.1	36.2
65–74 years	1,501	1,878	1,541	1,573	1,342	12.5	12.3	9.3	10.0	8.5
75–84 years	3,697	4,736	4,513	4,406	4,060	60.3	59.1	45.0	40.5	35.2
85 years and over	4,008	5,660	6,662	6,817	6,086	270.8	228.7	203.2	181.8	139.4
Black or African American[c]										
65 years and over, age-adjusted[b]	—	—	—	—	—	28.2	41.5	50.8	55.5	49.9
65 years and over, crude	377	820	1,229	1,459	1,454	22.0	35.0	45.5	51.0	47.7
65–74 years	122	225	296	303	345	11.1	15.4	18.5	18.2	20.2
75–84 years	134	306	475	587	546	26.7	45.3	57.8	66.5	55.5
85 years and over	121	290	458	569	563	105.7	141.5	168.2	182.8	160.7

—Category not applicable.

[a]Rates are calculated using estimates of the civilian population of the United States including institutionalized persons. Population data are from unpublished tabulations provided by the U.S. Census Bureau. The 2004 population estimates are postcensal estimates as of July 1, 2004, based on the 2000 census.

[b]Age-adjusted to the year 2000 population standard using the following three age groups: 65–74 years, 75–84 years, and 85 years and over.

[c]Starting with 1999 data, the instruction for the race item on the current resident questionnaire was changed so that more than one race could be recorded. In previous years, only one racial category could be checked. Estimates for racial groups presented in this table are for residents for whom only one race was recorded. Estimates for residents where multiple races were checked are unreliable due to small sample sizes and are not shown.

Notes: Residents are persons on the roster of the nursing home as of the night before the survey. Residents for whom beds are maintained even though they may be away on overnight leave or in a hospital are included. People residing in personal care or domiciliary care homes are excluded. Numbers have been revised and differ from previous editions of Health, United States. Data for additional years are available.

SOURCE: "Table 104. Nursing Home Residents 65 Years of Age and over, by Age, Sex, and Race: United States, Selected Years, 1973–2004," in *Health, United States, 2007. With Chartbook on Trends in the Health of Americans*, Centers for Disease Control and Prevention, National Center for Health Statistics, November 2007, http://www.cdc.gov/nchs/data/hus/hus07.pdf (accessed January 30, 2008)

11, November 2003) that a 1988 estimate placed costs of maintaining a pregnant woman in a PVS at $183,000 for nine weeks, and a 1996 estimate placed costs at $200,000 for twenty-seven weeks. The costs to maintain patients in a persistent vegetative state vary depending on the acuity of care needed (the type, degree, or extent of required services).

The End-Stage Renal Disease Program

Amendments to the Social Security Act in 1972 extended Medicare coverage to include end-stage renal disease (ESRD) patients. ESRD is the final phase of irreversible kidney disease and requires either kidney transplantation or dialysis to maintain life. Dialysis is a medical procedure in which a machine takes over the

function of the kidneys by removing waste products from the blood. Between 1994 and 2003 about three-quarters of ESRD patients underwent dialysis and the remaining quarter had kidney transplants. (See Table 9.12.) Over this period the percentage of transplants increased slightly, with a resultant slight decline in the percentage of those maintained on dialysis.

Medicare beneficiaries with ESRD are high-cost users of Medicare services. According to the Medicare Payment Advisory Commission, in *A Data Book: Healthcare Spending and the Medicare Program* (June 2006, http://www.medpac.gov/publications/congressional_reports/ Jun06DataBook_Entire_report.pdf), patients with ESRD made up only 0.4% of enrollees in 2003, yet they

TABLE 9.12

Growth in the number and percent of Medicare beneficiaries with end stage renal disease, 1994, 1998, and 2003

	1994		1998		2003	
	Patients (thousands)	Percent	Patients (thousands)	Percent	Patients (thousands)	Percent
Total	**272.3**	**100%**	**356.0**	**100%**	**453.0**	**100%**
Dialysis	200.4	74	260.4	73	324.8	72
In-center hemodialysis	167.7	62	230.5	65	296.8	66
Home hemodialysis	0.8	<1	1.6	<1	1.3	<1
Peritoneal dialysis	29.5	11	26.8	8	25.9	6
Unknown	2.3	<1	1.4	<1	0.8	<1
Functioning graft and kidney transplants	71.9	26	95.5	27	128.1	28

Notes: ESRD (end-stage renal disease). Totals may not equal sum of components due to rounding.
Functioning Graft = Patients who have had a successful kidney transplant.

SOURCE: "Chart 12–5. The ESRD Population is Growing, and Most ESRD Patients Undergo Dialysis," in *A Data Book: Healthcare Spending and the Medicare Program*, Medicare Payment Advisory Commission, June 2006, http://www.medpac.gov/publications/congressional_reports/Jun06DataBook_Entire_report.pdf (accessed March 15, 2008)

TABLE 9.13

Estimated numbers of AIDS diagnoses, deaths, and persons living with AIDS, 2001–05

	2001	2002	2003	2004	2005	Cumulative (1981–2005)
AIDS diagnoses	38,079	38,408	39,666	39,524	40,608	952,629
Deaths of persons with AIDS	16,980	16,641	17,404	17,453	16,316	530,756
Persons living with AIDS	331,482	353,249	375,511	397,582	421,873	NA

NA = Not applicable (the values given for each year in this row are cumulative).

SOURCE: "Estimated Numbers of AIDS Diagnoses, Deaths, and Persons Living with AIDS, 2001–2005," in *CDC HIV/AIDS Fact Sheet: A Glance at the HIV/AIDS Epidemic*, rev. ed., Centers for Disease Control and Prevention, June 2007, http://www.cdc.gov/hiv/resources/factsheets/PDF/At-A-Glance.pdf (accessed March 15, 2008)

accounted for 2.7% of Medicare spending in that year. Between 1994 and 2003 the ESRD population grew by 66%. (See Table 9.12.) In 1994 there were 272,300 ESRD patients in the Medicare system, and by 2003 this figure had grown to 453,000 ESRD patients.

PATIENTS WITH TERMINAL DISEASES
Acquired Immunodeficiency Syndrome

Acquired immunodeficiency syndrome (AIDS) is a set of signs, symptoms, and certain diseases occurring together when the immune system of a person infected with the human immunodeficiency virus (HIV) becomes extremely weakened. According to the Centers for Disease Control and Prevention (CDC), advances in treatment during the mid- to late 1990s slowed the progression of HIV infection to AIDS and led to dramatic decreases in AIDS deaths.

Deaths from AIDS fluctuated from 2001 through 2005. (See Table 9.13.) The number of AIDS diagnoses increased each year from 2001 to 2005. In 2001 an estimated 38,079 people had been diagnosed with HIV, and in 2005 this number had risen to 40,608. Cumulatively through 2005, 952,629 people had been diagnosed

with AIDS, 530,756 had died from the syndrome, and 421,873 were living with it.

Figure 9.7 shows federal funding for HIV/AIDS from the beginning of the AIDS epidemic through 2006. Funding began modestly, at less than $100 million. In 2006 the federal funding for all aspects of HIV/AIDS was $21.7 billion.

Figure 9.8 shows the categories of funding for HIV/AIDS and compares differences in categories of funding in fiscal years 1982, 1985, 1990, and 2006. At the beginning of the HIV/AIDS epidemic, 50% of federal funding was spent on research because at that time little was known about the disease, how to prevent it, and how to treat people who had contracted it. By 1985 and 1990, as medical researchers learned more about the disease, the proportion devoted to research shrank to 36% and 38%, respectively. By 2006 only 13% of federal HIV/AIDS funding went to research.

Likewise, the proportion of federal funds targeted for prevention have shrunk over the years as well. Twenty-five percent of federal funding went to prevention in 1982, 16% in 1985, 13% in 1990, and 4% in 2006.

FIGURE 9.7

Federal funding for HIV/AIDS, fiscal years 1981–2006

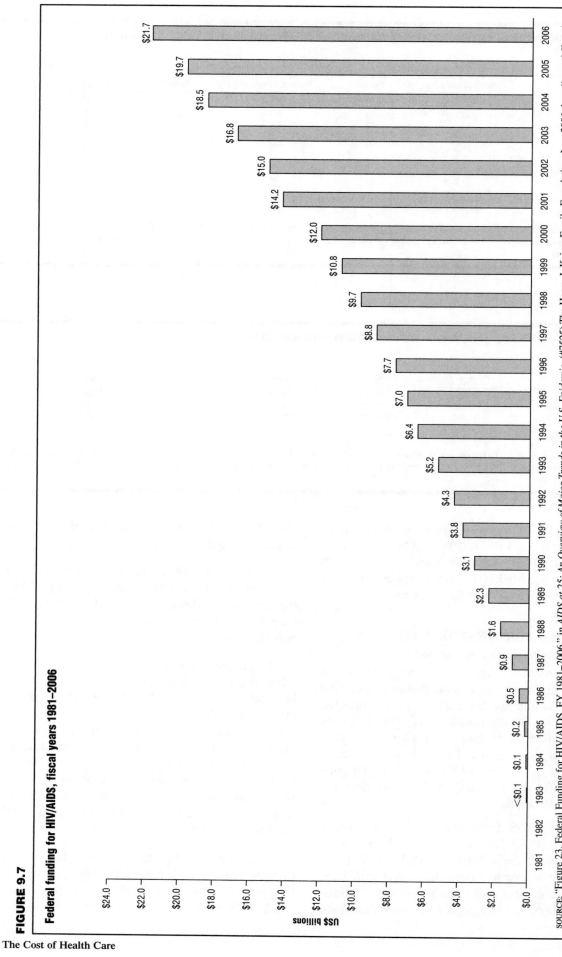

SOURCE: "Figure 23. Federal Funding for HIV/AIDS, FY 1981–2006," in *AIDS at 25: An Overview of Major Trends in the U.S. Epidemic*, (#7525) The Henry J. Kaiser Family Foundation, June 2006, http://www.kff.org/hivaids/upload/7525.pdf (accessed March 15, 2008). This information was reprinted with permission from the Henry J. Kaiser Foundation. The Kaiser Family Foundation, based in Menlo Park, California, is a nonprofit, private operating foundation focusing on the major health care issues facing the nation and is not associated with Keiser Permanente or Kaiser Industries.

FIGURE 9.8

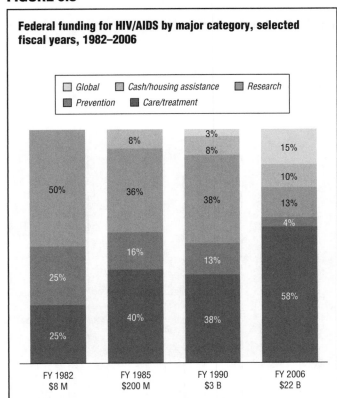

Federal funding for HIV/AIDS by major category, selected fiscal years, 1982–2006

Note: Funding for international research attributed to global category.
FY = Fiscal year

SOURCE: "Figure 24. Federal Funding for HIV/AIDS by Major Category, FY 1982–2006," in *AIDS at 25: An Overview of Major Trends in the U.S. Epidemic*, (#7525) The Henry J. Kaiser Family Foundation, June 2006, http://www.kff.org/hivaids/upload/7525.pdf (accessed March 15, 2008). This information was reprinted with permission from the Henry J. Kaiser Foundation. The Kaiser Family Foundation, based in Menlo Park, California, is a nonprofit, private operating foundation focusing on the major health care issues facing the nation and is not associated with Keiser Permanente or Kaiser Industries.

employers lose their coverage when they become too ill to work. These individuals eventually turn to Medicaid and other public programs for medical assistance.

Some people, whose employment and economic condition previously afforded the insurance coverage they needed, find their situation changed once they test positive for HIV. Some may become virtually ineligible for private health insurance coverage. Others require government assistance because insurance companies can declare HIV infection a preexisting condition, making it ineligible for payment of insurance claims. In addition, some insurance companies limit AIDS coverage to relatively small amounts.

THE RYAN WHITE COMPREHENSIVE AIDS RESOURCES EMERGENCY ACT. As of 2008 the Ryan White Comprehensive AIDS Resources Emergency (CARE) Act was the only federal program providing funds for the care, treatment, and support of low-income, uninsured, and underinsured men, women, children, and youth. The act is named after an Indiana teenager who had AIDS and worked against AIDS-related discrimination. The act was initially passed in 1990 and was reauthorized in 1996, 2000, and 2006. The Ryan White HIV/AIDS Treatment Modernization Act of 2006, which was the 2006 reauthorization, changed somewhat how Ryan White funds could be used and put an emphasis on life-saving and life-extending services for people living with HIV/AIDS. The appropriations of CARE funds follow the following formulas:

- Part A (formerly called Title I)—the federal government provides emergency assistance to metropolitan areas disproportionately affected by the HIV epidemic. To qualify for Part A financing, eligible metropolitan areas must have more than two thousand cumulative AIDS cases reported during the preceding five years and a population of at least five hundred thousand. The 2006 reauthorization gives priority to urban areas with the highest number of people living with AIDS. In addition, priority is also given to outreach, testing, and helping midsized cities and areas with emerging needs.

- Part B (formerly called Title II)—the federal government provides funds to state governments. Most of the Part B funds are allocated based on AIDS patient counts, while the remaining funds are distributed through competitive grants to public and nonprofit agencies. In addition, states receive funding to support AIDS Drug Assistance Programs, which provide medication to low-income HIV patients who are uninsured or underinsured.

- Part C (formerly called Title III)—federal funds are designated for Early Intervention Services (EIS) and planning. EIS grants support outpatient HIV services for low-income people in existing primary care systems,

Conversely, the percentage of federal funds devoted to the care and treatment of patients with HIV/AIDS has increased dramatically as more people acquire the disease and live longer with it. In 1982, 25% of federal funding was targeted for care and treatment of HIV/AIDS, and in 2006, 58% was spent on care and treatment. Figure 9.8 also shows that the federal government now spends money on the global fight against this disease. In 1990, 3% of the federal annual HIV/AIDS budget was used to help fight this disease globally. By 2006 this percentage had grown to 15% of the total federal HIV/AIDS budget.

MEDICAID ASSISTANCE. The financing of health care for AIDS patients has increasingly become the responsibility of Medicaid, the entitlement program that provides medical assistance to low-income Americans. This is due, in large part, to the rising incidence of AIDS among poor people and intravenous drug users—the groups least likely to have private health insurance. Furthermore, many patients who have private insurance through their

FIGURE 9.9

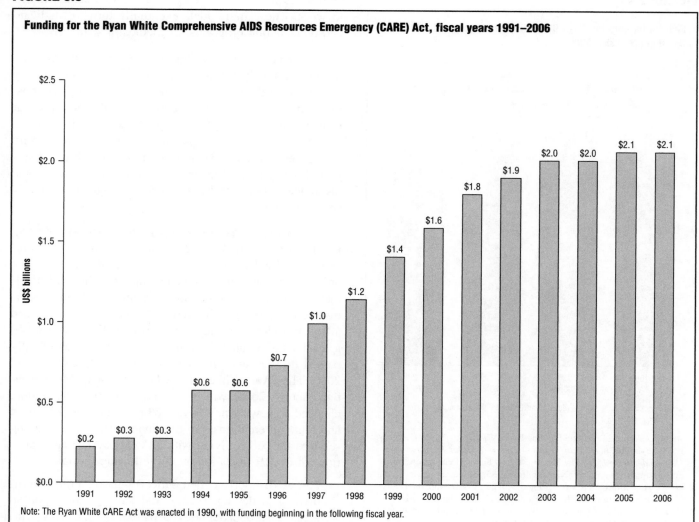

Funding for the Ryan White Comprehensive AIDS Resources Emergency (CARE) Act, fiscal years 1991–2006

Note: The Ryan White CARE Act was enacted in 1990, with funding beginning in the following fiscal year.

SOURCE: "Figure 29. Funding for the Ryan White CARE Act, FY 1991–2006," in *AIDS at 25: An Overview of Major Trends in the U.S. Epidemic*, (#7525) The Henry J. Kaiser Family Foundation, June 2006, http://www.kff.org/hivaids/upload/7525.pdf (accessed March 15, 2008). This information was reprinted with permission from the Henry J. Kaiser Foundation. The Kaiser Family Foundation, based in Menlo Park, California, is a nonprofit, private operating foundation focusing on the major health care issues facing the nation and is not associated with Keiser Permanente or Kaiser Industries.

and planning grants aid those working to develop HIV primary care.

• Part D (formerly called Title IV)—these federal programs focus on the development of assistance for women, infants, and children.

Figure 9.9 shows the annual funding for the Ryan White CARE Act from its inception in 1991 through 2006. Between 1991 and 2006 Ryan White CARE Act funding increased slightly more than tenfold, from $200 million to $2.1 billion. Figure 9.10 shows the locations of Ryan White HIV/AIDS Program providers across the United States.

Cancer

Cancer, in all its forms, is expensive to treat. Compared to other diseases, there are more options for cancer

treatment, more adverse side effects that require treatment, and a greater potential for unrelieved pain. According to the American Cancer Society, in *Cancer Facts & Figures 2008* (2008, http://www.cancer.org/downloads/STT/2008CAFFfinalsecured.pdf), the overall estimated cost of cancer to the nation in 2007 was $219.2 billion. Of this amount, $89 billion was due to direct medical costs. Of the remainder, $18.2 billion was the cost of lost productivity due to illness, and $112 billion was the cost of lost productivity due to premature death.

MEDICARE, CLINICAL TRIALS, AND CANCER. Some health insurance plans cover all or a portion of the costs associated with clinical trials (research studies that offer promising new anticancer drugs and treatment to enrolled patients). Policies vary, and some plans decide whether they will pay for clinical trials on a case-by-case basis. Some health plans limit coverage to patients for whom no

FIGURE 9.10

Locations of Ryan White CARE Act providers, 2005

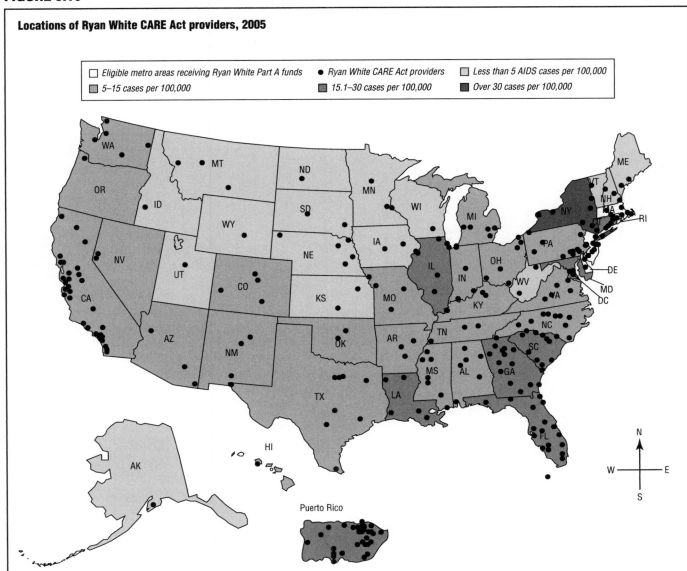

☐ *Eligible metro areas receiving Ryan White Part A funds*   ● *Ryan White CARE Act providers*   ☐ *Less than 5 AIDS cases per 100,000*
☐ *5–15 cases per 100,000*   ☐ *15.1–30 cases per 100,000*   ☐ *Over 30 cases per 100,000*

SOURCE: "The Ryan White HIV/AIDS Program Puts Health Care Where It Is Needed," in *HIV/AIDS Programs: Helping People with HIV/AIDS Live Longer and Better*, Health and Human Services, Health Resources and Services Administration, 2005, http://hab.hrsa.gov/hivmap.htm (accessed March 15, 2008)

standard therapy is available. Others cover clinical trials only if they are not much more expensive than standard treatment, and many choose not to cover any costs involved with clinical trials.

On June 7, 2000, President Bill Clinton (1946–) revised Medicare payment policies to enable beneficiaries to participate in clinical trials. Before this policy change, many older adults were prevented from participating in clinical trials because they could not afford the costs associated with the trials.

Alzheimer's Disease

The Alzheimer's Association (March 20, 2008, http://www.alz.org/alzheimers_disease_facts_figures.asp) notes that in 2008 there were 5.2 million people in the United States with Alzheimer's disease (AD). AD is a form of dementia characterized by memory loss, behavior and personality changes, and decreasing thinking abilities. The Alzheimer's Association also notes that the direct and indirect costs of AD and other dementias cost the United States over $148 billion annually.

CHAPTER 10
OLDER ADULTS

THE LONGEVITY REVOLUTION

As of the early twenty-first century, the United States was on the threshold of a longevity revolution. Richard J. Hodes (1943–), the director of the National Institute on Aging, recognized this revolution when he observed in "Director's Page" (February 16, 2008, http://www.nia.nih.gov/AboutNIA/DirectorsPages/) that "life expectancy has nearly doubled over the last century, and today there are 35 million Americans age 65 and older." What has fueled this new era of long life is a combination of better sanitation (safe drinking water, food, and disposal of waste), improved medical care, and reduced mortality rates for infants, children, and young adults.

In 1900 life expectancy in the United States was 47.3 years at birth; by 1970 it had increased to 70.8 years. (See Table 10.1.) By 2004 the National Center for Health Statistics projected that life expectancy for those born in that year was 77.8 years. Those who were sixty-five years old in 2004 could expect to live 18.7 more years, with women living an average of 20 more years and men 17.1 more years. In 2004 white men and women had longer life expectancies at age sixty-five than African-American men and women: 18.7 more years versus 17.1 more years.

AGING AMERICANS

According to the U.S. Census Bureau, 35.1 million (12.4%) of the U.S. population were aged sixty-five years and older in 2000. (See Table 10.2.) Those aged sixty-five years and older are projected to account for 20.7% of the population, or 86.8 million people, in 2050. Furthermore, 38.3 million (18.5%) men and 48.4 million (22.7%) women will be over sixty-five.

Who are the "older" Americans? Table 10.3 shows the characteristics of this group in 1990, 2000, 2005, and 2006. Nearly one-third (29.9%) of both men and women

in this age group were widowed in 2006. Breaking down this statistic by gender reveals the longevity gap between men and women: 42.4% of women were widowed, whereas only 13.1% of men were.

Table 10.3 also shows that a greater percentage of people aged sixty-five and older continued to work past this typical retirement age in 2006 (15%) than did people in 1990 (11.5%), 2000 (12.4%), and 2005 (14.5%). One-fifth (19.8%) of the sixty-five-and-over men were still working, whereas only one-tenth (11.4%) of women in this age group were still employed in 2006. Over these years, many of those aged sixty-five and older have pulled themselves above the poverty level. In 1990, 11.4% of those sixty-five and older lived below the poverty level, whereas in 2006, 10.1% did so. Nonetheless, more older women (12.3%) than older men (7.3%) lived below the poverty level in 2006.

Baby Boomers

The first children born during the post–World War II baby boom (1946–1964) will be turning sixty-five in 2011. Baby boomers, the largest single generation in U.S. history, will help swell the sixty-five and older population to approximately 54.6 million in 2020. (See Table 10.2.)

The Oldest Demographic

Americans aged eighty-five and older account for the most rapidly growing age group in the population. Predictions vary as to how fast this "oldest old" segment of the population is increasing. The Census Bureau's prediction is that there will be approximately 20.9 million people aged eighty-five and older by 2050. (See Table 10.2.) However, if life spans continue to increase, the Census Bureau may have to revise its calculation for this portion of the general population.

TABLE 10.1

Life expectancy at birth, at 65 years of age, and at 75 years of age, by race and sex, selected years, 1900–2004

[Data are based on death certificates]

Specified age and year	All races			White			Black or African American[a]		
	Both sexes	Male	Female	Both sexes	Male	Female	Both sexes	Male	Female
At birth					Remaining life expectancy in years				
1900[b,c]	47.3	46.3	48.3	47.6	46.6	48.7	33.0	32.5	33.5
1950[c]	68.2	65.6	71.1	69.1	66.5	72.2	60.8	59.1	62.9
1960[c]	69.7	66.6	73.1	70.6	67.4	74.1	63.6	61.1	66.3
1970	70.8	67.1	74.7	71.7	68.0	75.6	64.1	60.0	68.3
1980	73.7	70.0	77.4	74.4	70.7	78.1	68.1	63.8	72.5
1990	75.4	71.8	78.8	76.1	72.7	79.4	69.1	64.5	73.6
1995	75.8	72.5	78.9	76.5	73.4	79.6	69.6	65.2	73.9
1996	76.1	73.1	79.1	76.8	73.9	79.7	70.2	66.1	74.2
1997	76.5	73.6	79.4	77.1	74.3	79.9	71.1	67.2	74.7
1998	76.7	73.8	79.5	77.3	74.5	80.0	71.3	67.6	74.8
1999	76.7	73.9	79.4	77.3	74.6	79.9	71.4	67.8	74.7
2000	77.0	74.3	79.7	77.6	74.9	80.1	71.9	68.3	75.2
2001	77.2	74.4	79.8	77.7	75.0	80.2	72.2	68.6	75.5
2002	77.3	74.5	79.9	77.7	75.1	80.3	72.3	68.8	75.6
2003	77.5	74.8	80.1	78.0	75.3	80.5	72.7	69.0	76.1
2004	77.8	75.2	80.4	78.3	75.7	80.8	73.1	69.5	76.3
At 65 years									
1950[c]	13.9	12.8	15.0	—	12.8	15.1	13.9	12.9	14.9
1960[c]	14.3	12.8	15.8	14.4	12.9	15.9	13.9	12.7	15.1
1970	15.2	13.1	17.0	15.2	13.1	17.1	14.2	12.5	15.7
1980	16.4	14.1	18.3	16.5	14.2	18.4	15.1	13.0	16.8
1990	17.2	15.1	18.9	17.3	15.2	19.1	15.4	13.2	17.2
1995	17.4	15.6	18.9	17.6	15.7	19.1	15.6	13.6	17.1
1996	17.5	15.7	19.0	17.6	15.8	19.1	15.8	13.9	17.2
1997	17.7	15.9	19.2	17.8	16.0	19.3	16.1	14.2	17.6
1998	17.8	16.0	19.2	17.8	16.1	19.3	16.1	14.3	17.4
1999	17.7	16.1	19.1	17.8	16.1	19.2	16.0	14.3	17.3
2000	18.0	16.2	19.3	18.0	16.3	19.4	16.2	14.2	17.7
2001	18.1	16.4	19.4	18.2	16.5	19.5	16.4	14.4	17.9
2002	18.2	16.6	19.5	18.2	16.6	19.5	16.6	14.6	18.0
2003	18.4	16.8	19.8	18.5	16.9	19.8	17.0	14.9	18.5
2004	18.7	17.1	20.0	18.7	17.2	20.0	17.1	15.2	18.6
At 75 years									
1980	10.4	8.8	11.5	10.4	8.8	11.5	9.7	8.3	10.7
1990	10.9	9.4	12.0	11.0	9.4	12.0	10.2	8.6	11.2
1995	11.0	9.7	11.9	11.1	9.7	12.0	10.2	8.8	11.1
1996	11.1	9.8	12.0	11.1	9.8	12.0	10.3	9.0	11.2
1997	11.2	9.9	12.1	11.2	9.9	12.1	10.7	9.3	11.5
1998	11.3	10.0	12.2	11.3	10.0	12.2	10.5	9.2	11.3
1999	11.2	10.0	12.1	11.2	10.0	12.1	10.4	9.2	11.1
2000	11.4	10.1	12.3	11.4	10.1	12.3	10.7	9.2	11.6
2001	11.5	10.2	12.4	11.5	10.2	12.3	10.8	9.3	11.7
2002	11.5	10.3	12.4	11.5	10.3	12.3	10.9	9.5	11.7
2003	11.8	10.5	12.6	11.7	10.5	12.6	11.4	9.8	12.4
2004	11.9	10.7	12.8	11.9	10.7	12.8	11.4	9.9	12.2

—Data not available.

[a]Data shown for 1900–1960 are for the nonwhite population.

[b]Death registration area only. The death registration area increased from 10 states and the District of Columbia (DC) in 1900 to the coterminous United States in 1933.

[c]Includes deaths of persons who were not residents of the 50 states and DC.

Notes: Populations for computing life expectancy for 1991–1999 are 1990-based postcensal estimates of U.S. resident population. In 1997, life table methodology was revised to construct complete life tables by single years of age that extend to age 100 (Anderson RN. Method for constructing complete annual U.S. life tables. National Center for Health Statistics. Vital Health Stat 2(129). 1999). Previously, abridged life tables were constructed for 5-year age groups ending with 85 years and over. Life table values for 2000 and later years were computed using a slight modification of the new life table method due to a change in the age detail of populations received from the U.S. Census Bureau. In 2003, seven states reported multiple-race data. In 2004, 15 states reported multiple-race data. The multiple-race data for these states were bridged to the single-race categories of the 1977 Office of Management and Budget Standards for comparability with other states. Data for additional years are available.

SOURCE: "Table 27. Life Expectancy at Birth, at 65 Years of Age, and at 75 Years of Age, by Race and Sex: United States, Selected Years 1900–2004," in *Health, United States, 2007. With Chartbook on Trends in the Health of Americans*, Centers for Disease Control and Prevention, National Center for Health Statistics, November 2007, http://www.cdc.gov/nchs/data/hus/hus07.pdf (accessed January 30, 2008)

TABLE 10.2

Population and projected population, by age and sex, selected years, 2000–50

[In thousands except as indicated. As of July 1. Resident population.]

Population or percent, sex, and age	2000	2010	2020	2030	2040	2050
Population						
Total						
Total	282,125	308,936	335,805	363,584	391,946	419,854
0–4	19,218	21,426	22,932	24,272	26,299	28,080
5–19	61,331	61,810	65,955	70,832	75,326	81,067
20–44	104,075	104,444	108,632	114,747	121,659	130,897
45–64	62,440	81,012	83,653	82,280	88,611	93,104
65–84	30,794	34,120	47,363	61,850	64,640	65,844
85+	4,267	6,123	7,269	9,603	15,409	20,861
Male						
Total	138,411	151,815	165,093	178,563	192,405	206,477
0–4	9,831	10,947	11,716	12,399	13,437	14,348
5–19	31,454	31,622	33,704	36,199	38,496	41,435
20–44	52,294	52,732	54,966	58,000	61,450	66,152
45–64	30,381	39,502	40,966	40,622	43,961	46,214
65–84	13,212	15,069	21,337	28,003	29,488	30,579
85+	1,240	1,942	2,403	3,340	5,573	7,749
Female						
Total	143,713	157,121	170,711	185,022	199,540	213,377
0–4	9,387	10,479	11,216	11,873	12,863	13,732
5–19	29,877	30,187	32,251	34,633	36,831	39,632
20–44	51,781	51,711	53,666	56,747	60,209	64,745
45–64	32,059	41,510	42,687	41,658	44,650	46,891
65–84	17,582	19,051	26,026	33,848	35,152	35,265
85+	3,028	4,182	4,866	6,263	9,836	13,112
Percent of total						
Total						
Total	100.0	100.0	100.0	100.0	100.0	100.0
0–4	6.8	6.9	6.8	6.7	6.7	6.7
5–19	21.7	20.0	19.6	19.5	19.2	19.3
20–44	36.9	33.8	32.3	31.6	31.0	31.2
45–64	22.1	26.2	24.9	22.6	22.6	22.2
65–84	10.9	11.0	14.1	17.0	16.5	15.7
85+	1.5	2.0	2.2	2.6	3.9	5.0
Male						
Total	100.0	100.0	100.0	100.0	100.0	100.0
0–4	7.1	7.2	7.1	6.9	7.0	6.9
5–19	22.7	20.8	20.4	20.3	20.0	20.1
20–44	37.8	34.7	33.3	32.5	31.9	32.0
45–64	21.9	26.0	24.8	22.7	22.8	22.4
65–84	9.5	9.9	12.9	15.7	15.3	14.8
85+	0.9	1.3	1.5	1.9	2.9	3.8
Female						
Total	100.0	100.0	100.0	100.0	100.0	100.0
0–4	6.5	6.7	6.6	6.4	6.4	6.4
5–19	20.8	19.2	18.9	18.7	18.5	18.6
20–44	36.0	32.9	31.4	30.7	30.2	30.3
45–64	22.3	26.4	25.0	22.5	22.4	22.0
65–84	12.2	12.1	15.2	18.3	17.6	16.5
85+	2.1	2.7	2.9	3.4	4.9	6.1

SOURCE: "Table 2a. Projected Population of the United States, by Age and Sex: 2000 to 2050," in *U.S. Interim Projections by Age, Sex, Race, and Hispanic Origin*, U.S. Census Bureau, March 18, 2004, http://www.census.gov/ipc/www/usinterimproj/natprojtab02a.pdf (accessed February 2, 2008)

LEADING CAUSES OF DEATH AMONG THE ELDERLY

Six out of ten (59.8%) people aged sixty-five and older who died in 2004 were the victims of diseases of the heart, cancer (malignant neoplasms), or stroke (cerebrovascular diseases). (See Table 10.4.)

Coronary Heart Disease

Coronary heart disease (CHD) is the leading cause of death in the United States and remains the leading cause

of death among older Americans. Eight out of ten (81.8%; 533,302 out of 652,029) people who died of CHD in 2004 were aged sixty-five years and older. (See Table 10.4.) This figure is up from 1980, when a slightly lower percentage of those aged sixty-five and older died of CHD (78.3%; 595,406 out of 760,132). This shift is because more young people aged one to fourteen years and twenty-five to forty-four years died of CHD in 1980 than in 2004. In fact, fewer people in the sixty-five-years-and-older age group died from CHD in 2004 than in

TABLE 10.3

Characteristics of persons age 65 and older, by sex, selected years, 1990–2006

[As of March, except as noted]

Characteristic	Total 1990	Total 2000	Total 2005	Total 2006	Male 1990	Male 2000	Male 2005	Male 2006	Female 1990	Female 2000	Female 2005	Female 2006
Total (million)	**29.6**	**32.6**	**35.2**	**35.5**	**12.3**	**13.9**	**15.1**	**15.2**	**17.2**	**18.7**	**20.0**	**20.3**
Percent distribution												
Marital status												
Never married	4.6	3.9	4.1	3.6	4.2	4.2	4.4	3.8	4.9	3.6	3.9	3.6
Married	56.1	57.2	57.7	57.8	76.5	75.2	74.9	75.0	41.4	43.8	44.7	44.9
Spouse present	54.1	54.6	54.8	54.7	74.2	72.6	71.7	71.9	39.7	41.3	42.0	41.9
Spouse absent	2.0	2.6	2.9	3.0	2.3	2.6	3.2	3.1	1.7	2.5	2.7	3.0
Widowed	34.2	32.1	30.3	29.9	14.2	14.4	13.7	13.1	48.6	45.3	42.9	42.4
Divorced	5.0	6.7	7.9	8.7	5.0	6.1	7.0	8.1	5.1	7.2	8.5	9.1
Educational attainment												
Less than ninth grade	28.5	16.7	13.4	13.0	30.0	17.8	13.2	13.0	27.5	15.9	13.5	12.9
Completed 9th to 12th grade, but no high school diploma	16.1[a]	13.8	12.7	11.9	15.7[a]	12.7	11.9	11.0	16.4[a]	14.7	13.3	12.5
High school graduate	32.9[b]	35.9	36.3	36.7	29.0[b]	30.4	31.6	32.9	35.6[b]	39.9	39.9	39.5
Some college or associate's degree	10.9[c]	18.0	18.7	19.0	10.8[c]	17.8	18.4	17.4	11.0[c]	18.2	19.0	20.2
Bachelor's or advanced degree	11.6[d]	15.6	18.9	19.5	14.5[d]	21.4	24.9	25.6	9.5[d]	11.4	14.3	14.9
Labor force participation[e]												
Employed	11.5	12.4	14.5	15.0	15.9	16.9	19.1	19.8	8.4	9.1	11.1	11.4
Unemployed	0.4	0.4	0.5	0.4	0.5	0.6	0.7	0.6	0.3	0.3	0.4	0.3
Not in labor force	88.1	87.2	84.9	84.6	83.6	82.5	80.2	79.7	91.3	90.6	88.5	88.3
Percent below poverty level[f]	11.4	9.7	9.8	10.1	7.8	6.9	7.0	7.3	13.9	11.8	11.9	12.3

[a]Represents those who completed 1 to 3 years of high school.
[b]Represents those who completed 4 years of high school.
[c]Represents those who completed 1 to 3 years of college.
[d]Represents those who completed 4 years of college or more.
[e]Annual averages of monthly figures.
[f]Poverty status based on income in preceding year.

Notes: 29.6 represents 29,600,000. Covers civilian noninstitutional population. Excludes members of Armed Forces except those living off post or with their families on post. Data for 1990 are based on 1980 census population controls; 2000 data based on 1990 census population controls; beginning 2005, data based on 2000 census population controls and an expanded sample of households. Based on Current Population Survey.

SOURCE: "Table 34. Persons 65 Years Old and over—Characteristics by Sex: 1990 to 2006," in *Statistical Abstract of the United States: 2008*, U.S. Census Bureau, 2007, http://www.census.gov/compendia/statab/tables/08s0034.pdf (accessed March 15, 2008)

1980, even though the numbers of deaths from all causes in this group rose from 1.3 million in 1980 to nearly 1.8 million in 2004. Nonetheless, CHD is still the leading cause of death among older Americans.

The risk of dying from heart disease increases as a person ages. The death rate from CHD in 2004 for those aged seventy-five to eighty-four was 1,506.3 deaths per 100,000 population, almost three times the rate for those aged sixty-five to seventy-four (541.6 per 100,000). (See Table 10.5.) For those aged eighty-five and older, the death rate rose sharply to 4,895.9 deaths per 100,000 population—nine times the rate for those aged sixty-five to seventy-four. In 2004 females had a lower incidence of death from heart disease than did males at all ages, except for ages one to fourteen. At those ages the risk for both sexes was approximately the same.

In the sixty-five-and-older age group the death rate for males from heart disease has been consistently higher than the death rate for females of the same age group regardless of the race. For example, the death rate from heart disease for African-American males aged sixty-five to seventy-four years was 1,096.6 per 100,000 population in 2004, whereas the death rate from heart disease for African-American females was 656.5. (See Table 10.5.) In another example, the death rate from heart disease for Hispanic males aged sixty-five to seventy-four years was 572.2 per 100,000 population in 2004, whereas the death rate from heart disease for Hispanic females was 305.5.

Since the 1950s deaths from heart disease have consistently declined. (See Table 10.5.) Several factors account for this decrease, including better control of hypertension (high blood pressure) and cholesterol levels in the blood. Changes in lifestyle, such as the inclusion of physical exercise and a healthy diet, help decrease the incidence of heart disease. The expanding use of trained mobile emergency personnel (paramedics) in most urban areas has also contributed to the decrease, and the widespread use of cardiopulmonary resuscitation and new drugs have increased the likelihood of surviving an initial heart attack.

Until the 1990s almost all research on heart disease focused on white, middle-aged males. Researchers, physicians, and public health officials agree that more research and prevention efforts should be directed toward

TABLE 10.4

Leading causes of death and numbers of deaths, by age, 1980 and 2004

[Data are based on death certificates]

Age and rank order	1980		2004	
	Cause of death	Deaths	Cause of death	Deaths
Under 1 year				
—	All causes	45,526	All causes	27,936
1	Congenital anomalies	9,220	Congenital malformations, deformations and chromosomal abnormalities	5,622
2	Sudden infant death syndrome	5,510	Disorders related to short gestation and low birth weight, not elsewhere classified	4,642
3	Respiratory distress syndrome	4,989	Sudden infant death syndrome	2,246
4	Disorders relating to short gestation and unspecified low birthweight	3,648	Newborn affected by maternal complications of pregnancy	1,715
5	New born affected by maternal complications of pregnancy	1,572	Unintentional injuries	1,052
6	Intrauterine hypoxia and birth asphyxia	1,497	Newborn affected by complications of placenta, cord and membranes	1,042
7	Unintentional injuries	1,166	Respiratory distress of newborn	875
8	Birth trauma	1,058	Bacterial sepsis of newborn	827
9	Pneumonia and influenza	1,012	Neonatal hemorrhage	616
10	New born affected by complications of placenta, cord, and membranes	985	Diseases of circulatory system	593
1–4 years				
—	All causes	8,187	All causes	4,785
1	Unintentional injuries	3,313	Unintentional injuries	1,641
2	Congenital anomalies	1,026	Congenital malformations, deformations and chromosomal abnormalities	569
3	Malignant neoplasms	573	Malignant neoplasms	399
4	Diseases of heart	338	Homicide	377
5	Homicide	319	Diseases of heart	187
6	Pneumonia and influenza	267	Influenza and pneumonia	119
7	Meningitis	223	Septicemia	84
8	Meningococcal infection	110	Certain conditions originating in the perinatal period	61
9	Certain conditions originating in the perinatal period	84	In situ neoplasms, benign neoplasms and neoplasms of uncertain or unknown behavior	53
10	Septicemia	71	Chronic lower respiratory diseases	48
5–14 years				
—	All causes	10,689	All causes	6,834
1	Unintentional injuries	5,224	Unintentional injuries	2,666
2	Malignant neoplasms	1,497	Malignant neoplasms	1,019
3	Congenital anomalies	561	Congenital malformations, deformations and chromosomal abnormalities	389
4	Homicide	415	Homicide	329
5	Diseases of heart	330	Suicide	285
6	Pneumonia and influenza	194	Diseases of heart	245
7	Suicide	142	Chronic lower respiratory diseases	120
8	Benign neoplasms	104	In situ neoplasms, benign neoplasms and neoplasms of uncertain or unknown behavior	84
9	Cerebrovascular diseases	95	Influenza and pneumonia	82
10	Chronic obstructive pulmonary diseases	85	Cerebrovascular diseases	77
15–24 years				
—	All causes	49,027	All causes	33,421
1	Unintentional injuries	26,206	Unintentional injuries	15,449
2	Homicide	6,537	Homicide	5,085
3	Suicide	5,239	Suicide	4,316
4	Malignant neoplasms	2,683	Malignant neoplasms	1,709
5	Diseases of heart	1,223	Diseases of heart	1,038
6	Congenital anomalies	600	Congenital malformations, deformations and chromosomal abnormalities	483
7	Cerebrovascular diseases	418	Cerebrovascular diseases	211
8	Pneumonia and influenza	348	Human immunodeficiency virus (HIV) disease	191
9	Chronic obstructive pulmonary diseases	141	Influenza and pneumonia	185
10	Anemias	133	Chronic lower respiratory diseases	179

women, racial and ethnic minorities, and older adults. In *Heart and Stroke Statistics—2008 Update* (2008, http://www.americanheart.org/downloadable/heart/1200082005 246HS_Stats%202008.final.pdf), the American Heart Association notes that at age forty and older, 23% of women who have heart attacks die within the first year after the incident, compared to 18% of men.

The symptoms of heart attack can be significantly different for women than for men. Heart disease in

TABLE 10.4

Leading causes of death and numbers of deaths, by age, 1980 and 2004 [CONTINUED]

[Data are based on death certificates]

Age and rank order	1980		2004	
	Cause of death	Deaths	Cause of death	Deaths
25–44 years				
—	All causes	108,658	All causes	126,230
1	Unintentional injuries	26,722	Unintentional injuries	29,503
2	Malignant neoplasms	17,551	Malignant neoplasms	18,356
3	Diseases of heart	14,513	Diseases of heart	16,088
4	Homicide	10,983	Suicide	11,712
5	Suicide	9,855	Homicide	7,479
6	Chronic liver disease and cirrhosis	4,782	Human immunodeficiency virus (HIV) disease	6,294
7	Cerebrovascular diseases	3,154	Chronic liver disease and cirrhosis	3,108
8	Diabetes mellitus	1,472	Cerebrovascular diseases	2,928
9	Pneumonia and influenza	1,467	Diabetes mellitus	2,625
10	Congenital anomalies	817	Influenza and pneumonia	1,194
45–64 years				
—	All causes	425,338	All causes	442,394
1	Diseases of heart	148,322	Malignant neoplasms	146,476
2	Malignant neoplasms	135,675	Diseases of heart	101,169
3	Cerebrovascular diseases	19,909	Unintentional injuries	26,593
4	Unintentional injuries	18,140	Diabetes mellitus	16,347
5	Chronic liver disease and cirrhosis	16,089	Cerebrovascular diseases	16,147
6	Chronic obstructive pulmonary diseases	11,514	Chronic lower respiratory diseases	15,265
7	Diabetes mellitus	7,977	Chronic liver disease and cirrhosis	14,065
8	Suicide	7,079	Suicide	10,917
9	Pneumonia and influenza	5,804	Nephritis, nephrotic syndrome and nephrosis	6,030
10	Homicide	4,019	Septicemia	5,996
65 years and over				
—	All causes	1,341,848	All causes	1,755,669
1	Diseases of heart	595,406	Diseases of heart	533,302
2	Malignant neoplasms	258,389	Malignant neoplasms	385,847
3	Cerebrovascular diseases	146,417	Cerebrovascular diseases	130,538
4	Pneumonia and influenza	45,512	Chronic lower respiratory diseases	105,197
5	Chronic obstructive pulmonary diseases	43,587	Alzheimer's disease	65,313
6	Atherosclerosis	28,081	Diabetes mellitus	53,956
7	Diabetes mellitus	25,216	Influenza and pneumonia	52,760
8	Unintentional injuries	24,844	Nephritis, nephrotic syndrome and nephrosis	35,105
9	Nephritis, nephrotic syndrome, and nephrosis	12,968	Unintentional injuries	35,020
10	Chronic liver disease and cirrhosis	9,519	Septicemia	25,644

—Category not applicable.

SOURCE: "Table 32. Leading Causes of Death and Numbers of Deaths, by Age: United States, 1980 and 2004," in *Health, United States, 2007. With Chartbook on Trends in the Health of Americans*, Centers for Disease Control and Prevention, National Center for Health Statistics, November 2007, http://www.cdc.gov/nchs/data/hus/hus07.pdf (accessed January 30, 2008)

women is often due to coronary microvascular dysfunction, in which the small blood vessels of the heart do not dilate (widen) properly to supply sufficient blood to the heart muscle. This dysfunction may occur alone, or besides, blockages that reduce blood flow in the large coronary arteries as is often the case in men. Because of the differences in the sizes of the involved blood vessels, symptoms of a heart attack may differ between women and men. When the large vessels are blocked, symptoms may include pain, pressure, burning, aching, and tightness in the chest, along with shortness of breath, sweating, weakness, anxiety, and nausea. When small vessels are blocked, symptoms may be more subtle and may include discomfort spread over a wide chest area, exhaustion, depression, and shortness of breath. Nausea, back or jaw pain, shortness of breath, and chest pain may accompany these symptoms.

Cancer

Cancer (malignant neoplasms) is the second-leading cause of death among older adults. In 2004, 385,847 people sixty-five and older died of cancer. (See Table 10.4.) The risk of developing many types of cancers increases with age and varies by race and ethnicity. (See and Table 10.6 and Table 10.7.)

Regarding ethnicity, African-American males had the highest incidence of cancer of all types between 2000 and 2004 (663.7 per 100,000 population) and Native American and Alaskan Native females had the lowest incidence (282.4 per 100,000), followed closely by Asian-American and Pacific Islander females (285.8 per 100,000). (See Table 10.7.) African-American males also had the highest mortality rate from cancer between 2000 and 2004 at 321.8 deaths per 100,000 population. Asian-American and Pacific Islander females had the

TABLE 10.5

Death rates for diseases of the heart, by sex, race, Hispanic origin, and age, selected years, 1950–2004

[Data are based on death certificates]

Sex, race, Hispanic origin, and age	1950[a,b]	1960[a,b]	1970[b]	1980[b]	1990	2000[c]	2003	2004
All persons				Deaths per 100,000 resident population				
All ages, age-adjusted[c]	586.8	559.0	492.7	412.1	321.8	257.6	232.3	217.0
All ages, crude	355.5	369.0	362.0	336.0	289.5	252.6	235.6	222.2
Under 1 year	3.5	6.6	13.1	22.8	20.1	13.0	11.0	10.3
1–4 years	1.3	1.3	1.7	2.6	1.9	1.2	1.2	1.2
5–14 years	2.1	1.3	0.8	0.9	0.9	0.7	0.6	0.6
15–24 years	6.8	4.0	3.0	2.9	2.5	2.6	2.7	2.5
25–34 years	19.4	15.6	11.4	8.3	7.6	7.4	8.2	7.9
35–44 years	86.4	74.6	66.7	44.6	31.4	29.2	30.7	29.3
45–54 years	308.6	271.8	238.4	180.2	120.5	94.2	92.5	90.2
55–64 years	808.1	737.9	652.3	494.1	367.3	261.2	233.2	218.8
65–74 years	1,839.8	1,740.5	1,558.2	1,218.6	894.3	665.6	585.0	541.6
75–84 years	4,310.1	4,089.4	3,683.8	2,993.1	2,295.7	1,780.3	1,611.1	1,506.3
85 years and over	9,150.6	9,317.8	7,891.3	7,777.1	6,739.9	5,926.1	5,278.4	4,895.9
Male								
All ages, age-adjusted[d]	697.0	687.6	634.0	538.9	412.4	320.0	286.6	267.9
All ages, crude	423.4	439.5	422.5	368.6	297.6	249.8	235.0	222.8
Under 1 year	4.0	7.8	15.1	25.5	21.9	13.3	12.1	10.9
1–4 years	1.4	1.4	1.9	2.8	1.9	1.4	1.1	1.1
5–14 years	2.0	1.4	0.9	1.0	0.9	0.8	0.7	0.6
15–24 years	6.8	4.2	3.7	3.7	3.1	3.2	3.4	3.2
25–34 years	22.9	20.1	15.2	11.4	10.3	9.6	10.5	10.5
35–44 years	118.4	112.7	103.2	68.7	48.1	41.4	42.8	40.9
45–54 years	440.5	420.4	376.4	282.6	183.0	140.2	136.2	132.3
55–64 years	1,104.5	1,066.9	987.2	746.8	537.3	371.7	331.7	312.8
65–74 years	2,292.3	2,291.3	2,170.3	1,728.0	1,250.0	898.3	785.3	723.8
75–84 years	4,825.0	4,742.4	4,534.8	3,834.3	2,968.2	2,248.1	2,030.3	1,893.6
85 years and over	9,659.8	9,788.9	8,426.2	8,752.7	7,418.4	6,430.0	5,621.5	5,239.3
Female								
All ages, age-adjusted[d]	484.7	447.0	381.6	320.8	257.0	210.9	190.3	177.3
All ages, crude	288.4	300.6	304.5	305.1	281.8	255.3	236.2	221.6
Under 1 year	2.9	5.4	10.9	20.0	18.3	12.5	9.8	9.7
1–4 years	1.2	1.1	1.6	2.5	1.9	1.0	1.3	1.2
5–14 years	2.2	1.2	0.8	0.9	0.8	0.5	0.5	0.6
15–24 years	6.7	3.7	2.3	2.1	1.8	2.1	2.1	1.7
25–34 years	16.2	11.3	7.7	5.3	5.0	5.2	5.7	5.2
35–44 years	55.1	38.2	32.2	21.4	15.1	17.2	18.6	17.7
45–54 years	177.2	127.5	109.9	84.5	61.0	49.8	50.2	49.6
55–64 years	510.0	429.4	351.6	272.1	215.7	159.3	141.9	131.5
65–74 years	1,419.3	1,261.3	1,082.7	828.6	616.8	474.0	417.5	388.6
75–84 years	3,872.0	3,582.7	3,120.8	2,497.0	1,893.8	1,475.1	1,331.1	1,245.6
85 years and over	8,796.1	9,016.8	7,591.8	7,350.5	6,478.1	5,720.9	5,126.7	4,741.5
White male[e]								
All ages, age-adjusted[d]	700.2	694.5	640.2	539.6	409.2	316.7	282.9	264.6
All ages, crude	433.0	454.6	438.3	384.0	312.7	265.8	249.5	236.5
45–54 years	423.6	413.2	365.7	269.8	170.6	130.7	125.3	122.2
55–64 years	1,081.7	1,056.0	979.3	730.6	516.7	351.8	313.2	294.4
65–74 years	2,308.3	2,297.9	2,177.2	1,729.7	1,230.5	877.8	761.1	703.2
75–84 years	4,907.3	4,839.9	4,617.6	3,883.2	2,983.4	2,247.0	2,030.1	1,897.1
85 years and over	9,950.5	10,135.8	8,818.0	8,958.0	7,558.7	6,560.8	5,747.2	5,348.4
Black or African American male[e]								
All ages, age-adjusted[d]	639.4	615.2	607.3	561.4	485.4	392.5	364.3	342.1
All ages, crude	346.2	330.6	330.3	301.0	256.8	211.1	206.0	196.7
45–54 years	622.5	514.0	512.8	433.4	328.9	247.2	248.1	240.0
55–64 years	1,433.1	1,236.8	1,135.4	987.2	824.0	631.2	580.9	560.2
65–74 years	2,139.1	2,281.4	2,237.8	1,847.2	1,632.9	1,268.8	1,195.5	1,096.6
75–84 years[f]	4,106.1	3,533.6	3,783.4	3,578.8	3,107.1	2,597.6	2,426.6	2,235.5
85 years and over	—	6,037.9	5,367.6	6,819.5	6,479.6	5,633.5	4,850.3	4,637.3

lowest cancer death rate during this period at 96.7 deaths per 100,000 population.

Regarding age, the older people become, the higher their probability of developing invasive cancers. For example, the older a man gets, the more likely he is to develop prostate cancer. The chance of dying from pros-tate cancer also rises with age. The American Cancer Society reports in *Cancer Facts & Figures 2008* (2008, http://www.cancer.org/downloads/STT/2008CAFFfinal secured.pdf) that about 64% of men newly diagnosed with prostate cancer are older than sixty-five. The probability of developing prostate cancer is 1 in 10,553 for men who are younger than forty; 1 in 39 for forty- to

TABLE 10.5

Death rates for diseases of the heart, by sex, race, Hispanic origin, and age, selected years, 1950–2004 [CONTINUED]

[Data are based on death certificates]

Sex, race, Hispanic origin, and age	1950[a,b]	1960[a,b]	1970[b]	1980[b]	1990	2000[c]	2003	2004
				Deaths per 100,000 resident population				
American Indian or Alaska Native male[e]								
All ages, age-adjusted[d]	—	—	—	320.5	264.1	222.2	203.2	182.7
All ages, crude	—	—	—	130.6	108.0	90.1	98.5	91.4
45–54 years	—	—	—	238.1	173.8	108.5	116.7	94.1
55–64 years	—	—	—	496.3	411.0	285.0	293.5	260.7
65–74 years	—	—	—	1,009.4	839.1	748.2	655.6	590.0
75–84 years	—	—	—	2,062.2	1,788.8	1,655.7	1,309.9	1,252.1
85 years and over	—	—	—	4,413.7	3,860.3	3,318.3	3,266.5	2,812.6
Asian or Pacific Islander male[e]								
All ages, age-adjusted[d]	—	—	—	220.7	286.9	185.5	158.3	146.5
All ages, crude	—	—	—	119.8	88.7	90.6	86.3	81.4
45–54 years	—	—	—	112.0	70.4	61.1	62.7	56.6
55–64 years	—	—	—	306.7	226.1	182.6	152.9	138.9
65–74 years	—	—	—	852.4	623.5	482.5	398.3	347.7
75–84 years	—	—	—	2,010.9	1,642.2	1,354.7	1,145.1	1,047.0
85 years and over	—	—	—	5,923.0	4,617.8	4,154.2	3,524.6	3,416.7
Hispanic or Latino male[e,g]								
All ages, age-adjusted[d]	—	—	—	—	270.0	238.2	206.8	193.9
All ages, crude	—	—	—	—	91.0	74.7	72.2	70.2
45–54 years	—	—	—	—	116.4	84.3	79.6	77.6
55–64 years	—	—	—	—	363.0	264.8	235.6	224.6
65–74 years	—	—	—	—	829.9	684.8	625.0	572.2
75–84 years	—	—	—	—	1,971.3	1,733.2	1,543.5	1,489.0
85 years and over	—	—	—	—	4,711.9	4,897.5	3,874.5	3,496.8
White, not Hispanic or Latino male[g]								
All ages, age-adjusted[d]	—	—	—	—	413.6	319.9	286.9	268.7
All ages, crude	—	—	—	—	336.5	297.5	282.9	269.1
45–54 years	—	—	—	—	172.8	134.3	129.8	126.9
55–64 years	—	—	—	—	521.3	356.3	317.7	298.8
65–74 years	—	—	—	—	1,243.4	885.1	767.3	709.5
75–84 years	—	—	—	—	3,007.7	2,261.9	2,049.9	1,915.1
85 years and over	—	—	—	—	7,663.4	6,606.6	5,821.0	5,430.9
White female[e]								
All ages, age-adjusted[d]	478.0	441.7	376.7	315.9	250.9	205.6	185.4	172.9
All ages, crude	289.4	306.5	313.8	319.2	298.4	274.5	253.8	238.3
45–54 years	141.9	103.4	91.4	71.2	50.2	40.9	41.1	40.7
55–64 years	460.2	383.0	317.7	248.1	192.4	141.3	125.2	117.2
65–74 years	1,400.9	1,229.8	1,044.0	796.7	583.6	445.2	392.0	365.4
75–84 years	3,925.2	3,629.7	3,143.5	2,493.6	1,874.3	1,452.4	1,315.2	1,229.1
85 years and over	9,084.7	9,280.8	7,839.9	7,501.6	6,563.4	5,801.4	5,193.6	4,810.4
Black or African American female[e]								
All ages, age-adjusted[d]	536.9	488.9	435.6	378.6	327.5	277.6	253.8	236.5
All ages, crude	287.6	268.5	261.0	249.7	237.0	212.6	200.0	188.3
45–54 years	525.3	360.7	290.9	202.4	155.3	125.0	124.1	121.2
55–64 years	1,210.2	952.3	710.5	530.1	442.0	332.8	304.7	276.0
65–74 years	1,659.4	1,680.5	1,553.2	1,210.3	1,017.5	815.2	712.0	656.5
75–84 years[6]	3,499.3	2,926.9	2,964.1	2,707.2	2,250.9	1,913.1	1,699.6	1,622.9
85 years and over	—	5,650.0	5,003.8	5,796.5	5,766.1	5,298.7	4,976.5	4,534.7
American Indian or Alaska Native female[e]								
All ages, age-adjusted[d]	—	—	—	175.4	153.1	143.6	127.5	119.9
All ages, crude	—	—	—	80.3	77.5	71.9	75.9	73.6
45–54 years	—	—	—	65.2	62.0	40.2	45.4	49.5
55–64 years	—	—	—	193.5	197.0	149.4	153.4	116.9
65–74 years	—	—	—	577.2	492.8	391.8	390.3	317.4
75–84 years	—	—	—	1,364.3	1,050.3	1,044.1	950.3	894.1
85 years and over	—	—	—	2,893.3	2,868.7	3,146.3	2,284.1	2,449.1

fifty-nine-year-olds; and 1 in 15 for men aged sixty to sixty-nine. (See Table 10.6.) The odds rise to one in seven for men aged seventy and older.

Stroke

Stroke (cerebrovascular disease) is the third-leading cause of death and the principal cause of serious disabil-ity among older adults. In 2004, 130,538 people aged sixty-five and older died of a stroke. (See Table 10.4.) The death rate from stroke increases markedly with age. In 2004 the death rate from stroke for those aged sixty-five to seventy-four was 107.8 deaths per 100,000. (See Table 10.8.) This rate more than tripled for each succes-sive decade of age after that, to 386.2 deaths from stroke

TABLE 10.5

Death rates for diseases of the heart, by sex, race, Hispanic origin, and age, selected years, 1950–2004 [CONTINUED]

[Data are based on death certificates]

Sex, race, Hispanic origin, and age	1950[a,b]	1960[a,b]	1970[b]	1980[b]	1990	2000[c]	2003	2004
				Deaths per 100,000 resident population				
Asian or Pacific Islander female[e]								
All ages, age-adjusted[d]	—	—	—	132.3	149.2	115.7	104.2	96.1
All ages, crude	—	—	—	57.0	62.0	65.0	68.2	65.1
45–54 years	—	—	—	28.6	17.5	15.9	14.8	13.7
55–64 years	—	—	—	92.9	99.0	68.8	60.3	50.7
65–74 years	—	—	—	313.3	323.9	229.6	207.2	205.6
75–84 years	—	—	—	1,053.2	1,130.9	866.2	769.7	697.4
85 years and over	—	—	—	3,211.0	4,161.2	3,367.2	3,020.0	2,817.1
Hispanic or Latino female[e,g]								
All ages, age-adjusted[d]	—	—	—	—	177.2	163.7	145.8	130.0
All ages, crude	—	—	—	—	79.4	71.5	69.6	64.1
45–54 years	—	—	—	—	43.5	28.2	27.0	27.0
55–64 years	—	—	—	—	153.2	111.2	102.1	93.1
65–74 years	—	—	—	—	460.4	366.3	330.6	305.5
75–84 years	—	—	—	—	1,259.7	1,169.4	1,067.0	962.7
85 years and over	—	—	—	—	4,440.3	4,605.8	3,962.5	3,421.2
White, not Hispanic or Latino female[g]								
All ages, age-adjusted[d]	—	—	—	—	252.6	206.8	187.1	175.1
All ages, crude	—	—	—	—	320.0	304.9	285.1	269.1
45–54 years	—	—	—	—	50.2	41.9	42.4	42.2
55–64 years	—	—	—	—	193.6	142.9	126.6	118.9
65–74 years	—	—	—	—	584.7	448.5	394.8	368.6
75–84 years	—	—	—	—	1,890.2	1,458.9	1,324.0	1,241.2
85 years and over	—	—	—	—	6,615.2	5,822.7	5,232.2	4,862.4

—Data not available.

[a]Includes deaths of persons who were not residents of the 50 states and the District of Columbia.

[b]Underlying cause of death was coded according to the Sixth Revision of the International Classification of Diseases (ICD) in 1950, Seventh Revision in 1960, Eighth Revision in 1970, and Ninth Revision in 1980–1998.

[c]Starting with 1999 data, cause of death is coded according to ICD-10.

[d]Age-adjusted rates are calculated using the year 2000 standard population. Prior to 2003, age-adjusted rates were calculated using standard million proportions based on rounded population numbers. Starting with 2003 data, unrounded population numbers are used to calculate age-adjusted rates.

[e]The race groups, white, black, Asian or Pacific Islander, and American Indian or Alaska Native, include persons of Hispanic and non-Hispanic origin. Persons of Hispanic origin may be of any race. Death rates for the American Indian or Alaska Native and Asian or Pacific Islander populations are known to be underestimated.

[f]In 1950, rate is for the age group 75 years and over.

[g]Prior to 1997, excludes data from states lacking an Hispanic-origin item on the death certificate.

Notes: Starting with Health, United States, 2003, rates for 1991–1999 were revised using intercensal population estimates based on the 2000 census. Rates for 2000 were revised based on 2000 census counts. Rates for 2001 and later years were computed using 2000-based postcensal estimates. Census and Population Estimates. For the period 1980–1998, diseases of heart was coded using ICD-9 codes that are most nearly comparable with diseases of heart codes in the 113 cause list for ICD-10. Age groups were selected to minimize the presentation of unstable age-specific death rates based on small numbers of deaths and for consistency among comparison groups. In 2003, seven states reported multiple-race data. In 2004, 15 states reported multiple-race data. The multiple-race data for these states were bridged to the single-race categories of the 1977 Office of Management and Budget standards for comparability with other states. Data for additional years are available.

SOURCE: "Table 36. Death Rates for Diseases of Heart, by Sex, Race, Hispanic Origin, and Age: United States, Selected Years 1950–2004," in *Health, United States, 2007. With Chartbook on Trends in the Health of Americans*, Centers for Disease Control and Prevention, National Center for Health Statistics, November 2007, http://www.cdc.gov/nchs/data/hus/hus07.pdf (accessed January 30, 2008)

per 100,000 for those aged seventy-five to eighty-four, and 1,245.9 deaths per 100,000 population for those aged eighty-five and older.

Men aged sixty-five to seventy-four years and seventy-five to eighty-four years were more likely to have suffered a stroke in 2004 than females (121.1 versus 96.6 per 100,000 population, and 402.9 versus 374.9 per 100,000, respectively). (See Table 10.8.) However, in the eighty-five-years-and-older age group, women were more likely than men to have suffered a stroke (1,303.4 versus 1,118.1 per 100,000 population). This pattern was consistent from 1960 to 2004 for all ethnicities and generally for each ethnicity.

Stroke and Alzheimer's disease are two primary causes of dementia. Death rates from stroke have declined dramatically since the 1950s. (See Table 10.8.) Regardless, stroke leaves approximately one-third of the survivors with severe disabilities, and they require continued care.

DEMENTIA

Older people with cognitive (mental) problems were once labeled "senile," which had a derogatory connotation and meant an elderly person who was cognitively impaired. Researchers have found that physical disorders can cause progressive deterioration of cognitive and neurological functions. In the twenty-first century these disorders produce symptoms that are collectively known as dementia. Symptoms of dementia include loss of language functions, inability to think abstractly, inability to

TABLE 10.6

Probability of developing invasive cancers over selected age intervals, by sex, 2002–04 [a]

		Birth to 39 (%)	40 to 59 (%)	60 to 69 (%)	70 and older (%)	Birth to death (%)
All sites[b]	Male	1.42 (1 in 70)	8.58 (1 in 12)	16.25 (1 in 6)	38.96 (1 in 3)	44.94 (1 in 2)
	Female	2.04 (1 in 49)	8.97 (1 in 11)	10.36 (1 in 10)	26.31 (1 in 4)	37.52 (1 in 3)
Urinary bladder[c]	Male	0.02 (1 in 4,477)	0.41 (1 in 244)	0.96 (1 in 104)	3.50 (1 in 29)	3.70 (1 in 27)
	Female	0.01 (1 in 9,462)	0.13 (1 in 790)	0.26 (1 in 384)	0.99(1 in 101)	1.17 (1 in 85)
Breast	Female	0.48(1 in 210)	3.86(1 in 26)	3.51 (1 in 28)	6.95 (1 in 15)	12.28 (1 in 8)
Colon & rectum	Male	0.08 (1 in 1,329]	0.92 (1 in 109)	1.60 (1 in 63)	4.78 (1 in 21)	5 65 (1 in 18)
	Female	0.07 (1 in 1,394)	0.72 (1 in 138)	1.12 (1 in 89)	4.30 (1 in 23)	5 23 (1 in 19)
Leukemia	Male	0.16 (1 in 624)	0.21 (1 in 468)	0.35 (1 in 288)	1.18 (1 in 85)	1.50 (1 in 67)
	Female	0.12 (1 in 837)	0.14(1 in 705)	0.20 (1 in 496)	0.76 (1 in 131)	1.06 (1 in 95)
Lung & bronchus	Male	0.03 (1 in 3,357)	1.03 (1 in 97)	2.52 (1 in 40)	6.74 (1 in 15)	7.91 (1 in 13)
	Female	0.03 (1 in 2,964)	0.82 (1 in 121)	1.81 (1 in 55)	4.61 (1 in 22)	6.18 (1 in 16)
Melanoma of the skin	Male	0.15 (1 in 656)	0.61 (1 in 164)	0.66 (1 in 151)	1.56 (1 in 64)	2.42 (1 in 41)
	Female	0.26 (1 in 389)	0.50(1 in 200)	0.34 (1 in 297)	0.71 (1 in 140)	1.63 (1 in 61)
Non-Hodgkin lymphoma	Male	0.13 (1 in 760)	0.45 (1 in 222)	0.57 (1 in 174)	1.61 (1 in 62)	2.19 (1 in 46)
	Female	0.08(1 in 1,212)	0.32 (1 in 312)	0.45 (1 in 221)	1.33 (1 in 75)	1.87 (1 in 53)
Prostate	Male	0.01 (1 in 10,553)	2 54 (1 in 39)	6.83 (1 in 15)	13.36 (1 in 7)	16.72 (1 in 6)
Uterine cervix	Female	0.16 (1 in 638)	0.28 (1 in 359)	0.13 (1 in 750)	0.19 (1 in 523)	0.70 (1 in 142)
Uterine corpus	Female	0.06 (1 in 1,569)	0.71 (1 in 142)	0.79 (1 in 126)	1.23 (1 in 81)	2.45 (1 in 41)

[a]For people free of cancer at beginning of age interval.
[b]All sites exclude basal and squamous cell skin cancers and in situ cancers except urinary bladder
[c]Includes invasive and in situ cancer cases.

SOURCE: "Probability of Developing Invasive Cancers over Selected Age Intervals by Sex, US, 2002–2004," in *Cancer Facts and Figures 2008*, American Cancer Society, 2008, http://www.cancer.org/downloads/STT/2008CAFFfinalsecured.pdf (accessed March 15, 2008). Atlanta: American Cancer Society, Inc. Copyright © 2008 American Cancer Society, Inc. Reprinted with permission. Data from the National Cancer Institute.

care for oneself, personality change, emotional instability, and loss of a sense of time or place.

Dementia has become a serious health problem in developed countries, including the United States, because older adults are living longer than ever before. One indicator of diminished cognitive functioning in older adults is memory loss. Table 10.9 shows the percentage of people aged sixty-five and older with moderate to severe memory impairment. For each age shown, a higher percentage of men than of women show memory impairment. Nevertheless, in 2002 about one-third of men and women aged eighty-five and older exhibited memory impairment.

Alzheimer's Disease

Alzheimer's disease (AD) is the single most common cause of dementia. It is a progressive, degenerative disease that attacks the brain and results in severely impaired memory, thinking, and behavior. First described in 1906 by the German neuropathologist Alois Alzheimer (1864–1915), the disorder may strike people in their forties and fifties, but most victims are over age sixty-five.

Alzheimer's autopsy of a severely demented fifty-five-year-old woman revealed deposits of neuritic plaques and neurofibrillary tangles. The latter characteristic, the presence of twisted and tangled fibers in the brain cells, is the anatomical hallmark of the disease.

SYMPTOMS. The onset of dementia in AD is gradual, and the decline of cognitive function progresses over time. Mild or early AD is not easily distinguishable from the characteristics of normal aging—mild episodes of forgetfulness and disorientation. Gradually, the AD patient may experience confusion; language problems, such as trouble finding words; impaired judgment; disorientation in place and time; and changes in mood, behavior, and personality. The speed with which these changes occur varies, but eventually the disease leaves patients unable to care for themselves.

In the terminal stages of AD, patients require care twenty-four hours a day. They no longer recognize family members and need help with simple daily activities, such as eating, dressing, bathing, and using the toilet. Eventually, they may become incontinent, blind, and unable to communicate. The course of the disease varies widely—some patients die within a few years of diagnosis, whereas others live as long as twenty-five years.

PREVALENCE. In 2004, 65,313 deaths from AD were reported for those aged sixty-five and older. (See Table 10.4.) In that year AD was the fifth-leading cause of death in the sixty-five-and-older age group, whereas in 1980, AD was not even in the top-ten leading causes of death for this group. Figure 10.1 shows that the number of deaths from AD had increased 44.7% between 2000 and 2005, whereas the percentage change in numbers of deaths from heart disease, breast cancer, prostate cancer, and stroke had all decreased.

In "Prevalence of Dementia in the United States: The Aging, Demographics, and Memory Study" (*Neuroepidemiology*, vol. 29, nos. 1–2, 2007), Brenda L. Plassman et al. use data from the University of Michigan's Health

TABLE 10.7

Cancer incidence and mortality rates[a] by site, race, and ethnicity, 2000–04

Incidence	White	African American	Asian American and Pacific Islander	American Indian and Alaska Native[b]	Hispanic/ Latino[c, d]
All sites					
Males	556.7	663.7	359.9	321.2	421.3
Females	423.9	396.9	285.8	282.4	314.2
Breast (female)	132.5	118.3	89.0	69.8	89.3
Colon & rectum					
Males	60.4	72.6	49.7	42.1	47.5
Females	44.0	55.0	35.3	39.6	32.9
Kidney & renal pelvis					
Males	18.3	20.4	8.9	18.5	16.5
Females	9.1	9.7	4.3	11.5	9.1
Liver & bile duct					
Males	7.9	12.7	21.3	14.8	14.4
Females	2.9	3.8	7.9	5.5	5.7
Lung & bronchus					
Males	81.0	110.6	55.1	53.7	44.7
Females	54.6	53.7	27.7	36.7	25.2
Prostate	161.4	255.5	96.5	68.2	140.8
Stomach					
Males	10.2	17.5	189	16.3	160
Females	4.7	9.1	108	7.9	9.6
Uterine cervix	8.5	11.4	8.0	66	13.8
Mortality					
All sites					
Males	234.7	321.8	141.7	187.9	162.2
Females	161.4	189.3	96.7	141.2	106.7
Breast (female)	25.0	33.8	12.6	16.1	16.1
Colon & rectum					
Males	22.9	32.7	15.0	20.6	17.0
Females	15.9	22.9	10.3	14.3	11.1
Kidney & renal pelvis					
Males	6.2	6.1	2.4	9.3	5.4
Females	2.8	2.8	1.1	4.3	2.3
Liver & bile duct					
Males	6.5	10.0	15.5	10.7	10.8
Females	2.8	3.9	6.7	6.4	5.0
Lung & bronchus					
Males	72.6	95.8	38.3	49.6	36.0
Females	42.1	39.8	18.5	32.7	14.6
Prostate	25.6	62.3	11.3	21.5	21.2
Stomach					
Males	5.2	11.9	10.5	9.6	9.1
Females	2.6	5.8	6.2	5.5	5.1
Uterine cervix	2.3	4.9	2.4	4.0	3.3

[a]Per 100,000, age adjusted to the 2000 US standard population.
[b]Data based on Contract Health Service Delivery Areas (CHSD.A), 624 counties comprising 54% of the U.S. American Indian/Alaska Native population, for more information, please see: Espey DK, Wu XC, Swan J, et al Annual report to the nation on the status of cancer, 1975–2004, featuring cancer in American Indians and Alaska Natives.
[c]Persons of Hispanic/Latino origin may be of any race.
[d]Data unavailable from the Alaska Native Registry and Kentucky.
[e]Data unavailable from Minnesota, New Hampshire, and North Dakota

SOURCE: "Cancer Incidence and Mortality Rates by Site, Race, and Ethnicity, U S,2000–2004," in *Cancer Facts and Figures 2008*, American Cancer Society, 2008, http://www.cancer.org/downloads/STT/2008CAFFfinalsecured.pdf (accessed March 15, 2008). Atlanta: American Cancer Society, Inc. Copyright © 2008 American Cancer Society, Inc. Reprinted with permission. Data from the National Cancer Institute and the National Center for Health Statistics.

and Retirement Study to determine the prevalence of AD and other dementias in the United States. Table 10.10 shows some of the results from this study. Nearly 5% of all individuals aged seventy-one to seventy-nine suffered from a dementia of some type in 2002. Of these 5%, 2.3% suffered from AD and 0.9% suffered from vascular dementia, which is the second-most common form of dementia after AD. It is caused by problems with the

TABLE 10.8

Death rates for cerebrovascular diseases, by sex, race, Hispanic origin, and age, selected years, 1950–2004

[Data are based on death certificates]

Sex, race, Hispanic origin, and age	1950[a,b]	1960[a,b]	1970[b]	1980[b]	1990	2000[c]	2003	2004
All persons				Deaths per 100,000 resident population				
All ages, age-adjusted[d]	180.7	177.9	147.7	96.2	65.3	60.9	53.5	50.0
All ages, crude	104.0	108.0	101.9	75.0	57.8	59.6	54.2	51.1
Under 1 year	5.1	4.1	5.0	4.4	3.8	3.3	2.5	3.1
1–4 years	0.9	0.8	1.0	0.5	0.3	0.3	0.3	0.3
5–14 years	0.5	0.7	0.7	0.3	0.2	0.2	0.2	0.2
15–24 years	1.6	1.8	1.6	1.0	0.6	0.5	0.5	0.5
25–34 years	4.2	4.7	4.5	2.6	2.2	1.5	1.5	1.4
35–44 years	18.7	14.7	15.6	8.5	6.4	5.8	5.5	5.4
45–54 years	70.4	49.2	41.6	25.2	18.7	16.0	15.0	14.9
55–64 years	194.2	147.3	115.8	65.1	47.9	41.0	35.6	34.3
65–74 years	554.7	469.2	384.1	219.0	144.2	128.6	112.9	107.8
75–84 years	1,499.6	1,491.3	1,254.2	786.9	498.0	461.3	410.7	386.2
85 years and over	2,990.1	3,680.5	3,014.3	2,283.7	1,628.9	1,589.2	1,370.1	1,245.9
Male								
All ages, age-adjusted[d]	186.4	186.1	157.4	102.2	68.5	62.4	54.1	50.4
All ages, crude	102.5	104.5	94.5	63.4	46.7	46.9	42.9	40.7
Under 1 year	6.4	5.0	5.8	5.0	4.4	3.8	2.8	3.4
1–4 years	1.1	0.9	1.2	0.4	0.3	*	0.3	0.3
5–14 years	0.5	0.7	0.8	0.3	0.2	0.2	0.2	0.2
15–24 years	1.8	1.9	1.8	1.1	0.7	0.5	0.5	0.5
25–34 years	4.2	4.5	4.4	2.6	2.1	1.5	1.6	1.4
35–44 years	17.5	14.6	15.7	8.7	6.8	5.8	5.8	5.6
45–54 years	67.9	52.2	44.4	27.2	20.5	17.5	16.7	16.7
55–64 years	205.2	163.8	138.7	74.6	54.3	47.2	40.8	39.5
65–74 years	589.6	530.7	449.5	258.6	166.6	145.0	127.8	121.1
75–84 years	1,543.6	1,555.9	1,361.6	866.3	551.1	490.8	431.4	402.9
85 years and over	3,048.6	3,643.1	2,895.2	2,193.6	1,528.5	1,484.3	1,236.0	1,118.1
Female								
All ages, age-adjusted[d]	175.8	170.7	140.0	91.7	62.6	59.1	52.3	48.9
All ages, crude	105.6	111.4	109.0	85.9	68.4	71.8	65.1	61.2
Under 1 year	3.7	3.2	4.0	3.8	3.1	2.7	2.2	2.8
1–4 years	0.7	0.7	0.7	0.5	0.3	0.4	0.3	*
5–14 years	0.4	0.6	0.6	0.3	0.2	0.2	0.1	0.2
15–24 years	1.5	1.6	1.4	0.8	0.6	0.5	0.5	0.5
25–34 years	4.3	4.9	4.7	2.6	2.2	1.5	1.4	1.4
35–44 years	19.9	14.8	15.6	8.4	6.1	5.7	5.3	5.1
45–54 years	72.9	46.3	39.0	23.3	17.0	14.5	13.4	13.1
55–64 years	183.1	131.8	95.3	56.8	42.2	35.3	30.9	29.5
65–74 years	522.1	415.7	333.3	188.7	126.7	115.1	100.5	96.6
75–84 years	1,462.2	1,441.1	1,183.1	740.1	466.2	442.1	396.8	374.9
85 years and over	2,949.4	3,704.4	3,081.0	2,323.1	1,667.6	1,632.0	1,429.4	1,303.4
White male[e]								
All ages, age-adjusted[d]	182.1	181.6	153.7	98.7	65.5	59.8	51.7	48.1
All ages, crude	100.5	102.7	93.5	63.1	46.9	48.4	44.2	41.8
45–54 years	53.7	40.9	35.6	21.7	15.4	13.6	12.9	12.8
55–64 years	182.2	139.0	119.9	64.0	45.7	39.7	33.3	32.4
65–74 years	569.7	501.0	420.0	239.8	152.9	133.8	117.3	110.8
75–84 years	1,556.3	1,564.8	1,361.6	852.7	539.2	480.0	422.4	393.7
85 years and over	3,127.1	3,734.8	3,018.1	2,230.8	1,545.4	1,490.7	1,247.0	1,129.3
Black or African American male[e]								
All ages, age-adjusted[d]	228.8	238.5	206.4	142.0	102.2	89.6	79.5	74.9
All ages, crude	122.0	122.9	108.8	73.0	53.0	46.1	43.2	41.5
45–54 years	211.9	166.1	136.1	82.1	68.4	49.5	46.9	44.8
55–64 years	522.8	439.9	343.4	189.7	141.7	115.4	112.1	107.4
65–74 years	783.6	899.2	780.1	472.3	326.9	268.5	237.4	235.2
75–84 years[f]	1,504.9	1,475.2	1,445.7	1,066.3	721.5	659.2	588.9	551.0
85 years and over	—	2,700.0	1,963.1	1,873.2	1,421.5	1,458.8	1,180.3	1,061.0

supply of blood to the brain, such as when a person suffers a stroke, has chronic high blood pressure, or has diabetes.

Plassman et al. note that the prevalence of dementias increased dramatically in those aged eighty to eighty-nine from those aged seventy-one to seventy-nine. The prev-alence of any dementia increased fivefold to nearly 24.2%. Dementias more than tripled in males (from 5.3% to 17.7%), but increased nearly sixfold in females (from 4.8% to 27.9%). Likewise, the prevalence of AD increased dramatically from those in their seventies to those in their eighties. In men, the prevalence increased from 2.3% to 12.3%, and in women from 2.3% to 21.3%.

TABLE 10.8

Death rates for cerebrovascular diseases, by sex, race, Hispanic origin, and age, selected years, 1950–2004 [CONTINUED]

[Data are based on death certificates]

Sex, race, Hispanic origin, and age	1950[a,b]	1960[a,b]	1970[b]	1980[b]	1990	2000[c]	2003	2004
				Deaths per 100,000 resident population				
American Indian or Alaska Native male[e]								
All ages, age-adjusted[d]	—	—	—	66.4	44.3	46.1	34.9	35.0
All ages, crude	—	—	—	23.1	16.0	16.8	15.6	15.6
45–54 years	—	—	—	*	*	13.3	15.5	14.0
55–64 years	—	—	—	72.0	39.8	48.6	30.7	29.9
65–74 years	—	—	—	170.5	120.3	144.7	101.4	109.4
75–84 years	—	—	—	523.9	325.9	373.3	280.7	312.0
85 years and over	—	—	—	1,384.7	949.8	834.9	596.9	559.5
Asian or Pacific Islander male[e]								
All ages, age-adjusted[d]	—	—	—	71.4	59.1	58.0	48.5	44.2
All ages, crude	—	—	—	28.7	23.3	27.2	26.0	24.3
45–54 years	—	—	—	17.0	15.6	15.0	14.7	19.2
55–64 years	—	—	—	59.9	51.8	49.3	42.2	36.8
65–74 years	—	—	—	197.9	167.9	135.6	128.3	102.6
75–84 years	—	—	—	619.5	483.9	438.7	355.7	350.8
85 years and over	—	—	—	1,399.0	1,196.6	1,415.6	1,093.0	969.0
Hispanic or Latino male[e,g]								
All ages, age-adjusted[d]	—	—	—	—	46.5	50.5	43.0	41.5
All ages, crude	—	—	—	—	15.6	15.8	14.9	15.0
45–54 years	—	—	—	—	20.0	18.1	18.1	17.5
55–64 years	—	—	—	—	49.2	48.8	43.5	42.9
65–74 years	—	—	—	—	126.4	136.1	113.9	114.4
75–84 years	—	—	—	—	356.6	392.9	337.1	323.3
85 years and over	—	—	—	—	866.3	1,029.9	837.4	778.9
White, not Hispanic or Latino male[g]								
All ages, age-adjusted[d]	—	—	—	—	66.3	59.9	51.9	48.2
All ages, crude	—	—	—	—	50.6	53.9	49.7	47.0
45–54 years	—	—	—	—	14.9	13.0	12.1	12.1
55–64 years	—	—	—	—	45.1	38.7	32.1	31.1
65–74 years	—	—	—	—	154.5	133.1	116.9	110.0
75–84 years	—	—	—	—	547.3	482.3	426.0	396.9
85 years and over	—	—	—	—	1,578.7	1,505.9	1,264.2	1,145.3
White female[e]								
All ages, age-adjusted[d]	169.7	165.0	135.5	89.0	60.3	57.3	50.5	47.2
All ages, crude	103.3	110.1	109.8	88.6	71.6	76.9	69.5	65.3
45–54 years	55.0	33.8	30.5	18.6	13.5	11.2	10.0	10.1
55–64 years	156.9	103.0	78.1	48.6	35.8	30.2	25.8	25.1
65–74 years	498.1	383.3	303.2	172.5	116.1	107.3	92.1	89.0
75–84 years	1,471.3	1,444.7	1,176.8	728.8	456.5	434.2	389.9	366.8
85 years and over	3,017.9	3,795.7	3,167.6	2,362.7	1,685.9	1,646.7	1,442.1	1,315.7
Black or African American female[e]								
All ages, age-adjusted[d]	238.4	232.5	189.3	119.6	84.0	76.2	69.8	65.5
All ages, crude	128.3	127.7	112.2	77.8	60.7	58.3	54.8	51.9
45–54 years	248.9	166.2	119.4	61.8	44.1	38.1	36.0	33.9
55–64 years	567.7	452.0	272.4	138.4	96.9	76.4	71.8	65.0
65–74 years	754.4	830.5	673.5	361.7	236.7	190.9	175.3	166.8
75–84 years[f]	1,496.7	1,413.1	1,338.3	917.5	595.0	549.2	498.3	489.5
85 years and over	—	2,578.9	2,210.5	1,891.6	1,495.2	1,556.5	1,414.2	1,270.7
American Indian or Alaska Native female[e]								
All ages, age-adjusted[d]	—	—	—	51.2	38.4	43.7	34.2	35.1
All ages, crude	—	—	—	22.0	19.3	21.5	19.9	21.3
45–54 years	—	—	—	*	*	14.4	14.6	10.
55–64 years	—	—	—	*	40.7	37.9	26.0	24.5
65–74 years	—	—	—	128.3	100.5	79.5	94.8	110.9
75–84 years	—	—	—	404.2	282.0	391.1	304.7	258.8
85 years and over	—	—	—	1,095.5	776.2	931.5	569.1	710.1

The prevalence of AD in those ninety years and older declined to 9.7%—7.1% in men and 11.5% in women. This decline is due to deaths of those with AD.

Table 10.11 shows national estimates of the number of individuals with AD or any dementia (including AD). In 2002 approximately 2.4 million people seventy-one years and older were living with AD. About 3.4 million had dementias of some type.

DEPRESSION

According to Dan G. Blazer, in "Depression in Late Life: Review and Commentary" (*Journals of*

TABLE 10.8

Death rates for cerebrovascular diseases, by sex, race, Hispanic origin, and age, selected years, 1950–2004 [CONTINUED]

[Data are based on death certificates]

Sex, race, Hispanic origin, and age	1950[a,b]	1960[a,b]	1970[b]	1980[b]	1990	2000[c]	2003	2004
				Deaths per 100,000 resident population				
Asian or Pacific Islander female[e]								
All ages, age-adjusted[d]	—	—	—	60.8	54.9	49.1	42.6	38.9
All ages, crude	—	—	—	26.4	24.3	28.7	28.8	27.0
45–54 years	—	—	—	20.3	19.7	13.3	12.6	10.5
55–64 years	—	—	—	43.7	42.1	33.3	30.8	28.1
65–74 years	—	—	—	136.1	124.0	102.8	95.6	78.1
75–84 years	—	—	—	446.6	396.6	386.0	330.2	312.5
85 years and over	—	—	—	1,545.2	1,395.0	1,246.6	1,042.4	979.9
Hispanic or Latino female[e,g]								
All ages, age-adjusted[d]	—	—	—	—	43.7	43.0	38.1	35.4
All ages, crude	—	—	—	—	20.1	19.4	18.6	17.9
45–54 years	—	—	—	—	15.2	12.4	11.7	11.8
55–64 years	—	—	—	—	38.5	31.9	27.8	27.7
65–74 years	—	—	—	—	102.6	95.2	86.0	83.0
75–84 years	—	—	—	—	308.5	311.3	302.8	272.2
85 years and over	—	—	—	—	1,055.3	1,108.9	902.3	830.4
White, not Hispanic or Latino female[g]								
All ages, age-adjusted[d]	—	—	—	—	61.0	57.6	50.8	47.7
All ages, crude	—	—	—	—	77.2	85.5	78.2	73.7
45–54 years	—	—	—	—	13.2	10.9	9.7	9.8
55–64 years	—	—	—	—	35.7	29.9	25.5	24.7
65–74 years	—	—	—	—	116.9	107.6	92.1	89.0
75–84 years	—	—	—	—	461.9	438.3	393.6	371.6
85 years and over	—	—	—	—	1,714.7	1,661.6	1,461.3	1,335.1

—Data not available.

*Rates based on fewer than 20 deaths are considered unreliable and are not shown.

[a]Includes deaths of persons who were not residents of the 50 states and the District of Columbia.

[b]Underlying cause of death was coded according to the Sixth Revision of the International Classification of Diseases (ICD) in 1950, Seventh Revision in 1960, Eighth Revision in 1970, and Ninth Revision in 1980–1998.

[c]Starting with 1999 data, cause of death is coded according to ICD-10.

[d]Age-adjusted rates are calculated using the year 2000 standard population. Prior to 2003, age-adjusted rates were calculated using standard million proportions based on rounded population numbers. Starting with 2003 data, unrounded population numbers are used to calculate age-adjusted rates.

[e]The race groups, white, black, Asian or Pacific Islander, and American Indian or Alaska Native, include persons of Hispanic and non-Hispanic origin. Persons of Hispanic origin may be of any race. Death rates for the American Indian or Alaska Native and Asian or Pacific Islander populations are known to be underestimated.

[f]In 1950, rate is for the age group 75 years and over.

[g]Prior to 1997, excludes data from states lacking an Hispanic-origin item on the death certificate.

Notes: Starting with *Health, United States, 2003,* rates for 1991–1999 were revised using intercensal population estimates based on the 2000 census. Rates for 2000 were revised based on 2000 census counts. Rates for 2001 and later years were computed using 2000-based postcensal estimates. For the period 1980–1998, cerebrovascular diseases was coded using ICD-9 codes that are most nearly comparable with cerebrovascular diseases codes in the 113 cause list for ICD-10. Age groups were selected to minimize the presentation of unstable age-specific death rates based on small numbers of deaths and for consistency among comparison groups. In 2003, seven states reported multiple-race data. In 2004, 15 states reported multiple-race data. The multiple-race data for these states were bridged to the single-race categories of the 1977 Office of Management and Budget standards for comparability with other states. Data for additional years are available.

SOURCE: "Table 37. Death Rates for Cerebrovascular Diseases, by Sex, Race, Hispanic Origin, and Age: United States, Selected Years 1950–2004," in *Health, United States, 2007. With Chartbook on Trends in the Health of Americans*, Centers for Disease Control and Prevention, National Center for Health Statistics, November 2007, http://www.cdc.gov/nchs/data/hus/hus07.pdf (accessed January 30, 2008)

TABLE 10.9

Percentage of people age 65 and over with moderate or severe memory impairment, by age and sex, 2002

	Both sexes	Men	Women
	Percent		
65 and over	12.7	14.9	11.2
65–69	5.1	7.8	3.1
70–74	8.2	10.9	6.1
75–79	13.6	17.2	11.2
80–84	18.8	21.8	17.0
85 and over	32.1	33.9	31.2

SOURCE: "Percentage of People Age 65 and over with Moderate or Severe Memory Impairment, by Age Group and Sex, 2002," in *Older Americans Update 2006: Key Indicators of Well-Being*, Federal Interagency Forum on Aging-Related Statistics, 2006, http://agingstats.gov/agingstatsdotnet/Main_Site/Data/2006_Documents/Health_Status.pdf (accessed March 16, 2008)

Gerontology, vol. 58, no. 3, 2003), a review of depression in late life, it is difficult to get a definitive answer to the question of how many adults aged sixty-five and older suffer from depression. Blazer's review reveals a range of 9% to 16% of people aged sixty-five and older to have "clinically significant depressive symptoms." Other studies show an "overall estimate of the prevalence of major depression" in those aged sixty-five and older to vary from 0.15% to 2%, and an overall estimate of the prevalence of minor depression to be 12.9%. The National Institute of Mental Health notes in "Older Adults: Depression and Suicide Facts" (May 7, 2008, http://www.nimh.nih.gov/health/publications/older-adults-depression-and-suicide-facts.shtml) that "estimates of major depression in older people

FIGURE 10.1

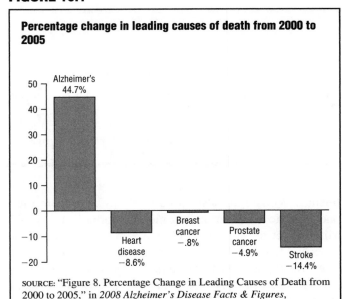

Percentage change in leading causes of death from 2000 to 2005

SOURCE: "Figure 8. Percentage Change in Leading Causes of Death from 2000 to 2005," in *2008 Alzheimer's Disease Facts & Figures*, Alzheimer's Association, 2008, http://www.alz.org/national/documents/report_alzfactsfigures2008.pdf (accessed March 18, 2008).

TABLE 10.11

Number of persons with dementia or Alzheimer's Disease, by age, 2002

Age	All dementia	Alzheimer's disease
71–79 years	712,000	332,000
80–89 years	1,996,000	1,493,000
≥90 years	699,000	556,000
Total	**3,407,000**	**2,381,000**

SOURCE: Adapted from B.L. Plassman et al., "Table 3. National Estimates of the Number of Individuals with Dementia or AD," in "Prevalence of Dementia in the United States: The Aging, Demographics, and Memory Study," Neuroepidemiology, vol. 29, no. 1–2, 2007, http://content.karger.com/ProdukteDB/produkte.asp?doi=109998 (accessed February 3, 2008). Reprinted with permission of S. Karger AG Basel.

living in the community range from less than 1 percent to about 5 percent, but rises to 13.5 percent in those who require home healthcare and to 11.5 percent in elderly hospital patients."

Family members and health-care professionals often fail to recognize depression among the elderly. Older people usually suffer from comorbidity (the presence of more than one chronic illness at one time), so depression may be masked by the symptoms of other disorders. In addition, older adults suffering from depression may mistakenly think that their depression is simply a reaction to an illness or loss, or is a consequence of aging. Many sufferers fail to divulge their depression because of the stigma associated with mental illness.

Suicide

According to the National Institute of Mental Health, in "Older Adults," depression is commonly associated with suicide in older people. Most suicidal older adults, up to 75%, visit their primary care physician during the month before ending their life. However, their depression apparently had not been accurately diagnosed or effectively treated.

Depression is especially common in nursing homes. Richard N. Jones, Edward R. Marcantonio, and Terry Rabinowitz determine in "Prevalence and Correlates of Recognized Depression in U.S. Nursing Homes" (*Journal of the American Geriatric Society*, vol. 51, no. 10, October 2003) that at least 20% of nursing home residents suffer from clinical depression. The researchers believe this may be an underrepresentation of the magnitude of the problem. They note that depression in long-term care settings such as nursing homes is often unrecognized. In addition, when depression is recognized it is often undertreated, treated inadequately, or treated inappropriately.

Feeling lonely, abandoned, or suffering financial woes, many depressed nursing home residents end their life by nonviolent means such as by starving themselves, failing to take prescribed medication, or ingesting large amounts of drugs. This type of suicide, as a result of depression, is different from that committed by the terminally ill who, not wishing to prolong the dying process, refuse life-sustaining medical treatment.

TABLE 10.10

Percentages of persons with dementia, Alzheimer's Disease and vascular dementia, by age, 2002

Age	All dementia			Alzheimer's disease			Vascular dementia		
	Combined	Male	Female	Combined	Male	Female	Combined	Male	Female
71–79 years	4.97	5.25	4.76	2.32	2.30	2.33	0.98	1.27	0.76
80–89 years	24.19	17.68	27.84	18.10	12.33	21.34	4.09	3.58	4.38
≥90 years	37.36	44.59	34.69	29.70	33.89	28.15	6.19	8.14	5.46
Total	**13.93**	**11.14**	**15.74**	**9.74**	**7.05**	**11.48**	**2.43**	**2.34**	**2.48**

SOURCE: Adapted from B.L. Plassman et al., "Table 2. National Prevalence of Dementia, AD and VaD, by Age Categories," in "Prevalence of Dementia in the United States: The Aging, Demographics, and Memory Study," *Neuroepidemiology*, vol. 29, no. 1–2, 2007, http://content.karger.com/ProdukteDB/produkte.asp?doi=109998 (accessed February 3, 2008). Reprinted with permission of S. Karger AG Basel.

TABLE 10.12

Sex ratio for population 25 years and over by age, 2000 and 2030

[Men per 100 women]

	2000						2030					
Country	25 to 54 years	55 to 64 years	65 to 69 years	70 to 74 years	75 to 79 years	80 years and over	25 to 54 years	55 to 64 years	65 to 69 years	70 to 74 years	75 to 79 years	80 years and over
United States	98	91	85	79	72	52	98	92	89	86	81	64

SOURCE: Adapted from Kevin Kinsella and Victoria A. Velkoff, "Table 6. Sex Ratio for Population 25 Years and over by Age: 2000 and 2030," in *An Aging World: 2001*, U.S. Census Bureau, November 2001, http://www.census.gov/prod/2001pubs/p95-01-1.pdf (accessed February 3, 2008)

In the United States the suicide rate generally increases with age. In 2004 the oldest old (eighty-five years and older) accounted for the second-highest rate at 16.4 suicides per 100,000 people. (See Table 6.1 in Chapter 6.) Those aged forty-five to fifty-four had a slightly higher rate at 16.6 per 100,000.

Men have a higher suicide rate than women. Men aged eighty-five years and older had the highest suicide rate of 45 per 100,000, whereas the rate among women was 3.6 suicides per 100,000 people. (See Table 6.1.)

By race, white men eighty-five years and older had the highest suicide rate in 2004 at 48.4 suicides per 100,000 people. (See Table 6.1.) In contrast, African-American men of this age had a suicide rate of fifteen. One generally held theory about the high rates of suicide among aged white men is that they have traditionally been in positions of power and thus have great difficulty adjusting to a life they may consider useless or diminished.

OLDER WOMEN
Women Live Longer Than Men

In the United States the life expectancy in 2004 for females born in that year was 5.2 years more than for males—80.4 years and 75.2 years, respectively. (See Table 10.1.) In 2000 there were eighty-five men aged sixty-five to sixty-nine for every one hundred women in the same age span. As both sexes age, the gap widens. For those aged eighty and older, there were only fifty-two men for every one hundred women. (See Table 10.12.) The U.S. Census Bureau (2007, http://www.census.gov/popest/national/asrh/NC-EST2007/NC-EST2007-02.xls) finds that in 2007 more than two-thirds of all people aged eighty-five years and older were women—approximately 3.7 million women, compared to approximately 1.8 million men.

Elderly Women Have More Chronic Diseases Than Do Elderly Men

Older women are more likely than men of the same age to suffer from chronic conditions, such as arthritis, osteoporosis and related bone fractures, AD, and incon-

tinence. Women are also more likely to have more than one chronic disorder at a time (comorbidity). Arnold Mitnitski et al. note in "Relative Fitness and Frailty of Elderly Men and Women in Developed Countries and Their Relationship with Mortality" (*Journal of the American Geriatric Society*, vol. 53, no. 12, 2005) that women, at any given age, are frailer than men, even though they have a lower mortality rate.

GERIATRICS

Geriatrics is the medical subspecialty concerned with the prevention and treatment of diseases in the elderly. In 1909 Ignatz L. Nascher (1863–1944) coined the term *geriatrics* from the Greek *geras* (old age) and *iatrikos* (physician). Geriatricians are physicians trained in internal medicine or family practice who obtain additional training and certification in the diagnosis and treatment of older adults. The Eastern Virginia Medical School's Glennan Center (November 7, 2007, http://www.evms.edu/services/geriatrics-glennan.html) explains that geriatricians rely on the findings of researchers and gerontologists (nonphysician professionals who conduct scientific studies of aging and older adults) to help older adults "maintain the highest possible degree of function and independence and avoid unnecessary and costly institutionalization."

Gerontology was unheard of before the nineteenth century, when most people died at an early age. Those who reached old age accepted their deteriorating health as a part of aging. In the early twentieth century gerontology was born when scientists began to investigate the pathological changes that accompany the aging process.

Even though many developed countries have recognized the need for more geriatrics education, the United States continues to lag in offering geriatrics courses in its medical schools. In "ACGME Requirements for Geriatrics Medicine Curricula in Medical Specialties: Progress Made and Progress Needed" (*Academic Medicine*, vol. 80, no. 3, March 2005), Elizabeth J. Bragg and Gregg A. Warshaw state that as of 2003 only 30% of the ninety-one nonpediatric accredited medical specialties offered in U.S. medical schools had specific geriatrics training requirements. Among those with specific requirements, curriculum expectations were considered modest by the Association of Directors of Geriatric Academic Programs' (ADGAP) team at the University of Cincinnati School of Medicine's Institute for Health Policy and Health Services Research.

Gregg A. Warshaw et al. report in "The Development of Academic Geriatric Medicine: Progress toward Preparing the Nation's Physicians to Care for an Aging Population" (*Journal of the American Geriatrics Society*, vol. 55, no. 12, December 2007) both positive and negative news on the topic: "From 2001 to 2005, more fellows and faculty [in geriatrics] have been recruited and trained, and some academic programs have emerged with strong education, research, and clinical initiatives. Medical student exposure to geriatrics curriculum has increased, although few academic geriatricians are pursuing research careers, and the number of practicing geriatricians is declining. An expanded investment in training the physician workforce to care for older adults will be required to ensure adequate care for aging Americans."

Decline in Numbers of Geriatricians in the United States

The ADGAP also reports that a tremendous shortage of physicians specializing in geriatrics exists, including those in the field of psychiatry known as geropsychiatrists. In "Fellows in Geriatric Medicine and Geriatric Psychiatry Programs" (*Training and Practice Update*, vol. 5, no. 2, October 2007), the ADGAP estimates that in 2007 there were only 7,128 active certified geriatricians practicing in the United States and 1,596 certified geriatric psychiatrists.

In "Geriatricians and Geriatric Psychiatrists" (*Training and Practice Update*, vol. 1, no. 2, May 2003), the ADGAP notes that Medicare, the primary payer for most clinical services provided by geriatricians, reduced the average reimbursement to physicians by 5.4% in 2002. The ADGAP suggests that "the growing gap between Medicare reimbursement and the actual costs of delivering medical care may affect the willingness of physicians to continue focusing their careers in geriatric medicine and geriatric psychiatry." The ADGAP explains in "Fellows in Geriatric Medicine and Geriatric Psychiatry Programs" that the low Medicare reimbursement rates leave community-based geriatricians with much lower salaries than physicians in other fields.

The Geriatric Care Act was introduced in 2003, which would help improve payment for geriatricians. This bill never became law, but two other related bills were pending as of May 2008. The Geriatric Assessment and Chronic Care Coordination Act of 2007 has the goal of providing financial incentives within Medicare to encourage the coordination of care for patients having multiple medical conditions and to bring down medical costs and increase the quality of care. The Caring for an Aging America Act of 2008 has the goal of providing federal funding to attract and retain trained health-care professionals and direct-care workers in the field of geriatrics.

CHAPTER 11
PUBLIC OPINION ABOUT LIFE AND DEATH

LIFE AFTER DEATH

Since the dawn of history, many people have believed that human beings do not simply cease to exist once they die. Many religions and cultures teach that the physical body may die and decompose but that some element of the person goes on to what many call the afterlife.

Between 1972 and 1982, when the Roper Center for Public Opinion Research (http://www.ropercenter.uconn.edu/) asked the American public, "Do you believe there is life after death?" 70% said they believed in an afterlife. In 1996, when the Roper Center asked the same question, 73% of respondents said yes. The National Opinion Research Center at the University of Chicago revealed similar results in its General Social Survey 2002 (http://www.cpanda.org/cpanda/getDDI.xq?studyID=a00079). Seventy-two percent of those polled said they believed that there is a life after death. More recently, the article "Poll: Majority Believe in Ghosts" (CBSNews.com, October 30, 2005) notes that 78% of adult Americans believe in life after death.

These data suggest that the proportion of the U.S. population believing in an afterlife is growing, from about 70% between 1972 and 1982 to about 78% in 2005. Data from the General Social Survey agree. (See Figure 11.1.) These data show that the percentage of Jewish Americans who said they believed in an afterlife rose dramatically between 1973 to 2004. In 1973, 16.7% of Jewish Americans believed in an afterlife, but by 2004 the percentage was 35.1%. The percentage of Protestant and Catholic Americans believing in an afterlife rose as well during this period. The percentage of Catholics who believed in an afterlife rose from 68.8% in 1974 to 77.3% in 2004. The percentage of Protestants who believed in an afterlife rose from 75.6% in 1973 to 77.7% in 2004.

Are there differences between those who attend religious services and those who do not? The article "Poll: Majority Believe in Ghosts" indicates what the most and the least religiously observant Americans said on the subject of afterlife. About 90% of those who attended religious services weekly or almost every week believed that humans transition to an afterlife after the physical body dies. About 70% of those who rarely or never attended religious services believed in an afterlife.

Frank Newport of the Gallup Organization notes in *Americans More Likely to Believe in God Than the Devil, Heaven More Than Hell* (June 13, 2007, http://www.gallup.com/poll/27877/Americans-More-Likely-Believe-God-Than-Devil-Heaven-More-Than-Hell.aspx) that when asked in polls about an afterlife and what that "eternal destination" might be, many Americans expressed a belief in heaven, where people who led a good life are eternally rewarded after death, and hell, where unrepentant people who led a bad life are eternally punished. Newport determines that belief in the existence of heaven and hell increased over time as has the more general belief in an afterlife. From 1997 to 2007 a majority of respondents (72% in 1997 and 81% in 2007) acknowledged a belief in heaven. (See Table 11.1.) In addition, a majority of respondents (56% in 1997 and 69% in 2007) acknowledged a belief that hell exists in the afterlife. (See Table 11.2.)

FEAR AND ANXIETY ABOUT DEATH

In "Poll Analysis: Aging in America" (*Los Angeles Times*, April 2, 2000), Susan Pinkus, Jill Richardson, and Elizabeth Armet find that people over age sixty-five think about and fear death the least, whereas those aged eighteen to twenty-nine think about and fear it the most. In 2000, 7% of those aged sixty-five and older said they were afraid to die, whereas 20% of eighteen- to twenty-nine-year-olds expressed a fear of dying.

Linda Lyons of the Gallup Organization indicates in *What Frightens America's Youth?* (March 29, 2005, http://www.gallup.com/poll/15439/What-Frightens-Americas-Youth.aspx) that those younger than eighteen are also

FIGURE 11.1

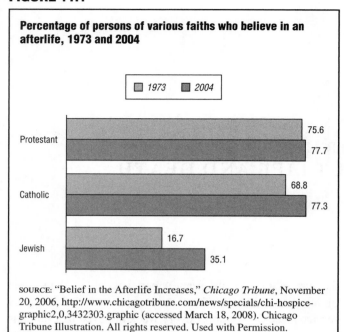

Percentage of persons of various faiths who believe in an afterlife, 1973 and 2004

□ 1973 ■ 2004

Protestant — 75.6 (1973), 77.7 (2004)
Catholic — 68.8 (1973), 77.3 (2004)
Jewish — 16.7 (1973), 35.1 (2004)

SOURCE: "Belief in the Afterlife Increases," *Chicago Tribune*, November 20, 2006, http://www.chicagotribune.com/news/specials/chi-hospice-graphic2,0,3432303.graphic (accessed March 18, 2008). Chicago Tribune Illustration. All rights reserved. Used with Permission.

TABLE 11.1

Public opinion on existence of heaven, selected years, 1997–2007

	Believe in	Not sure about	Don't believe in	No opinion
	%	%	%	%
2007 May 10–13	81	8	11	*
2004 May 2–4	81	10	8	1
2001 May 10–14	83	10	7	*
1997 May*	72	20	8	*

*Gallup/Nathan Cummings Foundation and Fetzer Institute Poll.

SOURCE: Frank Newport, "For Each of the Following Items I Am Going to Read You, Please Tell Me Whether It Is Something You Believe in, Something You're Not Sure about, or Something You Don't Believe in. First, … Next, …[RANDOM ORDER]? … D. Heaven," in *Americans More Likely to Believe in God Than the Devil, Heaven More Than Hell*, The Gallup Organization, June 13, 2007, http://www.gallup.com/poll/27877/Americans-More-Likely-Believe-God-Than-Devil-Heaven-More-Than-Hell.aspx (accessed March 27, 2008). Copyright © 2007 by The Gallup Organization. Reproduced by permission of The Gallup Organization.

TABLE 11.2

Public opinion on existence of hell, selected years, 1997–2007

	Believe in	Not sure about	Don't believe in	No opinion
	%	%	%	%
2007 May 10–13	69	8	22	1
2004 May 2–4	70	12	17	1
2001 May 10–14	71	13	15	1
1997 May*	56	22	20	2

*Gallup/Nathan Cummings Foundation and Fetzer Institute Poll.

SOURCE: Frank Newport, "For Each of the Following Items I Am Going to Read You, Please Tell Me Whether It Is Something You Believe in, Something You're Not Sure about, or Something You Don't Believe in. First, … Next, …[RANDOM ORDER]? … E. Hell," in *Americans More Likely to Believe in God Than the Devil, Heaven More Than Hell*, The Gallup Organization, June 13, 2007, http://www.gallup.com/poll/27877/Americans-More-Likely-Believe-God-Than-Devil-Heaven-More-Than-Hell.aspx (accessed March 27, 2008). Copyright © 2007 by The Gallup Organization. Reproduced by permission of The Gallup Organization.

concerned about death. She finds that death and dying was the second greatest fear of U.S. teens aged thirteen to seventeen in 2005. (See Figure 11.2.) This number-two spot was shared with a fear of spiders. The number-one fear of teens in this age group was terrorist attacks. Teens were more concerned about death than about war, gang violence, and not succeeding in life.

R. J. Russac et al. of the University of North Florida conducted studies not only to examine the consistent assertion in the medical literature that young adults typically report higher levels of concern about death than do older adults but also to examine the assertion that women

typically report higher levels of concern about death than men do. The researchers report in "Death Anxiety across the Adult Years: An Examination of Age and Gender Effects" (*Death Studies*, vol. 31, no. 6, July 2007) that the results of their studies support these findings and that anxiety about death peaks at about age twenty. Their results also support previous findings that women report higher levels of concern about death than men do. However, the results also show that the decline in death anxiety after age twenty differed between men and women. Concern about death declined after age twenty in both sexes, but in women a secondary peak in anxiety about death occurred in their early fifties.

Fearful Aspects of Dying

Russac et al. wondered why young people would be more anxious and fearful of dying than older people. Other researchers, they note, suggest that older Americans come to terms with death as they age. Other hypotheses include that death is more appealing to those in old age than to younger people (especially to older people with chronic conditions and illnesses), that older people are more religious and this affected their views, and that older people have more experience with death over their lifetime so are less anxious about it. Russac et al. instead consider why young people would be anxious about death and suggest that it might have to do with the concurrent peak in their reproductive years. Their concerns might actually be about their children and wondering what would happen to their youngsters if they were to die. Likewise, some researchers suggest that women report more anxiety about death than men because they are the primary caretakers, not only of children but also of the elderly and those who might be dying. One hypothesis for the peak of anxiety about death in the fifties is that women reach menopause during those years and this change of life may remind women that they are getting older and closer to death.

FIGURE 11.2

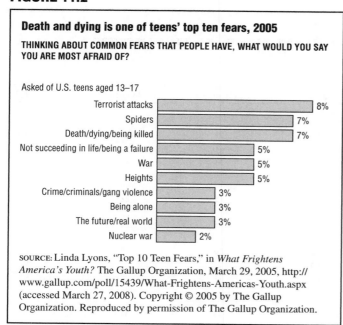

Death and dying is one of teens' top ten fears, 2005

THINKING ABOUT COMMON FEARS THAT PEOPLE HAVE, WHAT WOULD YOU SAY YOU ARE MOST AFRAID OF?

Asked of U.S. teens aged 13–17

Terrorist attacks	8%
Spiders	7%
Death/dying/being killed	7%
Not succeeding in life/being a failure	5%
War	5%
Heights	5%
Crime/criminals/gang violence	3%
Being alone	3%
The future/real world	3%
Nuclear war	2%

SOURCE: Linda Lyons, "Top 10 Teen Fears," in *What Frightens America's Youth?* The Gallup Organization, March 29, 2005, http://www.gallup.com/poll/15439/What-Frightens-Americas-Youth.aspx (accessed March 27, 2008). Copyright © 2005 by The Gallup Organization. Reproduced by permission of The Gallup Organization.

Even though they may not fear death or spend much time thinking about their own death, Americans are fearful about some aspects of dying. In a survey published in 2001 and conducted by Yankelovich Partners, *Time* magazine, and CNN, two-thirds of respondents expressed much or some concern about dying in pain. Another two-thirds said they were "very fearful" or "somewhat fearful" of leaving loved ones behind, and 43% of respondents were "very fearful" or "somewhat fearful" about dying alone.

The Yankelovich Partners/*Time*/CNN survey found that most people (73%) would prefer to die at home rather than in a hospital, hospice, or nursing home. Despite these expressed wishes to die at home, less than half (43%) believed they were likely to die at home—28% thought they were likely to die in a hospital, nursing home, or hospice.

The Seriously Ill Have Different Concerns

In "What Matters Most in End-of-Life Care: Perceptions of Seriously Ill Patients and Their Family Members" (*Canadian Medical Association Journal*, vol. 174, no. 5, February 28, 2006), Daren K. Heyland et al. find that when patients with advanced chronic illnesses and advanced cancer were asked whether they agreed or strongly agreed about the importance of a variety of end-of-life issues, their concerns were quite different from those of the general population. Even though dying at home appears to be a priority for many Americans, dying in the location of choice (home or hospital) was twenty-fourth on the patients' ranked list of concerns. Their top priorities (very or extremely important) were trusting their physician (ranked first), not being kept on life support when there was little hope (ranked second), having their physician communicate with them honestly

(ranked third), and completing things and preparing for death (resolving conflicts and saying good-bye) (ranked fourth). Seriously ill patients also revealed that they did not want to be a physical or emotional burden on their families (ranked fifth), wanted to have an adequate plan of home care were they to be discharged from the hospital (ranked sixth), and wanted to have relief from their symptoms (ranked seventh).

GETTING OLDER

Living to Age One Hundred

The ABC News/*USA Today* poll "Most Wish for a Long Life—Despite Broad Aging Concerns" (October 24, 2005, http://abcnews.go.com/images/Politics/995a1Longevity.pdf) reveals that in 2005 only one-quarter of a random national sample of one thousand adults wanted to live to be one hundred years or older. Twenty-three percent stated they would like to live into their nineties and 29% into their eighties.

Those surveyed by the ABC News/*USA Today* poll were asked how likely they thought it was that they would live to be one hundred years old and still have a good quality of life. Thirty-five percent thought it very or somewhat likely, whereas 64% thought it somewhat or very unlikely.

Concerns about Aging

The aging of the baby boomers (the generation born between 1946 and 1964) and the growing number of people living longer have focused much attention on concerns that come with aging. The ABC News/*USA Today* poll finds that even though respondents wanted to live longer, most were concerned about losing their health (73%). Seven out of ten worried about losing their mental abilities (69%) and losing their ability to care for themselves (70%). The respondents were also worried about being a burden to their families (54%) and living in a nursing home (52%).

Opinions on Nursing Homes

The Henry J. Kaiser Family Foundation conducted a national survey that included questions about nursing homes and reported its findings in *Toplines: Update on the Public's Views of Nursing Homes and Long-Term Care Services* (December 2007, http://www.kff.org/kaiserpolls/upload/7719.pdf). When asked if they thought that during the past five years "the quality of nursing homes in this country has gotten better, gotten worse, or stayed about the same," only 14% thought they had gotten better. Thirty-one percent thought nursing homes had gotten worse, whereas 32% felt that they had stayed about the same.

More than half (53%) of respondents felt nursing homes were understaffed, and only 19% believed nursing homes "have staff who are concerned about the well-being of their patients." (See Table 11.3.) Forty-three percent thought there was not enough government regulation of

TABLE 11.3

Public opinion on nursing homes, 2007

I'M GOING TO READ YOU SOME STATEMENTS PEOPLE HAVE MADE ABOUT NURSING HOMES. FOR EACH ONE, PLEASE TELL ME IF YOU AGREE OR DISAGREE WITH THE STATEMENT.

Statements about nursing homes	Strongly agree	Somewhat agree	Somewhat disagree	Strongly disagree	Don't know/ refused
They provide high-quality services for people who need them					
Total	12	38	21	19	10
18–64	12	39	22	18	8
65+	14	31	16	23	16
They provide an affordable way for people who need round-the-clock care to be able to get it					
Total	21	34	15	22	9
18–64	21	35	15	22	8
65+	23	28	14	24	10
The staff at nursing homes are often poorly trained					
Total	35	28	16	8	13
18–64	34	29	17	8	12
65+	43	24	11	6	16
They have staff who are concerned about the well-being of their patients					
Total	19	48	13	12	9
18–64	18	50	13	12	8
65+	20	41	12	14	13
There is not enough government regulation of the quality of nursing homes					
Total	43	21	10	9	16
18–64	44	23	10	9	14
65+	40	15	11	11	22
Nursing homes don't have enough staff					
Total	53	22	8	4	13
18–64	53	22	9	3	12
65+	56	19	6	5	14
Nursing homes are a decent place to stay					
Total	8	38	21	23	10
18–64	7	38	22	24	9
65+	12	39	14	23	13

SOURCE: "6. I'm Going to Read You Some Statements People Have Made about Nursing Homes. For Each One, Please Tell Me If You Agree or Disagree with the Statement," in *Toplines: Update on the Public's Views of Nursing Homes and Long-Term Care Services*, (#7719) The Henry J. Kaiser Family Foundation, December 2007, http://www.kff.org/kaiserpolls/upload/7719.pdf (accessed March 19, 2008). This information was reprinted with permission from the Henry J. Kaiser Foundation. The Kaiser Family Foundation, based in Menlo Park, California, is a nonprofit, private operating foundation focusing on the major health care issues facing the nation and is not associated with Keiser Permanente or Kaiser Industries.

these facilities. Only 12% believed that nursing homes provide high-quality services.

SUICIDE

The General Social Survey 2002 and the General Social Survey 2004, both conducted by the National Opinion Research Center (http://www.norc.org/homepage .htm), found that 58% of respondents in each survey approved of suicide if a person had an incurable disease, but only a small minority approved of it if the person had gone bankrupt (8% in 2002 and 11% in 2004), had dishonored his or her family (9% in 2002 and 11% in 2004), or was simply tired of living (15% in 2002 and 16% in 2004). In comparison, a survey from 1977 found that a much lower percentage of people (38%) thought suicide was acceptable if one had an incurable illness.

Suicide in other situations was also found less acceptable in the 1977 survey than in the 2002 and 2004 surveys.

According to the Centers for Disease Control and Prevention (March 20, 2008, http://www.cdc.gov/ncipc/wisqars/ default.htm), in 2005 suicide was the eleventh-leading cause of death in the United States, the second-leading cause of death among young people aged twenty-five to thirty-four, and the third-leading cause of death among young people aged ten to twenty-four. In *Nearly Half of Teens Aware of Peer Suicide Attempts* (May 25, 2004, http://www .gallup.com/poll/11776/Nearly-Half-Teens-Aware-Peer-Suicide-Attempts.aspx), Coleen McMurray of the Gallup Organization reports that 22% of American teens (aged thirteen to seventeen) had "ever talked or thought about committing suicide." Girls were more likely (28%) than boys (16%) to have had suicidal thoughts. When asked if

FIGURE 11.3

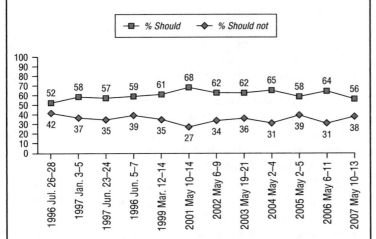

Public opinion on whether physicians should be allowed to assist the patient to commit suicide, selected years, 1996–2007

WHEN A PERSON HAS A DISEASE THAT CANNOT BE CURED AND IS LIVING IN SEVERE PAIN, DO YOU THINK DOCTORS SHOULD OR SHOULD NOT BE ALLOWED BY LAW TO ASSIST THE PATIENT TO COMMIT SUICIDE IF THE PATIENT REQUESTS IT?

SOURCE: Joseph Carroll, "When a Person Has a Disease That Cannot Be Cured and Is Living in Severe Pain, Do You Think Doctors Should or Should Not Be Allowed by Law to Assist the Patient to Commit Suicide If the Patient Requests it?," in *Public Divided over Moral Acceptability of Doctor-Assisted Suicide*, The Gallup Organization, May 31, 2007, http://www.gallup.com/poll/27727/Public-Divided-Over-Moral-Acceptability-DoctorAssisted-Suicide.aspx(accessed March 27, 2008). Copyright © 2007 by The Gallup Organization. Reproduced by permission of The Gallup Organization.

FIGURE 11.4

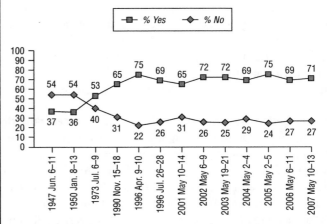

Poll respondents' support for euthanasia, selected years, 1947–2007

WHEN A PERSON HAS A DISEASE THAT CANNOT BE CURED, DO YOU THINK DOCTORS SHOULD BE ALLOWED BY LAW TO END THE PATIENT'S LIFE BY SOME PAINLESS MEANS IF THE PATIENT AND HIS FAMILY REQUEST IT?

SOURCE: Joseph Carroll, "When a Person Has a Disease That Cannot Be Cured, Do You Think Doctors Should Be Allowed by Law to End the Patient's Life by Some Painless Means If the Patient and His Family Request It?" in *Public Divided over Moral Acceptability of Doctor-Assisted Suicide*, The Gallup Organization, May 31, 2007, http://www.gallup.com/poll/27727/Public-Divided-Over-Moral-Acceptability-DoctorAssisted-Suicide.aspx (accessed March 27, 2008). Copyright © 2007 by The Gallup Organization. Reproduced by permission of The Gallup Organization.

they had ever tried to commit suicide, only 4% of boys and 9% of girls had.

PHYSICIAN-ASSISTED SUICIDE AND EUTHANASIA

Many advocates of physician-assisted suicide believe that people who are suffering from uncontrollable pain should be allowed to end their life with a lethal dose of medication prescribed by their physician. U.S. public opinion rose slowly from 1996 to 2001 in favor of physician-assisted suicide, from 52% in 1996 to 68% in 2001. After 2001 a slow decline occurred, with 56% in favor of physician-assisted suicide in 2007. (See Figure 11.3.) Results of the same polls show that, in general, a greater percentage of Americans support euthanasia—allowing a doctor to end the life of a patient who is suffering from an incurable disease and wants to die, without requiring the patient to administer the drugs to him- or herself. Figure 11.4 shows that support for euthanasia has increased considerably since the 1940s.

Joseph Carroll of the Gallup Organization indicates in *Public Divided over Moral Acceptability of Doctor-Assisted Suicide* (May 31, 2007, http://www.gallup.com/poll/27727/Public-Divided-Over-Moral-Acceptability-DoctorAssisted-Suicide.aspx) that in 2007 more Democrats than Republicans supported euthanasia (77% versus 64%, respectively) and physician-assisted suicide (62% versus 49%, respectively). Support of both euthanasia and physician-assisted suicide also varied by frequency of attendance of religious services. Those who seldom or never attended services were the most supportive of both euthanasia (84%) and physician-assisted suicide (73%). Those who attended almost weekly or attended monthly were the next most supportive: 70% supported euthanasia and 52% supported physician-assisted suicide. The least supportive were those who attended religious services each week: 47% supported euthanasia and 35% supported physician-assisted suicide.

Oregon Physician-Assisted Suicide Law

In 1994 Oregon became the first jurisdiction in the world to legalize physician-assisted suicide when its voters passed the Death with Dignity Act. Under the act, Oregon law permits physician-assisted suicide for patients with less than six months to live. Patients must request physician assistance three times, receive a second opinion from another doctor, and wait fifteen days to allow time to reconsider.

Before the Death with Dignity Act could take effect, opponents of the law succeeded in obtaining an injunction against it. Three years later, in November 1997, Oregon's legislature let the voters decide whether to repeal or retain the law. Voters reaffirmed the Death with Dignity Act. The Harris Poll indicates in "Majorities of U.S. Adults Favor Euthanasia and Physician-Assisted Suicide by More Than Two-to-One" (April 27, 2005, http://www.harrisinteractive .com/harris_poll/index.asp?PID=561) that in August 1997, before voters' reaffirmation of the law, 68% of those surveyed said they would approve of a similar law allowing physician-assisted suicide in their state. Asked again in 2001 whether they would favor or oppose such a law in their own state, 61% of respondents indicated they favored such legislation. In April 2005, 67% favored such a law.

Using Federally Controlled Drugs for Assisted Suicide

After the Death with Dignity Act took effect in November 1997, Timothy Egan reports in "Threat from Washington Has Chilling Effect on Oregon Law Allowing Assisted Suicide" (*New York Times*, November 19, 1997) that Thomas Constantine (1938–) of the U.S. Drug Enforcement Administration (DEA) announced that "delivering, dispensing, or prescribing a controlled substance with the intent of assisting a suicide" would be a violation of the federal Controlled Substances Act of 1970. The U.S. attorney general Janet Reno (1938–) overruled Constantine.

In November 2001 the U.S. attorney general John D. Ashcroft (1942–) overturned Reno's ruling in an attempt to again allow the DEA to act against physicians who prescribe lethal doses of controlled substances under Oregon's physician-assisted suicide law. In December 2001 the Harris Poll asked adults nationwide whether they considered Ashcroft's effort to overrule the proposition right or wrong. More than half (58%) of respondents believed his action was wrong. On April 17, 2002, Judge Robert E. Jones (1927–) of the U.S. District Court for the District of Oregon agreed, noting that "to allow an attorney general—an appointed executive . . .—to determine the legitimacy of a particular medical practice . . . would be unprecedented and extraordinary." Jones's ruling reaffirmed the Death with Dignity Act. The U.S. Department of Justice appealed the ruling to the Ninth Circuit Court of Appeals. On May 26, 2004, the court upheld Jones's ruling against Ashcroft.

In February 2005 the U.S. Supreme Court agreed to hear the Bush administration's challenge to Oregon's physician-assisted suicide law. The debate of this issue was heard in October 2005 before the High Court. On January 17, 2006, the Court ruled 6–3 that the state's authority overrode federal authority with regard to the Oregon's Death with Dignity Act, thereby upholding the lower courts' rulings.

WITHHOLDING NUTRITION AND HYDRATION: THE TERRI SCHIAVO CASE

The death of Terri Schiavo in March 2005 and the events leading up to her death resulted in an intense debate among Americans over end-of-life decisions and brought new attention to the question of who should make the decision to stop life support, most specifically nutrition and hydration. Schiavo died on March 31, 2005, after her feeding tube was withdrawn days earlier. Schiavo had been in a persistent vegetative state (PVS) since 1990. Her husband, Michael Schiavo, believing that she would never recover and saying that his wife did not want to be kept alive by artificial means, petitioned a Florida court to remove her feeding tube. Her parents, however, believed that she could feel, understand, and respond. They opposed the idea of removing the feeding tube. After years of legal disputes, the feeding tube was removed permanently and Schiavo died.

Two primary questions emerged as the nation watched the Schiavo case unfold: (1) If you were in a PVS would you want to be kept alive by artificial means?, and (2) Who should have the final say in the matter if you had not left an advance directive (living will)? Lydia Saad of the Gallup Organization reports in *Americans Choose Death over Vegetative State* (March 29, 2005, http://www.gallup.com/poll/15448/Americans-Choose-Death-Over-Vegetative-State.aspx) that in 2005, 53% of respondents worried "a great deal" about "the possibility of being vegetable-like for some period of time." In exploring this issue more deeply, Dalia Sussman and Gary Langer report in "Two-Thirds Back Spouse in Right to Die Cases" (March 15, 2005, http://abcnews.go.com/images/ Politics/975a3Schiavo.pdf) on an ABC News/*Washington Post* poll, which asked: "If you were in this condition [that of Terri Schiavo] would you want to be kept alive, or not?" Only 8% said "yes," whereas 87% said "no." When asked who should have the final say, 65% felt that the spouse should have the final say, whereas 25% believed it should be the parents.

It may be hard to determine the effect of the Terri Schiavo case on the American public, but in an attempt to do so, a FOX News/Opinion Dynamics poll (http://www .foxnews.com/projects/pdf/033105_poll.pdf) of March 31, 2005, asked the question: "Prior to the recent coverage of the Terri Schiavo case, had you ever discussed end of life medical decisions with your spouse, family or friends?" A huge majority (78%) reported that they had. Only 20% had not. Thus, a majority of the American public had dealt with this question before it was highlighted in the media. Nonetheless, the case appeared to generate strong interest in living wills as suggested by a March 25, 2005, poll (http:// www.srbi.com/TimePoll-Final_Report-2005-03-25.pdf) by *Time*/SRBI. Results of the survey revealed that 93% of respondents had heard of a living will, but only 37% had executed such a document. When those who had no living will were asked, "Has the Schiavo case made you think about drafting a living will or discussing with your family your wishes for medical treatment should you be unable to communicate them yourself?" 69% responded "yes."

IMPORTANT NAMES AND ADDRESSES

AARP
601 E St. NW
Washington, DC 20049
1-888-687-2277
URL: http://www.aarp.org/

Aging with Dignity
820 E Park Ave., Ste. D100
Tallahassee, FL 32301-2600
1-888-594-7437
FAX: (850) 681-2481
E-mail: fivewishes@agingwithdignity.org
URL: http://www.agingwithdignity.org/

Alzheimer's Association
225 N. Michigan Ave., Seventh Fl.
Chicago, IL 60601-7633
(312) 335-8700
1-800-272-3900
FAX: 1-866-699-1246
E-mail: info@alz.org
URL: http://www.alz.org/

American Association of Suicidology
5221 Wisconsin Ave. NW
Washington, DC 20015
(202) 237-2280
FAX: (202) 237-2282
E-mail: info@suicidology.org
URL: http://www.suicidology.org/

American Cancer Society
1599 Clifton Rd. NE
Atlanta, GA 30329-4251
(404) 320-33331-800-227-2345
URL: http://www.cancer.org/

American Foundation for Suicide Prevention
120 Wall St., Twenty-second Fl.
New York, NY 10005
(212) 363-3500
1-888-333-2377
FAX: (212) 363-6237

E-mail: inquiry@afsp.org
URL: http://www.afsp.org/

Centers for Disease Control and Prevention
1600 Clifton Rd.
Atlanta, GA 30333
(404) 498-1515
1-800-311-3435
URL: http://www.cdc.gov/

Children's Hospice International
1101 King St., Ste. 360
Alexandria, VA 22314
(703) 684-0330
1-800-242-4453
URL: http://www.chionline.org/

Compassion and Choices
PO Box 101810
Denver, CO 80250-1810
1-800-247-7421
FAX: (303) 639-1224
E-mail: info@compassionandchoices.org
URL: http://www.compassionandchoices.org/

The Hastings Center
21 Malcolm Gordon Rd.
Garrison, NY 10524-4125
(845) 424-4040
FAX: (845) 424-4545
E-mail: mail@thehastingscenter.org
URL: http://www.thehastingscenter.org/

Health Resources and Services Administration
5600 Fishers Lane
Rockville, MD 20857
URL: http://www.hrsa.gov/

International Task Force on Euthanasia and Assisted Suicide
PO Box 760
Steubenville, OH 43952
(740) 282-3810
URL: http://
www.internationaltaskforce.org/

March of Dimes
1275 Mamaroneck Ave.
White Plains, NY 10605
(914) 997-4488
1-888-663-4637
URL: http://www.marchofdimes.com/

National Association for Home Care and Hospice
228 Seventh St. SE
Washington, DC 20003
(202) 547-7424
FAX: (202) 547-3540
URL: http://www.nahc.org/

National Council on Aging
1901 L St. NW, Fourth Fl.
Washington, DC 20036
(202) 479-1200
URL: http://www.ncoa.org/

National Hospice and Palliative Care Organization
1700 Diagonal Rd., Ste. 625
Alexandria, VA 22314
(703) 837-1500
1-800-646-6460
FAX: (703) 837-1233
E-mail: nhpco_info@nhpco.org
URL: http://www.nhpco.org/

National Institute on Aging
31 Center Dr., MSC 2292
Bldg. 31, Rm. 5C27
Bethesda, MD 20892
(301) 496-1752
FAX: (301) 496-1072
URL: http://www.nia.nih.gov/

National Right to Life Committee
512 Tenth St. NW
Washington, DC 20004
(202) 626-8800
E-mail: NRLC@nrlc.org
URL: http://www.nrlc.org/

Older Women's League
3300 N. Fairfax Dr., Ste. 218
Arlington, VA 22201
(703) 812-7990
1-800-825-3695
FAX: (703) 812-0687
E-mail: owlinfo@owl-national.org
URL: http://www.owl-national.org/

United Network for Organ Sharing
700 N. Fourth St.
Richmond, VA 23218
(804) 782-4800
1-888-894-6361
FAX: (804) 782-4817
URL: http://www.unos.org/

Visiting Nurse Associations of America
900 Nineteenth St. NW, Ste. 200
Washington, DC 20006
(202) 384-1420
FAX: (202) 384-1444
E-mail: vnaa@vnaa.org
URL: http://www.vnaa.org/

RESOURCES

The National Center for Health Statistics (NCHS) provides in its annual publication *Health, United States* a statistical overview of the nation's health. The NCHS periodical *National Vital Statistics Reports* supplies detailed U.S. birth and death data. The Centers for Disease Control and Prevention (CDC) reports on nationwide health trends in its *Advance Data* reports, *Morbidity and Mortality Weekly Report*, *HIV/AIDS Surveillance Report*, *Trends in Health and Aging*, and *Longitudinal Studies of Aging*. The Centers for Medicare and Medicaid Services reports on the nation's spending for health care.

The U.S. Census Bureau publishes a wide variety of demographic information on American life. *U.S. Interim Projections by Age, Sex, Race, and Hispanic Origin* (March 2004) incorporate the results of the 2000 census and make projections to 2050.

The Alliance for Aging Research promotes scientific research on human aging and conducts educational programs to increase communication and understanding among professionals who serve the elderly.

The mission of the National Hospice and Palliative Care Organization (NHPCO) is "improving end of life care and expanding access to hospice care with the goal of profoundly enhancing quality of life for people dying in America and their loved ones." The Hospice Association of America represents hospices, caregivers, and volunteers who serve terminally ill patients and their families. The NHPCO and the Hospice Association of America both collect data about hospice care.

The United Network for Organ Sharing manages the national transplant waiting list, maintains data on organ transplants, and distributes organ donor cards. The primary goals of the U.S. Organ Procurement and Transplantation Network (OPTN) "are to increase the effectiveness and efficiency of organ sharing and equity in the national system of organ allocation, and to increase the supply of donated organs available for transplantation." The Scientific Registry of Transplant Recipients (SRTR) evaluates the scientific and clinical status of organ transplantation in the United States. Valuable information on these topics is available in the OPTN/SRTR annual reports.

The National Right to Life Committee can provide a copy of *The Will to Live*, an alternative living will, whereas Compassion and Choices provides news and bulletins on Oregon's Death with Dignity Act and other end-of-life legislation. The American Bar Association Commission on Law and Aging publishes information related to advance directives.

For cancer statistics, a premier source is the American Cancer Society's annual *Cancer Facts & Figures*.

Journals that frequently publish studies dealing with life-sustaining treatment, medical ethics, and medical costs include *Annals of Internal Medicine*, *Journal of the American Geriatrics Society*, *Journal of the American Medical Association*, the *Lancet*, and the *New England Journal of Medicine*.

The Gallup Organization, Harris Interactive, Polling Report, and Roper Center for Public Opinion Research have all conducted opinion polls on topics related to death and dying.

The Henry J. Kaiser Family Foundation provides a wealth of information on Medicare, Medicaid, health insurance, prescription drugs, HIV/AIDS, and nursing homes.

INDEX

Page references in italics refer to photographs. References with the letter t following them indicate the presence of a table. The letter f indicates a figure. If more than one table or figure appears on a particular page, the exact item number for the table or figure being referenced is provided.

A

AARP (American Association of Retired Persons), 155

ABC News/*USA Today* poll, 151

ABC News/*Washington Post* poll, 154

Abe Perlmutter, Michael J. Satz etc. v., 100

"ACGME Requirements for Geriatrics Medicine Curricula in Medical Specialties: Progress Made and Progress Needed" (Bragg & Warshaw), 146–147

Acquired immunodeficiency syndrome (AIDS)
death rates from HIV/AIDS, 23–24
diagnoses, deaths, persons living with, 125 (t9.13)
estimated numbers of deaths of persons with, 29t
funding for, 125, 127
HIV/AIDS, federal funding for, 126f, 127f
Ryan White CARE Act, 127–128
Ryan White CARE Act, funding for, 128f
Ryan White CARE Act providers, locations of, 129f

Active euthanasia, 14, 60

AD. *See* Alzheimer's disease

Addresses/names, of organizations, 155–156

ADGAP (Association of Directors of Geriatric Academic Programs), 147

Adkins, Janet, 75

Adolescents
death/dying fears of, 150, 151f
high school students who attempted suicide/whose suicide attempt required medical attention, 66t

high school students who attempted suicide/whose suicide attempt required medical attention, by sex, selected U.S. sites, 67t–68t
high school students who felt sad or hopeless, who seriously considered attempting suicide, who made suicide plan, by sex, race/ethnicity, grade, 68t
high school students who felt sad or hopeless, who seriously considered attempting suicide, who made suicide plan, by sex, U.S. sites, 69t–70t
medical decision making for older children, 57
suicidal ideation, suicide attempts/injuries among students in grade 9–12, 65t–66t
suicide among young people, 64–67, 69–70
suicide and, 152–153
suicide rates among persons aged 10–24 years, annual, 71t

Advance directives
additional instructions in, 90–93
advance health-care directive form, 91t–93t
combined advance directive laws, 93–94
communication for end-of-life care, 94
cultural differences in, 19
definition of, 81
durable power of attorney for health care, 90
"Five Wishes," states in which it is legally valid, 94f
health care power of attorney/combined advance directive legislation, 82t–89t
history of, 81
living wills, 81, 90
Patient Self-Determination Act, 94–95
public opinion on Terri Schiavo case, 154

African-Americans
cancer rates for, 136
death rate from heart disease, 134

infant mortality rate for, 43
life expectancy of, 46, 131, 132t
low birth weight and, 52
suicide among young people, 64
suicide rate of, 62, 146

Afterlife
percentage of persons of various faiths who believe in, 150f
public opinion on, 149
public opinion on existence of heaven, 150 (t11.1)
public opinion on existence of hell, 150 (t11.2)

Age
aging Americans, 131
Alzheimer's disease and, 140, 142–143
cancer risks and, 136, 137–138, 140t
death rates, by age, for 15 leading causes of death, 25t–28t
death rates for suicide, by sex, race, Hispanic origin, age, 61t–63t
death rates from HIV/AIDS and, 24
dementia, Alzheimer's disease, and vascular dementia, percentages of persons with, by age, 145 (t10.10)
dementia or Alzheimer's disease, number of persons with, by age, 145 (t10.11)
end-of-life care, who pays for, 116–117
fear/anxiety about death and, 149–150
leading causes of death by, 23
life expectancy, 132t
low birth weight and, 52
population and projected population, by age/sex, 133t
public opinion on aging, 151–152
sex ratio for population 25 years and over by age, 146t
stroke risk and, 138–139
suicide rate and, 62, 146
See also Older adults

C

CAA (Child Abuse Amendments of 1984), 56–57

California Natural Death Act of 1976, 81

Cancer
    health-care costs for, 128–129
    incidence/mortality rates by site, race, ethnicity, 141t
    invasive, probability of developing, 140t
    as leading cause of death, 23, 136–138

Cancer Facts & Figures 2008 (American Cancer Society), 128, 137–138

Cancer patients, terminal
    euthanasia and assisted suicide, 20
    hospice use, Medicare expenditures and, 118
    physician-assisted suicide, patients with/without interest in, 21t
    physician-assisted suicide, symptoms and concerns of patients with/without interest in, 22 (t3.4)
    reasons for assisted suicide requests, 73–74
    reasons for being for/against legalization of, 22 (t3.5)
    requesting assisted suicide/euthanasia, 72
    substituted judgment court case, 99

Cardiac arrest, 31

Cardiopulmonary resuscitation (CPR), 30, 31

CARE Act. *See* Ryan White Comprehensive AIDS Resources Emergency (CARE) Act

"Care of the Dying Adolescent: Special Considerations" (Freyer), 57

Caring Connections, 31

Caring for an Aging America Act of 2008, 147

Carroll, Joseph, 153

Catechism of the Catholic Church
    on end-of-life ethics, 13, 14
    on suicide, 60

Catholic Church, 60, 149

CBS, 75

CBSNews.com, 149

CDC. *See* Centers for Disease Control and Prevention

Cemeteries, 2–3

Center for Health Law and Ethics at the University of New Mexico, 94

Center to Improve Care of the Dying (CICD), 93–94

Centers for Disease Control and Prevention (CDC)
    on birth defects, 46
    on circumstances of suicide, 62–64
    contact information, 155
    death rates from HIV/AIDS, 23–24
    on Down syndrome, 50
    on HIV/AIDS, 125

on infant mortality, 43
on low birth weight, 51–52
on neural tube defects, 48
on spina bifida, 50
on suicide, 152

Centers for Medicare and Medicaid Services, 119

Cerebral insult and coma, flow chart of, 32f

Cerebral palsy, 51

Cerebrovascular disease (stroke)
    death rates for, 142t–144t
    as leading cause of death among elderly, 23, 138–139

Cessation, 9

"Changing the Rules on CPR for Cardiac Arrest" (*Harvard Women's Health Watch*), 31

"Characteristics of Patients Requesting and Receiving Physician-Assisted Death" (Meier et al.), 72

Charles S. Soper, as Director of Newark Developmental Center et al. v. Dorothy Storar, 99

CHD (coronary heart disease), 133–136, 137t–139t

Chemotherapy, 99

Chest compressions, 31

Child Abuse Amendments of 1984 (CAA), 56–57

"Child Welfare versus Parental Autonomy: Medical Ethics, the Law, and Faith-Based Healing" (Hickey & Lyckholm), 57

Children, seriously ill
    anencephalus cases/rates, number of live births, 50 (t5.5)
    anencephalus rates, 49f
    birth defects, 46–51
    births with selected medical or health characteristics, 56t
    costs (economic) for certain developmental disabilities, 52t
    deaths, life expectancy at birth, by race/sex; infant deaths, mortality rates, by race, 46t
    infant, neonatal, postneonatal mortality rates, by race/Hispanic origin of mother, 44t–45t
    infant deaths, mortality rates, by age, race, Hispanic origin, 45t
    infant deaths/infant mortality rates, ten leading causes of, 47t–48t
    infant mortality, causes of, 46
    infant mortality, life expectancy at birth, 43–46
    low birth weight, 51–52
    low birthweight, number/percent of, number of live births, 53t–54t
    low-birthweight live births, by mother's race, Hispanic origin, smoking status, 55t
    medical decision making for infants, 52, 55–57

medical decision making for older children, 57
    prematurity, 52
    spina bifida cases/rates, number of live births, 50 (t5.6)
    spina bifida rates, 50f

Children's Health Act of 2000, 51

Children's Hospice International, 155

Chinese, ancient, 1

Choice in Dying (CID), 59

Christian Scientists, 14

Christianity
    beliefs about death, 2
    end-of-life ethics, 13–15
    public opinion on afterlife, 149
    suicide, views of, 60

Chromosomes, 50–51

Chronic noninfectious diseases, 23

CICD (Center to Improve Care of the Dying), 93–94

CID (Choice in Dying), 59

Cigarette smoking, 51–52

"A Circumscribed Plea for Voluntary Physician-Assisted Suicide" (Cohen-Almagor), 75

Classical Age, death in, 1–2

"The Clinical Criteria of Brain Death throughout the World: Why Has It Come to This?" (Wijdicks), 9

"Clinical Diagnosis of Prolonged States of Impaired Consciousness in Adults" (Wijdicks & Cranford), 9

Clinical trials, for cancer, 128–129

Clinton, Bill, 51, 129

CNN, 151

Cohen, Joel W., 122

Cohen-Almagor, Raphael, 75

Coma
    cerebral insult and coma, flow chart of, 32f
    court case on rights of nursing home, 102–103
    court cases on rights of hospital, 101–102
    government redefinition of death and, 9
    Karen Ann Quinlan case, 97–98
    liability of doctors for terminating life support, 101
    as new criterion for death, 7–8
    outcomes of, 32–33

Combined advance directive laws
    health care power of attorney/combined advance directive legislation, 82t–89t
    of states, 93–94

Comfort care, 91

Comity provision, 94

Committee for Pro-Life Activities of the National Conference of Catholic Bishops, 14

Communication
    for end-of-life care, 94
    between physicians, patients, 30

dementia, Alzheimer's disease, and vascular dementia, percentages of persons with, by age, 145 (*t*10.10)

Vaud University Hospital Center, Lausanne, Switzerland, 79

"The Vegetative and Minimally Conscious States: Consensus-Based Criteria for Establishing Diagnosis and Prognosis" (Giacino), 33

Ventilation, mechanical, 31

Very-low-birth-weight infants, 51, 52

Victor, Maurice, 103

Vision impairment, 51

Visiting Nurse Associations of America, 156

Voluntary Euthanasia Society, 59

W

Wachtler, Sol, 99, 104

Wade, Roe v., 71, 98

Waiting list, organ transplant, 34, 38*t*

Wantz, Marjorie, 75

Warne, Tony, 70

Warshaw, Gregg A., 146–147

Washkansky, Louis, 7

Wells, H. G., 59

Westchester County Medical Center, 104–105

What Frightens America's Youth? (Gallup Organization), 149–150

"What Length of Hospice Use Maximizes Reduction in Medical Expenditures Near Death in the U.S. Medicare Program?" (Taylor et al.), 117–118

"What Matters Most in End-of-Life Care: Perceptions of Seriously Ill Patients and Their Family Members" (Heyland et al.), 151

"When Is Physician Assisted Suicide or Euthanasia Acceptable?" (Frileux et al.), 71

whites
  infant mortality rate for, 43
  life expectancy of, 46, 131, 132*t*
  low birth weight and, 52
  suicide among young people, 64, 67
  suicide rate of, 146

"Why Oregon Patients Request Assisted Death: Family Members' Views" (Ganzini et al.), 74

Wickett, Ann, 74

Widows/widowers, older adults as, 131

Wijdicks, Eelco F. M., 9

"Will to Live" (NRLC), 90

Wills. *See* Last will and testament; Living wills

Wilson, Keith G., 20

Wishes, of patient, 103–105

Women
  fear/anxiety about death, 150
  life expectancy of, 131
  older women, 146
  suicide rate for, 61–62
  See also Gender

World Medical Association, 16

"World's Suicide Capital—Tough Image to Shake" (Prideaux), 60

Y

Yamamoto, Takamitsu, 33

Yankelovich Partners, 151

York, Nancy L., 19

Youk, Thomas, 75

Young people
  annual suicide rates among persons aged 10–24 years, 71*t*
  fear/anxiety about death, 149–150
  high school students who attempted suicide/whose suicide attempt required medical attention, by sex, race/ethnicity, grade, 66*t*
  high school students who attempted suicide/whose suicide attempt required medical attention, by sex, selected U.S. sites, 67*t*–68*t*
  high school students who felt sad or hopeless, who seriously considered attempting suicide, who made suicide plan, by sex, race/ethnicity, grade, 68*t*
  high school students who felt sad or hopeless, who seriously considered attempting suicide, who made suicide plan, by sex, U.S. sites, 69*t*–70*t*
  suicidal ideation, suicide attempts/injuries among students in grade 9–12, 65*t*–66*t*
  suicide among, 64–67, 69–70
  suicide as leading cause of death among, 152